SHRIKES

A GUIDE TO THE SHRIKES

OF THE WORLD

SHRIKES

A GUIDE TO THE SHRIKES

OF THE WORLD

NORBERT LEFRANC

ILLUSTRATED BY TIM WORFOLK

YALE UNIVERSITY PRESS
NEW HAVEN AND LONDON

Published 1997 in the United Kingdom by Pica Press (an imprint of Helm Information Ltd)
and in the United States by Yale University Press.

ISBN 0-300-07336-4

Library of Congress Cataloging in Publication Number 97-60716

A catalogue record for this book is available from the British Library.

The paper in this book meets the guidelines for permanence and durability of the Committee
on production Guidelines for Book Longevity of the Council on Library Resources.

10 9 8 7 6 5 4 3 2 1

Contents

To Jocelyne and Marina

NL

To Carolyn, Jack and Sally

TW

INTRODUCTION

Shrikes are a peculiar group of small or medium-sized passerines known to have similarities to raptors, in both morphology and habits. The extraordinary impaling behaviour of members of the genus *Lanius* contributes special appeal. The fact that populations of the well-studied species living in Europe and North America are declining puts the whole family, represented throughout the world's continents except in Australia and South America, under the spotlight. Novel technologies have been used recently to study these birds such as DNA fingerprinting, radio-telemetry and ptilochronology. The breeding biology and ecology of some African and Asian species is, however, still very little known; the shortcomings are highlighted here in the hope of encouraging research in the appropriate directions. Those becoming infected by the 'shrike virus' will find a few useful addresses at the end of the introductory chapters. They may also skim through the bibliography and notice, among other things, that the genus *Lanius* was treated in a keystone monograph more than 50 years back by Olivier (1944) in his *Monographie des Pies-grièches du genre Lanius*. Other more recent books give treatments of the shrikes of the Palearctic (Panov 1983), the western Palearctic (Cramp and Perrins 1993, Lefranc 1993), central Europe (Glutz von Blotzheim and Bauer 1993) or South Africa (Harris and Arnott 1988). Important contributions can be found in many ornithological reviews. The proceedings of the first (Yosef and Lohrer 1995) and the second (in press) International Shrike Symposium are essential reading for every 'shrikeologist'.

The present book is primarily an identification guide and the first of its kind giving detailed descriptions of species and some of the races considered to be valid and recognisable in the field. It also aims to give precise, up-to-date information on this fascinating family of 31 bird species.

ACKNOWLEDGEMENTS

The present work, as is obvious from a glance at the bibliography, relies heavily on published material; it owes much to the work both of 'generalists' interested in local avifaunas and to dedicated shrike specialists. Many of the latter were kind enough to give or send reprints of their studies to NL, mainly since the publication of the book in French devoted to the 'Pies-grièches'.

NL is also particularly grateful to the persons who have read and commented on parts of the text: Patrice Christy, Robert J. Dowsett, Christian Erard, Paul Isenmann, Dries van Nieuwenhuyse, Satoshi Yamagishi and Steve Zack.

Many others have helped in some way or other. Marc Ameels, Ian J. Andrews, Thiery Bara, Bruno Bruderer, Clide Carter, Douglas M. Collister, Marc Herremans, Paul Koenig, Heinz Kowalski, Michel Lepley, Fred Lohrer, Steve Madge, David C. Moyer, Anne Nason, Vibhu Prakash and Martin Schön have provided useful additional and often still unpublished information. John H. Fanshawe readily published a plea for information in the *Bulletin of the African Bird Club*, and J.T.R. Sharrock did the same with a request concerning photographs in the magazine *British Birds*. Michael Rank took great pains in translating several Chinese texts into English! Many thanks also to Reuven Yosef and Fred Lohrer who had the excellent idea of organising a shrike symposium in Florida, at the Archbold Biological Station, Lake Placid, and of inviting many people outside the USA including NL.

Several people sent photos or drawings. Special thanks are due to Serge Nicolle for the loan of his field drawings and paintings of the two races of the Chinese Grey Shrike, to Bernard Hiolle and Daniel Haubreux who respectively sent drawings and photos of an adult hybrid Woodchat/Red-backed Shrike observed in northern France. Alain Saunier kindly provided a series of his impressive photos of shrikes; most of the line drawings in this book are heavily inspired from his work whereas the drawing of the predation by a Northern Goshawk on a Great Grey Shrike's nest is after an extraordinary photo by Igor I. Byshnev (Berezinsky Biosphere Reserve). Philip W. Atkinson kindly offered copies of a series of the first and probably only colour slides of a Newton's Fiscal caught alive in the wild.

Richard Ranft, curator of the wildlife section of the British Library Sound Archive was very helpful in providing tapes of the calls and songs of shrikes. Claude Chappuis made a visit to NL's study area of the Great Grey Shrike and recorded several types of calls and songs. He also kindly provided a cassette with all his recordings of that species and of the various races of the Southern Grey Shrike.

TW would like to give special thanks to Mark Andrews, John Archer, Phil Atkinson, David Brewer, Alan Burtenshaw, Patrick Buys, Hugh Chambers, Gerald Driessens, David Griffin, Alan Hands, John Holmes, David Johnson, Jerry Lewis, Guy Manners, Phil Mountain, Karno Mikkola, David Ogle, David Pearson, Per Smitterberg, Simon Stirrup and Ray Tipper.

We are both very grateful to the staff at the Natural History Museum at Tring, England, and particularly to Robert Prys-Jones, Peter Colston, Mark Adams and Michael Walters for permitting access to the skin and egg collections. Effie Warr, librarian at the same museum, managed to track down many papers desperately sought by NL. The latter enjoyed the many weeks spent in a typical small English town and also spent much time at the Muséum National d'Histoire Naturelle in Paris, where Christian Erard, director of the Laboratoire d'Ornithologie et Mammalogie was very helpful, as was Mrs Evelyne Brémond, the librarian. David Agro of the Museum of the Academy of Natural Sciences, Philadelphia, kindly arranged a loan of a skin of an adult Chinese Grey Shrike of the race *giganteus*.

Finally we are very grateful to Nigel Redman, who believed in the project from the start and encouraged us to do it, to Christopher Helm for his great patience and understanding (all the more so since the fruition was longer than expected), and to Julie Reynolds and Marc Dando who dealt with the technical side of the production. NL also wishes to thank Brigitte Nouguès who typed the text in English and stoically accepted all additions and changes right to the end.

We extend our gratitude to our families. NL owes a great debt to his wife Jocelyne and to his daughter Marina, often neglected because of the numerous shrike trips all over the world, but always very tolerant and supporting.

TAXONOMY AND RELATIONSHIPS

One of the major recent standard works concerned with traditional taxonomy is Peters's *Check-list of Birds of the World*. The family Laniidae, as treated by Austin L. Rand (1960) in volume IX, comprises 74 species grouped in four subfamilies and twelve genera as follows (the number of species concerned is indicated after each genus):

Subfamily Prionopinae, the helmet-shrikes
- Genus *Eurocephalus*   2
- Genus *Prionops*   7

Subfamily Malaconotinae, the bush-shrikes
- Genus *Lanioturdus*   1
- Genus *Nilaus*   1
- Genus *Dryoscopus*   6
- Genus *Tchagra*   6
- Genus *Laniarius*   10
- Genus *Telephorus*   10
- Genus *Malaconotus*   5

Subfamily Laniinae, the true shrikes
- Genus *Corvinella*   2
- Genus *Lanius*   23

Subfamily Pityriasinae, the Bornean Bristlehead
- Genus *Pityriasis*   1

Morony, Bock and Farrand (1975) in their *Reference List of the Birds of the World,* and Bock and Farrand (1980), did not change anything in Rand's list of the Laniidae.

All these 74 species have certain features in common: a hooked bill with a variably obvious 'tooth' in the upper mandible and a corresponding notch in the lower; strong legs and feet, and sharp claws; wings with 10 primaries and a tail with 12 rectrices.

However, the Bornean Bristlehead, from the lowland forests of Borneo, heavily built, about 25cm long, with a massive hooked bill and a striking red head, certainly has little in common with any other of the subfamilies recognised by Rand. Voous (1985), following others, placed it in a family of its own, Pityriasidae.

Benson, Brooke, Dowsett and Irwin in *Birds of Zambia* (1971) erected the exclusively African Malaconotinae into a family, Malaconotidae, doubting that its members had any close connections with the birds of the genus *Lanius*. These authors took the view that the bush-shrikes had been placed with the Laniidae merely on account of their generally similar size and above all because of their hooked bills, which they regarded as probably a result of convergence.

The Malaconotidae are characterised by contrasting colour-patterns and soft, elongated rump feathers, particularly in the genera *Laniarius* and *Dryoscopus*. They have loud distinctive calls, but no warbling song like *Lanius* shrikes, and mainly inhabit thickets in savanna woodland or forest edge. They are almost exclusively insectivorous, but their foraging techniques differ markedly from those of the true shrikes, as they never adopt the sit-and-wait strategy so characteristic of the latter. Instead, most of them are strictly arboreal feeders, gleaning inside vegetation like giant warblers. All tchagras as well as probably most *Laniarius* species and sometimes also the Rosy-patched Shrike *Rhodophoneus cruentus* – placed with the tchagras by Rand (1960), but in the genus *Rhodophoneus* by Hall and Moreau (1970) – feed near or on the ground, inside thickets. The nests of bush-shrikes vary a great deal, but are generally rather small, inconspicuous and neatly made; the clutch only consists of two or three eggs.

Voous (1985) retained the bush-shrikes as a subfamily of the Laniidae where he recognised only one other subfamily, the Laniinae. Like others, he placed the helmet-shrikes in a family of their own, the Prionopidae.

Traditionally (Rand 1960, Hall and Moreau 1970, Voous 1985) the helmet-shrikes often comprised two genera: *Prionops* and *Eurocephalus*. The seven species of the genus *Prionops* are all endemic to the Afrotropical region. They are characterised by stiff forehead feathers projecting forward and covering the nostrils; they also show distinctly coloured eye-wattles and are unusual in having the tarsus scutellated on both side and front. Helmet-shrikes are highly sociable, occurring in groups of 6-12 birds throughout the year; normally a group has only one active nest and one breeding female. These shrikes are almost exclusively insectivorous, searching for prey on trunks, branches and leaves. Their nest is a neatly formed shallow cup in which three or four eggs are usually laid.

In traditional taxonomy, the true shrikes, whether regarded as a subfamily of the Laniidae (Rand 1960, Voous 1985 among others) or as a family in themselves (Benson *et al.* 1971, Benson and Benson 1977), always included the genera *Lanius* and *Corvinella*, the Magpie Shrike *Corvinella melanoleuca* even sometimes being regarded as a *Lanius* shrike. Ecologically, these birds differ markedly from bush-shrikes and helmet-shrikes as they are almost all typical of more or less open country. They mainly hunt from a perch from which they drop to the ground to pick up food, mostly insects but also small vertebrates. *Lanius* shrikes also commonly impale some of their prey in larders.

In the early 1980s, new sources of taxonomic data began to be used. They promised to be even more useful than comparative studies of egg-white proteins (Sibley 1970) and were based on comparisons of the genetic material (DNA) of different species, the idea being that the more alike genetically two species are, the more recently in geological time they shared a common ancestor and thus the more closely related they are to one another. The laboratory method used for determining these degrees of genetic similarity is DNA-DNA hybridisation; for details see Monroe (1992), who gives an easy-to-follow explanation of how these similarities are measured. A few years ago, two bulky and 'revolutionary' volumes were published: *Phylogeny and Classification of Birds* by Sibley and Ahlquist (1990) and *Distribution and Taxonomy of Birds of the World* by Sibley and Monroe (1990). These authors place all the bird species in a DNA-based classification, and update all the taxonomic information pertinent to that listing. This classification is certainly not perfect, but it has at least one big advantage: it is totally objective, based entirely on a single value showing genetic relationships. In this system, the family Laniidae only consists of three genera, *Lanius*, *Corvinella* and *Eurocephalus*, which represent the true shrikes. It is of course still placed in the order Passeriformes, in the suborder Passeri, in the parvorder Corvida and finally in the superfamily Corvoidea.

The other species traditionally placed in the Laniidae also appear as members of the superfamily Corvoidea, but in another family, the Corvidae. The Bornean Bristlehead is now ascribed to the subfamily Corvinae in the tribe Artamini with the currawongs and wood-swallows. DNA comparisons of that species with a wide array of passerine taxa clearly show that it is an artamine, not a shrike, despite the relatively recent opinion of Raikow *et al.* (1980), based on similarities in limb musculature. The bush-shrikes and helmet-shrikes appear in the subfamily Malaconotinae, but in separate tribes: Malaconotini for the bush-shrikes, including the boubous, tchagras and gonoleks, and Vangini for the helmet-shrikes, vangas and the genera *Batis* and *Platysteira*. DNA hybridisation confirmed that the bush-shrikes and helmet-shrikes were not closely related to the true shrikes, a fact which, as mentioned above, had already been strongly suggested on purely ecological and behavioural grounds. More surprisingly perhaps, the DNA comparisons showed that the Malaconotinae are even farther from the true shrikes than the drongos, orioles and cuckoo-shrikes.

In 1993, Monroe and Sibley published *A World Checklist of Birds* based on their previous volume and including some changes and corrections. They listed the following 30 true shrikes in the family Laniidae (a few English names have been changed or, in the case of *Lanius dorsalis*, slightly altered; the changes affect the species marked *):

Genus *Lanius* (26 species):
    Tiger Shrike *Lanius tigrinus*
    Bull-headed Shrike *Lanius bucephalus*
    Red-backed Shrike *Lanius collurio*
  * Isabelline Shrike *Lanius isabellinus*
    Brown Shrike *Lanius cristatus*
    Burmese Shrike *Lanius collurioides*
    Emin's Shrike *Lanius gubernator*
    Sousa's Shrike *Lanius souzae*
    Bay-backed Shrike *Lanius vittatus*

Long-tailed Shrike *Lanius schach*
Grey-backed Shrike *Lanius tephronotus*
Mountain Shrike *Lanius validirostris*
Lesser Grey Shrike *Lanius minor*
Loggerhead Shrike *Lanius ludovicianus*
* Great Grey Shrike *Lanius excubitor*
Chinese Grey Shrike *Lanius sphenocercus*
Grey-backed Fiscal *Lanius excubitoroides*
Long-tailed Fiscal *Lanius cabanisi*
* Taita Fiscal *Lanius dorsalis*
Somali Fiscal *Lanius somalicus*
Mackinnon's Shrike *Lanius mackinnoni*
Common Fiscal *Lanius collaris*
Newton's Fiscal *Lanius newtoni*
Uhehe Fiscal *Lanius marwitzi*
Woodchat Shrike *Lanius senator*
Masked Shrike *Lanius nubicus*

Genus *Corvinella* (2 species):
Yellow-billed Shrike *Corvinella corvina*
Magpie Shrike *Corvinella melanoleuca*

Genus *Eurocephalus* (2 species):
White-rumped Shrike *Eurocephalus rueppelli*
White-crowned Shrike *Eurocephalus anguitimens*

Monroe and Sibley (1993) also list a certain number of 'well-marked subspecies that have been considered to be species in the recent past, or may be so recognised in the future'. Among these forms in the Laniidae, they mention the Southern Grey Shrike *Lanius* (*excubitor*) *meridionalis*. This bird is given specific status in the present book, which otherwise follows Monroe and Sibley's list. It must, however, be emphasised that the DNA-DNA technique cannot establish exact relationships in lower taxonomic categories (below tribe level). So questions remain open concerning genera and especially species. These points are developed in some detail below. For descriptions and comments on subspecies see 'Geographical Variation' in the species accounts.

NOTES ON GENERA AND SPECIES TAXONOMY IN TRUE SHRIKES

SPECIES PROBLEMS IN THE GENUS *LANIUS*

The *collurio/isabellinus/cristatus* group

Three small, largely allopatric Eurasian shrikes, the Red-backed Shrike *Lanius collurio*, the Isabelline Shrike *L. isabellinus* and the Brown Shrike *L. cristatus* are undoubtedly closely related. They also share a long common 'capricious' taxonomic history, as Voous (1979) put it when speaking of the Isabelline Shrike!

Various authorities combined them into:

one species: *Lanius cristatus* (Stresemann 1927, Voous 1960, etc);

two species: *Lanius collurio* including *isabellinus*, and *Lanius cristatus* (Stegmann 1930, Hartert and Steinbacher 1933, Vaurie 1959, etc);

three species: (Olivier 1944, Stresemann and Stresemann 1972, Voous 1977, etc);

four species: (Panov 1983, 1995, Kryukov 1995); the fourth species – 'Turkestan Red-backed Shrike' *Lanius phoenicuroides* – results from a split of the Isabelline Shrike, for which four subspecies are generally recognised (see species account).

Things are clearly complicated in this group. However, from various studies already mentioned above or other discussions (e.g. Nielsen 1981, Glutz von Blotzheim and Bauer 1993, Cramp and

Perrins 1993, Lefranc 1993, etc), the following points arise. (1) The Brown Shrike *Lanius cristatus* is a good species. It is phenotypically well distinguished from the Red-backed Shrike; the breeding ranges of the two birds overlap in a wide area, but only two hybrid specimens exist. These shrikes may occur in the same habitats and in sometimes neighbouring territories. A long zone of sympatry also exists between the Brown and Isabelline Shrike, race *speculigerus*, and the two species generally prefer different types of habitat; only one possible hybrid has been described (Sokolov and Sokolov 1987). (2) The Red-backed Shrike *Lanius collurio* and the Isabelline Shrike *L. isabellinus* can be regarded as distinct biological species (see criteria: Glutz von Blotzheim and Bauer 1982: 505). This case is, however, more controversial, as the degree of reproductive isolation between these two forms is still relatively low: mixed pairs and hybrids regularly occur in the zones of overlap (see under Isabelline Shrike). These birds are typical semi-species and form a superspecies. (3) The so-called 'Turkestan Shrike' may need further research. The recent opinion of Russian authors is, however, to be taken seriously as it is based on vast field experience, on morphological considerations as well as on observations concerning behaviour and voice.

The *schach/tephronotus/validirostris* group

The Long-tailed Shrike *Lanius schach*, Grey-backed Shrike *L. tephronotus* and Mountain Shrike *L. validirostris* appear to be closely related, although their taxonomy is still not altogether clear. Rand (1960) followed Dunajewski (1939) and recognised two species: *L. schach* with twelve races, and *L. validirostris*, confined to the Philippines, with four. Biswas (1950, 1962), however, recognised the validity of the third species, *L. tephronotus*. Despite contrary opinion (e.g. Rand and Fleming 1957) recent observations (e.g. Ali and Ripley 1972, Inskipp and Inskipp 1991) confirm that the latter bird, a high-elevation form sometimes called Tibetan Shrike, is a good species, having large zones of sympatry with *L. schach* and not interbreeding with it. Its race *lahulensis*, confined to parts of northern India (see under 'Geographical Variation' in Grey-backed Shrike) is, however, a puzzling bird, appearing morphologically intermediate between *L. tephronotus* and *L. s. erythronotus*. It may constitute a stabilised hybrid population (Panov 1983). *Lanius validirostris* is phenotypically very close to *L. tephronotus* but somewhat smaller and with a thicker bill. As its English name suggests, it is also a mountain bird. Because of their similarities, Biswas (1950) treated them as a single species; this view is generally not followed, but it certainly deserves further consideration.

The *excubitor/meridionalis* group

The Great Grey Shrike *Lanius excubitor*, the Southern Grey Shrike *L. meridionalis* and the exclusively North American Loggerhead Shrike *L. ludovicianus* are undoubtedly closely related species. The little-studied Chinese Grey Shrike *L. sphenocercus*, although more distantly related, could also be attached to this group, which forms a clear superspecies.

For the Great Grey Shrike, Vaurie (1959) distinguished the northern group *excubitor* and the southern group *meridionalis*. The latter group is here given specific status following Grant and Mackworth-Praed (1952), Panov (1983, 1995) and Isenmann and Bouchet (1993).

Races of *excubitor* tend to be slightly larger, with more rounded wings, a less graduated tail, broader rectrices, and slightly shorter legs. At least nominate *excubitor* shows, compared to *meridionalis*, a relatively distinct sexual dimorphism, males having more white in their plumage (Dohmann 1985, Schön 1994a). Some *excubitor* races, particularly nominate *excubitor* and, even more so, *homeyeri*, often show a double wing-bar formed by white at the base of the primaries and secondaries (both vanes of the latter are white). Races of *excubitor* in juvenile plumage have barred underparts in some degree and barring may even still occur in some adults including nominate *excubitor*; it is quite regular in adults of the dark races *funereus* and *mollis*. *Lanius excubitor* is predominantly a northern taiga species which has also adapted to semi-open grass-rich agricultural land dotted with copses and hedges; pairs, or single birds in winter, live in rather large territories covering 30-100ha or more; they mainly feed on insects and small vertebrates, particularly voles; in central Europe, the average nest height is c. 8m.

Races of *meridionalis* have only one white wing-patch confined to the base of the primaries, this being particularly obvious in nominate *meridionalis* and in *pallidirostris*, the 'Steppe Grey Shrike'; however, some races, for instance *elegans* and *lahtora*, have some white on the secondaries, but only on the inner vanes. Adults of *meridionalis* races never have barred underparts; faint vermiculations may, however, sometimes be found in juveniles of nominate *meridionalis* and of *koenigi*. *Lanius meridionalis* is mainly an Afro-asian species living in warm areas such as scrublands, steppes and deserts; territory size is generally small, between 5-15ha (for exceptions, see species account) and the diet comprises mainly insects but also small invertebrates, above all lizards; the nest-site sometimes reflects a difference in habitat from *excubitor*, as it is generally only at a height of 1-2m in bushes or small trees.

The breeding ranges of *excubitor* and *meridionalis* nearly touch in south-western France; they may even have overlapped at some time in Aquitaine, but so far the available data remain inconclusive. More interestingly, a definite zone of sympatry exists near the easternmost end of the respective breeding ranges, in Mongolia. There, the race *mollis* of the Great Grey Shrike and the race *pallidirostris* of the Southern Grey Shrike coexist geographically and not infrequently syntopically: *mollis* mainly occupies open mountain forests from the base of the slopes to the alpine zone, whereas *pallidirostris* is confined to the *Caragana* steppe. This spatial and ecological segregation is, however, not very strict and pairs of *mollis* can sometimes be found in typical *pallidirostris* habitat; even in those cases no mixed pairs have so far been found which, like nominate *excubitor* and nominate *meridionalis* in south-west France, show sharp differences in their general appearance (Lefranc 1995, Panov 1995).

Recent studies concerning base-sequencings of the cytochrome-b gene of mitochondrial DNA confirm that *excubitor* and *meridionalis* are good allospecies. The differences between them is almost as great as between *excubitor* and *ludovicianus*. Interestingly, *meridionalis* seems to be closer to the latter species than to *excubitor*; this point, however, needs further research (A. Helbig *in litt.*).

The *collaris/newtoni/marwitzi* group

The Common Fiscal *Lanius collaris* is widespread in sub-Saharan Africa, whereas the Uhehe Fiscal *L. marwitzi* is confined to highlands in south-western Tanzania and the very rare Newton's Fiscal *L. newtoni* to the island of São Tomé in the Gulf of Guinea.

The specific status of the two latter shrikes is controversial; they have been regarded as races of the Common Fiscal, for instance by White (1962). Rand (1960) only gave specific status to *newtoni*; this view has been reinforced by recent observations confirming rather marked plumage as well as ecological differences between *collaris* and *newtoni* (see species accounts). The form *marwitzi*, elevated to species level by such authorities as Hall and Moreau (1970), shows less obvious differences from the Common Fiscal; Dowsett-Lemaire (1993) have no doubt that it is just a race of the latter, and point out that the white eyebrow so striking in *marwitzi* also occasionally appears in the population of *L. c. capelli* which lives on the Nyika Plateau in Malawi. The Uhehe Fiscal is, however, treated as a good species here; this may at least encourage further research on this very little known bird. Further proposals concerning the already complicated taxonomy of the Common Fiscal exist: Harris and Arnott (1988) and Harris (1995) suggest that it might be composed of a northern and southern species; they base their hypothesis, still to be firmly tested, on sexual plumage dimorphism and above all on differences in visual and vocal displays; see map showing respective breeding distributions of these two possible species in Harris and Arnott (1988).

THE GENUS *CORVINELLA*

In the true shrikes, the genera *Lanius* and *Eurocephalus* are well defined as they each obviously concern groups of very closely related species. The genus *Corvinella* with its two species, the Yellow-billed Shrike *C. corvina* and the Magpie Shrike *C. melanoleuca* is, on the contrary, sometimes split in two with the latter bird placed in its own genus *Urolestes*, even in recent works (Dowsett and Dowsett-Lemaire 1993). Further research may well confirm this, but Monroe and Sibley (1993) follow White (1962) and Hall and Moreau (1970) among others in considering that the two African 'long-tailed shrikes', though different in colour and pattern, are alike in structure, have similar sociable habits, and occupy similar habitats in acacia savanna north and south of the equator. Hall and Moreau (1970) also suggested that these two shrikes were perhaps divergent members of a superspecies. Historically were also sometimes placed with the *Lanius* shrikes on morphological and behavioural grounds. Sibley and Ahlquist's (1985) DNA analyses confirmed that *Corvinella* and *Lanius* are two closely related genera.

THE GENUS *EUROCEPHALUS*

The genus *Eurocephalus* has often been attached to the helmet-shrikes Prionopidae or Prionopinae. They are now placed with the true shrikes on mainly morphological or behavioural grounds (Harris and Arnott 1988), or on arguments based on osteology (Olson 1989) or genetics (Sibley and Monroe

1990). Two geographically separated species are generally recognised, following for instance Hall and Moreau (1970): the White-rumped Shrike *E. rueppelli*, confined to eastern Africa, and the White-crowned Shrike *E. anguitimens*, occurring in southern Africa.

OVERVIEW OF THE GENUS *LANIUS*

NAMES

In Latin, *Lanius* means butcher. In the same language *laniare* means to tear in pieces. Clearly, the scientific name given to the genus is a reference to the shrikes' habit of impaling their prey on a spike or thorn (Gotch 1981, Lefranc 1993). The fact that they use, as it were, a 'butchering device' (see *Food, feeding habits and larders* below) has given them, or at least gave them for a long time, a reputation for cruelty reflected in their names in several languages. A common English name used for the whole genus is 'butcher-bird'. In eastern and southern Africa one very suggestive name of the Common Fiscal is 'jacky hangman' (Vincent 1935); early Dutch settlers in South Africa called it 'canary biter' (Harris and Arnott 1988). Things are not much better in Germany where one of the common names of the Red-backed Shrike is *Neuntöter*, the murderer with nine victims: the story went that the bird killed nine poor innocent creatures before having a rest. The common German name of the Great Grey Shrike, *Raubwürger*, is also frightening to perfection as it comes from the verb *rauben*, which means to steal using violence, and from the noun *Würger* = strangler! All shrikes are given the latter name in German. The French word *pies-grièche* sounds somewhat better, but loosely according to the *Robert de la Langue Française* (1985 edition) '*grièche*' comes from a gallo-roman term meaning 'hard, painful'. Thus a *pie-grièche* would be loosely translated as a sadisitic Magpie. From 1656 onwards the word has also been used to designate a bad-tempered, quarrelsome woman. In Languedoc-Roussillon, in southern France, shrikes used to be called *tarnagas* which means something like 'perfect idiot' in the local dialect (Hugues 1932); this reputation for stupidity was certainly due to the fact that shrikes, as birds of open habitats, were relatively easy to trap, as indeed is still the case in Taiwan for instance (Severinghaus 1991).

The generic word 'shrike' also has a pejorative connotation as it refers to the reputedly unpleasant vocalisations of these birds. The specific English names reflect morphological characteristics (Long-tailed Shrike, Great Grey Shrike, Lesser Grey Shrike, Bull-headed Shrike), dominant colours (Brown Shrike, Isabelline Shrike, etc), geographical areas (Burmese Shrike, Chinese Grey Shrike, Somali Fiscal) and sometimes names of persons, Sousa's Shrike for instance, named after I. A. de Sousa, director of the Lisbon Museum towards the end of last century. The name 'loggerhead' may refer both to the fact that the head of the species in question, and of shrikes in general, is relatively large compared to its body size and, again, to its reputation for stupidity as it also means 'blockhead' (Yosef 1996). The word 'fiscal' is more dignified as it derives from the title of senior judicial officers of the Cape settlement in South Africa who dressed in black and white (Harris and Arnott 1988). It was first used to name the Common Fiscal and now appears in the names of seven pied African species.

MORPHOLOGY, PLUMAGES AND MOULT

Lanius shrikes are small to medium-sized birds. The smallest species is Emin's Shrike of Central Africa, which is about 15cm in length with an average body mass of 20-25g, while the largest is the Chinese Grey Shrike, particularly its high-elevation race *giganteus*, measuring about 32cm and weighing on average about 100g.

One of the most striking features of these shrikes is their raptor-like bill, indicative of a predatory and carnivorous mode of feeding. It is generally very strong with a sharp hook on the end; the upper mandible shows a subterminal tomial tooth on each side and the lower mandible has corresponding incurvations. This shape bears strong similarities to that of falcons (Cade 1995); it is, however, interesting to note that in shrikes the hooked bill and tomial teeth only become apparent when the young birds are about four weeks old. Large jaw muscles are needed so that such a beak can give a powerful bite, hence the shrikes' relatively large head. Whereas their bill shape is very similar to those of falcons their feet are markedly different; a relatively powerful grip is, however, possible thanks to a hind limb muscular specialisation apparently unique among passerine birds (Raikow *et al.* 1980).

Comparison of Great Grey Shrike *L. excubitor* **with Common Kestrel** *Falco tinnunculus* **showing similarity of bill shape.**

Another typical shrike feature is the 'highwayman's' facial mask, dark brown or black in adults. Always covering the ear-patches, and very often the lores, it sometimes extends over the base of the bill and occasionally even well up onto the forehead as in the Lesser Grey Shrike, Bay-backed Shrike or the Grey-backed Fiscal. In some species with a black 'cap', particularly African ones like the Common Fiscal, the facial mask may be difficult to distinguish as such, at least in the field.

Four main colours occur in the plumages of *Lanius* shrikes: black, grey with its various shades, white and reddish-brown; the latter colour can tend towards brown, particularly in young birds, or to deep chestnut or even yellowish or orange. The wings are generally dark, often with a varyingly conspicuous white or whitish patch generally confined to the base of the primaries, but occasionally also extending to the base of the secondaries as in the case of some European races of the Great Grey Shrike. White scapulars can be found in a variety of species. The underparts of adults are generally white or off-white, sometimes partly tinged yellowish, orange, rose, etc; they are never really dark except in the '*fuscatus*' morph of the Long-tailed Shrike. Sexual dimorphism is generally low; it is obvious only in a very few species, particularly the Red-backed and to a lesser extent Emin's, Bull-headed and Tiger Shrikes. In a few species, it is even, as far as is known, impossible to tell males from females on plumage characteristics alone; this is the case for the Loggerhead, Southern Grey, Grey-backed and Mountain Shrikes and Somali Fiscal.

Young birds are characteristically brown and heavily vermiculated both on the upperparts and underparts; these vermiculations generally disappear after the moult into first-summer plumage except in females of a few species: Red-backed, Bull-headed and Tiger Shrikes, where they remain very conspicuous. They are also regularly present in adults of both sexes of a few races of the Great Grey Shrike, particularly in *mollis* and *funereus*. Remarkably, barring even occurs on the upperparts of adults of one species, the Tiger Shrike; hence its name.

Much has still to be learnt about moult in *Lanius* shrikes and only a general picture, mainly based on data from Holarctic species, can be given here.

Young shrikes spend about two weeks or a little more in their nest. During that time they acquire the typical heavily vermiculated brown plumage. A post-juvenile moult involves almost exclusively the body feathers, but is generally very partial and starts very early when the young are only three or four weeks old, immediately after fledging. A complete or almost complete moult into first-summer plumage takes place in winter. Some unmoulted feathers make it possible, at least in the hand or at close quarters, to tell first-summer birds from older adults. This is for instance the case in the Woodchat Shrike, Masked Shrike, and often the Long-tailed Shrike.

The moult strategy in adults varies with their migratory status. Sedentary shrikes tend to have a complete moult soon after breeding. Migrant species, or populations, generally begin their moult while still on the breeding grounds; it can then be suspended during migration and resumed in the winter quarters, where all the remaining old feathers are generally renewed. This pattern is typical of passerines. Two shrikes, remarkably, appear to have two complete or almost complete moults, a post-breeding one on the breeding grounds and a pre-breeding one in the wintering area: the Brown Shrike (race *cristatus*) and the Tiger Shrike (Stresemann and Stresemann 1971). Prys-Jones (1991) only lists seven passerine species of six different families with such a moult strategy, including the well-studied Willow Warbler *Phylloscopus trochilus*. He also mentions a few other species in which the available evidence remains ambiguous. This may in fact also be the case in the Brown Shrike (see Neufeldt 1981).

ORIGINS, PRESENT DISTRIBUTION, MIGRATIONS AND WINTERING AREAS

Sibley and Ahlquist (1990), who base their opinion on the results of their DNA-DNA hybridisation experiments, think that the ancestor of the true shrikes emigrated from Australia, probably to Asia. This event might have taken place c. 20-30 million years ago, during the Tertiary period, when Australia drifted northwards. *Corvinella* and *Eurocephalus* only occur in Africa; the genus *Lanius* probably radiated first in Africa and Eurasia; it appears obvious that it arrived more recently in North America, possibly during the Pleistocene and probably, like Man, through what is now the Bering Strait. The Loggerhead Shrike may represent a first wave of *Lanius* immigrants to the New World, pushed south by a glacial epoch and followed much later, probably after the last ice age, by another wave of very similar birds, the Great Grey or Northern Shrike (Salomonsen 1948). A fossil bird, apparently already having much in common with these shrikes, is known from Miocene deposits in south-west France (Milne-Edwards in Farner *et al.* 1985); it has been given the name of *Lanius miocaenus*. According to these findings, the genus *Lanius* already existed in western Europe c. 25-30 million years ago. Panov (1983) is convinced of the African origin of the genus and of its progressive spread into Eurasia and finally into North America. Of the 27 species listed in the present book, twelve breed in Africa and four others have, as it were, kept a link with that continent in so far as their wintering range mainly, if not entirely, lies within its limits. The migration pattern of the Red-backed Shrike might even partly reflect the progressive invasion by a southern species of northern latitudes after the retreat of the glaciers about 12,000 years ago. The resident ancestor of the Red-backed Shrike might be the very similar Emin's Shrike, now distributed in a belt from central-west to central-east Africa (for a general review of the possible evolution of the Palearctic-African migration system, see Safriel 1995). East Africa is particularly rich in *Lanius* shrikes, the combined check-lists of Uganda, Kenya and Tanzania totalling 14 species (Dowsett and Dowsett-Lemaire 1993). Certain species like the Long-tailed Shrike probably evolved in Asia; interestingly China is also very rich in *Lanius* shrikes, with eleven breeding species (Cheng 1987). Whatever their past history, *Lanius* shrikes are now widespread over almost the whole world except Australia and South America; their absence from Madagascar is also noteworthy.

According to latitude, geographical area and food habits, *Lanius* shrikes can be either long-distance, partial or altitudinal migrants. Those populations breeding in various types of tropical climate, as for instance the different races of the Common Fiscal, find enough food all the year round and are mainly, if not exclusively, resident. Local movements may, however, occur; not well documented, they are probably linked to significant shifts in weather conditions such as rain or drought. Shrikes breeding in subarctic or temperate areas or at relatively high latitudes in Asia are, by contrast, rarely resident. All the smaller species, which depend almost exclusively on insects, completely vacate their breeding areas in autumn: Red-backed Shrike, Isabelline Shrike (with a few possible exceptions in Central Asia), Brown Shrike and Tiger Shrike. Three mainly insectivorous Eurasian species nesting in climatically mediterranean or continental areas also vacate their breeding range: Woodchat Shrike, Masked Shrike and Lesser Grey Shrike. Larger species, such as Chinese Grey Shrike, Great Grey Shrike, Loggerhead Shrike and even the somewhat smaller Bull-headed Shrike, which are able to catch small vertebrates and to adapt to relatively harsh weather conditions, are partial migrants. They are almost migratory in the north of their respective breeding ranges, but tend to be resident further south, the proportions of birds migrating being lower in areas with reduced snow cover in winter. Other partial migrants are Burmese Shrike, Bay-backed Shrike, Long-tailed Shrike and Grey-backed Shrike. Some populations of the two latter species are altitudinal migrants, for instance in Nepal. The same might hold true for the very little-known Mountain Shrike, endemic to the Philippines. The Southern Grey Shrike is mainly a resident species over its vast breeding range; local movements do, however, occur and the northern populations of the race *pallidirostris*, breeding in Kazakhstan, are long-distance migrants, spending the winter as far south as Sudan and Ethiopia.

The longest migratory movements are performed by two Palearctic species wintering in southern Africa, the Red-backed Shrike and Lesser Grey Shrike; some populations of these birds may well travel over 10,000km each way; the Lesser Grey Shrikes breeding in the north-western part of the Chinese autonomous region of Xinjiang (Cheng 1987) and wintering somewhere in Botswana or Namibia (Dowsett 1971) may even travel nearly 11,000km. The nominate race of Brown Shrike in the eastern Palearctic covers a distance of 5,000-8,000km each way between its Siberian breeding grounds and its wintering area in the Indian subcontinent and South-East Asia; its Chinese race *lucionensis* migrates to the Philippines and some of these birds even reach Borneo and Sulawesi, thus covering almost 4,000km each way (Panov 1983).

The migrations of some species are unusual. The western European populations of both Red-backed and Lesser Grey Shrike fly south-east in autumn, largely avoiding Africa west of 20°E (c. 25°E for *Lanius minor*). The same populations of both species are also loop-migrants, passing further east in spring than in autumn (Moreau 1972). This may be explained by climatic patterns (Pearson and Lack 1992) or by differences in the wind patterns (Verheyen 1951). Woodchat and Masked Shrike may also make loop migrations (see species accounts).

Lanius shrikes, like all birds, put on fat before migrating (Alerstam 1990) but they carry a much smaller percentage of fat than other passerines (Moreau 1972, Jakober and Stauber 1980a). This could be accounted for by the fact that they migrate in relatively short stages, particularly in autumn; they also easily find food en route, including smaller, weakened migrant passerines (Moreau 1972). Observations have shown that even the slightly built Masked Shrike with its rather weak bill does not hesitate to attack handicapped migrants (e.g. Watson 1967). In the Palearctic-African migration system, the Lesser Grey Shrike is one of only two passerine species whose populations winter entirely south of the Equator, the other being the Icterine Warbler *Hippolais icterina*. The Lesser Grey Shrike also shows the most extreme example of a Eurasian bird having a smaller wintering than breeding range. The latter is estimated to cover an area seven times greater than the wintering area in south-western Africa (Dowsett 1971, Newton 1995).

Migrating shrikes travel singly, never in flocks, but several can turn up on the same morning at the same stopover. Most species are predominantly night-migrants, except the Loggerhead Shrike (Yosef 1996); the Great Grey Shrike may occasionally also start its migration flights in the afternoon (Glutz von Blotzheim and Bauer 1993).

HABITAT

Lanius shrikes are widespread over a range of habitats roughly stretching between the Arctic Circle and c. 33°S in southern Africa. A few populations of the Great Grey and Brown Shrike breed even further north, near c. 70°N. The Laniidae are thus present in almost all types of climate. They can be found from near sea-level to c. 5,000m; the latter altitude is reached by the race *giganteus* of the Chinese Grey Shrike; other typical high-elevation shrikes are the Grey-backed (or Tibetan) Shrike breeding in the Himalayas, and the Mountain Shrike, confined to the Philippines.

The rounded wings of some supposedly primitive species like the Great Grey Shrike and the Grey-backed Fiscal might indicate that ancestors of *Lanius* shrikes lived in woodlands, presumably in Africa (Stegmann in Panov 1983). This idea draws support from the fact that a few species can almost be regarded as 'forest shrikes': Sousa's Shrike in *Brachystegia* woods in Central Africa, the Masked Shrike in open oak and pine forests in the Middle East, and the Tiger Shrike in light deciduous woodlands in far-eastern Asia. At least the two latter species have, however, also expanded into more open terrain and, as a whole, true shrikes can be considered as birds of more or less open habitats, avoiding dense forests.

Species differ in their precise ecological requirements, but they all need: (a) at least a few trees or bushes as shelters against enemies, as nesting-sites and, for most species, also as larder sites; (b) a variable number of watch-posts, natural or not, essential for these birds which are mainly 'sit-and-wait' predators, taking most of their prey on the ground; (c) open hunting grounds scattered with perches and characterised by large herbaceous patches or even bare soil where insects or small vertebrates are easily detectable and accessible.

It is of course of particular interest to study the precise requirements of various species living in the same geographical area. Lewis and Pomeroy (1989) for instance have shown that, in Kenya, the presence, absence or frequency of different shrikes is at least partly related to a moist–arid gradient. The difference between the extremes, Mackinnon's Shrike, typical of rather humid areas, and the Somali Fiscal, characteristic of arid habitats, is very clear. See also Ullrich (1971) and Lefranc (1980) for habitat differences in four Palearctic shrikes living largely in sympatry. Bruderer (1994) gives some details on niche separation in southern Africa between the Common Fiscal, two Palearctic wintering shrikes (Red-backed and Lesser Grey), and another sit-and-wait hunter, the Marico Flycatcher *Melaenornis mariquensis*. Where all species have to co-exist the basic difference is probably prey size, correlated with perch height and attack distance.

SOCIAL ORGANISATION AND GENERAL BEHAVIOUR

The vast majority of *Lanius* shrikes breed in pairs, each defending a territory. However, two highly social species, possibly sister taxa (Hall and Moreau 1970), occur in Africa. One of these, the little-studied Long-tailed Fiscal, may also be found in pairs with individual territories (van Someren 1956); the other, the Grey-backed Fiscal, well studied near Lake Naivasha in Kenya, more regularly appears to breed in groups of up to at least eleven birds (Zack and Ligon 1985a,b, Zack 1986a). Cooperative breeding may be an ancestral trait in *Lanius* shrikes; in fact it may be the ancestral condition of the Laniidae as a whole, as it is still regular in the genera *Eurocephalus* and *Corvinella*. Non-cooperative breeding with dispersal of young at maturity is assumed to be derived for the majority of *Lanius* shrikes (Zack 1995). In cooperative *Lanius* shrikes, normally only one pair nests per group; the other members aid with the rearing of young. They also help defend the territory against intruders; territorial rallies are frequent, noisy and accompanied by much wing-beating and tail-fanning 'dances' somewhat reminiscent of *Turdoides* babbler behaviour (Banage 1969, Zack 1986a). Members of a group, at least in the case of the Grey-backed Fiscal in East Africa, remain all year round in the same home range in which individuals disperse widely; they come together only during their frequent rallies, near the nest, near abundant localised food or at a common roosting-site.

Lanius shrikes are typically monogamous. A few cases of polygyny have, however, been observed in the Southern Grey Shrike, presumably race *aucheri*, in the Negev Desert in Israel (Yosef and Pinshow 1988b), and in the Loggerhead Shrike (Verner and Wilson in Yosef 1992b and Yosef 1992b).

Pair-bonds from one season to the next are rarely renewed in non-social *Lanius* shrikes. In migrant species like the Red-backed, Woodchat and Lesser Grey Shrike such events can only be occasional as females show a much lower site-fidelity than males (Cramp and Perrins 1993). Pair-bonds are more regular, but by no means the rule, in resident shrikes. Thus in southern Japan, Yamagishi and Nishiumi (1994) followed 47 females of the sedentary Bull-headed Shrike which bred in more than two successive seasons: in 14 cases

Red-backed Shrike, alarmed at presence of observer; tail is cocked vertically and wings are slightly flicking.

(30%) the female paired with the previous year's mate and in 33 cases (70%) with a new mate despite the fact that 19 previous mates were still present in the same area; so there was at least a 40% divorce rate. Contrary to supposition (Cramp and Perrins 1993), renewals of pair-bonds appear to be only very occasional in resident or partly resident populations of Great Grey and Southern Grey Shrikes: males tend to stay all their life in the same territory, whereas the females disappear as soon as the young become independent; they probably do not move far, but are rarely found again in their previous mate's territory (Dohmann 1985, Cruz Solis *et al.* 1990, Yosef 1992a, Schön 1994b).

The sexual life of shrikes is receiving more and more attention and at least three species can now be added to the list of birds in which extra-pair copulations (EPCs) have been recorded: the Red-backed Shrike (Jakober and Stauber 1994 among others), the Great Grey Shrike (Lorek 1995b) and the Bull-headed Shrike (Yamagishi *et al.* 1992). Detailed field observations in Poland (Lorek 1995b) have shown that in clumped territories of the Great Grey Shrike male intruders regularly seek EPCs with paired females from neighbouring territories; females appear to have little choice but to participate, possibly forced by physically dominant males. Sixty-nine intrusions resulted in 23 EPCs, that is a 'success rate' of 33.3% despite intensive mate-guarding behaviour by the resident males during the fertile period of their respective females. The observed EPCs were generally quickly followed by a copulation by the female's mate probably in order to reduce the extra-pair male's chances of successful fertilisation due to sperm precedence. Yamagishi *et al.* (1992) analysed parentage in a wild population of the Bull-headed Shrike in southern Japan by DNA fingerprinting. They found that among 99 nestlings from 24 clutches, 10 (10%) from 4 (17%) clutches had extra-pair paternity, but all were offspring of the females.

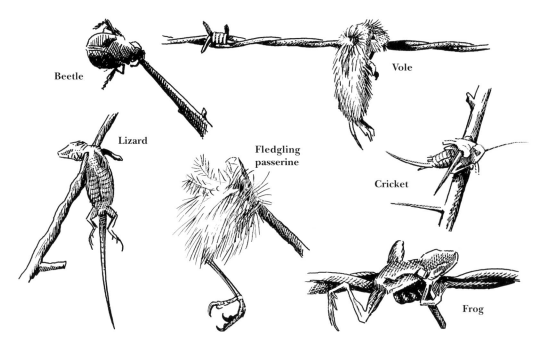

Beetle

Vole

Lizard

Fledgling
passerine

Cricket

Frog

Prey impaled at larder.

FOOD, FEEDING HABITS AND LARDERS

Many studies have been carried out on the food of shrikes in the Holarctic region. Earlier this century they were mainly based on stomach analyses, for instance in Miller (1931) for the Loggerhead Shrike and Madon (1934) for West Palearctic shrikes. Nowadays, particularly for the Great Grey Shrike, most precise data come from pellet analyses. Pellets are regularly regurgitated by shrikes and can be picked up under their favourite perches or near their nests. Those of the Great Grey Shrike measure on average about 25 x 12mm, weigh about 1-1.5g and generally can be easily handled as they usually (though not always) contain a lot of fur of small mammals, besides bones, skulls, feathers, chitinous remains, etc. Pellets of mainly insectivorous shrikes, like those of the Lesser Grey Shrike, measure about the same size, but are much more fragile and break easily. For examples of pellet analyses, among many others, see the recent works by Wagner (1993) for the Red-backed Shrike, Wagner and Hölker (1995) for the Great Grey Shrike, Hernandez et al. (1993) for the Southern Grey Shrike, the Woodchat Shrike and the Red-backed Shrike, Scott and Morrison (1990) for the Loggerhead Shrike, Ogawa (1977) for the Bull-headed Shrike, and Winter (1987) for the Chinese Grey Shrike. The food of 6–10-day-old nestling Red-backed Shrikes has been studied by a few workers

through collar-sampling (e.g. Mansfeld 1958, Lefranc 1979, Mann 1983). Monitoring of larder-sites also provides useful information; see for instance Lefranc 1979 for the Red-backed Shrike, Hernandez and Salgado (1993) for the Southern Grey Shrike, Grünwald (1986a,b) and Olsson (1986) for the Great Grey Shrike and Severinghaus and Liang (1995) for the Brown Shrike. Direct observations can also be very helpful, all the more so as they give clues on foraging habits, preferred perch-heights, prey selection, etc. (for instance Solari and Schudel 1988 for the Red-backed Shrike). Less usual techniques have been tried by Hernandez (1993b), who studied the nestling diet of the Southern Grey, Woodchat

Juvenile Great Grey Shrike ejecting pellet.

and Red-backed Shrikes through faecal sac analysis and identification of vertebrate remains found in nests.

All the techniques listed above have their advantages and limits; one of the drawbacks of pellet analyses, for instance, is that they somewhat underestimate the part played by soft-bodied insects (Cade 1967, Olsson 1986), whereas impaling records are obviously biased towards the larger prey items. All the studies, however, confirm that shrikes are opportunistic, insectivorous birds, able to exploit a wide array of species and to have seasonal, annual and geographical variations in their diet. Opportunism and selection of prey may go together in favourable circumstances. Thus studies on the Red-backed Shrike have shown that the species mainly feeds its young nestlings on spiders, insect larvae and soft-bodied insects like flies (Korodi Gal 1969, Lefranc 1979), that it almost never takes prey measuring less than 4mm (except ants when in abundance: Wagner 1993) and that it readily profits from plague years or temporary high populations of easily accessible insects such as chafers *Melolontha*, *Hoplia*, *Phyllopertha*, etc, or small rodents (Cramp and Perrins 1993, Lefranc 1993).

All *Lanius* shrikes are, at least occasionally, able to catch small vertebrates although definite proof is currently lacking for a few smaller, little-studied species like Emin's and Sousa's Shrikes in Africa and Bay-backed and Burmese Shrikes in Asia. Larger species regularly take small animals, which may represent up to 90% of the prey biomass of the Great Grey Shrike, particularly in winter (Glutz von Blotzheim and Bauer 1993). In Europe, the Great Grey has occasionally been known to kill animals the size of a European Mole *Talpa europaea*, a young Black Rat *Rattus rattus* or a Song Thrush *Turdus philomelos* (Glutz von Blotzheim and Bauer 1993, Lefranc 1993), but such attacks are rare and possibly induced by severe hunger or easy opportunities offered by sick, handicapped animals. The main prey items of the species are voles, particularly of the genus *Microtus*; the bird probably selects the size of its victims, preferring those which would be easier to catch to larger prey requiring more energy expense (see Slack 1975).

Shrikes kill small vertebrates by striking them repeatedly with the bill at the back of the head; the tomial teeth are used to disarticulate cervical vertebrae, exactly as in falcons (Cade 1967, 1995). Unlike some raptors the feet never serve as killing weapons; they may, however, be helpful for destabilising small birds in flight, which are quickly killed by blows to the nape. They are also used to hold relatively small prey items, like large insects, against a perch in order to pull them apart. This technique cannot be employed for larger victims like voles, lizards, passerines (Cramp and Perrins 1993, Cade 1995). Small vertebrates have to be carried to a larder where they are either impaled or, more often, wedged. A shrike that regularly or occasionally consumes small vertebrates can carry prey weighing up to approximately its own weight. Red-backed Shrikes, weighing on average c. 30g, have for instance been seen carrying full-grown small passerines like Greenfinches *Carduelis chloris*, Yellowhammers *Emberiza citrinella* or Common Crossbills *Loxia curvirostra* (Glutz von Blotzheim and Bauer 1993). Larger prey is carried with difficulty and frequent pauses may be necessary, even on the ground, every 20-30m (Cramp and Perrins 1993). Experiments carried out on the Loggerhead Shrike (average weight c. 50g) with laboratory mice *Mus musculus* ranging in size up to 62g, have shown that the species was able to carry prey weighing up to 129% of its own body mass (Yosef 1993b). The same study confirmed that small prey was transported in the beak, intermediate prey in beak and then feet, and heavy prey only in the feet.

Red-backed Shrike feeding at larder.

Lanius shrikes, as far as is known, are the only members of the family to use larders regularly; impaling of food has, however, exceptionally been recorded in captive bush-shrikes of the genus *Laniarius* (Sonnenschein and Reyer 1984). The habit has not yet been recorded in a *Lanius* species, in Sousa's Shrike for instance, but this may simply reflect low levels of observation. The habit is obviously very rare in some species like the Lesser Grey Shrike and somewhat irregular in others like the Woodchat. Even some Red-backed Shrikes, mainly those living in warm lowlands where food is plentiful, appear never to use larders, although the habit is, as a rule, widespread in that species (Lefranc 1993). Many types of thorn can be used for impaling as well as sharp twigs, crotches, barbed wire, etc. Vertebrates are always killed first and then carried away and wedged into a fork or, when they are merely 'stored', often impaled through the neck. Insects are usually impaled through the thorax and can remain alive a long time. Not all cached prey is utilised by shrikes: in north-west Spain Hernandez (1995) observed that Southern Grey Shrikes (nominate *meridionalis*) only used 62% (n = 162) and Red-backed Shrike 88% (n = 556) of stored prey. The former tended to leave pilose lepidopteran larvae unused and ate most of its cached prey within nine days of storage. Only 2% of the prey stored by the Red-backed Shrike was recovered later than 24 hours following storage. Other animals can profit from stored food: Hernandez (1995) noted that 6% of the prey cached by Red-backed Shrikes was pilfered, especially by wasps and occasionally by ants and at least once by a Blackbird *Turdus merula*. Other birds and particularly corvids can be important pilferers; thus in Sweden, Magpies *Pica pica* took more than half of the prey stored by wintering Great Grey Shrikes (Olsson 1985). Shrikes tend to hide some of their food in the inner parts of shrubs, presumably in order to avoid such thefts; there might even be a link between prey colour and the colour of shrubs used, a point to be confirmed (Hernandez 1995). On the other hand items may be deliberately positioned well in view, particularly at the beginning of the breeding season, and might have a communicating function (see below).

Impaling and wedging of prey is, at least to a certain extent, innate. Both captive and wild young shrikes, when aged three to four weeks, perform what Smith (1973b) calls 'dabbing'. This behaviour, recognisable as being related to impaling, consists of taking an object in the bill, turning it sideways and placing it on the perch beside the bird. A little later a pulling component appears, called 'dragging' by Smith (1973b). The same author suggests that 'dabbing' may have originally been performed by an ancestor of *Lanius*, simply when not hungry enough to eat its prey; in thorny country, presumably tropical Africa, pieces of food may occasionally and accidentally have become caught on thorns; thus 'dabbing', a behaviour also noted in other species like the Black-capped Chickadee *Parus atricapillus* and Blue Jay *Cyanocitta cristata* may have been the original motor pattern that eventually led to the impaling behaviour now typical of most *Lanius* species. For the ontogeny of impaling behaviour in shrikes see also the experiments by Lorenz and Saint Paul (1968).

Impaling or wedging behaviour appears to have several functions:

(1) It is useful and even necessary in order to enable shrikes to dismember small vertebrates which they are unable, unlike raptors, to hold down with their talons. The victims have to be well anchored at a 'butchering site' before the birds begin tearing off bite-size pieces, each jerk being accompanied by a slight flip of the wings (see for instance Olsson 1985).

(2) It guarantees a certain food supply as a 'larder' or a 'cache', available in bad weather when insects are less active. Observations on the Red-backed Shrike in north-east France, for instance, have shown that stored prey items quickly disappear in wet weather (Lefranc 1979). General data also suggest that Red-backed Shrikes are more prone to impale prey in areas of more unstable weather: the habit is rarely recorded in the African winter quarters (Harris and Arnott 1988, Cramp and Perrins 1993, Lefranc 1993). In north-western Spain, Hernandez (1995) observed that the number of cached prey increased throughout the Red-backed Shrike's breeding season and that there was a positive relationship between rate of food-storing and number of nestlings.

(3) It enables at least one species, the Loggerhead Shrike, to consume toxic insects like the Monarch butterfly *Danaus gilippus* and a frog *Gastrophyne carolinensis*, usually avoided by avian predators. These prey items are left impaled for three days or more and then eaten, presumably after poisons have degraded (Yosef and Whitman 1992, which also see for details on the relationships between the Loggerhead Shrike and the chemically defended lubber grasshopper *Romalea guttata*).

(4) It may serve as mate attraction. In the Negev Desert in Israel, Yosef and Pinshow (1989) have shown that cache size influences female mate-choice in the Southern Grey Shrike (presumably race *aucheri*), so that it was positively correlated with male mating success. A study in north-east France (Lefranc unpublished) has revealed that impaled crickets *Gryllus campestris* were well distributed,

very conspicuous and often left uneaten all over the territories of Great Grey Shrikes at the beginning of the breeding season. They might have a communicating function, as may a variety of impaled 'objects' which can occasionally be found in shrike territories, for instance the dates impaled by the Southern Grey Shrike (race *elegans*) in North Africa (review in Cramp and Perrins 1993).

FORAGING BEHAVIOUR

Lanius shrikes are almost exclusively 'sit-and-wait' predators that scan the surrounding ground and air, from a great variety of natural or man-made perches. Most prey items are caught on the ground where they are easily spotted as they move about. Shrikes may, however, also be able to detect images as suggested by observations on the Loggerhead Shrike (Yosef 1996). Movement may not be essential in prey recognition, but it certainly makes things easier. As in the case of the Red-backed Shrike (Carlson 1985), a perched bird raises its head from time to time and sometimes assumes a sleek erect posture, which probably shows it is on the lookout for predators. A shrike having difficulty in finding prey may occasionally flick and/or swing its tail as it often does in other circumstances to express annoyance or excitement. Some birds, particularly Great Grey Shrikes, intently watching rodent holes, may stay in the same spot for half an hour or more, but, as a rule, shrikes often change perches, patrolling favourite parts of their territory. In a study area in southern Sweden wintering Great Grey Shrikes observed for a total of 94 hours spent on average about eight minutes per perch (Olsson 1984c).

Each species appears to have its favourite average perch-height. In small shrikes, like the Red-backed, Isabelline and Brown, it is close to about two metres (pers. obs.). These species catch most of their prey within a radius of c. 10m, but favourite perch-height as well as average attack-distance may vary with the structure of the foraging area, the height of the grass layer, the density, size and availability of prey, etc. Carlson's (1985) experiments on the Red-backed Shrike have shown, not surprisingly, that the probability of detecting prey decreased with increasing distance and that there was a tendency for less precision in the strike with increasing attack-distance. Whereas 'sit-and-wait' is by far their most common hunting technique, shrikes also indulge in a variety of other feeding strategies. Hovering is very common in the Lesser Grey Shrike, a typical steppe bird, less so in the Great Grey, Loggerhead and Chinese Grey Shrikes, and occasional in other species. Shrikes may also sometimes be seen hopping on the ground like wheatears *Oenanthe* spp. (see species accounts). Bird-hunting is relatively rare but regular in some larger species like the Great Grey Shrike, which may then adopt a flight recalling a Sparrowhawk *Accipiter nisus* (Cramp and Perrins 1993); in Alaska, the Great Grey Shrike has also been seen flashing its wings in order to flush small passerines out of bushes (Cade 1962). Larger species of bird like Hoopoes *Upupa epops* are normally not potential victims, but they may occasionally be kleptoparasitised even by relatively small shrikes like the Woodchat (Harris 1994). Finally, shrikes are occasional scavengers (Cramp and Perrins 1993, Lefranc 1993). Anderson (1976) observed Loggerhead Shrikes exploiting remains of prey left by hawks.

When an insect is taken, it is either eaten immediately, for instance where it was caught on the ground, or, more frequently, brought back to a perch for consumption. At least four species – Loggerhead, Great Grey, Red-backed and Woodchat — are able to devenomise stinging Hymenoptera (Cade 1995). The experiments of Gwinner (1961) on captive Red-backed Shrikes, showed that birds destroyed the stinging apparatus by thoroughly squeezing the tip of the abdomen and rubbing it against the substrate; this work also showed that the recognition of sting-bearing Hymenoptera was innate and suggested that the most essential sign-stimulus was the specific elasticity of the insect body, particularly the thorax.

When a small vertebrate is caught it has, as already mentioned, to be impaled or wedged. Killing an adult vole may take a Great Grey Shrike a good minute; such a relatively big victim, as a rule, can provide three meals, each one lasting 5-15 minutes (Olsson 1984c, 1985).

Red-backed Shrike feeding on the ground.

NESTS, EGGS AND BREEDING BEHAVIOUR

Nests of *Lanius* shrikes are of the simple, cup-shaped type, made of a variety of materials such as twigs, rootlets, etc. At high latitudes or in mountainous areas, wool, hair and feathers are often present in the lining, but they may also be used elsewhere. At least some species readily include man-made materials; for instance, in the south of France the Lesser Grey Shrike regularly uses small strings and ribbons found in vineyards. This species is also remarkable for incorporating a high proportion of aromatic flowers in its nest.

Shrike nests are well structured, but not necessarily neatly made. There is, however, at least one exception: the relatively small, nicely built cup of the Masked Shrike (Lefranc 1993). The nest of Sousa's Shrike also appears to be somewhat peculiar, being neatly bound round with plant down and old cobwebs and at least sometimes reminiscent of the nests of bush-shrikes of the genera *Prionops* or *Nilaus* (Took 1966). Abnormal nests are found from time to time like the 'feather-nests' of the Great Grey Shrike (Cramp and Perrins 1993, Lefranc 1993). Most species nest either in bushes or in trees; the Lesser Grey Shrike is however largely, if not exclusively, a tree-nester, at least in Europe. Other species such as Southern Grey Shrike, Red-backed Shrike and Isabelline Shrike are mainly bush-nesters. Remarkably, in some areas of the Far East, the Brown Shrike regularly builds its nest on the ground, often at the base of a small tree or bush. Nests of other birds, e.g. Carrion Crow *Corvus corone*, Black-billed Magpie *Pica pica* or raptors are occasionally used by Great Grey, Southern Grey and Lesser Grey Shrike (Panov 1983, Lefranc 1993). In Minnesota, USA, occasional Loggerhead Shrike nests have been located in old nests of Common Grackle *Quiscalus quiscula* and Gray Catbird *Dumetella carolinensis* (Bent 1950).

Schönwetter and Meise (1970) in their *Handbuch der Oologie* (part 18) recognise two main types of egg in *Lanius* shrikes: the *collurio*-type and the *excubitor*-type. The latter includes the Great Grey, Southern Grey and Loggerhead Shrike; the eggs of these species are normally subelliptical and heavily marked all over their surface with small blotches roughly varying from grey-brown to brown; variations do occur, of course, but are less well marked than in the *collurio* type, which involves all the other species. The *collurio*-type eggs appear much less uniform and duller. They are also normally subelliptical with the small end blunt, generally slightly glossy and often variable in their ground colour, particularly in the Red-backed, Brown and Burmese Shrike, where this colour can be whitish, yellowish, greenish, brownish and even reddish. The ground colour appears to be less variable in a few other species, for instance in Sousa's Shrike, where it is greenish. In almost all cases, and much more so than in the *excubitor*-type, the ground colour is fairly obvious. The very variable markings are usually in the form of a zone, generally at the large end, though occasionally in the middle or at the small end of a shell.

As far as is known, the eggs of three species, Emin's Shrike, Newton's Fiscal and Mountain Shrike, have not yet been described.

Average size of eggs (in mm) of most species, mainly based on the general review of Schönwetter and Meise (1970), are as follows: Tiger Shrike: 22.0 x 16.7; Bull-headed Shrike: 23.2 x 17.6; Red-backed Shrike: 22.3 x 16.7; Isabelline Shrike (*phoenicuroides*): 22.2 x 17.2; Brown Shrike (*cristatus*): 21.8 x 16.9; Burmese Shrike: 21.1 x 16.4; Sousa's Shrike: 20.9 x 16.2; Bay-backed Shrike: 21 x 16.5; Long-tailed Shrike (*erythronotus*): 23.7 x 18.1, (*schach*): 25.2 x 19.4; Grey-backed Shrike: 25.3 x 18.7; Lesser Grey Shrike: 25.2 x 18.2; Loggerhead Shrike (*ludovicianus*): 24.5 x 18.8; Great Grey Shrike (*excubitor*): 26.3 x 19.5, (*invictus*): 26.9 x 20.4; Southern Grey Shrike (*meridionalis*): 27.3 x 19.6, (*koenigi*): 25.6 x 19.1, (*lahtora*): 26 x 19.8, (*leucopygos*): 24.5 x 18 (only one egg); Chinese Grey Shrike (*sphenocercus*): 27.3 x 20.4; Grey-backed Fiscal: 24.2 x 18.4; Long-tailed Fiscal: 25.5 x 18.8. Somali Fiscal: 23.4 x 18.6; Common Fiscal (*collaris*): 25 x 17.8, (*humeralis*): 22.8 x 17.2; Uhehe Fiscal: 23 x 17.4. Woodchat Shrike (*senator*): 23 x 17, (*niloticus*): 22.8 x 16.8; Masked Shrike: 20.5 x 15.8.

The full clutches of *Lanius* shrikes normally comprise between three and eight eggs. Clutch-size varies markedly with latitude both within the genus and within populations of the same species. The extreme cases are the Great Grey Shrike (race *invictus*), which has a modal clutch-size of eight eggs in arctic Alaska (Cade 1995), and Sousa's Shrike of south-central Africa, which never lays more than three eggs (Harris and Arnott 1988). For variations within a species see account of Long-tailed Shrike, and for a general discussion of geographical variation in clutch-size of passerines see Ricklefs (1980).

At the beginning of the breeding season, males, which are generally present before the females, establish an all-purpose territory serving for courtship, nesting, feeding and raising young. They are then generally very demonstrative and conspicuous. The notions of territory (= a defended area)

Red-backed Shrike displaying.

and of home range (= an area occupied by a pair) are thus interchangeable or almost so for most shrike species. Overlapping home ranges do, however, occur; although very limited in the case of the Red-backed Shrike, which defends a large core area around its nest (Fornasari *et al.* 1993). It is more regular in the extreme case of the Lesser Grey Shrike, in which several adults may be seen foraging without apparent quarrels in the same 'neutral' area (Lefranc 1993, Panov 1983). Territory sizes vary according to the requirements of the different species and, within a species, with the quality of the habitat (structure and, above all, sufficient food availability). Smaller territories only cover 1-1.5ha and concern small species like the Red-backed Shrike. The largest territories are inhabited by the Great Grey Shrike, which generally needs between 25 and 100ha, sometimes more (Cramp and Perrins 1993, Lefranc 1993, Schön 1994e).

Pair formation in shrikes is accompanied by displays varying in detail between species and characterised by much wing-shivering, tail-spreading, bowing, movements of the head, etc. Display-flights are regular in some species like Red-backed, Lesser Grey and Bull-headed Shrikes; they are rare in others like the Loggerhead and apparently non-existent in most, if not all, races of the Southern Grey Shrike. Distinct advertising calls are often very typical and more audible than songs. Some species like the Long-tailed and Red-backed Shrikes are excellent mimics; others like the Great Grey or Loggerheads are not. Duets have been performed by Woodchat and Great Grey Shrikes during group meetings (Cramp and Perrins 1993, Lefranc 1993, Yosef 1996).

Nesting territories are mainly, although not exclusively, defended by males; in the cooperative breeding Grey-backed Fiscal such defences can lead to noisy rallies with the participation of most members of the group (see species accounts). In the Red-backed Shrike, the male is particularly aggressive towards his congeners from the time of his arrival until the end of the fertile period of the female. Studies of males caught in their breeding territories in Italy showed that levels of testosterone were highest at the time of the birds' arrival and declined abruptly after a few days. These findings suggest that aggressive motivation is particularly helpful when the boundaries of territories are being established; lower levels are apparently sufficient for sexual behaviour, while elevated aggression could negatively influence mate choice by the female and make courtship rather ineffective (Fornasari *et al.* 1992). Red-backed Shrikes threaten their congeners as well as other birds with a typical hunched posture as they crouch with ruffled plumage. Loggerheads, particularly males, give a typical 'flutter display' when

Woodchat Shrike displaying.

another shrike is present in their territory at the beginning of the breeding season: they adopt a horizontal position, flex their legs, bow their heads, droop their wings slightly away from the body and flutter them rapidly while generally emitting notes similar to those of juveniles begging for food (Smith 1973). Great Grey and Southern Grey Shrikes show rather similar displays also based on wing-fluttering (Cramp and Perrins 1993). Such displays, which may be mistaken for sexual behaviour, also occur in individual winter territories. They probably indicate a high attack tendency. Real fights are relatively rare, but see Dohmann (1985) for the Southern Grey Shrike.

Male courtship-feeding is probably regular in all *Lanius* shrikes. Females solicit food, often but not always with much wing-shivering and 'begging calls' very similar to those of hungry fledglings. In a study in Sweden, female Red-backed Shrikes responded to experimentally enhanced courtship feeding by significantly increasing their clutch-size (Carlson 1989). Observations on the Bull-headed Shrike in Japan suggest that the function of courtship-feeding is directly beneficial to the female as its frequency is highest in cold seasons and at critical breeding stages: egg-laying, incubation (Yamagishi and Saito 1985). Other observations on the Loggerhead Shrike (Woods 1995) and on the Great Grey Shrike (pers. obs.) suggest that delivery of large food items by the male and subsequent holding of the food by the female appeases the latter and prevents her from pecking at the male while he is mounting her. As in many other species, courtship-feeding has probably various functions: to entice females to copulate, strengthen the pair-bond and divert surplus energy into offspring production.

During the fertile period of the females, male shrikes tend to stay in close contact with them, the risks of extra-pair copulations being far from negligible at least in some, and possibly in all, species (see *Social organisation and general behaviour*). It is possible that extra-pair copulations are necessary to ensure genetic diversity. If several pairs occur in the same area 'aggregates' can form enabling the birds to have a 'normal' sexual life. Mate-guarding in shrikes will probably receive increasing attention in the future, particularly as it may have some importance in the adoption of conservation strategies (van Nieuwenhuyse 1996).

As a rule in *Lanius* shrikes it seems that the male advertises a variety of possible nest-sites to the female, which may have the final choice. As a rule also, it appears that nest-building is a shared business, the male, however, being mainly a provider of material and the female mainly undertaking the actual construction.

Incubation is almost entirely or exclusively done by the female, who is largely dependent on the male for food from the start of laying until the young are about a week old. For instance, a female Loggerhead Shrike at a nest with eggs, watched for 942 minutes, spent 82% of the time incubating. Incubation bouts averaged 23 minutes in length, ranging from one to 94 minutes, while absences ranged from 0.5 to 28 minutes, averaging five minutes. Nine times the female left the nest in response to the arrival of her mate with food, and thirteen times she left independently. The male fed his mate on or near the nest about once in 23 minutes (Johnson 1940).

At least in well-studied species, it has been observed that incubation tends to start before the clutch is complete, generally with the penultimate egg (Miller 1931, Cramp and Perrins 1993, Lefranc 1993). Hatching is thus asynchronous and occurs over c. 24-36 hours. For about a week or more after the eggs have hatched, depending on the weather, the female broods her young and distributes the food brought by the male. From time to time she leaves the nest in order to preen or to procure some of the food herself, whether from a larder or not.

Potential nest predators are vigorously attacked by the male, and the female may join in. The Great Grey Shrike for instance makes dive-attacks with rattle-calls, particularly on crows and raptors. Intruders may also be frightened off by threat postures, chasing and bill-snapping (Cramp and Perrins 1993). A remarkable passive anti-predator behaviour has been witnessed in Israel in the Southern Grey Shrike. At eight nests containing young aged 9-18 days which had been disturbed by possible predators or human observers (for ringing), the females were subsequently seen forcing the nestlings out by prodding them with the bill; after they had tumbled to the ground from their nests, located low in bushes, the young were coaxed to move to cover some distance from their nests (Yosef and Pinshow 1988a).

At least in some species – Great Grey, Lesser Grey and Red-backed Shrikes – family groups split up some time after fledging, each adult taking charge of one part of the progeny in different parts of the territory (Cramp and Perrins 1993, Glutz von Blotzheim and Bauer 1993). Young shrikes, as a rule, become independent a few weeks after fledging and leave the natal territory; retention of offspring well into adulthood is, however, regular in the cooperative-breeding Grey-backed Fiscal (Zack 1986a). Remarkably, Macdonald (1980) found that juveniles of the non-cooperative Common Fiscal remained months longer in their respective natal territories in tropical Ghana than juveniles of the same species in South Africa.

Juvenile Great Grey Shrike begging for food.

ASPECTS OF POPULATION DYNAMICS

Studies of ringed populations of West Palearctic shrikes and on the North American Loggerhead Shrike show that at least these species, and presumably all *Lanius* shrikes, breed for the first time when nearly one year old, that is in the first spring after hatching (Cramp and Perrins 1993, Yosef 1996).

The life span of shrikes apppears normally to lie between seven and eight years. Among the records listed in *The Ring* (1973, 1974) are a Bay-backed Shrike which lived at least seven years, eleven months and eight days, and a Red-backed Shrike which lived seven years and four days. Jakober and Stauber (in Glutz von Blotzheim and Bauer 1993), in their long-term study of the latter species in south-west Germany, recorded a male which was ringed as a nestling ten years and two months before. A captive bird of the same species reached an age of eleven years (Rabiger in Glutz von Blotzheim and Bauer 1993). A Great Grey Shrike ringed in Finland and recovered in Germany was at least seven years and four months old (Schüz 1957) and a Woodchat Shrike aged six years has been recorded in Germany (Ullrich 1987). The age record for the Loggerhead Shrike is twelve years and six months (Klimkiewicz *et al.* in Collister 1994).

According to the very few detailed long-term studies, survival of adults from one year to the next appears to be close to 50%, which closely corresponds to what is known for passerines in general closely (Dorst 1971). In south-west Germany, 51.3% of 421 male Red-backed Shrikes more than a year old were thus back the following year in or near the same territories. Of course the percentage given above underestimates somewhat the real survival, as some birds certainly settled outside the 18km^2 study area. The survival of female Red-backed Shrikes is probably similar, but cannot be estimated as they show a much lower site-fidelity than males (Jakober and Stauber 1987 and in Glutz von Blotzheim and Bauer 1993). Interesting data also come from Alsace, in north-east France, concerning an isolated population of about 40 pairs of Woodchat Shrike under close observation and dispersed over an area of c. 400km^2, lying at the present northern limit of the species' range. Between 1990 and 1994 the annual return rate of adults was on average 45.5%; the strong variations, from 26% to 66%, appeared at least partly to be linked with prevailing meteorological conditions in spring at the time of arrival (Bersuder and Koenig 1995). Adult survival rates have also been calculated for some Loggerhead Shrike populations. Collister (1994) for instance, for an entirely migrant Canadian population breeding in south-east Alberta, found that nearly 40% of the adults survived from one year to the next. As for other studies, these figures are probably confounded by undetermined levels of dispersal between breeding seasons (Yosef 1996), and are thus somewhat underestimated. In Africa, Zack (1986a), who studied a population of the Grey-backed Fiscal for two-and-a-half years near Lake Naivasha in Kenya, found a relatively high survival in that species: 67.2% and 64.2%, each time between two successive months of August. These percentages are probably also somewhat too low, as some birds might not have died but emigrated. For the Common Fiscal, more prone to wander than the previous species, Zack (1986b) found a minimum survival rate of 39%.

Mortality of adult shrikes during the breeding season has been estimated at 4-5% for the Red-backed Shrike (Jakober and Stauber 1987) and 5% in the case of the Great Grey Shrike (Lefranc 1993). It is also thought to be low in the Loggerhead Shrike (Collister 1994).

Adult and immature shrikes die in a variety of ways. Not much is known about diseases or the possible effects of endo- or ectoparasites; flies of the genus *Ornithomya* are often present on nestling and adult Red-backed Shrikes (Ash 1970), but should have adverse effects only on birds already weakened for other reasons. Also for the Red-backed Shrike, Harrison (in Peakall 1962) thought that a parasitic worm *Contortospiculum nodosum* might help explain fluctuations in the bird's population, but this view needs confirming. Shrikes not infrequently die accidentally; many are killed by cars as they fly low to the ground across roads in order to get from one bush to another or in pursuit of insects. Flickinger's (1995) long-term observations on Loggerhead Shrike fatalities on a highway in Texas even suggest that road mortality may be a major factor in reducing that species below the number that could otherwise be supported by available habitat. In France near Montpellier one of the two last populations of the Lesser Grey Shrike almost exclusively nests on trees bordering busy roads; juveniles when leaving the nest are particularly at risk (Bechet *et al.* 1995, pers. obs.). Other less common types of accident are chronicled in the ornithological literature such as death by trains or drowning in drinking troughs (see Lefranc 1993). There is even a case of a Woodchat Shrike caught by a grass *Briza maxima* in southern France: without the aid of the observer the shrike would have been unable to get free (Pons 1993).

Predation of Great Grey Shrike nest by Northern Goshawk.

Predation is the most important cause of death. Shrikes are often well in view when looking for prey or, in the case of males, when advertising their territory. Raptors are the main threat. For various parts of central Europe, Glutz von Blotzheim *et al.* (1971) mention 761 Red-backed Shrikes caught by Eurasian Sparrowhawks *Accipiter nisus* out of a total number of 61,873 prey-items – that is 1.2%. Walter's (1968) observations on the diet of Eleonora's Falcon *Falco eleonorae* are more impressive. This falcon breeds on sea cliffs mainly on Mediterranean islands and here and there along the Moroccan Atlantic coast; its breeding season begins late as its young are reared on autumn migrant birds. Among these migrants, shrikes play a particular role: at Paximada, a small island near Crete, the Red-backed Shrike is the second most important (15%) prey-item after the Willow Warbler *Phylloscopus trochilus* (16%); the Lesser Grey Shrike and the Woodchat Shrike are also taken in great numbers. The latter is the most important bird taken (18%) between August and September by falcons nesting on Mogador near Essaouira (Morocco). Owls also take a toll: Ullrich (1987) for instance argued that in Germany conservation measures should not be taken for the Woodchat Shrike and the Little Owl *Athene noctua* in the same areas, as the owl commonly catches the shrike. In Israel, the observations of Yosef (1993c) show the extreme vulnerability of recent fledglings of the Southern Grey Shrike to Little Owl predation; they also demonstrate that Little Owl presence has an adverse impact on shrike hunting success and on the amount of time spent hunting.

Human persecution has become exceptional in developed countries, but as a whole it is still a significant problem. Even in Europe, in countries bordering the Mediterranean Sea, the illegal hunting of protected birds remains widespread (see McCulloch *et al.* 1992 for a general analysis and review). In Greece, on the island of Chios alone the amazing number of 400,000 Red-backed Shrikes is reputedly shot each autumn (Choremi and Spinthakis in Bayle 1994); it must be remembered that a very high percentage of this bird's European population converges on Greece and its islands in autumn, before crossing the sea towards Egypt. In Turkey, numerous Red-backed Shrikes are caught and then blindfolded in order to be used as decoys to net Eurasian Sparrowhawks. The latter in turn are used to catch Common Quail *Coturnix coturnix*. Thousands of birds of prey are shot to feed the shrikes and sparrowhawks (see *World Birdwatch* 1987, vol. 9, no. 4, p. 3 and *World Birdwatch* 1988, vol. 10, no. 1, p. 4). Many birds including shrikes are also killed in the Middle East and North Africa: for example the Masked Shrike rarely manages to rear young in the Damascus area in Syria as adults are regularly shot near their nest (Baumgart and Stephan 1987; also other references in Lefranc 1980, 1993). Birds are also trapped in Asia and some detailed information exists on the hunting of the 'Chinese' race *lucionensis* of the Brown Shrike in Taiwan, where it is a winter resident or a passage migrant to or from the Philippines. Shrikes have been traditionally caught with bamboo foot traps made by local villagers, some of whom have become virtually professional trappers. It has been estimated that 53.5% of the shrikes migrating through the Heng Chun peninsula at the southern end of the country are caught. In 1967, 8,695 shrikes were sold for food in Heng Chun; about an equal number were directly eaten by the trappers and their families. Since then, their market value has markedly increased, as 2.8 million tourists now visit Ken Ting National Park every year; so barbecued wintering shrikes and birds of other species are sold all year round (Severinghaus 1991).

Many migrating shrikes may also die from exhaustion, at least those encountering adverse weather conditions. Desert crossings are particularly hazardous for migrants, especially when the birds are faced with sand storms or strong winds. In the Iraqi desert, Moore and Boswell (1957) saw migrant Red-backed and Lesser Grey Shrikes forced to crouch on tussocks in a dust storm. In an oasis near Gabès (Tunisia), lying just north of the Sahara, Castan (1960) caught and weighed 1,054 Woodchat Shrikes which, on their spring migration, had just crossed the desert and were on their way back to their European breeding grounds. The average weight of the birds was only 30g, compared to their average weight of 35g in their breeding territories. Most birds appeared to stay only one day, but many stayed in the oasis three to five days (up to 16 days in a few cases) in order to obtain the food necessary to enable them to travel further. However, it was apparently already too late for 4.5% of the birds; weighing only between 21g and 25g on arrival, they were probably too wasted to survive.

The difficulty of obtaining enough food in harsh, snowy winters may also be a problem for the Great Grey Shrike, especially when voles *Microtus* sp. are in short supply. Heavy mortality in such winters has been known for a long time in Europe, although it is difficult to quantify (Glutz von Blotzheim and Bauer 1993, Lefranc 1993). Vole densities obviously have an effect on the survival of adult Great Grey Shrikes and presumably also on their breeding success which would explain the striking fluctuations in numbers of the species on their wintering grounds in the southern USA. Davis (1937) presented some evidence for cyclic emigrations affecting both Great Grey Shrike and Snowy Owl *Nyctea scandica*; these 'invasions' coincided with the maximum abundance of the Arctic Fox *Alopex lagopus* which also largely preys on *Microtus* sp. During good rodent years, the number of predators increases; when the rodents disappear, the predators first exhaust other prey and then either migrate or die. The subject has recently been reviewed by Atkinson (1995), who found that only the members of the Great Grey Shrike's eastern race *invictus* were cyclic between 1969 and 1989 and that the most significant cycles were of eight years' duration. Another example showing the relationship between vole numbers and Great Grey Shrikes comes from the French Jura at 800m in the winters 1992-1993 and 1993-1994. Remarkable densities of the shrike coincided with an impressive peak of vole populations. Locally, there were at least 18 birds on 56km², both in December 1992 and October 1993. Snow cover, later in both seasons, seriously reduced the number of birds, and this was probably due to emigration (Kéry *et al.* 1996).

Breeding success in shrikes is highly variable. According to a few detailed studies it is particularly low in tropical species. Out of 55 Grey-backed Fiscal nests found by Zack (1986a) in Kenya, only eight (14.5%) fledged young. The results, in the same area, for the Common Fiscal were not much better: of 20 attempts, young were produced in only three cases (15%) (Zack 1986b). The fact that these shrikes may breed several times in twelve months, depending on the rainy season, and possess a relatively high adult survival rate at least in the case of the Grey-backed Fiscal, possibly compensates for such high losses. In the Holarctic region, information from various studies indicates that in general a little over 50% of nests produce fledglings (see tables in Lefranc 1993 for West Palearctic shrikes, and review in Yosef 1996 for the Loggerhead Shrike). In detailed European studies of the Red-backed Shrike involving between 56 and several hundred nests, this percentage varied between 39% and 61% (Lefranc 1993). The average number of fledglings produced by successful pairs of this species is similar in various countries: 4.1 in England (Ash 1970), 4.2 in eastern France (Lefranc 1979) and in south-west Germany (Jakober and Stauber 1987), 4.3 in Sweden (Olsson 1995b) and 4.6 in north-eastern Moravia (Holan 1993). The number of fledglings produced by a given population is variable and depends on the percentage of pairs unable to produce any young at all. In the Red-backed Shrike, this figure can reach 36% (Jakober and Stauber 1987). Many nests are destroyed by predators, most of them birds. In Europe for instance, corvids such as Black-billed Magpie *Pica pica*, Carrion Crow *Corvus corone* and Eurasian Jay *Garrulus glandarius* play a prominent role, but raptors such as Northern Goshawk *Accipiter gentilis* or Common Buzzard *Buteo buteo* also take their share. A number of mammals prey on shrikes' nests, too: in Europe, nests of Great Grey Shrikes can be plundered by Red Squirrels *Sciurus vulgaris*; those of the Red-backed Shrike by Stoats *Mustela erminea*, and feral and Wild Cats *Felis silvestris*. (Lefranc 1993). In Cyprus, most unsuccessful nests of the Masked Shrike are probably predated by large lizards (Flint and Stewart 1992).

Some shrike species are regularly parasitised by cuckoos. Red-backed Shrikes are particularly affected in eastern Europe. In north-eastern Moravia (Czech Republic) during 1987-1992, Holan (1993) found one young Common Cuckoo *Cuculus canorus* for every 70 shrike nests; it was markedly less, however, than for the period 1970-1974 when he came across one young Cuckoo for every 18-20 nests. This could possibly indicate a decrease in the number of cuckoos.

In more or less stable habitat, the pressure of predation is probably constant. In south-west Germany, only 8.6% of 140 clutches of the Woodchat Shrike found in nine years were destroyed by predators (Ullrich 1993); this remarkably low percentage is, however, far from the general rule (see Glutz von Blotzheim and Bauer 1993 and Lefranc 1993 for West Palearctic shrikes). At the other extreme are the heavy losses mentioned above concerning the nests of two tropical shrike species, Grey-backed and Common Fiscals, attributed to an array of bird predators, including Lilac-breasted Rollers *Coracias caudata* and Grey Hornbills *Tockus nasutus* (Zack 1986a,b).

A very important factor in Holarctic shrike breeding success is weather. Low temperatures combined with rain have an adverse effect on clutch-size and on the average number of young produced per pair. The following table, adapted from Rudin (1990) and Lefranc (1993), gives some details of the influence of general weather conditions on Red-backed Shrike breeding success. It shows that the average clutch-size is lower in cold and rainy seasons than in fine ones. This appears to be at least partly due to a delayed laying period ('calendar effect'). The table also indicates (last column) that more young are produced per pair under favourable conditions. In bad weather, nests are re-built to replace nests abandoned when under construction or with eggs. In rainy weather some young may die of starvation as the adults struggle to find food. The youngest nestlings (hatching usually being asynchronous) die first. All the young may perish if conditions become really hard, with persistent strong rain and cold temperatures (for details see Stauber and Ullrich 1970, Lefranc 1979). Occasionally, in very bad weather, adult shrikes may even eat (and kill?) their young; this has been observed in the Lesser Grey Shrike (Lierath 1954).

Sources and locations	Years	Meteorological conditions: + fine; - cold & rainy; ± variable	Average Clutch-size	Average no. of young fledged per nest built	Average no. of young produced per pair
Korodi Gal (1969), Romania	1967	+	5.7 (n = 56)	3.5	
Stauber and Ullrich (1970)	1964	+	5.3 (n = 45)	3.6	
South-west Germany	1969	-	4.6 (n = 61)	1.6	
Lefranc (1979)	1969	-	4.4 (n = 18)	1.4	2.3
North-east France	1971 – 74	+	4.8 (n = 117)	2.9	3.7
	1975	±	4.5 (n = 52)	2.1	3.2
Jakober and Stauber (1987)	1964 – 84				
South-west Germany	(8 yrs)	-			2.5
	(8 yrs)	+			3.2
Rudin (1990)	1988	-	4.9 (n = 38)	1.6	2.1
North-east Switzerland	1989	+	5.2 (n = 25)	2.6	3.6

Weather and breeding performances in Red-backed Shrikes.

Mortality often occurs during the period from fledging through to independence. In Indiana, mortality of young Loggerhead Shrikes during the first week after fledging was 46% (Burton in Collister 1994); in south-east Alberta in two successive years it varied between 33% (n = 13) and 53% (n = 15) during the first ten days after fledging (Kiliaan in Collister 1994).

Mortality in first-year birds is certainly higher than mortality in adults, but few precise data exist. In California only 29% of 59 Loggerhead Shrikes ringed between 1980 and 1982 as nestlings and recovered later had reached adulthood (Scott and Morrison 1990).

Jakober and Stauber (1987) estimated that a population of Red-backed Shrikes in Germany would be stable if the mortality of young shrikes, from fledging through to the next breeding season, did not exceed 63%. They based their calculations on an annual adult mortality rate of 50% (see above) and on an average production of 2.7 young per pair per year.

POPULATION CHANGES AND THEIR PRESUMED CAUSES

Trends in population over the last 100 years are only relatively well known for Great Grey, Lesser Grey, Woodchat and Red-backed Shrikes in Europe and Loggerhead Shrike in North America. Anecdotal data exist for a few Asian species like the Long-tailed and Tiger Shrikes, but almost nothing is known about possible changes in African shrike numbers. The known history of various shrikes is summarised in each species account; see also Lefranc (1993, 1997) and Tucker and Heath (1994) for the European species and Peterjohn and Sauer (1995) and Yosef (1996) for the Loggerhead Shrike.

All the species mentioned above are of conservation concern, as they show evidence of overall decline. However, they still have large breeding areas and none of them is as yet globally threatened. A few subspecies may, nevertheless, be in a critical situation. This is the case with two races of the Loggerhead Shrike, *mearnsi* confined to San Clemente, an island of 145km² lying off southern California, and *migrans* (not always recognised as a valid subspecies) which has declined markedly in numbers and range in north-eastern Canada and U.S.A. (Peterjohn and Sauer 1995). From a conservation point of view well-defined subspecies represent irreducible taxa. Under the Phylogenetic Species Concept (PSC) most of these distinct taxa would be recognised as good species (for a general review of this point see Hazevoet 1994).

One of the rarest shrikes is undoubtedly Newton's Fiscal, which exists only in the virgin forests of São Tomé, an island of 857km² lying in the Gulf of Guinea. For a long time this bird was even thought to be extinct, as it was not seen between 1928 and 1990. Recent reports suggest that its total population might amount to several hundred pairs (Atkinson *et al.* 1991, Sargeant 1994, P. Christy pers. comm.).

The decline of shrikes in Europe and North America has generally been ascribed to two main causes: climatic fluctuations and habitat deterioration. Other influences such as the use of pesticides may also be involved. Some details are given below on these aspects (see also *Aspects of population dynamics* for human persecution and road-kill factors).

Significant climatic fluctuations have affected northern and central Europe over the last 150 years. Between roughly 1850 and 1950, a change towards a more maritime climate took place with strikingly higher mean winter temperatures, particularly in northern areas, and also with significantly cooler summers in central Europe (Salomonsen 1948, Kalela 1949, Williamson 1975, Burton 1995). Periodic series of cold wet summers are thought to have had adverse effects on the food availability and reproductive success of shrikes. Ornithological data strongly suggest that the two species that flourish most in warm weather, the Woodchat and Lesser Grey Shrikes, have suffered most. Their respective breeding ranges have markedly contracted towards the south. In the 1950s, both species were, however, in good shape and had relatively thriving populations as far north as north-east France or central-east Germany (see species accounts). The last phase of their rapid decline started at the beginning of the 1960s. They have not recovered since, probably because their regression was also, and still is, largely linked to habitat deterioration (Niehuis 1968, Lefranc 1978, 1993, 1997, Glutz von Blotzheim and Bauer 1993). Local climatic fluctuations also occur in Africa. The arid acacia savannas of the Sahel zone, which stretch across the continent in a wide belt between the southern borders of the Sahara and the broad-leaved/acacia woodlands of the Sudan zone, have known three prolonged droughts since the beginning of the twentieth century. The longest, from 1968 to 1973, might have caused the death of up to about 150,000 people in the French-speaking countries of West Africa alone (Ramade 1987). This was also the time when the Whitethroat *Sylvia communis*, which winters in the Sahel zone, suffered a drastic reduction in breeding numbers in Europe. In Britain, this crash was measured by the Common Bird Census of the British Trust for Ornithology as a fall of 71% of the previous year's population (Winstanley *et al.* 1974). Other Palearctic migrants were also affected (Marchant 1992), among them possibly the Woodchat Shrike the northern part of whose wintering range lies in the Sahel.

In Europe, from Neolithic times onwards, scythes and domestic grazing progressively created cultivated land, pastures and meadows at the expense of densely wooded areas. Extensive farming systems beneficial to shrikes and other birds of semi-open habitats gradually altered the shape of the rural landscape. This long 'golden age' for *Lanius* species came rather abruptly to an end in the 1950s with the foundation of the Common Agricultural Policy (CAP). After World War II and fears of food shortages, this policy had one major objective: increased agricultural production. This goal, forty years later, has certainly been achieved, creating chronic problems of overproduction. The landscape has of course changed enormously in the countries concerned, particularly in lowlands, under the pressure of a high level of mechanisation. Areas of mixed cultivation have largely given way to vast monocultures. Fields have become much larger, hedges have been removed (in France for instance two million kilometres of hedgerows disappeared between 1950 and 1980), as well as traditional orchards, copses, marshes, banks, ditches and even paths. Grasslands on the other hand have been replaced by arable land; thus in France 25% of the area covered by meadows disappeared between 1970 and 1995. Many of the remaining grasslands have been made more productive and no longer support a diversified flora or a high insect population. The use of pesticides has overall contributed to a reduction in potential shrike food (Institut Français de l'Environnement 1996, Pain and Pienkowski 1997, Lefranc 1997).

Agricultural intensification has also resulted in the abandonment of farming in areas considered uneconomic. Large areas of former fields or pastures are either planted, generally with conifers, or allowed to regenerate into forest naturally. Such transformations in the landscape particularly affect medium-altitude mountainous areas, as for instance the famous 'Causses' in the south of the Massif Central in France. There, wooded habitats tend to be closing around more open ones, as farmers and their sheep gradually disappear; and there is a corresponding reduction in numbers of three species of shrike – the Southern Grey, Woodchat and Red-backed. Other birds of semi-open habitats such as the Ortolan Bunting *Emberiza hortulana* are also locally at risk. Thus shrikes, along with many other species, are subject on the one hand to agricultural intensification and on the other to the complete abandonment of agriculture (Lefranc 1997). The least threatened European species by far is the small Red-backed Shrike, a pair of which only needs on average 1.5ha of suitable habitat. Everywhere in Europe it has largely disappeared from lowlands where huge fields given over to one crop cover the plains; but it remains widespread in suitable forest clearings or, as in Switzerland, at medium altitudes, in regions which are still (but for how long?) farmed traditionally. More thermophilic species like the Woodchat or Lesser Grey Shrike are unfortunately not to be found in 'refuges'. Neither is the Great Grey Shrike, a pair of which may need up to 100ha of semi-open habitat situated on flat or relatively flat land. This species has also suffered greatly in lowlands where 'untidy' open landscapes rich in grasslands and associated with low-intensity farming have given way to a monotonous and 'shrike-unfriendly' succession of woods and vast tracts of open fields. In France the best populations are now to be found on the northern plateaus of the Massif Central, at altitudes of c. 1,000m in areas characterised by the presence of extensively managed pastures (Lefranc 1993, 1997). The Great Grey Shrike appears to fare somewhat better in Nordic countries where it breeds in open taiga forests, reminiscent of primeval habitats and mainly composed of pines and birches and dotted with marshes and raised bogs. It also exploits recently cleared forest land, as it does, very locally, in Germany (Olsson 1980, Fischer 1994b). After a strong increase in the breeding population and an expansion southwards, until around 1975, the species has undergone a sharp decline in numbers in Sweden and Finland. In the latter country the large-scale drainage of wetlands, concentrated in the period 1965-1975, may have contributed to the population increase mentioned above, as diked, drying moors offer more suitable habitats than wet mires. Since then, large areas of natural breeding habitats have been lost on account of the peat industry and afforestation of marshland. The fact that newly clear-cut areas only partly compensate for the afforestation of earlier ones may also explain the downward trend (Hildén and Hildén 1996). The decline of the Great Grey Shrike is worrying, but the most threatened species in western Europe is the Lesser Grey Shrike. Because of its climatic requirements (hot dry summers) it is (or was) almost exclusively present in lowlands or in well-exposed hilly areas. Strictly insectivorous, this steppe bird is particularly attracted by agricultural landscapes with large areas of short grass or bare soil such as vineyards. It has very likely suffered from a reduction of available prey because of pesticides, and is also most likely to suffer from the direct effects of pesticides as it often picks up its prey in cultivated fields (Lefranc 1993, 1997, Bara 1995). At higher latitudes, in north-east and central France, south-west Germany and eastern Switzerland, the future of the Woodchat depends on what happens to the grazed traditional orchards that still remain around certain villages. It is not particularly reassuring to note that in Switzerland, for instance, ten million fruit trees disappeared between 1950 and 1980. Further south, in its

Mediterranean strongholds, the habitats of the species, as well as those of the Southern Grey Shrike, are increasingly threatened by agricultural abandonment and subsequent forest regeneration. Both these species benefit, however, from fires in forests (for the importance of fires and of non-climax vegetation for the original avifauna of mediterranean ecosystems, see Prodon 1987).

In North America, the decline of the Loggerhead Shrike has been linked with habitat degradation, particularly in the north-eastern part of its range. Historically, within Canada, the clearing of forest by European settlers for cultivation and pasture probably permitted or at least favoured the extension of its breeding range eastwards, throughout southern Ontario and into Quebec and the Maritimes. Until the middle of the twentieth century, the species continued to increase. Since that time, the population has been shrinking, presumably because of changes in land use and in particular a severe loss in the area covered by unimproved pasture, a favoured habitat of the species. In Quebec, generally speaking, the area of pastureland and the numbers of Loggerhead Shrikes show a constant relationship since the shrike became established (Robert and Laporte 1991). Further west, in Alberta and Saskatchewan, regions showing large declines in breeding shrikes lost 39% of their unimproved pasture area through conversion to cropland between 1946 and 1986 and up to 79% of their pre-settlement pasture area. Regions where shrikes declined less lost only 12% of their unimproved pasture to cropland. In the probable winter range of these populations, in Texas, pasture area has also declined due to encroachment by cropland and brush (Telfer 1992). The Loggerhead Shrike also suffers from a reduction of other types of more 'natural' habitats localised in its strongholds in the arid shrubland and desert regions of the western states: in Idaho, for example, about 70% of its original sagebrush habitat has been destroyed by man-caused fires, livestock grazing and a sagebrush eradication programme to convert rangelands to farmland or improve range quality for cattle (Woods in Yosef 1996, Woods and Cade 1996). The history of the San Clemente Loggerhead Shrike (race *mearnsi*) is an interesting case: its nesting habitat on a Californian island has been degraded by feral domestic goats *Capra hircus* which eat the low shrub used for nesting sites (Scott and Morrison 1990).

Intensification of agriculture is accompanied by the deliberate use of fertilisers and large quantities of pesticides. Active nutrient input from modern chemicals, as well as passive input in the form of nitrous oxides emitted by industry and transport, cause eutrophication that eliminates many plant species and causes the grass vegetation to grow early, dense and high. This changes the living conditions of insects, reduces them in numbers and diversity, and makes them less available for shrikes and other predators (Ellenberg 1986). Fertilisers, including those certified by federal agencies for use in the USA, may also have direct negative effects on shrike populations. In central Florida, Yosef (1994) documented the immediate and disastrous consequences of sodium ammonium nitrate spraying on a Loggerhead Shrike population breeding on cattle pastures.

The precise impact of pesticides on shrike populations remains unclear. At best, they considerably reduce the populations of prey, a fact which is by no means negligible. They may also have worse effects as suggested by Busbee's (1977) experiments, which showed that Loggerhead Shrikes treated with food containing a 2 ppm daily diet of dieldrin died within about three months, and that pesticides also induced behavioural changes; such doses may be, or may have been, 'available' in some agricultural regions for shrikes and other birds (Korshgen in Busbee 1977). Anderson and Duzan (1978) also claim that the Loggerhead Shrike experienced eggshell thinning at least in southern Illinois; nesting success of the species, however, remained high in the study area. In Europe, Poltz (1975) presented some data on the pesticide problem: in southern Germany he detected no difference in the clutch-size of the Red-backed Shrike between the years 1948 and 1973, neither could he find any significant difference in the egg-shell thickness in that species for the years 1850, 1900 and 1973. However, he recorded a high and unexplained mortality during the hatching period. The worst pesticides – those with a really bad reputation such as DDT and dieldrin – were banned or restricted by the early 1970s in most developed countries. This enabled many raptor populations to recover (see for instance Ratcliffe 1993 for the Peregrine Falcon *Falco peregrinus*). Organochlorine pesticides are, however, still widely used in third world countries. In Africa, DDT is still used to control tsetse fly, which transmits sleeping sickness to both man and cattle; dieldrin was still used a few years ago on a large scale to control desert locusts in North Africa. Despite their shorter persistence rate in hot climates there is evidence that pesticides accumulate in food chains and affect the egg-shell thickness of some African raptors (Crick 1990). They could also have harmful effects on a wide variety of animals and insectivorous birds, including shrikes.

CONSERVATION

For a very long time, shrikes suffered from a bad reputation (see above under *Names*). They shared this with raptors and were often regarded as miniature birds of prey. Interestingly, Linnaeus in the tenth edition of his *Systema Naturae* (1758), which marks the start of modern systematics, placed the five shrike species known at that time alongside diurnal and nocturnal raptors in the order Accipitres, but in their own genus *Lanius*. To it, however, he added a few other small birds very superficially possessing a 'shrikish' or rapacious appearance, including the Waxwing *Lanius garrulus* (now *Bombycilla garrulus*) with its black facial mask and slightly hooked bill.

Shrikes, as well as raptors, used to be seen as harmful birds which had to be eliminated by all means in order to protect other birds and particularly the chicks of game species. This was mainly the view of hunters and gamekeepers, but some well-known ornithologists did not like them either. Examples include some early famous French authors: Crespon (1840), for instance, says that 'the Red-backed Shrike, in order to devour young birds, attracts them by imitating their song'. Bailly (1853) writes that 'male and female Great Grey Shrikes want their young as early as possible to have a taste for still palpitating flesh and to be bloodthirsty; so they kill and tear apart a lot of small birds just in front of their progeny'. Much later, Madon (1934) states that no species is useful: the Red-backed, Woodchat and Lesser Grey Shrike are said to be 'rather harmful' whereas the Great Grey Shrike, not surprisingly in that context, is declared to be 'particularly harmful'. Similarly the latter used not to be highly regarded in its wintering quarters in the United States. Bent (1950) calls it a 'bloodthirsty rascal' and recalls that towards the end of the last century men were employed to shoot the shrikes on Boston Common, as it was feared that they could destroy the populations of the 'English' Sparrow *Passer domesticus* which was then in its early days in North America. He also mentions the winter invasion of 1926-1927 when Great Grey Shrikes were unusually plentiful in the north-eastern states; of seventy that were caught by bird ringers over six months, only eight were ringed and released, all the others were destroyed.

Things have changed; raptors and shrikes have been rehabilitated and attract the interest of increasing numbers of birdwatchers, both professionals and amateurs. During the last 30 years or so, a wealth of papers has been published on these birds both in the New World and in various European countries, particularly Germany. An increasing number of them are devoted to conservation problems; and conservation was certainly on the minds of the 71 participants of the First International Shrike Symposium organised at the Archbold Biological Station, Lake Placid, Florida, USA, in January 1993 under the chairmanship of Reuven Yosef. The ensuing proceedings (Yosef and Lohrer 1995) include 60 papers, of which 34 are directly concerned either with population trends in six *Lanius* shrikes or with problems linked to their conservation and management. One of the positive consequences of that meeting, followed by another at Eilat (Israel) in March 1996, was the creation of the International Shrike Working Group, subdivided into three geographical sections. On a national scale such a group already existed in Germany (see *Useful addresses* below).

The most threatened shrike species, as already mentioned, remains the very localised and recently rediscovered Newton's Fiscal, endemic (as well as 15 other bird species) to the West African island of São Tomé. Remarkably, this shrike is strictly to be found in relatively open lowland primary rain-forests. It occurs neither in secondary forests nor in cultivated areas. The contrast with the Common Fiscal in habitat selection is thus striking; the Common Fiscal has largely become a parkland or even a garden bird. Five other São Tomé endemic birds also only exist in primary forests; the conservation of the latter is thus a priority. It is reassuring to note that the creation of national parks (*Zonas Ecológicas*) is underway and adequate areas have been officially designated by the government (Atkinson *et al.* 1994, Peet and Atkinson 1994).

In Europe and North America the conservation of the few remaining patches of more or less primary habitats, whatever they may be, is of course of the highest importance, but rarely to the benefit of shrikes, which have become birds of man-modified habitats. The chief exception is the Loggerhead Shrike, as it is one of the American species locally occurring in native sagebrush habitats typical of semi-arid, cold desert ecosystems in the western USA (Woods 1995).

The Loggerhead race *mearnsi* receives particular attention as it is confined to a Californian island with a current population of fewer than 50 individuals (Mundy and Woodruff 1996). The conservation plan for this species includes field studies, predator control, habitat restoration, captive propagation and reintroduction. Artificial rearing started in 1991 when a breeding flock was established at the San Diego Zoo from eggs and chicks taken on the island where the birds renested following removal of their initial clutch. As early as 1992, eight chicks, hatched that year, were released on the island (Morrison *et al.* 1995). Reintroductions might also be part of an Action Plan in north-eastern Canada for the race *migrans* (Canadian Wildlife Service 1992).

The following paragraphs briefly deal with shrike conservation as seen through species protection, site protection and conservation of the wider environment.

In North America and Europe, the seven shrike species concerned are given legal protection, as far as is known, in all countries. Regrettably, however, illegal destruction still affects many migrant birds even in European Union countries like France, Italy and Greece. Because of their autumn migratory routes the European Red-backed and Lesser Grey Shrike populations are particularly at risk in Greece (see above *Aspects of population dynamics*). Shrikes and other birds may also have problems in many African and Asian countries where conservation laws be unenforceable. Conservation efforts are currently underway in Taiwan and particularly concern the Grey-faced Buzzard-Eagle *Butastur indicus* and the Brown Shrike, the latter being locally particularly appreciated when barbecued (see above and Severinghaus 1991). Public education is targeted at local villagers, students and tourists using slide presentations, lectures, radio shows and posters. A less conventional technique has been used by a local tourism bureau which in an effort to deter people from eating barbecued shrikes, showed that the birds had many internal parasites. The Ken Ting National Park offices are particularly busy with shrike conservation, providing a videotape freely distributed to all the local primary and middle schools (Severinghaus 1991).

Providing site protection to shrikes is not easy. In the European Union, regrettably only two species, the Red-backed and Lesser Grey Shrike are listed on Annex I of the Wild Birds Directive 79/409, the aim of which is to protect wild birds and their habitats through the designation of Special Protection Areas (SPAs). However, not even these two species can profit from the creation of nature reserves if, as in France, they are established in areas recognised as exceptional mainly from a habitat point of view: estuaries, strips of primary forest, lakes important for waterbirds, high mountain areas, small islands, etc. There are, however, a few notable exceptions: the Southern Grey Shrike is thus well represented in an SPA created in the Crau, a unique habitat in southern France, a stony desert rich in insects, grazed by sheep and dotted with bushes where shrikes can hide their nests. The Red-backed Shrike occasionally profits from protected areas including those, generally small in size, acquired by conservation bodies with the help of private and/or public money (Lefranc 1997). Acquiring land for the conservation of shrikes as the main goal happens very rarely. Locally it may, however, be a solution, as for instance in south-east Alberta where a still important Loggerhead Shrike population nests along a Canadian Pacific Rail right of way (Collister 1994). Buying and adequately managing traditional orchards still frequented by the Woodchat Shrike near its present northern limits in north-east France, south-west Germany and eastern Switzerland might be a good solution for this species; but it would be essential at the same time to maintain the numbers of cattle, horses and sheep that graze these orchards.

Clearly, however, the future of shrikes and many other birds of semi-open habitats, both in North America and Europe, will depend less on site protection than on the conservation of what has been called the 'wider environment', and particularly of landscapes shaped by 'extensive' types of farming. Such landscapes have already disappeared over large areas following the intensification of agriculture or, more rarely, the complete abandonment of agriculture in zones where such activity is considered uneconomic. In the European Union, great hopes are placed on management agreements which can be taken out under the Agri-environment Regulation (EC Reg. 2078/92) of the Common Agricultural Policy. Such measures are unfortunately very limited both in space and time. Furthermore farmers often have alternative choices, more attractive from a financial point of view and less 'friendly' to the environment. Sadly also the Agri-environment Regulation is only an 'Accompanying Measure'; real progress would be made if environmental protection became a central objective of the Common Agricultural Policy. That time may come, not so much because of an impoverishment of biological diversity, but because soil, water and landscape quality are more and more seriously affected, and also because many people are becoming worried about their health, and about the quality of the food they are given (Tucker and Heath 1994, Lefranc 1997, Pain and Pienkowski 1997).

Meanwhile, it is already possible to help shrike populations in Europe using existing tools (protected areas, agri-environment regulations, etc), and also in North America Canadian Wildlife Service 1992 (Collister 1994). Where agreements with landowners have been reached, simple measures affecting the habitat can be adopted. Providing extra perches at the right height can be useful as they improve the shrikes' chances of catching prey in otherwise unsuitable areas. A perch 1-2m high, about every 12m, seems to be ideal for the Red-backed Shrike. The latter, as all *Lanius* species, also favours a mosaic of tall and short vegetation. This can be achieved by temporal-spatial rotations of hay mowing. Its nesting opportunities can also be increased by planting suitable shrubs in potential or existing territories, either in isolation or in linear hedges. Piles of trimmed branches of thorny shrubs are also readily accepted (van Nieuwenhuyse 1996). Management of Red-backed Shrike habitats is relatively easy and can quickly produce excellent results as measured in numbers of breeding territories in a given area (van Nieuwenhuyse 1996, Steiof and Ratzke 1990). For possible management of Great Grey Shrike territories in central Europe, see Schön (1994e) and for a general review Lefranc (1993).

An example of recent collaboration between conservationists and farmers comes from one of the two last strongholds of the Lesser Grey Shrike in southern France, in Languedoc-Roussillon. In this famous vineyard, the vines play an important role as Lesser Grey Shrikes are undoubtedly much attracted by bare soil. The difference from the surrounding areas is that high trees are also present as well as meadows, still harmoniously interwoven with the vines; all this gives rise to a mosaic landscape rich in potential nesting sites and food. Other bird species nesting in the same area include Great Spotted Cuckoo *Clamator glandarius*, European Roller *Coracias garrulus* and Ortolan Bunting *Emberiza hortulana*. Application of an agri-environment measure has recently given hope for the future of this 'island reserve', as many grape farmers have accepted schemes incorporating favourable management techniques including the restriction of pesticide use. A special cuvée (vintage) of wine named *Pie-grièche à poitrine rose* (= Lesser Grey Shrike) was produced in June 1996, the label being painted by the French bird artist Serge Nicolle. It is being sold with a contribution of two francs per bottle towards the enhancement and sensitive management of Lesser Grey Shrike habitat. Wildlife in general and the landscape itself should benefit from this step in the right direction.

OVERVIEW OF THE GENUS *CORVINELLA*

The two 'giant' species of this genus are almost unmistakable birds, one brown and one black, both with long, strongly graduated tails. Both have a relatively short, stout bill with a curved culmen and stiff upstanding bristles at the base. The Yellow-billed Shrike is grey and brown and streaked darker; the sexes are almost alike but with slightly different colour patches on their flanks. In the black-and-white Magpie Shrike, sometimes called Long-tailed Shrike, the sexes are also very similar, but the adult female has distinct white patches on her flanks.

Both *Corvinella* shrikes are mainly resident, although local movements are suspected, particularly in the Yellow-billed Shrike in the Sahel zone of West Africa. These are probably related to seasonal changes in weather. Both are arboreal species, often occurring in park-like savannas, particularly in *Acacia* stands, but also in other types of woodland. The Yellow-billed Shrike has locally become a parkland or even a garden bird.

These shrikes are gregarious, noisy species, breeding cooperatively, but unfortunately still relatively little studied, except for the valuable observations of group behaviour and the breeding biology of the Yellow-billed Shrike by Grimes (1980), a study conducted within the campus of the University of Ghana at Legon. Only one female breeds in a group and she alone incubates. She and the nestlings are fed by the other members of the group (see species accounts).

Yellow-billed Shrike and Magpie Shrike catch most of their prey in typical *Lanius* manner, by swooping to the ground from a perch. They eat all kinds of insects, spiders, worms, etc. and small vertebrates like frogs, reptiles and mice. Birds have not yet been recorded in the diet, and no larder has ever been found.

Both species build a rather bulky, untidy and roughly constructed cup-shaped nest, generally well concealed in the foliage of thorny trees, about 1.5-10m above the ground. They usually lay between three and five glossy eggs. The eggs of the Yellow-billed Shrike have a buff or cream ground colour and are spotted, speckled and scrawled with yellow-brown and undermarkings of grey (Bannerman 1953). They measure on average 22.4 x 18.3mm (n = 36, in Ghana) (Grimes 1980). In the Magpie Shrike the ground colour of the eggs varies from cream to salmon-pink, spotted all over, but most densely in a zone around the big end with small dots, and a few short zig-zag markings of rufous-brown, burnt sienna and slate-grey (Sclater 1901). They measure on average 26.8 x 19.7 (n = 166, in southern Africa) (Maclean 1993).

Adult survival is known in the case of the Yellow-billed Shrike studied in Ghana (Grimes 1980). Of 61 adults at least one year old, ringed at the beginning of the study, 44 (72%) were alive after one year, 37 (60%) after two years, 25 (40%) after three years, 10 (16%) after four years and 7 (11%) after five years. The same study provides data on fledging success. Over five years, five well-studied groups raised three broods per year on seven occasions, two broods per year on eleven occasions, and one brood per year on three occasions. Of 159 nestlings in broods of different sizes, only 70 (44%) successfully fledged. The fledging success expressed as the percentage of total eggs laid that survived to produce fledglings was 25%. Of 66 nestlings ringed that left their nest, at least 29 (44%) were alive a year later.

Nothing is known about the population trends in the two species, which are not globally threatened.

OVERVIEW OF THE GENUS *EUROCEPHALUS*

Both species are rather big and heavy, easy to identify with a mainly brown and white plumage and a snow-white crown. The wings are long and pointed; the tail is also long, but shorter than the wings and slightly rounded. Both shrikes also have a relatively short, strong black bill with a culmen evenly curved beyond the stiff frontal feathers, which point forward and partly conceal the nostrils. The sexes are indistinguishable. Juveniles are overall paler, with a mottled crown, pale bill, and underparts variably tinged with brown. Adults presumably undergo only one moult each year, after the breeding season. In the White-rumped Shrike a detailed study of moult would probably confirm that there are no subspecies (see species accounts).

White-rumped and White-crowned Shrikes are largely resident species; movements may, however, occur on a local scale; the White-crowned might even sometimes be nomadic. *Eurocephalus* shrikes are mainly arboreal species, typical of dry *Acacia* steppes. They can occur in open parkland.

Both species are noisy and gregarious, often met with in small groups. Their respective social organisations are not yet well known, but both appear to be cooperative breeders, although definite monogamous pairs have also been recorded.

Prey is caught in 'true shrike' fashion, mostly on the ground but also sometimes in the air. Food is usually carried in the bill and occasionally, at least in the case of the White-crowned Shrike, in the feet. It is generally held down with one foot against a perch while being torn apart with the bill. Both in the wild and in captivity the White-crowned Shrike has been seen to transfer food to the bill with the foot, with tarsus resting on perch (Dorka 1975, Harris and Arnott 1988), a fact also recorded in *Lanius* shrikes such as the Great Grey and the Woodchat (Dorka 1975, Glutz von Blotzheim and Bauer 1993). All kinds of insects are eaten, also millipedes and occasionally fruit. No larder has ever been recorded .

Eurocephalus shrikes build a very neat, relatively small, compact, cup-shaped thick-walled nest. Made of plant fibres, it is lined with spider webs and placed on a horizontal branch several metres above the ground. Both species usually lay three or four eggs. They are glossy, white or cream, sparsely and irregularly spotted with grey, violet-grey and brown blotches; in White-crowned Shrike, the eggs measure on average 27.2 x 21.3 mm (for n = 94), and in White-rumped Shrike about 25.5 x 21 mm (Moreau and Moreau 1939, Vincent 1949, Archer and Godman 1961, Harris and Arnott 1988).

Nothing is yet known about population dynamics.

STYLE AND LAYOUT OF THE BOOK

INTRODUCTORY CHAPTERS

TAXONOMY AND RELATIONSHIPS

The section starts with some general considerations concerning these aspects set against a historical background; both traditional and DNA-based taxonomy are taken into account. Detailed notes on some difficult, controversial points follow.

OVERVIEW OF THE GENERA *LANIUS*, *CORVINELLA* AND *EUROCEPHALUS*

The first of these three overviews is fairly substantial as the genus *Lanius* contains the great majority of species in the family (27 out of 31), some of them being well studied. The plan adopted is as follows: names; morphology, plumages and moult; origins, present distribution, migrations and wintering areas; habitat; social organisation and general behaviour; food, feeding habits and larders; foraging behaviour; nests, eggs and breeding behaviour; aspects of population dynamics; population changes and their presumed causes; conservation.

SPECIES ACCOUNTS

The species accounts contain up to thirteen sections; the coverage of general aspects of behaviour and ecology of course varies greatly from species to species.

IDENTIFICATION

This section begins with an indication of the species' average total length in centimetres and with a brief outline of its breeding range. The more obvious and useful criteria to facilitate rapid identification to species level are then given for male, female, juvenile and, when considered relevant, first-winter birds. Comparisons with similar sympatric species are made, special attention being given to some difficult cases.

DESCRIPTION

This invariably concerns the nominate subspecies, unless otherwise stated. The plumages of adult male, adult female and juvenile, always in that order, are described in some detail, but without involving a feather-by-feather description. The specific highlights given in the previous section are expanded. The pattern followed for the description of a bird is the same throughout the book and successively concerns the head, upperparts, tail, wings, underparts and undertail. The terminology used for plumage descriptions is shown on the topography of a typical shrike (see page 44). It is important to remember that when wing formulae are considered, the primaries have been numbered ascendently (the short outer primary being the first), following Svensson (1992). Description of the bare parts is presented separately.

MEASUREMENTS

The standard measurements of wing, tail, bill and tarsus, expressed in millimetres, have mainly been compiled from the literature and concern both museum skins and live birds. They can be taken as an initial guide and are certainly very useful for a comparison between species and sometimes of subspecies, but should be treated with some caution as several methods of measurement, rarely stated by the authors, exist. On the other hand it is well known that a slight shrinkage may affect measurements taken on dry skins. Weights are in grams; an average weight is often given as well as known extremes; in only a very few cases could no data on weight be found.

DISTRIBUTION AND STATUS

This section concerns the breeding range. It expands on the information conveyed by the maps, giving particular attention to the geographical limits reached by the species. It is of course to be used in conjunction with the section devoted to habitat, as a given bird does not occur everywhere inside its range.

Whenever possible, the recent history, population trends and what is known about the present status in various countries have been summarised at the end of that paragraph. Various sources have been used for the last point, for Europe for instance, mainly the work by Tucker and Heath (1994) modified by more recent or precise data.

GEOGRAPHICAL VARIATION

Species with a large breeding range generally exhibit pronounced geographical variation. The subspecies recognised by modern authorities are listed here and described by comparisons between them or with the nominate form; comments are made on some difficult, controversial points. Most races which can be reasonably separated in the field are shown on the plates. For some of them their approximate distribution is also shown on the species map; but the 'boundaries' between various races in mainland areas are, of course, purely indicative, as intergradation over vast zones can be frequent, resulting in birds not easily assignable to a given race. This is, for instance, true for the Loggerhead Shrike, Southern Grey Shrike in North Africa and in the Middle East, and Long-tailed Shrike.

HYBRIDS

Details are given when relevant; only a few Palearctic species are involved.

MOVEMENTS

This section gives the migratory status of each species. For migrant shrikes the limits of the wintering range are then indicated in some detail as well as the migration routes. The paragraph continues with data relating to phenology: departure from the breeding grounds, autumn passage dates, arrival in and departure from the wintering range, passage dates in spring and subsequent return to the breeding territories. When judged relevant, some information is given on observations of vagrants outside their normal range. The *European News* sections of the magazine *British Birds* have been very helpful as far as the western Palearctic is concerned.

MOULT

The plumage sequences are known in some detail only for some Holarctic species; the general progression is summarised in the 'overview' paragraphs. The English terminology used here is as explained in *British Birds* vol. 78, 1985. The main terms are listed below with the American alternatives in brackets:

> Juvenile (Juvenal)
> First-winter (First Basic)
> First-summer (First Alternate)
> Adult Breeding (Definite Alternate)

VOICE

Shrikes are rarely first detected in the field by their songs although some species readily sing and are excellent mimics. Special attention is given here to the advertising, alarm and general contact calls. The vocalisations have been transcribed by giving priority, when possible, to English transcriptions found in the literature after direct comparisons with our own notes and with the sound recordings provided by the National Sound Archive of the British Library.

HABITAT

This section first deals with the general types of climate occurring in the range of the species. It then gives details of the altitudes reached and of the main types of habitat and habitat structures where the birds are to be found, both in summer and winter.

HABITS

As far as possible the following points are considered in this section: conspicuouness of the species and behaviour at the beginning of the breeding season, densities, territorial behaviour, site-fidelity, possible nesting associations with other birds, preferred perch-heights and hunting strategies, and finally impaling behaviour when relevant.

FOOD

The main known characteristics of the diet are given with special emphasis on the respective importance of invertebrate and vertebrate prey.

BREEDING

This section generally starts with a brief discussion of pair-formation and continues with data concerning known egg-laying seasons, number of normal clutches and repeat clutches, nest-building, nest-sites, nest description, clutch-size, incubation, nestling period and the time needed by juveniles to reach independence. When relevant, information is given on parasitism by cuckoos.

REFERENCES

The references cited are those considered to have been the most useful during the compilation of the species accounts. For the western Palearctic, a certain priority has been given to recent works which could not be covered by the three important volumes published in 1993 (see Introduction). All references are given in full in the Bibliography.

PLATES

The 16 plates depict 140 individuals and show not only birds of the nominate race (generally when relevant: adult male, adult female, juvenile), but also many races when typical birds are recognisable in the field. Two hybrids are also shown. The plates are arranged largely in taxonomic sequence; the very few exceptions are for practical reasons.

On a given plate all the birds are drawn to scale.

SHRIKE TOPOGRAPHY

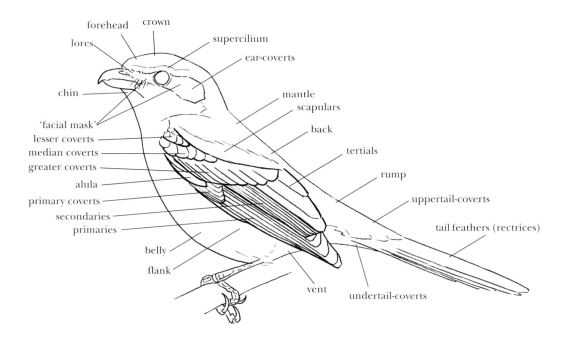

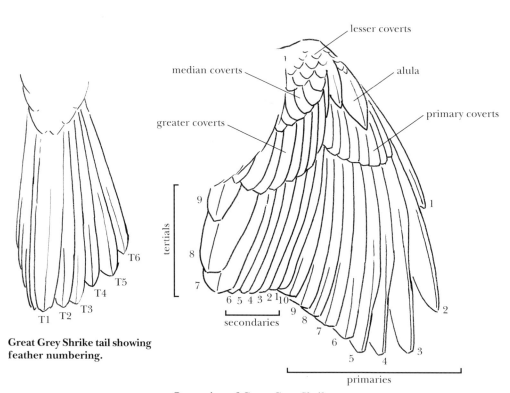

Great Grey Shrike tail showing feather numbering.

Open wing of Great Grey Shrike.

Useful Addresses

An International Shrike Group was founded during the first International Shrike Symposium in Florida in January 1993. At least one section, the Afro-European, is still very active and regularly publishes a newsletter in English. The coordinator is:

Dries van Nieuwenhuyse,
'Het Speihuis' Speistraat 17,
B-9550 Sint-Lievens-Esse (Herzele),
Belgium.

A national group exists in Germany. It is also very active and publishes a *Rundschreiben* in German. If interested write to:

Heinz Kowalski,
Wallstr. 16,
D-51702 Bergneustadt,
Germany.

A national shrike group has also recently been created in the Czech Republic. For details write to:

Czech Society for Ornithology,
Homomecholupska 34,
CZ-10200 Praha,
Czech Republic.

In the USA there is a specialised library on shrikes:

The Shrike Library,
Western Foundation of Vertebrate Zoology,
439 Calle San Pablo,
Camarillo CA-93012,
USA.

PLATES
1-16

PLATE 1: ASIAN SHRIKES I

1   Tiger Shrike *Lanius tigrinus*   Text and map page 83

Breeding range in the extreme eastern Palearctic, mainly China and Japan. Migratory, wintering chiefly in the Oriental region, from northern Vietnam and Laos southwards to Thailand, the Malay Peninsula and the Greater Sunda islands as far south as Java and Bali. Inhabits open forests or agricultural country well dotted with trees, occasionally suburban parks or gardens.

> **1a**   **Adult male** Unmistakable: brightly coloured and with a thicker bill than other shrikes. Bluish-grey crown and a 'tigered' rufous back; pure white underparts.
>
> **1b**   **Adult female** Duller than male with distinct black bars on sides. Lores mainly whitish.
>
> **1c**   **Juvenile** Rufous-brown ground colour; confusion with juvenile Bull-headed Shrike conceivable, but small size and thick bill are diagnostic.

2   Bull-headed Shrike *Lanius bucephalus*   Text and map page 85

Breeding range mainly in China and Japan and almost identical to that of Tiger Shrike, but extends further north, reaching 50°N on Sakhalin island. Migrant and resident, wintering area lying further south, particularly in south-east China. Japanese birds are resident or undertake local movements. Occurs in a wide range of fairly open habitats, including clearings, cultivated land, etc.

> **2a/b**   **Adult male** (nominate; whole breeding range except Gansu province, China) Rufous crown, grey back, dark tail and rather small white primary patch. Underparts washed orange-buff. See text for race *sicarius*.
>
> **2c**   **Adult female** (nominate) Duller, browner than male with no white spot on wings. Fine wavy bars on underparts.
>
> **2d**   **Juvenile** (nominate) A rather pale, rufous-tinged and heavily barred individual is shown. Larger than Tiger Shrike with, proportionally, a smaller bill.

6   Burmese Shrike *Lanius collurioides*   Text and map page 104

A species of South-East Asia, widespread in Burma as its name suggests; eastwards the range extends to southern China. Migrant and resident; limits of wintering range not well known. Regularly occurs in northern Thailand in winter, but can also be found further south (see map). Occurs in typical open *Lanius* habitats, forest edges, cultivated fields, etc.

> **6a/b**   **Adult male** (nominate; whole breeding range except southern Vietnam) Almost unmistakable; slight risk of confusion with races of the somewhat larger Long-tailed Shrike. Dark ashy crown, bright chestnut back and black tail fringed and tipped white are characteristic. Note distinct white primary patch.
>
> **6c**   **Adult female** (nominate) Distinguished from male by both paler lores and nasal feathers.
>
> **6d**   **Juvenile** (nominate) Note greyish-brown crown and nape and pale rufous back; primary patch, not seen on individual shown, may already be apparent.
>
> **6e**   **Adult male** (*nigricapillus*; southern Vietnam) Generally with more sooty-black on crown than nominate; note also richer chestnut back in this individual (variable).

PLATE 2: RED-BACKED AND BROWN SHRIKES

3 Red-backed Shrike *Lanius collurio* Text and map page 87

Breeds over large parts of Europe east to western Siberia in temperate, Mediterranean and steppe climates. Migratory, wintering in eastern and southern Africa. Inhabits open terrain with bushes, particularly thorn hedges.

3a/b **Adult male** Typical bird from western Europe. Unmistakable with bluish-grey crown, chestnut back and black tail with white sides. Note grey rump and inverted black T on tail, best seen in flight.

3c **Adult male** Less brightly coloured individual. Such birds, and even duller ones, can be seen throughout the range. Note here a very small white primary patch, which occurs occasionally.

3d **Adult female** Typical bird with brown to rufous-brown upperparts and wings; dark brown tail tinged rufous and slightly fringed white. Underparts distinctly scalloped with dusky-brown crescents. Individual variation in colour of upperparts and tail can be relatively wide (see text).

3e **Juvenile** Resembles adult female; ground colour of upperparts also variable but always closely barred dark brown. In Europe confusion is conceivable with juvenile Woodchat and Masked Shrikes; in the eastern part of its range with immature Isabelline Shrike.

5 Brown Shrike *Lanius cristatus* Text and map page 99

An East Palearctic species breeding from middle Irtysh and Tomsk east to Sakhalin, Japan and China. Almost all populations are migratory. Winters in the Indian subcontinent, South-East Asia and southern China. Like Red-backed Shrike, found in a variety of semi-open habitats; locally, however, more of a 'forest' shrike.

5a **Adult male** (nominate; north-western part of range) Relatively 'bull-headed', with strong bill and slim, graduated tail. Almost uniform russet-brown upperparts; distinct broad white supercilium.

5b **Adult female** (nominate) Similar to male, and not always separable; often slightly duller with supercilium tinged cream and breast and flanks finely vermiculated dusky.

5c **First-winter** (nominate) after juvenile moult; underparts still heavily barred in this individual, which already shows the plain upperparts of adults.

5d **Adult male** (*superciliosus*, Japan) Upperparts much more rufous than in other races and white frontal patch wider; underparts also more rufous.

5e **Adult male** (*lucionensis*, Korea, China; in winter mainly Taiwan and the Philippines) Upperparts much greyer than in other races; forecrown pale grey, grading into pale ashy on top of crown.

4   Isabelline Shrike *Lanius isabellinus*   **Text and map page 94**

Mainly breeding in Central Asia and wintering south of the Sahara in north-east Africa, in the south of the Arabian Peninsula and from southern Iraq east to north-west India. Occurs in open country with scattered bushes, particularly in semi-deserts, but also in cultivated and sometimes marshy areas.

4a   **Adult male** (nominate; north-western China) Typical bird. Pallid appearance with uniform sandy-grey upperparts; poorly defined head pattern with just a small dark brown spot on lores; small white primary patch. Tail generally less rufous than in next race (variable).

4b/c **Adult male** (*phoenicuroides*; western part of range, from Iran to Xinjiang) Typical, well-contrasted individual with well-marked head pattern showing rather large, jet black facial mask extending to lores, and distinct white supercilium. Rufous crown and tail contrast with grey-brown back. Small but distinct white primary patch. Underparts almost pure white in bird shown; can be tinged vinous-pink.

4d   **Adult male** (*phoenicuroides*) Less typical individual with greyer upperparts and a weaker face pattern, the supercilium being less pronounced and buff.

4e   **Adult male** (*speculigerus*; Mongolia, north-central China) Intermediate between *isabellinus* and *phoenicuroides*. Particularly resembles greyer individuals of the latter race with its typical drab grey upperparts. Note well-defined facial mask, prominent white primary patch and dark wings, all reminiscent of *phoenicuroides*, but also subdued supercilium and creamy underparts, which recall *isabellinus*.

4f   **Adult female** (*phoenicuroides*) Browner and smaller facial mask than in male; lores paler and supercilium less well defined; upperparts somewhat browner and primary patch only faintly indicated.

4g   **First-winter** (*phoenicuroides*) Rather pallid appearance. Note plain mantle; barring has disappeared (or is sometimes limited to crown and rump). More and more such birds are being found in western Europe in autumn. See text for differences with juvenile Red-backed Shrike.

4h   **Juvenile** (*phoenicuroides*) Very similar to Red-backed Shrike, but somewhat paler with a more rufous tail (though this can also occur in young *collurio*: see text).

4i   **Hybrid** Dark individual, presumably a hybrid between *phoenicuroides* and Red-backed Shrike. Hybrids are extremely variable, which explains the description by Russian ornithologists of six new 'species' and two new 'races' in a 17-year period towards the end of the last century. In the bird illustrated here note the blackish tail reminiscent of a male Red-backed Shrike, dark grey upperparts and small white primary patch.

10   Long-tailed Shrike *Lanius schach*   **Text and map page 111**

Vast breeding area, mainly over large areas of Asia; occurs as far west as Turkmenistan (and possibly Iran) and east to the Pacific coast of China, South-East Asia and New Guinea. The extreme western part of the breeding range is completely vacated in winter (see map). Elsewhere the species is a partial migrant or resident. Mainly a scrub jungle bird, also widespread in lightly wooded or cultivated country.

Only males are shown below, the sexes in all races being identical or almost so.

10a   **Adult male** (nominate; eastern and southern China) Unmistakable with dark grey and deep rufous upperparts and long, black, strongly graduated tail. Black band on forehead relatively wide (up to c. 2cm) and white primary patch conspicuous.

10b   **Adult male** (of melanistic form '*fuscatus*'). Confined to parts of south-west China, including Hainan, and northern Vietnam (see map). 'Mixed' pairs of typical *schach* and '*fuscatus*' have been recorded.

10c/d **Adult male** (*erythronotus*; western part of range) Similar to nominate, but distinctly smaller with grey and rufous of upperparts lighter. Black band of forehead narrower.

10e   **Juvenile** (*erythronotus*) Orange-buff tinges in plumage; no obvious primary patch.

10f   **Adult male** (*caniceps*; western and southern India, Sri Lanka) Similar to previous race, but less rufous on upperparts, generally only on rump and uppertail-coverts.

10g   **Adult male** (*tricolor*, Nepal eastwards to Yunnan and northern Thailand) Black cap, deep rufous upperparts, small greyish area on upper mantle. Intermediate birds between *erythronotus* and *tricolor* are frequent in a large zone in India and Nepal.

10h   **Adult male** (*nasutus*; the Philippines) Rather similar to previous race but with upper back grey, not rufous-chestnut.

10i   **Adult male** (*stresemanni*; New Guinea) Looks like previous race, but with less grey on upper back and deeper rufous on rest of upperparts.

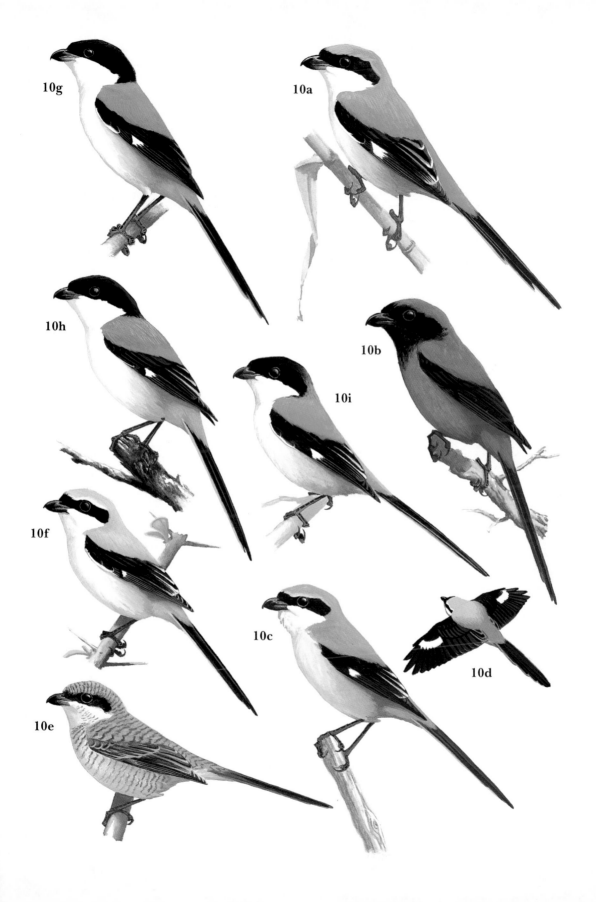

10g

10a

10h

10b

10i

10f

10c

10d

10e

9   Bay-backed Shrike *Lanius vittatus*   Text and map page 108

Mainly an Asian species, breeding from south-east Iran east to India where it is widespread. Mostly resident, except in western and northern parts of range. Inhabits a variety of semi-open habitats including parks and gardens.

9a/b   Adult male (nominate; western Pakistan and India) In coloration not unlike a male Red-backed Shrike, but with a distinct wide black band on forehead and white primary patches which are very conspicuous, particularly in flight. Note also white rump area and rusty-coloured flanks. Sexes similar.

9c   Adult male (*nargianus*; western part of range) Paler, less brightly coloured than nominate, but with high variation in plumage; sexes generally more easily separable than in nominate as female is generally duller than male.

9d   Juvenile (nominate) moulting into **First-winter**; note upperparts tinged rufous on mantle, indication of a whitish primary patch, and rufous-brown tail.

11   Grey-backed Shrike *Lanius tephronotus*   Text and map page 115

A high-elevation species also appropriately called Tibetan Shrike, breeding mainly in the Himalayas. Resident and migratory, birds occurring further south in winter, for instance in northern Thailand. Altitudinal movements are also characteristic. Nests up to at least 4,500m in open scrub; in winter at lower altitudes, in cultivated areas in valleys and plains.

Sexes similar in plumage.

11a/b Adult (nominate; Nepal, Sikkim, Bhutan, Arunachal Pradesh and parts of China and Tibet) Dark grey back, rufous on upperparts confined to rump area and chestnut-brown tail are diagnostic. See text for race *lahulensis*.

11c   Juvenile (nominate) Darker above than juvenile Long-tailed Shrike.

12   Mountain Shrike *Lanius validirostris*   Text and map page 117

Confined to the Philippines where it is common in mountainous areas. Little-known species.

Sexes similar in plumage.

12   Adult (nominate; northern Luzon) Very similar to the allopatric Grey-backed Shrike, but with a distinctly thicker bill and no, or much less, rufous on rump area. See text for other races.

17   Chinese Grey Shrike *Lanius sphenocercus*   Text and map page 144

Breeds in far-eastern Russia (Amur region) and in north-eastern and central China. Resident and migrant; the wintering area extends to south-east China. The high-elevation race *giganteus* is probably mainly a resident or an altitudinal migrant; in summer it occurs at 3,000-5,000m in stunted vegetation stands. Nominate is to be found in habitats recalling those of the Great Grey Shrike in central Europe, for instance in grasslands dotted with trees.

Sexes similar.

17a/b Adult (nominate; far-eastern Russia, north-eastern and central China) Like a large Great Grey Shrike of nominate race, with prominent white supercilium, large white patches in wings, and long, graduated tail. White under-parts. When seen well, confusion is unlikely with the races *mollis* and *sibiricus* of the Great Grey Shrike which may occur in same areas, particularly in winter.

17c   **Adult** (*giganteus*; eastern Nan Shan and eastern Tibet) Even larger than nominate. Upperparts darker; less white in plumage, no white supercilium; underparts not so white, but rather lavender-grey.

13   Lesser Grey Shrike *Lanius minor*   Text and map page 118

The breeding range extends over warmer parts of Eurasia from south-east Spain in the west to the Altai region in the east. Has become very rare in western Europe. Migratory, wintering in south-ern Africa, mainly Namibia and Botswana. A steppe species which has adapted well to cultivated areas with short vegetation and bare soil.

Main confusion species are Great Grey and Southern Grey Shrikes. Note different structure of *minor* with thick, relatively short bill, rather short tail, but long, pointed wings with a long primary projection.

13a/b Adult male Mainly grey, black and white. Characteristic features apart from structure are: a wide black band on forehead, conspicuous white primary patch and pinkish-washed underparts.

13c   **Adult female** Generally somewhat duller than male, often with a certain amount of brownish, not black feathers on forehead and less pinkish underparts.

13d   **First-winter** No vermiculations left on bird shown, which still lacks a black band on the forehead. Some individuals on autumn migration in Africa may show a more yellowish ground colour with some vermiculations still remaining on upperparts.

13e   **Juvenile** Paler than adults with brownish- (yellowish-) grey upperparts barred brown-grey. Vermiculations on underparts few and mainly on sides of breast.

17a

17b

17c

13a

13c

13b

13e

13d

PLATE 7: NORTH AMERICAN SHRIKES

14 **Loggerhead Shrike** *Lanius ludovicianus* **Text and map page 123**

Only endemic species in North America. Breeds in some southern parts of Canada and in most of the USA and Mexico. Has, however, markedly declined in many areas in recent decades, particularly in south-eastern Canada and the north-eastern United States. Winters mainly south of 40°N. Occurs in a variety of semi-open habitats; presence often correlated with agricultural land rich in grasslands and/or pastures, well dotted with shrubs and trees.

Slightly smaller than Great Grey Shrike with a distinctly shorter bill in proportion to body size. Generally darker upperparts.

Sexes similar in plumage.

14a/b **Adult** (nominate; south-eastern USA) Dark grey upperparts; dull white supercilium often noticeable; underparts generally white, can be washed greyish. White scapulars, white primary patch in black wings. Tail black, fringed white. Note black facial mask extending just above eyes and narrow black line over base of bill; these are diagnostic features when bird seen well (compare with Great Grey Shrike below).

14c **Juvenile** (nominate) Brownish-grey upperparts, paler than adults. Fairly distinctly barred overall.

14d **Adult** Individual from the west coast with dark upperparts and greyish underparts showing faint indications of barring. Probably to be included in the variable race *mexicanus* (see text).

14e **Adult** (*excubitorides*; Great Plains of the west) A pale race with generally more white in the plumage than other northern races. Often a rather distinct white supercilium. Note also white rump area.

14f **Adult** (*mearnsi*; San Clemente Island, California) An endangered subspecies. Note dark upperparts, white rump area and pale underparts. Averages smaller than other Californian races.

15 **Great Grey Shrike** *Lanius excubitor* (1) **Text and map page 128**

Occurs in many races in a vast belt stretching over the north of Eurasia and North America; mainly an open taiga species but also extending into central Europe and in winter can be found as far south as northern Spain, northern Italy and Turkey.

A black, white and grey bird with a long, strong bill, a long tail and round wings, quite different in structure from the Lesser Grey Shrike. More difficult to separate from Loggerhead Shrike in winter in the United States (see under that species).

15a **Adult** (*borealis*; eastern part of range in North America; very similar to other American race *invictus* and to Eurasian race *sibiricus*) Upperparts pale blue-grey as in nominate, but rump area generally paler. White wing patch always confined to primaries. Underparts greyer than in nominate and distinctly vermiculated on breast, sides and flanks.

15b **Juvenile** (*borealis*) Quite different from nominate. Wood-brown or buffy-brown above; underparts heavily vermiculated. **First-winter** birds have greyer upperparts, but are still easily separable from Loggerhead Shrike in winter when both species may occur in same areas.

14a

14d

14c

14b

14e

14f

15a

15b

15 Great Grey Shrike *Lanius excubitor* (2)   **Text and map page 128**

15c/d Adult male (nominate; western and northern Europe, eastwards through Russia) Individual with a 'double wing-bar', with white on base of primaries and secondaries. Such birds mainly occur in France and western Germany, but can also be found elsewhere, including Scandinavia. Supercilium is not always well marked.

15e **Adult male** (nominate) Individual with only one wing-bar, with white confined to base of primaries. Such birds tend to have slightly darker upperparts and show faint traces of vermiculations on underparts (variable), particularly in Scandinavia.

15f **Adult female** (nominate) Bird from central Europe, with double wing-bar. As a rule, has less white in plumage than male, although this may not be easy to appreciate in the field (see text). Also shows tendency to faint barring on upper breast, possibly birds in their second calendar year.

15g **Juvenile** (nominate) Upperparts grey-brown. Underparts off-white with fairly conspicuous vermiculations. Note pale tips to greater coverts, still present on first-winter birds.

15h **Adult** (*homeyeri*; from Bulgaria east through south-east Russia to western Siberia) Paler than nominate with white supercilium always prominent, large white wing-patch over primaries and secondaries, rump area often whitish not grey, and more white at base of tail.

15i **Adult** (*leucopterus*; western Siberia to the Yenisey) Even paler with more white than previous race, with which it intergrades.

15j **Adult** (*mollis*; Russian Altai, north-west Mongolia) A dark race with a small white wing-patch. Underparts dingy and heavily vermiculated even in adults.

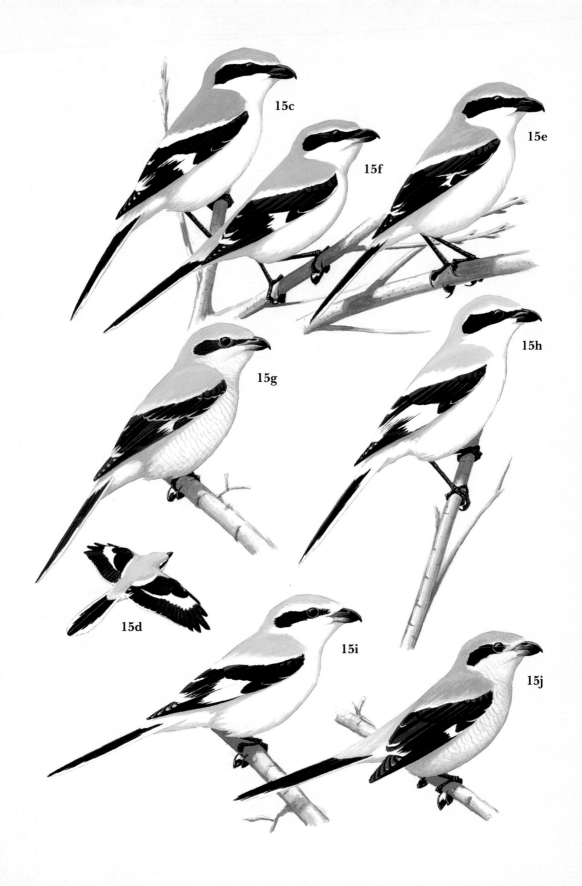

PLATE 9:   SOUTHERN GREY SHRIKE (1)

16   Southern Grey Shrike *Lanius meridionalis*   **Text and map page 137**

A Saharo-Sindian arid zone shrike breeding mainly in parts of North Africa, the Middle East, Central Asia and the northern part of the Indian subcontinent. Nominate *meridionalis* nests in the Iberian peninsula and southern France. Most races or populations are resident but there are exceptions: thus *pallidirostris*, the 'Steppe Grey Shrike', is a partial long-distance migrant. Inhabits hot, dry areas dotted with mainly thorny bushes.

Sexes similar in all races as far as known.

16a/b Adult (nominate; Iberian peninsula, southern France) Easily told from nominate *excubitor*, characteristic features are: dark plumbeous-grey upperparts, a white, thin, but conspicuous supercilium, a white primary patch (no white at base of secondaries), and vinous-tinged underparts.

16c   Juvenile (nominate) Generally no vermiculations on underparts; faint barring may, however, occur in some individuals (as well as in juveniles of next two races).

16d   Adult (*algeriensis*; North Africa) Similar to nominate, but with off-white or greyish underparts (variable); white supercilium lacking or poorly indicated.

16e   Adult (*koenigi*; Canary Islands) Similar to previous race, but smaller; white supercilium almost always present.

16f   Adult (*elegans*; northern fringes of Sahara and oases) Much paler than previous races with much white in plumage (variable). Underparts pure white or almost so.

16g   Adult (*leucopygos*; southern fringes of Sahara) Even paler than *elegans* and rump area whiter; also distinctly smaller.

16a

16c

16b

16e

16d

16g

16f

PLATE 10: SOUTHERN GREY SHRIKE (2)

16 Southern Grey Shrike *Lanius meridionalis*   Text and map page 137

16h **Adult** (*aucheri*; northern Ethiopia, Eritrea, from Sinai north to Syria, Iraq and southern Iran; also Arabian Peninsula) Similar to *elegans*, but with less white in plumage, a narrow black band at base of bill and underparts variably washed greyish.

16i **Adult** (*buryi*; Yemen) A dark race recalling *algeriensis*, but with distinctly less white on scapulars; underparts also generally darker, even on throat.

16j **Adult** (*lahtora*; eastern Pakistan, northern India) Rather similar to *aucheri*, but with more white on upperparts and in wings; underparts also whiter; a distinct, relatively wide black frontal band.

16k/l **Adult** (*pallidirostris* 'Steppe Grey Shrike'; mainly Central Asia; in winter, birds occur as far south as Sudan and Ethiopia) Typical pale bird with whitish lores and horn-coloured bill; underparts may be faintly salmon-tinged (variable).

16m **Adult** (*pallidirostris*) Head of less typical bird with black on lores and bill.

16n **First-winter** (*pallidirostris*) Note pale plumage, pale lores, reduced dark brown mask and typical pale bill with dark tip. As in adults, the underparts can be tinged pale pinkish-buff in fresh plumage. Such birds are occasionally found in the western Palearctic.

16k

16m

16n

16j

16l

16h

16i

PLATE 11: AFRICAN SHRIKES I

7 Emin's Shrike *Lanius gubernator*

Text and map page 105

A very little-known species confined to parts of western and central Africa north of the Equator, roughly from Ivory Coast east to northern Uganda. Mainly resident as far as known, but at least local movements appear possible. Can be found in semi-open habitats like degraded Guinea savanna, forest clearings, cultivated areas, etc.

7a **Adult male** Striking resemblance to a small male Red-backed Shrike, but rump area chestnut like back, not blue-grey. Wings with a small but conspicuous white primary patch, only very occasional in *collurio* and then very small. Note also tawny underparts (washed salmon-pink in Red-backed Shrike).

7b **Adult female** Differs little from male, but duller. Ground colour variable; rather well-contrasted individual shown. Unlike adult female Red-backed Shrike, does not show any barring on underparts, which are variably washed pale rufous.

7c **Juvenile** Rather similar to a relatively small dark juvenile Red-backed Shrike, but note underparts washed tawny.

8 Sousa's Shrike *Lanius souzae*

Text and map page 107

A relatively little-known species occurring in Central Africa from Gabon (rare) east to western Tanzania and south to southern Angola, Zambia and Malawi. Mainly if not exclusively resident. May be called a 'forest' shrike, being typical of light miombo woodland.

8a **Adult male** (nominate; southern Congo, southern Zaïre, Angola) Crown, nape and mantle grey recalling male Red-backed Shrike, but rest of upperparts brown, not chestnut. A whitish supercilium and white scapulars are generally conspicuous. Note also long, dark brown and particularly narrow tail. See text for other races.

8b **Adult female** (nominate) As in male, ground colour somewhat variable but generally duller than male with distinct tawny patch on flanks.

8c **Juvenile** (nominate) Upperparts brown or russet-brown; indication of pale supercilium may already be noticeable. Note also whitish scapulars barred blackish.

18 Grey-backed Fiscal *Lanius excubitoroides*

Text and map page 146

Breeds in central-eastern Africa, roughly from south-east Mauritania east to the Rift Valley. Mainly resident except perhaps for some western populations living in typical Sahel areas. Occupies open woodlands, cultivated areas well dotted with rather high trees, parks and gardens, etc. Often in small, noisy groups. A cooperative-breeding species.

A large, relatively bulky, long-tailed, black, grey and white shrike. Sexes very similar but female has distinct chestnut patch on flanks.

18a/b Adult male (nominate; western part of range) Grey upperparts contrast with black wings in which a white primary patch is very conspicuous. Note also characteristic black band on forehead and typical tail pattern with mainly white basal half and black terminal half. Unmistakable when seen well; the main problem may be adult Lesser Grey Shrike (different structure, much smaller tail, etc.). See text for other races.

18c **Juvenile** (nominate) Already shows some typical features of adults: white wing-patch and typical tail pattern.

68

7a

7b

7c

8a

8b

8c

18a

18c

18b

PLATE 12: AFRICAN SHRIKES II

19 Long-tailed Fiscal *Lanius cabanisi*
Text and map page 149

Range restricted to East Africa in parts of Kenya, Tanzania and Somalia. Occupies drier habitats than the Grey-backed Fiscal with which it is largely allopatric; occurs in shrubby, almost treeless savannas, open woodlands and cultivated patches. Lives in groups.

19a/b Adult male Almost unmistakable with its mainly dark upperparts, white rump and typical long, mainly black tail. Wings also black with a distinct white primary patch. Pure white underparts.

19c Adult female Similar to male, but note chestnut patch on flanks.

19d Juvenile Grey-brown upperparts with whitish rump area. Long tail and white primary patch on mainly dark wings.

20 Taita Fiscal *Lanius dorsalis*
Text and map page 150

Range confined to six countries in East Africa; well distributed in Kenya. Inhabits dry open bushed habitats.

Medium-sized and relatively stocky. Sexes very similar, but female has, at least sometimes, some chestnut streaks on flanks.

20a Adult male Black cap, sides of head and tail contrast with rest of upperparts, which are pale grey. Note white scapulars and wholly black wings except for a conspicuous white primary patch.

20b Immature bird moulting into adult plumage.

21 Somali Fiscal *Lanius somalicus*
Text and map page 151

Occurs almost exclusively in the Horn of Africa; as its name suggests, it is common and widespread in Somalia. Frequents sparsely bushed habitats in arid areas. Rarely in contact with the very similar Taita Fiscal, which is less tolerant of such extreme conditions.

Sexes almost similar, but female has axillaries brownish ashy-grey, not black; unlike female Taita Fiscal does not show indications of a chestnut patch on flanks.

21a/b Adult male Differs from adult Taita Fiscal in having a little more white in plumage. Note characteristic rather broad white tips to the secondaries, a mainly white rump (grey in Taita Fiscal) and tail broadly fringed white. Undertail wholly white when tail closed (see text).

21c Juvenile Some characteristic features of adults are already visible.

23 Common Fiscal *Lanius collaris* Text and map page 154

Most common and widespread *Lanius* shrike south of the Equator. Absent, however, from certain geographical areas like the Horn of Africa. Mainly resident. Inhabits a vast range of open savanna habitats in lowlands and highlands, and has locally become a garden bird.

Mainly black and white. Females generally somewhat duller and in most races with some chestnut on flanks.

23a/b Adult male (nominate; parts of southern Africa) Blackish-brown upperparts with grey gloss and black tail contrasting with striking white scapulars and conspicuous white primary patch. Note grey or pale grey rump. Underparts off-white, often finely vermiculated grey from breast to belly.

23c Adult female (nominate) Similar to male, but duller above (variable). Usually some chestnut on flanks.

23d Juvenile (nominate) Ash-brown above with dirty grey scapulars; underparts greyish, finely barred.

23e Adult male (*humeralis*; eastern Africa) Upperparts dull black; rump generally pale grey; much white in tail; underparts almost pure white.

23f Adult male (*smithii*; western Africa) Distinct bluish gloss on black upperparts. Note also distinct white tips on tertials and some secondaries. Less white in tail than previous race, but underparts pure white.

23g Adult male (*subcoronatus*; south-west Africa) Most distinct feature is a distinct white supercilium joining a white area on lores and base of forehead.

23h Adult female (*subcoronatus*) Note conspicuous chestnut patch on flanks.

25 Uhehe Fiscal *Lanius marwitzi* Text and map page 159

Little-known; confined to highlands in south-central Tanzania. Sexes similar as far as is known.

25 Adult Conspicuous white supercilium and thin white frontal band are diagnostic. Not unlike *subcoronatus* race of Common Fiscal, but dark grey, not white, rump. Rather small white primary patch.

24 Newton's Fiscal *Lanius newtoni* Text and map page 157

The rarest *Lanius* shrike, only found on São Tomé island in the Gulf of Guinea. Strictly confined to open lowland primary rainforest. Rediscovered in July 1990 when an individual was caught and photographed.

24 Adult Illustration based on a photograph of the captured individual mentioned above. The yellowish colour of the underparts is not visible on the few known museum specimens.

22 Mackinnon's Shrike *Lanius mackinnoni* Text and map page 152

Range lies in Central Africa and surrounds the huge rainforest areas. An apparently strictly resident and typical forest-edge shrike which favours relatively moist or humid areas.

Female similar to male, but with distinct patch of chestnut on flanks.

22a Adult male The fairly broad white supercilium and white scapulars contrast with the sooty-grey upperparts, the wholly black wings and the mainly black tail. Underparts off-white; may be washed pale buff.

22b Juvenile Heavily barred overall. Note conspicuous whitish scapulars and dark wings.

23c

23d

23a

23e

23b

23g

23f

23h

25

22b

24

22a

PLATE 14: WOODCHAT AND MASKED SHRIKES

26 Woodchat Shrike *Lanius senator* Text and map page 159

Most of the breeding range lies in the Mediterranean climatic zone of the western Palearctic; but it also extends into the temperate zone within the July isotherm of 19°C and eastwards to Iran. Migratory, wintering south of the Sahara and north of the Equator. More arboreal than Red-backed Shrike; generally occurs in lowlands, not over 600-900m, in open woodlands, old orchards, roadside trees, etc. In Africa mainly in dry *Acacia* savanna and cultivated patches.

26a/b **Adult male** (nominate; western part of range) Unmistakable; black and white with rufous crown and hindneck, white scapulars, rump and conspicuous primary patch; tail black, fringed white. Feathers of wings fringed pale rufous in fresh plumage.

26c **Adult female** (nominate) Close to male, but generally duller or much duller (variable) with facial mask mottled brown-buff and somewhat browner upperparts.

26d **Juvenile** (nominate) Overall slightly whiter, 'greyer' than young Red-backed Shrike. Also larger, more angular head. Clear indications of whitish scapulars, rump and primary patch recalling adult pattern.

26e **Adult male** (*badius*; western Mediterranean islands) White primary patch absent or much reduced.

26f **Adult male** (*niloticus*; eastern part of range) More white in plumage, wings and base of tail.

26g **Adult hybrid** Woodchat x Red-backed Shrike after photographs and paintings of a bird near Valenciennes (France) in June 1995.

27 Masked Shrike *Lanius nubicus* Text and map page 166

Breeding range almost entirely confined to eastern part of the Mediterranean zone in the western Palearctic: Greece, Turkey, Cyprus, and the Levant eastwards to Iran. Migratory; in winter in sub-Saharan Africa, mainly Sudan and Ethiopia westwards to eastern Mali. Also in the south-western part of the Arabian peninsula. Almost a 'forest' shrike, often in areas with high tree cover such as: open woodlands, olive groves, gardens and parks.

27a/b **Adult male** Uniform black from crown to tail with bold white forehead and white supercilium; also white scapulars and conspicuous white primary patches. Flanks distinctly rufous or rusty-chestnut. A slim, rather delicate shrike with a graceful flight.

27c **Adult female** Similar to but duller than male.

27d **Juvenile** Overall distinctly slimmer build and greyer upperparts than young Woodchat Shrike. Unlike latter, has dark rump, concolorous with back; pale forehead and indication of whitish supercilium already recall adult pattern.

28   Yellow-billed Shrike *Corvinella corvina*   Text and map page 169

Breeds in a wide belt crossing the African continent south of the Sahara, but generally north of the Equator, except in the extreme eastern part of the range. Mainly resident; local movements do, however, occur particularly in the Sahel in western Africa. An arboreal species occurring in *Acacia* savannas, but also in well-wooded parks and gardens. Often in small groups, conspicuous and noisy. A cooperative breeder.

Female similar to male, but with a slightly different colour-patch on flanks (patches hidden by closed wings).

28a/b Adult male (nominate; western part of range) Unmistakable giant brown shrike characterised by a strong yellow bill, streaked upperparts and a very long, dark brown, graduated tail. Note also pale, but distinct, broad supercilium, conspicuous orange-buff patch in wings, and pale buff, narrowly streaked underparts.

28c   Juvenile (nominate) Already very similar to adult. Note barred, not streaked, upperparts and underparts.

28d   Adult male (*affinis*; eastern part of range) Distinctly more greyish-brown above than nominate; orange-buff patch in wings smaller.

29   Magpie Shrike *Corvinella melanoleuca*   Text and map page 172

Breeding range entirely south of the Equator in eastern and southern Africa. Mainly resident; vagrants sometimes occur outside 'normal' range. Typical of park-like savannas with rather tall *Acacia* trees. Gregarious, breeding cooperatively.

29a/b Adult male (nominate; southern Africa) Unmistakable, large, mainly black shrike with a strong black bill and a very long graduated tail. Note also striking white scapulars and white primary patch. See text for race *aequatorialis*.

29c   Adult female (nominate) Similar to male, but with a conspicuous large white patch on flanks.

28a

28d

28c

28b

29c

29b

29a

PLATE 16: *EUROCEPHALUS* SHRIKES

30   White-rumped Shrike *Eurocephalus rueppelli*   Text and map page 174

Range limited to East Africa. Mainly resident. A tree-dwelling species, and a typical inhabitant of *Acacia* woodlands; also occurs in parks and gardens. Sociable and often noisy, sometimes breeding cooperatively.

Sexes similar in plumage.

  30a/b Adult A fairly unmistakable, stocky species with a powerful bill and brown upperparts except for the crown and rump, which are white. Underparts off-white with some brownish patches. Butterfly-like flight interspersed with glides on stiff wings.

  30c   Juvenile Note head pattern different from adults, with dark crown; underparts rather heavily washed brown.

31   White-crowned Shrike *Eurocephalus anguitimens*   Text and map page 175

A southern African shrike, allopatric from previous species. Mainly resident although local movements exist. Lives in open thorny woodlands, particularly in light *Acacia* forest; also occurs in parkland near human habitations. Generally sociable, noisy and obvious; at least in some degree a cooperative breeder.

Sexes similar in plumage.

  31a/b Adult Unmistakable with its white crown, ashy-brown upperparts and dark tail and wings. Note also ashy-brown colour on underparts between lower belly and vent.

  31c   Juvenile In moult with greyish-white crown; underparts washed ashy-brown all over.

30a

30c

30b

31b

31a

31c

SYSTEMATIC
SECTION

1   TIGER SHRIKE
Lanius tigrinus   Plate 1

Other name: Thick-billed Shrike

IDENTIFICATION Length c. 17.5cm. A rather small, brightly coloured monotypic Asian shrike, both of whose two common English names suit it well. Its bill is proportionately thicker than those of the somewhat larger Bull-headed and Brown Shrikes which occur in approximately the same geographical area. The species is also 'tigered' insofar as both sexes show barred upperparts in adult plumage. Males have a mid-grey cap which extends down to the nape and contrasts with the bright rufous of the back and tail. The flight feathers of their dark brown wings are edged pale rufous and the underparts are pure white. Females are very similar, but duller with a browner mantle. They can easily be distinguished in the field as they show very distinct black bars on their breast and belly and also whitish, not black, lores. Juveniles resemble young Bull-headed Shrikes but are smaller with a proportionately larger bill, and live in a different habitat (see under Bull-headed Shrike).

The species is generally less conspicuous than other small shrikes as it keeps more to relatively closed habitats, open forest or forest edge.

DESCRIPTION
Adult male Facial mask black over lores, eyes, ear-coverts and anterior part of forehead. Supercilium whitish, very faint behind eye. Upperparts mid-grey from forehead to base of nape. Mantle, back, scapulars, rump and uppertail-coverts rufous, heavily and rather coarsely barred blackish. Tail brown-rufous and graduated (graduation c. 2cm); outer tail feathers paler and all rectrices faintly tipped whitish. Wings dark brown, tertials paler; all feathers fringed pale rufous. Underparts white. Undertail pale brown.
Adult female Similar to male but variably duller with upperparts slightly browner, less rufous. Lores always whitish, not black. Underparts with very distinct black bars on sides of breast and flanks.
Juvenile Facial mask dark brown faintly marked over lores, eyes and ear-coverts. Upperparts rufous-brown and heavily barred, becoming brighter rufous on lower back, rump and uppertail-coverts. Tail brown-rufous. Wings dark brown as in adults. Underparts off-white, washed pale buff, with coarse barring overall except on chin. Undertail pale brown.
Bare parts Bill strong, very deep and bluish-black. Legs plumbeous-grey. Iris brown.

MEASUREMENTS Wing 83-90 (females averaging probably slightly smaller than males); tail c. 75-80; bill (culmen) 17-18; tarsus c. 22-25. Weight: no data.

DISTRIBUTION AND STATUS The Tiger Shrike breeds in the extreme eastern Palearctic, but winters in the Oriental region. The breeding range is rather restricted. In far-eastern Russia it mainly covers the Primorskiy Kray, and more precisely the area around Ussuriysk along the coasts of Peter the Great Bay

reaching its northern limits at c. 44°N. After apparently a gap in the north-eastern Korean peninsula, the range extends through the rest of North Korea, reaching the Seoul area in South Korea. However, *Lanius tigrinus* is mainly a Chinese bird, inhabiting the extreme north-east and southern parts of the country. It is widely distributed in the north-east and in Hebei and Shandong provinces; southwards the range extends to the Chang-jiang and Zhejiang rivers, and the Tropic of Cancer appears to be a good limit; westwards the Tiger Shrike occurs as far as the southern part of Shaanxi, Sichuan and Guizhou. The western boundary lies in the two latter provinces at c. 101°E. Some populations also nest here and there on Honshu, the main Japanese island. They are mainly to be found in the central and northern parts, from the Kanto plain north to Aomori-ken. The species also breeds on Sado and in Miyazaki-ken, but its status in Shikoku, most of Kyushu and Tsushima is not well known.

There are few precise data on population trends. At least in the northern parts of its breeding range, far-eastern Russia and Japan, the Tiger Shrike has declined markedly over the last 30-40 years. In Japan it was once common and widespread, occurring even in parks in the suburbs of Tokyo, but it is now a very local, uncommon summer visitor.

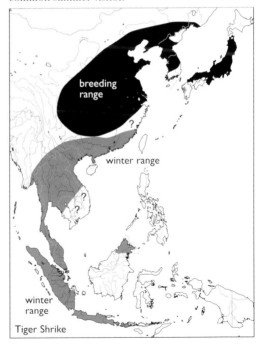

Tiger Shrike

GEOGRAPHICAL VARIATION None known. Monotypic.

HYBRIDS A hybrid male *tigrinus* x *cristatus* has been observed in far-eastern Russia, nesting with a typical female Brown Shrike. When found, the pair had a nest with five young ready to fledge.

MOVEMENTS All populations are migratory or almost so (a few individuals remain in winter in Japan). The northern boundaries of the wintering range lie apparently just south of the breeding range and pass through south-east China, where wintering or at least migratory birds can be found in the south-eastern part of Yunnan as well as in Guangxi, Guangdong, Hunan and Fujian. The Tiger Shrike also winters in northern Vietnam, northern Laos and Thailand, where it has been reported on migration or in winter from the northern plateau (Lamphun, Phrae), the central plains (Bangkok) and the peninsular provinces from Prachuap Khiri Khan to the extreme south. In Burma, it is known as a rare straggler to southern Tenasserim. Further south, in the Malay Peninsula, the bird occurs throughout, south to Singapore. It has also been recorded on passage or wintering on the islands of Terutao, Pulan Paya, Penang, Tenggul, Jarak, Pisang, Ayer Merbau and Ubin. It is an irregular winter visitor throughout the Greater Sundas (including the many small islands), being rather common in Sumatra and also in northern Borneo, but observed as far south as Java and Bali.

Tiger Shrikes from far-eastern Russia leave their breeding grounds as early as August. Most of them depart in the last ten days of that month; there are very few observations from the beginning of September when passage birds can still be seen on the islands in Peter the Great Bay. Russian birds come back late, at the end of May or the beginning of June. Japanese birds also leave in late August or early September; they are back in early to mid-May. The same holds for the Nanking area in China. In the Malay Peninsula, migrants have been seen as early as 26 August in Phangnga and as late as 7 May at Fraser's Hill. At the latter locality, night-flying migrants have been netted from 9 September to 2 November and then again from 11 April to 7 May. In Sumatra, this winter visitor has been recorded between 3 September and 22 April.

Tiger Shrikes may appear outside their normal breeding or wintering ranges. In Japan the species is accidental in Hokkaido, where it was first recorded on Yagishiri on 19 June 1951. It is also a vagrant to Hong Kong, with two records up to 1986: single females or immatures at Cheung Chau on 5 September 1979 and Tai Po Kau on 26 September 1984.

MOULT Very similar to the moult of the Brown Shrike. Adult *tigrinus* renew their entire plumage, including the flight feathers, twice every year. A complete or almost complete moult (the six outer secondaries perhaps remain unmoulted) takes place while the birds are still on their breeding territories; it begins at the start of July and is finished in August or at the start of September. A new moult begins in the winter quarters at the end of December or start of January; it is completed by the end of March. This prenuptial moult is accomplished over a somewhat longer period than the postnuptial moult. Winter and summer plumages are perfectly alike.

VOICE The song may be resonant and musical, but at the beginning of courtship, when the male is perched near the female, it is subdued and does not carry very far. A characteristic territorial call is quite different from those of other small *Lanius* sp.; in fact it sounds like the alarm calls which are typical of the family. It is repeated in series and may be transcribed as *tcha tcha tcha tcha*. Another very subdued but sharp call can be described as *tchik*.

HABITAT The Tiger Shrike breeds in a temperate climate and is mainly found in lowlands or low hills (in Japan usually below 800m and never above 1,200m). It is almost a 'forest' shrike, occupying more open mixed or deciduous woods and partial to the outskirts of forests. It can also occur in forest glades, agricultural country well dotted with trees, and occasionally even suburban parks, as used to be the case in Tokyo. In far-eastern Russia it nests at low elevations (c. 150m), among deciduous woods composed mainly of elms *Ulmus propinqua*, *U. japonica*, alders *Alnus japonica*, oaks *Quercus mongolica*, etc., growing along rivers or on gentle slopes. In its winter quarters, in tropical or subtropical climates, this shrike can be met with at the edges of primary and secondary forests and hills up to c. 900m, as in Sumatra, or in cultivated areas and even gardens.

HABITS The Tiger Shrike is relatively inconspicuous in its rather closed habitat. At the beginning of the breeding season unpaired males can, however, commonly be observed on the tops of trees. There they may deliver their quiet song or their very loud, energetic territorial calls. While doing so, they hold their heads rather upright and flutter their wings. They also, still while calling, perform rapid, powerful display-flights over their territories. The Tiger Shrike is a solitary nester and densities are generally low. In far-eastern Russia, it has been estimated that there is one pair per 2.5-3km². However in the same region, three pairs have been found nesting close together, their nests only being separated by 10-12m. It can be assumed from this that territories are rather small, but precise data are lacking. A degree of site-fidelity has been proved for wintering birds: at Jelebur Pass (Negri Sembilan, Malay Peninsula) a bird ringed on 2 November was retrapped at the same place on 20 October the following year; another ringed on Singapore was caught again on the same wintering grounds two seasons later. Insects are caught in typical *Lanius* manner but the birds prefer perching in trees or skulking in scrub to hawking from a prominent place in the open. Unsurprisingly, therefore much more frequently than other *Lanius* species, it catches insects from branches and leaves and particularly in the foliage of trees. There are no records of its using larders.

FOOD Almost exclusively insects and mainly Orthoptera and Coleoptera. In far-eastern Russia, the stomachs of six adults contained grasshoppers (chiefly *Gampsacleis ussuriensis*), Pentatomidae, Elateridae (*Selatosomus aeneus*), Scarabaeidae, Lepidoptera, etc. In the same area, six-day-old chicks were mainly given grasshoppers (*Gampsacleis* sp.). Attacks on small birds have been recorded.

BREEDING In far-eastern Russia, the first birds that arrive towards the end of May are mostly males. Many

females arrive, however, at the same time. Pair formation takes place very quickly and it is possible that it
may sometimes occur during migration stopovers. In
the northern parts of the breeding range, far-eastern
Russia and Japan, breeding starts very late, between
the end of May and mid-June. It ends in July. This
species is usually single-brooded, but repeat clutches
are frequent. Both male and female build the nest in
about 5-7 days, probably immediately after pair formation. In Russia and Japan, it is placed fairly high,
generally between 2-6m, in a deciduous tree (oak, elm,
apple, etc.) and, as a rule, on a horizontal side-branch
1-4.5m from the trunk; it may be partly hidden by
creeping plants such as wild vines. In southern China,
nests have been recorded in brambles and low bushes.
The nest itself is a rather small compact cup with substantial, well-defined walls, composed of weed- stems,
grasses, pliable bark, other pliable material and, occasionally, moss. Its outer diameter measures c. 13cm and
its overall height c. 7.5cm. Clutch-size varies from 3 to
6 eggs ; in Russia there are 5 or, more rarely, 6 eggs
(mean 5.3, n = 11). Incubation, done exclusively by
the female, lasts 15-16 days and the young stay in the
nest for about two weeks. After fledging they stay in
the vicinity of the nest for about another two weeks.

REFERENCES Austin & Kuroda (1953), Brazil (1991),
Caldwell & Caldwell (1931), Chalmers (1986), Cheng
(1987), Deignan (1945, 1963), Jahn (1942), La Touche
(1925 - 1930), Loskot *et al.* (1991), MacKinnon & Phillipps (1993), Medway & Wells (1976), Panov (1983),
Smythies (1960, 1986) Stresemann & Stresemann
(1971).

---

2   BULL-HEADED SHRIKE
Lanius bucephalus   Plate 1

IDENTIFICATION Length c. 20cm. A medium-sized,
colourful Asian species (two races) with a relatively
long dark brown tail. The adult male has a characteristic rufous crown which shades into olive-brown on
the upperparts. A white supercilium is very obvious, as
is a white primary patch on the black wings. On the
otherwise whitish underparts, bright rufous appears
on the sides of the throat, breast and flanks, which
may faintly be barred with dark brown vermiculations.
The duller, slightly browner female has no white primary patch and much more heavily vermiculated
underparts. Juveniles have dark rufous, heavily barred
upperparts and off-white underparts, slightly washed
buff and also heavily barred. They may be confused
with young Tiger Shrikes, but are distinctly larger with
a proportionately smaller bill.

The Bull-headed Shrike occupies a variety of semi-
open habitats. It is one of the most characteristic and
widespread birds of the Japanese rural landscape.

DESCRIPTION *L. b. bucephalus*
Adult male Facial mask jet black over eyes and ear-
coverts. Supercilium white, very obvious behind eyes,
thinner in front, and joining very narrowly over base

of bill. Forehead, crown and nape rufous. Upperparts
olive-brown from mantle and scapulars to uppertail-
coverts. Tail dark brown, very faintly tipped white and
graduated (graduation c. 2.5cm); central pair of
rectrices darker than rest, appearing tipped blackish.
Wings dark brown with a distinct white patch on
primaries; greater wing-coverts and tertials fringed pale
buff. Underparts off-white washed orange-buff, particularly on breast and flanks (almost same colour as cap);
dark brown barring may occur on breast and flanks.
Undertail grey-brown.
Adult female Similar to male, but facial mask browner, not jet black. Supercilium whitish, more creamy and
often less obvious. Forehead, crown and nape rufous.
Upperparts more olive-tinged. Wings dark brown as
in male, but without white primary patch. Underparts
off-white, washed orange-buff and much more heavily
barred than in male.
Juvenile Facial mask dark brown over lores, eyes and
ear-coverts. Upperparts dark rufous, heavily barred
blackish from forehead to back, becoming paler on
scapulars and rump area. Uppertail-coverts dark
rufous. Tail brown-rufous. Wings dark brown; tertials
dark, fringed buff, creating a distinctive pale zone.
Underparts off-white, washed buff and heavily barred.
Undertail light brown.
Bare parts Bill black, lighter at base of lower mandible. Legs black. Iris dark brown.

MEASUREMENTS (*bucephalus*) Wing 79-92 (mean c.
86); tail 89-103 (mean c. 93); bill 15-16.5; tarsus 23-26.
Weight: mean c. 40; in a study in central Japan (Yamagishi & Saito 1985), the mean body weight of 66 females
in the incubation stage was c. 45 (range 37.3-54.4); in
October- November, the mean body weight of 37
females was c. 39 (range 35.5-43.2).

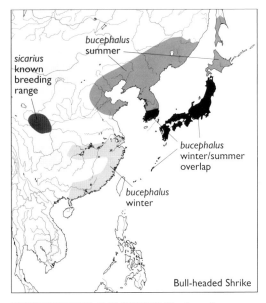

Bull-headed Shrike

DISTRIBUTION AND STATUS The breeding range
of the Bull-headed Shrike lies in the far-eastern Palearctic. It is rather similar to that of the Tiger Shrike,

but extends further north. The species reaches c. 50°N in Russian territories, in southern Ussuriland and on Sakhalin. It also nests between 44° and 49°N in the Kuril islands, also belonging to Russia. Further south, the breeding range covers the Koreas, Japan and north-east China. In the latter country, the species nests in the north-east provinces (middle Changbai Mts, around Dandong), Hebei (in the hilly country in Donling and Xiling) and Shandong. An isolated population (race *sicarius*) occurs further south-west in Gansu province (south-western part) and in Sichuan (Wushan). In Japan, the Bull-headed Shrike is widespread in Kyushu, Shikoku, on the main island, Honshu, and on the northern island, Hokkaido. It also nests on smaller islands or group of islands: Oki, Tsushima, the Goto Islands, from Oshima to perhaps Torishima, Tanegashima, Yakushima. In 1988, breeding was first proved on Chichijima in the Ogasawara Islands. This may be the southernmost breeding site for the species.

GEOGRAPHICAL VARIATION Two subspecies are recognised. The race *sicarius* was described in 1928 and, for a long time, only known from a female specimen. Details concerning the characters of the male were given for the first time by Zheng and Wang (1985).

L. b. bucephalus (southern Ussuriland, Sakhalin, Japan, the Korean peninsula, north-east China) Described above.

L. b. sicarius (Gansu province in southern China) Structure possibly very slightly different from nominate, with tip of the first primary closer to the second. Male with darker grey back and a less conspicuous primary patch. Female differs from nominate in having very heavily barred underparts.

MOVEMENTS Most populations are migratory; some, however, are more or less sedentary or undertake local movements. The wintering grounds lie south of but include some breeding areas: particularly parts of South Korea and three of the four main islands of Japan – Kyushu, Shikoku and Honshu – and small numbers may even winter in northernmost Honshu and occasionally in Hokkaido. In Japan, as a rule, northern breeders and those from higher elevations move to warmer regions or to lowlands. In winter, this shrike is largely, if not completely, absent from the Russian territories and from north-east China. As a passage migrant or wintering bird, the Bull-headed Shrike occurs in the following provinces of south-east China: Shaanxi (southern part), Henan, Sichuan (central part), Hubei, Hunan, Jiangsu, Anhui, Zhejiang, Fujian and Guangdong. It is rare in Taiwan, where it was recorded for the first time on 22 November 1932. The migration routes are not well known, but in autumn the birds presumably take a south or south-easterly direction and in spring a north or north-westerly one.

Migrant birds start leaving their breeding grounds in August. Late birds have been seen on the Kuril islands on 23 September and 6 October, and on Sakhalin between 8 and 20 September. In Ussuriland, the last birds are generally recorded towards the end of September, exceptionally at the beginning of October. In spring, the Bull-headed Shrikes nesting in the north of the breeding range are back in their territories as early as the beginning of April. In Ussuriland and the Kuril islands, the first birds are generally seen between 5 and 12 April, but there are new arrivals at least until the end of the month. On Hokkaido, the first shrikes also arrive in early April.

MOULT The juvenile moult begins soon after fledging and involves the body feathers and wing-coverts. In central Japan, this moult is finished as early as the end of August. It is then difficult to tell first-year birds from adults. Young birds, however, retain some unmoulted primary coverts until May of their second calendar year. These feathers, easy to recognise as they are buff-tipped, constitute a reliable criterion for identifying birds in their first-summer plumage (see Yamagishi 1982).

VOICE The song is rather loud and somewhat reminiscent of that of a Marsh Warbler *Acrocephalus palustris*. It includes clear whistles and imitations of other birds or even of insects like cicadas. A trilling call given by the male at the beginning of the breeding season is very characteristic (see also Habits). Another common call is a noisy chattering *ju-ju-ju* or *gi-gi-gi*.

HABITAT The breeding range lies in a temperate type of climate; in winter some populations penetrate into subtropical zones. The species may be found from sea-level up to c. 2,700m in the Japanese Alps; on Honshu, however, the Bull-headed Shrike is rarely found above 1,600m and, in winter, rarely above 600m. Remarkably, the first specimen of the race *sicarius* was found at an altitude of 2,750m in southern China. A wide range of fairly open habitats are used by this rather ubiquitous shrike. In Ussuriland, it is found in light hill forests opened up by foresters and fires; there it can be regarded as a forest-edge shrike, but it also nests along lines of trees crossing meadows, light riverine forests, reed-beds, etc. In the Kuril islands, it breeds in clearings created by man in mixed taiga forest or bamboo stands. In Japan, where it is widespread, the Bull-headed Shrike occurs in the same types of habitats, but also in open cultivated land with scattered trees, along roadsides with shrubs and trees, etc. It is also a common sight in villages and readily breeds in suburban parks and gardens, even in large towns.

HABITS A quite conspicuous, confiding and often noisy shrike. In resident populations in central Japan, the male and female have individual winter territories; at the end of January, females begin to wander about males' territories until they select a mate. Most females settle within 1km of their winter territory. Males can be of two types: strictly sedentary, remaining and breeding in their winter territory, and 'floaters', which leave their winter territory to nest elsewhere. At the beginning of the breeding season, unpaired males are very demonstrative. They sing loudly from vantage points and often change perches, performing a display-flight which takes them from tree-top to tree-top. This zigzag flight is accompanied by loud trilling calls. When a male notices a female it gives short, harsh *kew* calls, repeated three or four times, and sometimes a trilling *kürrrrririri*. When displaying close to the female, the male continues to sing, but in a more subdued way. Densities of breeders are variable; they can be remarkably high, as for instance in Oizumi city park (Japan) where up to 32 pairs nest each year in an area of c. 70ha. In winter, the same area includes the individual territories of c. 55 birds, but the boundaries of the territories overlap somewhat. Not surprisingly, at this site the pair-bond is rather strong and from one year to the next c. 30% of the females can be found again with the same male in the same territory. However, a slightly higher percentage of females, c. 40%, switch to a new mate even when the one from the previous season is present in the area. A female generally stays in her mate's territory 50 to 90 days or even, much more rarely, 100 to 150 days in the case of two successive broods. The territory size varies from c. 2 to 12ha; birds rarely move more than 200m from their nest. In good-quality habitats and when the density is high, territories may be smaller than 2ha. The species hunts in the usual shrike manner, generally flying down to the ground from a relatively high perch. Larders are common throughout the year; in Japan, two birds were recorded making respectively 68 and 48 caches during the autumn and early winter.

FOOD Most of the prey items are invertebrates. A study of 151 pellets collected in Hokkaido from October to April (Ogawa 1977) resulted in the identification of 1,470 prey items, most of them insects consisting of 57 genera. Coleoptera represented 57.5% of the total, Harpalidae being particularly favoured. Pyrrhocoridae and Vespidae came next in importance. Other invertebrates included spiders and centipedes. Some vertebrates also appeared in the analyses: birds, voles and frogs. A few plant seeds were recorded only in October. Other observations reveal that the Bull-headed Shrike also catches worms Oligochaeta, crustaceans, lizards and even small fish. The diet of this opportunistic feeder varies throughout the year. Studies at a few nests in Ussuriland showed that the young were fed exclusively on insects; at an early stage they were mainly given Noctuidae caterpillars; later they received mostly crickets Acrididae and cicadas Cicadidae.

BREEDING In resident populations in central Japan, pair formation starts at the end of January when females start entering males' winter territories (see Habits). In Ussuriland, where the species is a migrant, the first birds back at the beginning of April are generally males. Many birds, however, appear to be already paired on arrival; in other cases, pair formation is very rapid except for some males unable to attract females. These birds are, of course, very easy to see and hear. In southern Japan, laying may start as early as late February; in a study of a central Japan population, the majority of males had obtained their mates by the end of February and laying peaked towards mid-March. In Ussuriland, it only begins in the last ten days of April, in the Kuril islands and northern Japan (Hokkaido) at the beginning of May,

and on Sakhalin about a month later. The breeding season is very protracted, and the Bull-headed Shrike appears to be double-brooded over most, if not all, of its range. Replacement clutches are also frequent and fresh eggs can still be found in July, particularly in northern populations. Both sexes participate in nest-building, but the female takes by far the larger share. In fine weather, the nest is finished in 5-6 days. Made of twigs, bark, leaves, moss and lined with rootlets and hair, it can be hidden in a variety of trees and bushes or in bamboo thickets at a height of 0.5-4.5m above ground. In a study in Hokkaido early breeders nested in dwarf bamboos or the vines of shelterbelts at an average height of 0.75m (0.30-1.03m), and late breeders in green shrubs at an average height of 1.35m (0.80-2.24m). Not uncommonly, thorns and nettles surround the nest, which is relatively large: the external diameter may reach 16cm and the internal 8cm, with a depth of c. 10cm. Large size and thick walls are probably associated with egg-deposition starting so early in the season. The Bull-headed Shrike lays between (2) 4 and 7 eggs, generally between 5 and 7. There might be a geographical variation as northern breeders appear to have larger clutches on average; more data are, however, needed to confirm this. The female alone incubates the eggs for c. 14-15 days. The nestling stage lasts about two weeks and both parents feed their young in their territory for about another 15 days. The nests of this shrike are regularly parasitised by the Common Cuckoo *Cuculus canorus* and the Himalayan Cuckoo *C. saturatus*.

REFERENCES Austin & Kuroda (1953), Brazil (1991), Cheng (1987), Chiba (1990), Chong (1938), Gore & Won (1971), Haas & Ogawa (1995), Jahn (1942), Ogawa (1977), Panov (1983), Shaw (1936), Takagi & Ogawa (1995), Yamagishi (1982), Yamagishi & Saito (1985), Yamagishi *et al.* (1992), Yamashina (1961), Zheng & Wang (1985).

3 RED-BACKED SHRIKE
Lanius collurio   Plate 2

IDENTIFICATION Length c. 17cm. By far the commonest shrike of the western Palearctic, only slightly larger, but slimmer, than a House Sparrow *Passer domesticus*. The Woodchat Shrike is somewhat bulkier, bigger-headed and longer-winged. The sexes are dissimilar. The male displays 'exotic' features and is unmistakable with its bluish-grey head, bright chestnut back, black, white-edged tail and salmon-pink underparts. The rather 'sparrow-like' female is very variable, but basically warm brown above and whitish below with dusky-brown crescents on breast and flanks. Juveniles and first-winter birds are very similar to adult females, but with distinctly barred upperparts.

Adult females and young birds may be confused with young Woodchats, adult or young Isabelline Shrikes, and adult or young Brown Shrikes (see under those species). Adult males are very similar to adult Bay-backed Shrikes. Both species may be seen in south-eastern Turkmenistan, parts of Iran, Afghanistan and the extreme north-west of the Indian subcontinent, particularly during passage periods. Unlike the Bay-backed Shrike, the male Red-backed Shrike has no well-marked dark frontal band and no well-defined white speculum.

DESCRIPTION *L. c. collurio*

Adult male Facial mask black over base of upper mandible (generally a thin line), over lores, just over and under eyes and on most of ear-coverts. Supercilium whitish, more or less distinct, merging into a pale area sometimes present on forehead. Upperparts bluish-grey from forehead to lower mantle, usually bright chestnut on lower mantle and scapulars; rump and uppertail-coverts bluish-grey. Tail black, edged and slightly tipped white (fresh plumage); central pair of rectrices wholly black; other pairs white at base; outer pair with outer web completely white; the black central tail feathers and the terminal black band form an inverted T on a white background, particularly obvious in flight. Wings dark brown with distinct chestnut margins on wing-coverts, secondaries and tertials; tips of secondaries bordered whitish, particularly in fresh plumage; tiny white primary patch apparent in a few individuals. Underparts mainly salmon-pink except on chin, throat and undertail-coverts, which are white; dark barring occasionally present on flanks (in 4% of 775 individuals caught for ringing in Germany) whatever the age. Undertail grey-white with large dark terminal band and whitish tips.

Adult female (very variable) Facial mask limited to dark warm brown ear-coverts; lores cream-white with some dark feathers in front of eyes. Supercilium cream-white variably speckled black. Upperparts mainly warm brown or rufous-brown (sometimes grey-brown) on crown, mantle, scapulars and back; rear-crown, nape and particularly rump area generally distinctly tinged greyish. Traces of dark juvenile barrings may still be present particularly on the scapulars and rump. Tail generally dark brown but may be rufous-brown, with every possible intermediate; fringed and tipped white. Wings as in adult males, but with much duller, paler fringes, more cinnamon, not so deep chestnut. Underparts cream, often washed pale pink-buff on sides of breast and flanks; chin, mid-belly and vent whitish; rest of underparts fairly heavily barred blackish particularly on cheeks, breast and flanks. Undertail generally dull grey.

Juvenile Very similar to adult female, but shows fresh and generally less contrasting plumage. The heavy barring on the upperparts is diagnostic.

Bare parts Bill black or dark brown in breeding adults; not so dark, more grey-brown or blue-slate from base outwards between July-August and the next spring migration; bills of young birds generally paler. Legs black or dark brown in adult males; generally paler, more grey-brown in females and dull grey-brown in juveniles. Iris dark brown.

MEASUREMENTS
Wing 87-100 (mean c. 95); tail 69-79; bill (to skull) 16.5-20 (mean c. 18); tarsus 22.5-25. Weight 23-40 (mean c. 29).

DISTRIBUTION AND STATUS
The breeding range of the Red-backed Shrike, widely distributed in the western Palearctic, extends somewhat into the eastern Palearctic. From west to east, it lies between north-west Portugal and Siberia (Russia), where it reaches the area lying north-east of Tomsk between the rivers Ob and Yenisey. The western limits follow the northern coast of the Iberian peninsula and the French Atlantic coast as far as Brittany, which with Normandy is largely avoided. The species is also absent, or almost so, from the western parts of Belgium and the Netherlands. In Scandinavia, it is present in south-east Norway and in the southern third of Sweden, where it breeds along the eastern coast as far north as 66°30'N; in Finland, isolated breeding pairs may occur as far north as Rovaniemi, very near the Arctic Circle. In European Russia, the northern boundary roughly follows 64°30'N; further east, in the Urals, the bird is apparently not found above 58°N, but it again reaches 64°N in western Siberia. The southern limits are fairly well known in the Mediterranean area. They cross the northern mountainous parts of the Iberian peninsula, then southern France, the western coast of Italy, Greece and southern Turkey. In all these areas, the hot plains near the sea are almost completely avoided by breeders. The species is widespread on Corsica and Sardinia but rare in Sicily and Crete, and definite proof of breeding is still lacking for Cyprus. Rather isolated populations nest in mountainous areas of Syria (Anti-Lebanon), Israel (Mount Hermon) and also Lebanon where breeding was first confirmed in spring 1996 (Thiery Bara). Further to the north, the boundary crosses the northern part of Turkey, the north-east of Iran (Zagros Mountains), then follows the western coast of the Caspian Sea and goes further north as far as about 49°N in Russia before turning east and even south-east, towards the area lying just north of the Aral Sea in Kazakhstan; the southern limits then run slightly north-wards, north of Lake Balkhash and as far east as the Chrebet Tarbagataj near the Chinese border.

The Red-backed Shrike remains a common species, but a general fall in numbers and contraction of range has been witnessed in most European populations, particularly in the last 20-30 years. The decline has been severe in north-west Europe. Sweden lost over 50% of its population between 1970 and 1990. In the Netherlands there were 5,000-15,000 pairs in the 1900s and only c. 200-280 pairs in 1990. In Belgium the population was estimated at c. 5,000 pairs in the 1950s and at only 550-900 pairs in the 1980s. The recent history of the species in Great Britain is well documented; in the 1900s the Red-backed Shrike was still widespread in most parts of England and Wales; by 1940 the range had started to contract markedly into the south-east part of the country; the last strongholds were in Hampshire, particularly in the New Forest and in the Norfolk/Suffolk area. In 1960 there were only c. 253 pairs left, all in southern and south-eastern England; in 1971 only 81 pairs were known; in 1976 there were probably less than 40 pairs; and only six pairs in 1985, three in 1986, one in 1987 and none in 1989. The species bred in Scotland during 1977-1979 and again in

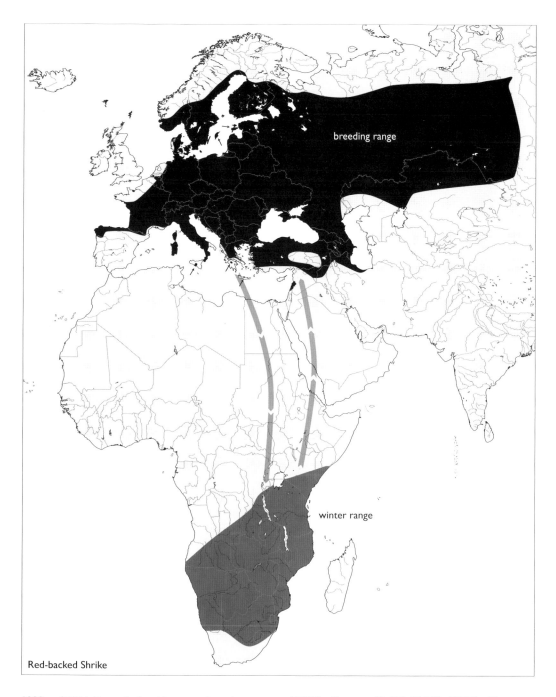

breeding range

winter range

Red-backed Shrike

1992 and 1994. Recently, local increases have been reported from several countries including Belgium, the
Netherlands, Germany and France, with a general
upward trend also noted in Norway. Recent estimates
(of pairs) exist for a good number of countries: Austria:
10,000-15,000 (1992), Belarus: 50,000-70,000 (1990),
Belgium: 550-900 (1990), Denmark: 1,500-3,000
(1986), Finland: 50,000-80,000 (1992), France:
160,000-360,000 (1994), Germany 50,000-140,000

(1993), Greece: 20,000-50,000 (1976), Hungary:
60,000-90,000 (1976), Italy 30,000-60,000 (1976), Luxembourg: 300-500 (1992), Netherlands: 150-220
(1992), Norway: 50,000-100,000 (1990), Poland:
80,000-300,000 (1990), Portugal: 100-1,000 (1989),
Romania: 600,000-800,000 (1992), Russia: 100,000-
1,000,000 (1989), Spain: 240,000-500,000 (1989),
Sweden: 20,000-100,000 (1987), Switzerland 8,000-
12,000 (1981), Ukraine 200,000-210,000 (1986).

GEOGRAPHICAL VARIATION The species is classically regarded as polytypic. For what can be called the *collurio* group (as opposed to the *isabellinus* group), Rand (1960) lists four races. Vaurie (1955, 1959) recognises the same races; but Panov (1983) mentions five subspecies. Stepanyan (1978), on the other hand, considers this shrike monotypic. Recent observations and particularly those by Jakober and Stauber (in Glutz von Blotzheim and Bauer 1993) and Bruderer (in prep.) strongly support this view, which is shared here. Cramp and Perrins (1993) also think that the species is perhaps better considered monotypic. The paragraphs below list the four often recognised races and the main characters used to typify them.

L. c. juxtus (Great Britain) Upperparts darker on mantle of males than in nominate; more chestnut, less brightly rufous. Williamson (1973) could not discern any difference in the shade of reddish-brown of birds from different parts of Britain, western and south-eastern Europe concluding that *juxtus* is a synonym of *L. c. collurio*.

L. c. collurio (Europe and Asia Minor except western Siberia and Transcaucasia) Described above. Variable; even in western Europe, individual males may show characters of different 'races'. In males, the chestnut of the mantle varies in brightness, shade and extent. In south-west Germany, out of 771 males examined c. 17% showed a restricted chestnut band on the back (Jakober and Stauber in Glutz von Blotzheim and Bauer 1993). These birds could probably have passed for perfect representatives of race *kobylini*. Females can also be variable; in south-west Germany brown, reddish and grey types were found with many intermediates.

L. c. pallidifrons (western Siberia) Upperparts of males paler than in nominate, especially on the crown and neck.

L. c. kobylini (Crimea to Iran) Variable, but the chestnut of the mantle in males is duller and sometimes darker, not so bright as in nominate *collurio*; it is also generally more reduced, sometimes almost absent. Crown and hindneck paler or very much paler than in nominate.

HYBRIDS See under Isabelline Shrike, Brown Shrike, Lesser Grey Shrike and Woodchat Shrike.

MOVEMENTS All the populations are migratory and spend the winter in eastern and southern Africa. A few birds may stay in southern Sudan, but the regular wintering range lies south of the Equator and southeast of the Congo River basin. The species is present in south-east Kenya from c. 1°22'S at Kitui southwards; some birds also winter in western Kenya and Uganda. The Red-backed Shrike is present in western Tanzania and southern Angola, but the bulk of the wintering population is found from southern Zambia and Malawi southwards. This shrike is thus very common in Mozambique south of the Rio Save, in Zimbabwe, in the less dry areas of Botswana and Namibia. In South Africa it is absent or rare in the southern Cape Province and the Drakensberg highlands. Insofar as different races can be recognised, it can be said that their winter quarters substantially overlap.

The migration routes of the Red-backed Shrike are concentrated on the eastern end of the Mediterranean and the Middle East. This holds true even for birds breeding in south-west France, northern Spain and Portugal; in autumn they travel east, then south-east. European birds undertake a loop migration rather similar to that of the Lesser Grey Shrike. In autumn they converge on Greece and its islands, and North Africa is entered between c. 20°and 33°E, i.e. between eastern Libya and the Suez Canal in Egypt. This corridor is roughly followed, mainly over Sudan, as far south as north-eastern Zaïre. South of the rainforests, movements occur on a wider front towards the south of the continent. In spring, the species follows a more easterly course and this is already obvious south of the Equator where birds are much more common than in autumn in Tanzania and Kenya. Spring migrants are also numerous in Ethiopia, northern Somalia, Eritrea, the Red Sea coasts of Sudan and Saudi Arabia; they largely avoid Sudan and Egypt (except Sinai where they are, however, scarce). From the African Red Sea coast, European birds apparently travel on a relatively broad front towards the Middle East; passage is strong over Jordan, Israel, Lebanon and also, more than in autumn, over Iraq. Many migrants appear on Cyprus and in Turkey, but few birds turn up at this time in southern Greece, on the southern islands of the Aegean Sea or on Crete. Eastern Palearctic birds probably follow roughly the same routes both ways. Siberian birds cross Kazakhstan, Iran, Saudi Arabia and the Red Sea coast of Africa. Those from the extreme eastern part of the range pass, in small numbers, through the north-west of the Indian subcontinent: western Pakistan and extreme western Rajasthan and northern Gujarat in India.

In the breeding range, post-nuptial movements begin as early as the beginning of July for adults which have nested early and successfully or which have lost their young at the end of June or the beginning of July. In central Europe, most adults leave their territories between mid-July and the second week of August. Families with young can, however, still be seen until the beginning of September, sometimes even later. There seems to be little difference in autumn departure throughout the breeding range. The last birds are generally juveniles. Adults, and particularly males, migrate on average earlier. Observations become very rare in October and are exceptional later. The first birds appear in Egypt at the end of the first ten days of August, but the well-known passage over the Balkans and the eastern Mediterranean peaks at the end of that month and in early September. Records are known from Kenya at the end of October, from Zimbabwe from 20 October to mid-November, and from Namibia at the start of November. In southern Africa, the species's arrival is associated with the rain fronts in late November and early December. Roughly speaking, it takes a bird about 100 days to reach its winter quarters. It arrives there at a very favourable time. Despite strong territorial behaviour and site-fidelity, local movements are possible depending on meteorological conditions. The return migration starts in the second half of March; it peaks at the beginning of April in Zimbabwe, Tanzania and Kenya, although birds remain until the beginning of May, sometimes even later. The first birds turn up in Sinai (eastern Egypt) at the beginning of April, in Israel and Romania generally towards 20 April. As a rule, the first birds, mostly males, arrive on their Palearctic territories between the end of April (eastern and southern European countries) and the end of May (for countries as far north as Sweden or Norway). Things are faster in spring; there are fewer stopovers. On average it takes a central European bird 45-50 days to return to its breeding territory.

MOULT The post-juvenile moult takes place a few weeks after fledging, when the young birds are (23) 28-45 (65) days old, at a time when the flight feathers and the tail may not even be fully grown. It involves the body feathers as well as the lesser and median coverts and, very occasionally, a few greater coverts. A complete moult takes place in the African winter quarters when the primary coverts, wing feathers and tail feathers are also renewed. In South Africa, it is possible to sex 50% of the young birds in January and all in February. Adults, particularly those which leave late, may undergo a partial head and body moult towards the end of the breeding season, when some of them also change one, two or all tertials. For these birds, moult is suspended during migration; others do not start moult before migrating, although they may do so on stop-overs. Before the autumn migration starts, the lost wing feathers, and particularly the lost tail feathers, are replaced. Adults, like first-winter birds, have a complete moult in Africa where they start replacing their feathers slightly in advance of the young birds. A complete primary moult, which spans the moult of most other feathers, takes 80-85 days. In South Africa it has been estimated that c. 40% of the Red-backed Shrikes start their moult in November, with another 6% in December; in January, however, most birds are in moult. In March half of the shrikes have changed their feathers and the moult is complete for all birds in the first half of April.

VOICE The song is neither frequent nor loud. It is a long warble including much good mimicry; a study in Ukraine revealed that the songs of 97 males included imitations of 33 local bird species and also of a cricket. The species is regularly heard singing in its winter quarters, where it incorporates in its phrases calls and parts of songs of both African and European birds. On the breeding grounds and in the presence of a female, the song can become more rapid and excited. The most characteristic note is the advertising call of the male, a kind of harsh, somewhat nasal *kscha* typically given from vantage points before the arrival of the female. Unlike the song, it can be heard from a distance and so is very useful for locating birds. Other calls, including a rapid *ki-jet, ki-jet*, are commonly heard at that time during display-flights. When the bird is on the alert it may give a *gek gek gek* and when the danger is very close the sound can become a typical, 'shrikish'

tskek, tskek, tskek, sometimes prolonged by a drawn-out note recalling the male's advertising call. When the female solicits food from the male, she utters a nasal begging-call, a *kwee-ee-ee* which sounds like the food calls of the young once they are out of the nest (see Blase 1960 for a detailed study both in captivity and in the wild).

HABITAT The Red-backed Shrike breeds in temperate and Mediterranean types of climates. It is one of the most cold-tolerant of European shrikes, but is absent from areas which are both cool and rainy in summer, as for instance Brittany in France or the west coast of Norway. It also tends to avoid very dry areas like some of the Mediterranean plains; in Spain it is thus mainly regarded as a 'mountainous' bird. It breeds up to 2,050m in the French Alps, and even up to 3,200m on subalpine meadows in the Caucasus, but these are rather isolated cases. The species is much more common at lower levels and can be abundant in plains, in hill regions or at mid-altitudes (in Switzerland regularly up to 900-1,000m) in sunny, flat or gently sloping and open areas dotted sometimes with tall trees and always with bushes and low trees (1-3m high) providing suitable perches and nest-sites. Among the original habitats of this shrike there were probably ecotones between forests and grasslands, and chaotic-looking forest clearings created by regenerating stages, fires, the action of insects and storms, large herbivores etc. Deer may in fact have had a special importance as they do not browse shrubs like blackthorn *Prunus spinosa* or hawthorn *Crataegus* sp., which are still today among the favourite nesting-sites of the Red-backed Shrike. Locally young plantations, particularly of spruce *Picea excelsa*, are also occupied. Shrubs and trees cover from 5-60% of the territory, and foraging areas mainly include grasslands (meadows and pastures) but the substrate can be very variable, from dry heathland to boggy areas. Spaces with alternately long and short grass are appreciated, as are patches of bare soil where insects are easily seen. A suitable perch every c. 20m offers the best hunting conditions. The Red-backed Shrike can be found in hedges crossing meadows, pastures, marshes, and along roads or railway-lines. The species also inhabits forest clearings, young plantations (particularly of conifers), neglected fields, orchards, gardens and even city parks.

In its southern African winter quarters, the Red-backed Shrike uses habitats with a vegetation structure similar to those used in the breeding season. It occurs widely in the savanna biome, particularly in semi-arid parts, and south of 22°S its distribution mainly coincides with that biome; it also spreads into the grassland and to the nama-karoo biomes, but is much scarcer there (see maps in Bruderer and Bruderer 1993). In northern Transvaal it shows a preference for low scrub (1-3m high) and open bush (10-50% coverage is preferred to either dense coverage or open grassland). It uses perches 1.5-2m high in open areas with a herbaceous layer rich in insects.

HABITS The Red-backed Shrike is generally easy to detect on one of the many perches which have to be

Red-backed Shrike adopting typical horizontal posture when anxious.

present in its territory; it may, however, be relatively elusive in certain more closed habitats like forest clearings. At the beginning of the breeding season, the advertising call of the male betrays its presence; the bird is then well in view at the top of a bush or one of the highest trees in its territory. A zigzag fluttering flight performed between vantage points and accompanied by fairly quiet calls also makes it quite conspicuous before the arrival of a female (see Voice). The Red-backed Shrike tends to breed in small, loose groups, and in good habitats up to six or seven pairs may be found on 10ha, each one, as a rule, strictly remaining in its territory. Densities are often much lower and isolated pairs not rare. In its African non-breeding strongholds, densities can be remarkable with 5-30 birds per 10ha and peak densities of 8 birds per ha. In the breeding season territory-size averages c. 1.5ha (1-3.5); neighbouring and occupied nests may be less than 100m apart; in north-east France, two pairs had their nests separated by only 25m, but the foraging areas did not overlap while there were young in the nest. The species is also highly territorial outside the breeding season, even on migration halts. Site-fidelity is high from one spring to the next. In a long-term study in south-west Germany c. 45% of the breeding males were back in their territories the following year. The highest fidelity rate was found in old males which had used their territories for two seasons or longer. Breeding success obviously causes a stronger tie to the former territory; females are less site-faithful and the majority of first-year birds do not return to their natal area. Data from the winter quarters also suggest a high return rate (23%) to the non-breeding territories of the previous winter; this figure is among the higher rates reported for any Palearctic migrant in southern Africa. In certain parts of eastern Europe, an interesting nesting association exists with the Barred Warbler *Sylvia nisoria*. The habitat requirements of both species are not exactly the same (see detailed study by Neuschulz 1988) but they have often occupied nests only 4.5-12m apart, occasionally even only 1m. Both species probably benefit from this association when their respective nests are threatened by a potential predator.

The Red-backed Shrike uses a great variety of natural or artificial perches. When looking for prey, in a typical sit-and-wait strategy, it is generally perched between 1-4m from the ground and most of the time at a height of c. 2m. Most insects are caught on the ground within a radius of 10m. In good weather, flying insects are taken in the air and may represent up to 30% of the captures; they can be pursued up to 20m or even 30m from the ground. In cold, wet weather or when a meadow has just been mown the bird may be seen hopping on the ground. The prey is almost always brought back to a perch to be dealt with. Small vertebrates are regularly impaled (rather than wedged), as are insects particularly in areas with unstable weather. The habit is less well developed in drier areas and in the south of the breeding range. In north-east France up to 28 prey items have been found impaled in the same territory on the same day.

Red-backed Shrike with bill open, suffering from the heat.

FOOD The diet, well studied in the Palearctic breeding range, includes a great number of invertebrates: snails, worms, spiders, centipedes, but above all insects. Almost all insect orders may be exploited (see list in Cramp and Perrins 1993), but most of them belong to the Coleoptera, Orthoptera and Hymenoptera, generally in that order of importance. As a rule, they are large or medium-sized, but very small insects (less than 4mm long) may occasionally be taken, ants for instance. Small or soft prey, like spiders, caterpillars or Diptera, are regularly fed to small nestlings. The Red-backed Shrike is an opportunistic feeder; there can be significant yearly, seasonal or geographical changes in the composition of its diet. Large numbers of chafers (*Melolontha*) are taken in plague years. This also applies to voles (*Microtus*). Small vertebrates are regularly taken, but they rarely exceed 5% of the captures. In normal years, however, they represent between 25 and 50% of the whole prey biomass. Most of them are voles, more rarely other small mammals (genera *Apodemus, Mus, Clethrionomys, Sorex*). Even a bat *Pipistrellus pipistrellus* has been recorded. Amphibians, particularly frogs and reptiles (mainly lizards but also slow-worms and exceptionally young grass snakes), are also common victims. Individuals that specialise in preying on birds have been noted but adult birds are very rarely killed in the breeding season; nestlings and fledglings are taken from time to time. Killing of exhausted or otherwise handicapped small passerines appears to be regular on migration halts. At the end of summer and in autumn the diet of the Red-backed Shrike is sometimes complemented by berries, for instance those of *Prunus avium* or *Sambucus nigra*. 'Red berries' are at least occasionally taken even in the African winter quarters.

Female Red-backed Shrike feeding young at nest.

BREEDING In Europe, males generally arrive on the breeding grounds a few days before the females (0-5 days). Pair formation is fairly rapid and takes place as a rule in the breeding territory. Some observations, however, suggest that it may occasionally occur during spring stopovers. Adult males rarely mate with partners of the previous year, which are not very faithful to their former territories. Throughout Europe laying begins in May, generally in the middle ten days of that month, exceptionally earlier; it peaks in the last ten days of May and at the beginning of June. Occasional clutches can be started as late as the end of July. Normal second broods occur, but are very rare; a few definite records exist for Belgium, France and Germany. Replacement clutches are very frequent particularly in the second half of June; they are always laid in a new nest which is

generally only a short distance (2-60m) from the first; but can be built in a different territory more as far as 150m away. Up to four attempts have been recorded. Within-season divorces are not exceptional after a breeding failure. The nest-site is chosen by the male. The nest is built generally in 4-6 days, by both sexes, but the female does most of the work particularly in the last stages. A wide variety of bushes, mainly but not exclusively thorny ones, are used: blackthorn, hawthorn, bramble and dog-rose are favoured. Nests may also be found in young trees, for instance spruce or fruit trees in orchards. In most studies the average height of the nest above the ground is 1-1.5m with extremes ranging from 0.3 to 5m. Odd nests have been located on the ground, in reeds or high up in trees (25m in a pine *Pinus*, but the case is probably unique). The nest looks rather untidy with loose foundations; its main structure is made of various grass stems and may include man-made material like strings or pieces of paper; rootlets, lichen, moss and sometimes bird-feathers are also used for this construction, in which the outer diameter varies between 12 and 18cm for an overall height of c. 8cm. The Red-backed Shrike lays between (1) 3 and 7 (8) eggs. In western Europe first clutches generally have 4 to 6 eggs; during the course of the season clutch-size declines, replacement clutches having fewer eggs on average. A geographical variation also exists, as 7-egg clutches are much more frequent in eastern than in western Europe, except Corsica. Incubation lasts 14-16 days; it is assumed almost exclusively by the female, but definite males (and not females with male-type plumage) have been seen and even photographed on the eggs. Normally the young stay in the nest for 14-16 days; they may stay longer, up to 18 or even 20 days, in very bad weather or by contrast jump out of the nest when only 11 days old in the presence of a predator. At 25 days young may already try to catch insects, but they only become really independent when they are c. 42 days old.

Red-backed Shrike removing faecal sac from nest.

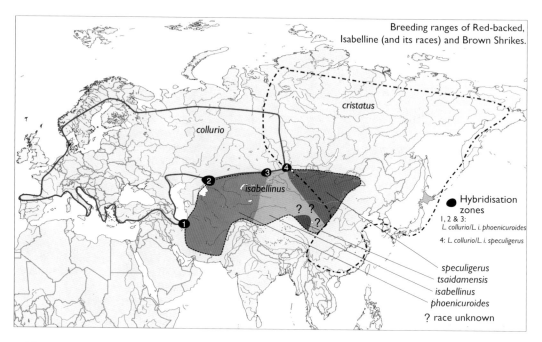

Breeding ranges of Red-backed, Isabelline (and its races) and Brown Shrikes.

Hybridisation zones
1, 2 & 3:
L. collurio/L. i. phoenicuroides
4: L. collurio/L. i. speculigerus

speculigerus
tsaidamensis
isabellinus
phoenicuroides
? race unknown

The Red-backed Shrike is fairly regularly parasitised by the Common Cuckoo *Cuculus canorus* in certain parts of its breeding range: eastern parts of Germany (particularly Sachsen), Poland, Romania, Russia, etc, and a few northern countries, Denmark and Finland. Few records have been published for central-western Europe: but there was a successful case in Suffolk, England, in 1939 and three unsuccessful attempts in south-west Germany in 1978.

REFERENCES Ali & Ripley (1972), Bechet & Moes (1992), Blase (1960), Brandl *et al.* (1986), Bruderer (1994), Bruderer & Bruderer (1993, 1994), Clancey (1973), Cramp & Perrins (1993), Glutz von Blotzheim & Bauer (1993), Harris & Arnott (1988), Hernandez (1993a,b), Herremans (1994), Herremans & Herremans-Tonnoeyr (1995), Holan (1993, 1994), Hölzinger (1987), Jakober & Stauber (1980a,b, 1987, 1989, 1994), Kowalski (1993), Lefranc (1979, 1993), Massa *et al.* (1993), Moes (1993), Neuschulz (1988), van Nieuwenhuyse (1992), van Nieuwenhuyse & Vandekerkhove (1992), Olsson (1995a,b), Panov (1983), Peakall (1995), Shirihai (1995), Simonetta & Sierro (1996), Stepanyan (1978), Tucker & Heath (1994), Wagner (1993), Williamson (1973).

4 ISABELLINE SHRIKE
Lanius isabellinus **Plate 3**

Other names: Red-tailed Shrike, Rufous-tailed Shrike

IDENTIFICATION Length 17.5cm. The size and structure of this eastern Palearctic, polytypic shrike are similar to those of the Red-backed Shrike but its tail is slightly longer. The Isabelline Shrike also has a plainer plumage and shows a much less well pronounced sexual dimorphism. Its most conspicuous feature lies

in the contrast between its relatively dull upperparts and its rufous rump and tail. Of the four recognised subspecies, two have been recorded in Europe.

The nominate race *isabellinus*, which breeds in the eastern part of the species's range, possesses a very plain, pallid plumage. The upperparts of the adult male are sandy-grey tinged with buff; rump and tail are somewhat brighter but still a rather pale rufous colour. The lores are pale and the facial mask is reduced to a relatively small dark brown, not black, eye-patch. A creamy or buff supercilium is present, but relatively dull. The underparts are sandy-buff and pink-tinged. This race has only a vestigial primary patch, sometimes absent in females, which are also slightly duller than males but only separable at close range. As in the Red-backed Shrike, juveniles are scalloped; from their first autumn following the juvenile moult they are however plain on the upperparts with a rather subtle scalloping still present on the crown, breast and flanks.

The westernmost race *phoenicuroides* occurs more often in the western Palearctic. When seen well, typical adults of the two races are not difficult to separate: *phoenicuroides* is much less pale with a grey-brown back contrasting with a strongly rufous rump and tail. The adult male often shows a rufous crown contrasting with mantle, a rather large black facial mask extending from lores to upper ear-coverts, a well-marked white supercilium and a small but distinct white patch at the base of the primaries. The underparts are almost pure white. The female is somewhat duller with a less well marked head-pattern and with a sometimes smaller but usually obvious white primary patch. The underparts may show distinct crescent-shaped barring on the breast and flanks.

The confusion species are the Red-backed Shrike except the adult male, and the Brown Shrike. The breeding ranges of *collurio* and *isabellinus* overlap to

L. cristatus   *L. isabellinus phoenicuroides*   *L. collurio*

Wing outlines of Brown Shrike (left), Isabelline Shrike (centre) and Red-backed Shrike (right). Note that the outer webs of 3rd-5th primaries are emarginated in *cristatus* and *isabellinus* , but only outer webs of 3rd and 4th primaries in *collurio*. In *collurio*, the 2nd primary is generally longer than the 5th whereas the opposite is true for *isabellinus*. *Cristatus* and *isabellinus* have a very similar wing structure; the latter is longer winged with a distance of 42-52mm between 1st primary and tip of wing against 35-42mm for *cristatus* (Svensson 1992).

some extent and hybrids are regular in those areas (see below and map). On migration, the two species may be seen in the same countries, particularly in the Middle East and East Africa. The Isabelline Shrike also occurs as a rare but regular vagrant to western Europe. The eastern part of the breeding range of Isabelline overlaps with the range of Brown Shrike, but only one possible hybrid is known. Both species locally occur in the same wintering areas in northern India.

Adults or first-winter Isabelline Shrikes can usually be fairly easily identified when seen well. A contrast between distinctly rufous tail, uppertail-coverts, lower rump and a pallid grey-brown or sandy mantle is a good indicator. First-winter birds, regularly seen in western Europe, in contrast to first-winter Red-backed Shrikes, show a plain, unbarred, not scalloped mantle. Difficulties may arise from females or young *collurio* showing a significant rufous component to both tail and lower rump. Subsidiary characters of Isabelline Shrike include the lack of discreet white margins to the tail and, especially in immatures and in the nominate race, a pellucid pink-tinged base to the bill.

The structure of the Brown Shrike is different from that of *isabellinus* and *collurio*. It is more powerfully built with a larger bill and more graduated tail. Birds of the nominate race have a russet mantle and rump, whereas the tail is russet-brown rather than rufous. There is normally no well-marked white primary patch and the underparts frequently display an extensive russet flush.

DESCRIPTION *L. i. phoenicuroides* (westernmost race)
Adult male Facial mask black, very narrow over base of upper mandible, lores, just below eyes and on ear-coverts. Supercilium white and distinct, sometimes extending narrowly across forehead. Forehead and crown rufous-cinnamon contrasting with the drab brown of the upperparts from nape to mantle including scapulars. Rump and uppertail-coverts bright rufous-cinnamon. Tail rufous-brown; outer rectrices rather rufous-cinnamon; all tail-feathers very narrowly

tipped buff when fresh. Wings dark brown with distinct white primary patch (5-10mm visible on closed wings); inner primaries fringed pale; wing-coverts, secondaries and particularly tertials fringed buff; secondaries narrowly tipped pale. Underparts white variably tinged vinous-pink on sides of breast and upper flanks. Undertail pale rufous-brown.

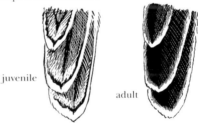

juvenile   adult

Tertial patterns of *L. i. phoenicuroides*

Adult female Resembles male, but with a browner and smaller facial mask (lores paler) and a less well defined supercilium. Upperparts may be duller, somewhat browner. Primary patch also smaller. Underparts with usually indistinct scaling on sides of throat, breast and flanks.

Juvenile Upperparts grey-brown with black scaling. Very similar to a young Red-backed Shrike, but somewhat paler and with a rufous-brown tail. Underparts creamy with brown vermiculations except on middle of throat, breast, belly and undertail-coverts.

First winter Pallid appearance. Facial mask still poorly indicated. On upperparts dark barring subdued and confined to crown and rump; mantle plain with only occasional indications of barring. Tertials, greater coverts and tail with subterminal contour lines. Primary patch whitish; may be absent. Underparts as in adult female.

Bare parts Bill black in adult breeding males and sometimes in adult breeding females; otherwise in adults or juveniles it may be bluish-horn or pale brown with a darker tip. Legs dark grey or dark brown. Iris brown.

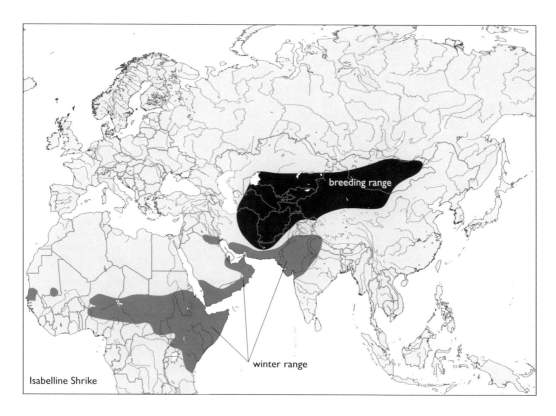

Isabelline Shrike

breeding range

winter range

MEASUREMENTS (*phoenicuroides*) Wing 91-97 (mean c. 93); tail 74-82 (mean c. 77); bill (to skull) 17.5-18.5; tarsus 24-25.5. Weight 24-38, usually 26-30.

DISTRIBUTION AND STATUS The Isabelline Shrike breeds in central Eurasia. The north-western limits of its breeding range lie at c. 50°N 57°E; from there, the western boundary runs south over western Kazakhstan before passing just west of the Aral Sea and through western Uzbekistan and western Turkmenistan, where it reaches the south-eastern fringes of the Caspian Sea and eastern Iran as far south as about Kazerun and Shiraz at c. 29°N 52°E. The southern limits cross southern Iran (Khuzestan, Kerman, Baluchistan) and central-western Pakistan before running north-eastwards, well west of the Indus plains towards the Pamir region. From there the range extends east over parts of Mongolia and north-west China, where the southern limits appear to be in Qinghai province very roughly at c. 33°50'N (race *tsaidamensis*). The north-east limits cross north-west Inner Mongolia and the north-easternmost areas reached lie at 50°N 120°E (race *speculigerus*). The northern boundary has the shape of an irregular line drawn between that point and the area lying north of the Aral Sea in Kazakhstan.There are no detailed accounts of possible recent changes in status.

GEOGRAPHICAL VARIATION Four races are generally recognised (Vaurie1959) with two 'groups' (Cramp and Perrins 1993): the *phoenicuroides* group with *phoenicuroides* and *speculigerus*, and the *isabellinus* group with

isabellinus and *tsaidamensis*. Recent Russian authors treat these two groups as separate species (Neufeldt 1978) or even regard *phoenicuroides* as a monotypic species (Panov 1983, 1995, Kryukov 1995).

L. i. phoenicuroides (western part of the breeding range, from Iran north-east to the Chinese region of Xinjiang through parts of Turkmenistan, Afghanistan, western Pakistan, Uzbekistan, southern Tajikistan and southern Kazakhstan) Typical *phoenicuroides* described above, but plumage variable. A colour variety is known as *karelini*. Such birds show greyer upperparts, the crown being only very slightly tinged cinnamon when the plumage is fresh. Their face-pattern is also less well marked with a less pronounced buff supercilium and sometimes shorter eye-stripe due to paler front part of lores. Their underparts are tinged buff, not vinous-pink. *Karelini* birds appear to be mainly found in lowlands whereas *phoenicuroides* predominates in mountainous areas. It has also been shown that that colour variety mainly occurs in hybrid zones or in areas lying between distinct populations of typical *phoenicuroides* and the Red-backed Shrike. *Karelini*-like birds might thus well be results of hybridisation. Of course, intermediates between the two described colour phases occur. Hybrids between *phoenicuroides* and *isabellinus* also probably exist and might cause further confusion (see Panov 1983).

L. i. speculigerus (south-eastern Altai in Russia, Mongolia; north-central China) Intermediate in appearance between typical *phoenicuroides* and *isabellinus*. The male resembles *phoenicuroides* (particularly birds of the *karelini* type) in that it shows a prominent white primary patch, relatively dark wings contrasting with body, a well-defined black facial mask and a black bill. However, creamy underparts and a relatively subdued supercilium recall *isabellinus*. Moreover, *speculigerus* shows a light grey crown and otherwise typical drab grey upperparts. Females are very similar to females *phoenicuroides*, but tend to be more isabelline-yellow, particularly on the underparts.

L. i. isabellinus (north-western China, province of Xinjiang) Plumages also variable, but appearance pallid. Typical males of nominate race have almost uniform drab grey or rather sandy-grey upperparts from crown to lower back with forehead and supercilium tinged isabelline. Their face pattern is poorly defined with dark brown on lores limited to a small spot in front of eyes. The tail is uniformly dull cinnamon, not so rufous as in *phoenicuroides*. A small primary patch may be visible – white, creamy or tinged isabelline. The underparts are fairly uniform sandy-pink, the middle of the belly being white or creamy-white in the breeding season. Females are similar, but with pale lores and brown ear-patches; they rarely show a primary patch. Faint vermiculations may be visible on throat and sides of breast. Very faint barring can often be seen on the tail.

L. i. tsaidamensis (north-central China, province of Qinghai) Very similar in coloration to nominate, but slightly paler; also markedly larger with wing-length of males up to 102mm (88-94 in *isabellinus*).

Note that both *isabellinus* and *speculigerus* may have to be renamed, as it appears that the type of *L. isabellinus*, described from Arabia, is in fact an example of *speculigerus* (see Cramp and Perrins 1993: 455).

HYBRIDS Four regular hybrid zones between the Isabelline Shrike and the Red-backed Shrike are known (see map). Three of these concern the race *phoenicuroides* and one the race *speculigerus*. The breeding ranges of Red-backed Shrike and *phoenicuroides* overlap in two relatively small areas which respectively lie (1) just south-east of the Caspian Sea in southern Turkmenistan and northern Iran, and (2) north-east of the Aral Sea in Kazakhstan; a larger zone of overlap exists in eastern Kazakhstan, east-north-east of Lake Balkhash. There, the portion of phenotypically intermediate birds reaches its maximum in the foothills of the Saur Mountains. The ranges of Red-backed Shrike and *speculigerus* overlap in the south-eastern Altai Chua steppe with 44% of hybrids in the centre of that steppe, all the others being Isabelline Shrikes; a small population of Red-backed Shrikes only occurs in the northern part of that area. It is worth noting that single hybrids can be found breeding almost throughout the whole range of *phoenicuroides* (see map in Kryukov 1995). Colour variation of the hybrids is great and the observer can be much confused. Not surprisingly, up to thirteen 'species' or 'subspecies' of shrike were described in all these zones last century. A hybrid has

also been described between the race *speculigerus* and the Brown Shrike.

MOVEMENTS All the populations are migratory and spend the winter south-west to west-south-west of their breeding range. *Phoenicuroides* and *speculigerus* regularly occur in Africa, south of the Sahara, but largely north of the regular winter range of the Red-backed Shrike. The status of nominate *isabellinus* in Africa remains unclear; it may only be an occasional straggler (see Pearson 1979). In winter *phoenicuroides* is said to occur in small numbers in north-west India, in northern Gujarat and Kutch; at the same time it is widespread in the southern part of the Arabian Peninsula and in north-east Africa, particularly in Sudan, Ethiopia, Somalia, Kenya and north-east Uganda. Southwards, it reaches Dar es Salaam, in Tanzania, at 6°48'S. Very few birds are seen further south; two vagrants have been recorded in Malawi, one of them, on the eastern Nyika Plateau, as recently as 26 November 1996. Westwards, it is probably mainly, if not exclusively, that race which reaches Zaïre, Chad, northern Cameroon, Nigeria, Mali and even, occasionally, the Gambia (four records), Mauritania and Senegal where in Djoudj National Park, four birds (three caught) were seen in the winter 1991-92 and two were trapped in the winter 1992-93. *Speculigerus* also winters in the Arabian Peninsula and in north-east Africa; its regular western limits probably lie in Sudan (confirmation needed). *Isabellinus* winters from north-west India (chiefly west and north of a line from Khandesh through Sehore in Madhya Pradesh to Gorakhpur in Uttar Pradesh) westwards through Pakistan (Punjab plains down to the coast of Sind), Afghanistan, Iran and southern Iraq. Some birds also appear to winter regularly in south-east Uzbekistan, Tajikistan and possibly Turkmenistan. Southwards this race can also be regularly met with in parts of the Arabian Peninsula. The wintering grounds of the north-central Chinese race, *tsaidamensis*, are not well known; it apparently reaches at least southern Iran.

All populations of the Isabelline Shrike migrate on a south-west bearing in autumn. Some *isabellinus* from north-west China might, however, first move north into north-east Kazakhstan in order to avoid the high range of the Tien Shan. Birds reaching West Africa, presumably *phoenicuroides*, probably head due west at some time within Africa. As far as is known, the return migration in spring follows the same routes. The passage is strong all through Central Asia and the Arabian Peninsula. Iran is probably one of the few countries where the four races appear at some time or other.

Post-nuptial movements become important in the second half of August for *phoenicuroides*; this race is common on passage in Central Asia until the end of September, adults preceding young birds. It already appears in Iraq in early September and some birds have even been found in the Arabian Peninsula as early as mid-August. Prolonged stopovers probably occur in the latter area as most Isabelline Shrikes only arrive in East Africa from the beginning of November. They stay there until the end of March or early April. The peak return passage through the Gulf is in mid-April, but movements there begin as early as mid-February and are probably due to local wintering birds. Arrivals on the breeding grounds are between early March and early (late) May depending on geographical area and meteorological conditions. Males arrive a few days before females. Few details are known about *speculigerus*. It is the commonest form recorded in Israel, being regular in autumn in the southern parts of the country, in southern Arava and Eilat. Birds have been observed there between 19 September and 8 December, the 'bulk' of the passage taking place between the second week of October and the first week of November. Far fewer birds are seen in spring, between 2 April and 5 June (at Eilat mainly between 20 April and 10 May). Birds of the race *isabellinus* also start to move in August; some juvenile dispersal may even take place as early as the end of June. The passage through Central Asia is also important in September, but many birds of this race are still in these areas in October and a few stragglers are even seen in November. In Pakistan, where only this subspecies is present in winter, most birds arrive at the end of September and most have gone by the second week of March; they also leave north-west India in March. In Kazakhstan the last migrant *isabellinus* are seen in April when the first *phoenicuroides* appear. The first birds are back on their Chinese breeding grounds in the second half of March.

The Isabelline Shrike is a rare vagrant to Egypt with a few records from September, October and March; it is also rarely seen in Europe, although it is being more frequently recorded as the numbers of observers increase.

Small islands off the coast of Britain and western Europe, offer good chances of an encounter with Isabelline Shrike. In Britain it is almost an annually recorded vagrant. The bird may, however, turn up in unusual places, such as the one found dead in March 1994 in Richmond, Greater London. In many cases, racial assessments of birds seen in Europe have not been possible; when opinions are expressed they generally refer to *phoenicuroides* which, purely on geographical grounds, is the most likely race to occur in Europe.

MOULT The post-juvenile moult of *phoenicuroides* and *isabellinus* is similar to that of the Red-backed Shrike. However, an unknown proportion of young birds not only change their body feathers, but also their tertials and all their tail feathers. First-winter birds show much plainer upperparts, most of the barring having gone; this is a useful clue for specific identification (see Identification for comparison with Red-backed Shrike). The post-breeding moult of adults lasts from July to September. It involves the body feathers, but also the tertials and, remarkably, all the tail feathers. The latter are renewed rather quickly in *phoenicuroides* and so grow more or less together with few differences in length. First-winter birds, as well as adults, undergo a complete moult in the winter quarters from November to February; however, a few immatures keep the three or four old innermost primaries until the next moult in winter. The moult strategy of eastern populations of *isabellinus*, those wintering in Pakistan and India, and of most individuals of *speculigerus* is strikingly different from the general pattern. These birds have a complete moult in summer when they are still

on their breeding grounds.

VOICE The song, very similar to that of the Red-backed Shrike, is a prolonged babbling and warbling containing both harsh sounds and relatively melodious whistles. Many birds are imitated including the Thick-billed Warbler *Acrocephalus aedon* with its rich, varied phrases. The Isabelline Shrike often sings in its winter quarters. The main advertising call of the male at the beginning of the breeding season sounds like that of the Red-backed Shrike. It is, however, somewhat softer, quieter and less 'nasal' in quality; it can be transcribed as *zea*. As far as is known, there are no obvious differences in the voice of the various subspecies.

HABITAT In its eastern Palearctic breeding range this shrike inhabits rather dry steppes or semi-deserts generally at low or middle altitudes. In arid mountainous areas, it can, however, occur up to c. 3,000m. Locally, it can even be regarded as a high-elevation bird, as for instance in Pakistan (Baluchistan), where the race *phoenicuroides* does not nest below c. 2,100m. In the Pamir range in Tajikistan a nest of the same subspecies has been found at an altitude of 3,533m. In northern Mongolia, *speculigerus* is numerous in the semi-desert of the Lacustrine Depression, but also in the barren mountains of the Gobi Altai, and in central Gobi. Whatever the elevation, the structure of the breeding habitat is the same and is very similar to that inhabited by the Red-backed Shrike. The Isabelline Shrike needs very open terrain dotted with bushes, particularly thorny ones, and can adapt to a variety of situations. In southern Turkmenistan it can, thus, be found in tamarisks growing in river valleys, in dry steppes rich in scrub, near pistachio *Pistacia* groves, in juniper *Juniperus* stands growing on mountain slopes, etc. It occupies cultivated areas and may also occur in open woodland.

In its East African winter quarters, the Isabelline Shrike is, not surprisingly, a bird of rather lower and drier country than the Red-backed Shrike. It is common in a variety of dry, open, bushed and wooded habitats up to c. 2,000m. It avoids over-moist conditions and is for instance absent from the semi-arid country around Lake Baringo during years with above-average rainfall, particularly if rains are frequent in January or February. It can, however, be seen on the verge of marshy areas as for instance in Chad or near Lake Tana in Ethiopia.

HABITS Very similar to those of the Red-backed Shrike at least as far as *phoenicuroides* and *speculigerus* are concerned. At the beginning of the breeding season the males can be located by their advertising calls. Display-flights are also then frequent; those performed by *speculigerus* end in a long glide. Densities and territory sizes are virtually the same as in the Red-backed Shrike. The favoured height of perches is also c. 2m and most prey are caught within a radius of 8-10m, generally on the ground (c. 75%), but less frequently in the air or from leaves of trees and bushes. Prey is impaled regularly.

FOOD Consists mostly of insects, particularly beetles and grasshoppers; other invertebrates such as spiders and snails are taken. Small vertebrates are also taken all the year round. In Turkmenistan, rodents and birds play an important part early in the breeding season when there are still relatively few active insects of adequate size. Birds are also regularly caught on migration and in the winter quarters; among the most frequent victims are wagtails *Motacilla* sp. and warblers *Phylloscopus* sp. Other vertebrates found in the diet include: lizards, amphibians and even fish.

BREEDING As in the Red-backed Shrike, males of *phoenicuroides* and *speculigerus* generally arrive in their breeding territories a few days before the females, but again like *L. collurio* there are observations suggesting that some pairs may form during stopovers. Such behaviour has been noted for *phoenicuroides* in mid-May in the United Arab Emirates. For *phoenicuroides*, egg-laying starts at the end of April in southern Turkmenistan and two to four weeks later further north, in Kazakhstan. In the Altai region the first eggs of *speculigerus* are laid only at the end of May. The few data concerning nominate *isabellinus* show that it begins nesting as early as mid-April and that eggs may still be laid at the start of June. There are marked differences between areas and subspecies. Replacement clutches are frequent; second normal broods have been suspected so far only in *isabellinus* (confirmation needed). The nest-site is chosen by the male; in *phoenicuroides* he also initiates building. While doing so, he tries to get the female interested in his job: he calls and sometimes sings perched on the nest, displaying with breast pressed down on the nest, wings extended (white wing-patches conspicuous) and tail raised upwards. The female soon joins in and the work can then be completed in a few days. All over its range, the species builds its nest mostly in bushes, often thorny ones, and more rarely small trees. Most nests of *phoenicuroides* are c. 1m above the ground; they can be up to 3-5m in trees like *Pistacia* or *Populus tremula*. Nests of *isabellinus* and *speculigerus* are rarely found more than 1.5m from the ground. The latter race, in parts of its range, often hides its nest in *Caragana* bushes. The nest resembles that of the Red-backed Shrike; it is built with the materials most readily available and its dimensions are variable with an outer diameter of 9-20cm and an overall height of 4-10cm; the nests of *phoenicuroides* in or near the reed-beds growing along Lake Balkhash (Kazakhstan) are, thus, almost entirely made of whatever reeds can offer (leaves, stems, etc.). *Phoenicuroides* lays (3) 4-6 (7) eggs, the mean clutch-size in northern Iran and parts of former USSR being c. 5 eggs (n = 58). *Speculigerus* lays mostly 5 or 6 eggs (range 4-8), and nominate *isabellinus* 4-5. In all races, incubation is probably done exclusively by the female. It lasts 13-17 days and the young stay in the nest 13-16 days. *Phoenicuroides* is regularly parasitised by the Common Cuckoo *Cuculus canorus*. In the Lake Balkhash area, 13 out of 90 controlled nests contained a Cuckoo's egg. The parasite is readily accepted and raised by the adoptive parents. One case is known where an adult *phoenicuroides* brought food to two Cuckoo fledglings.

REFERENCES Ali & Ripley (1972), Andrews (1995), Capello *et al.* (1994), Cheng (1987), Cramp & Perrins (1993), Dean (1982), Dement'ev & Gladkov (1968), De Smet & BAHC (1994), Dymond *et al.* (1989), Fraticelli & Sorace (1992), Glutz von Blotzheim & Bauer (1993), Gore (1990), Inskipp & Inskipp (1991), Kozlova (1933), Kryukov (1995), Lefranc (1993), Mauersberger & Portenko (1971), Panov (1983, 1995), Pearson (1979, 1981), Richardson (1990, 1991), Rodwell *et al.* (1996), Roberts (1992), Robertson (1996), Shirihai (1995), Sokolov & Sokolov (1987), Stresemann & Stresemann (1972), Ticehurst (1922), Voous (1979).

5   BROWN SHRIKE
Lanius cristatus   Plate 2

IDENTIFICATION Length c. 18cm. A medium-sized, polytypic (four races), eastern Palearctic species, slightly larger than the Red-backed Shrike. It is heavily built, rather bull-headed with a strong bill often ending in a prominent hook, and with a long, slim, graduated and rounded tail. The strong head pattern is characterised by a solid black facial mask and a broad white supercilium extending to the forehead. The species is aptly named as its russet-brown upperparts and wings are almost uniform. They contrast with the whitish underparts washed pale rufous. The sexes are almost identical. Juveniles have poorly defined head markings and are barred above and below. First-year birds are rather similar, still marked by dark but rather faint crossbars; a whitish supercilium is already well indicated.

The confusion species are female and immature Red-backed Shrike and Isabelline Shrike (see under latter species).

DESCRIPTION *L. c. cristatus*
Adult male Rather 'bull-headed'. Facial mask black over lores, eyes and ear-coverts. Supercilium broad and pure white, from base of bill to back of ear-coverts, particularly wide over and just behind eye, joining a buff-white patch on forehead which grades into dull brown on forecrown. Crown and nape rufous, contrasting generally only slightly with rather russet-brown mantle, back and scapulars. Rump and uppertail-coverts tend to be as rufous as cap. Tail light rufous with fringes and tips of outer rectrices paler. Wings dark brown; most wing-coverts, inner secondaries and tertials fringed buff-white. Underparts off-white, washed with pale rufous except on throat. Undertail light brown-grey.
Adult female Almost identical to male and not always separable, but facial mask generally slightly less distinct in front of eyes, supercilium tinged cream and breast and flanks finely vermiculated dusky.
Juvenile Facial mask dark brown over ear-coverts. Supercilium dull whitish, but already visible. Upperparts more rufous than in adults and heavily barred from forehead to uppertail-coverts. Tail as in adults. Wings brown; wing-coverts, outer secondaries and tertials fringed buff. Underparts off-white heavily barred, except on chin, upper throat and belly. Undertail light grey-brown.

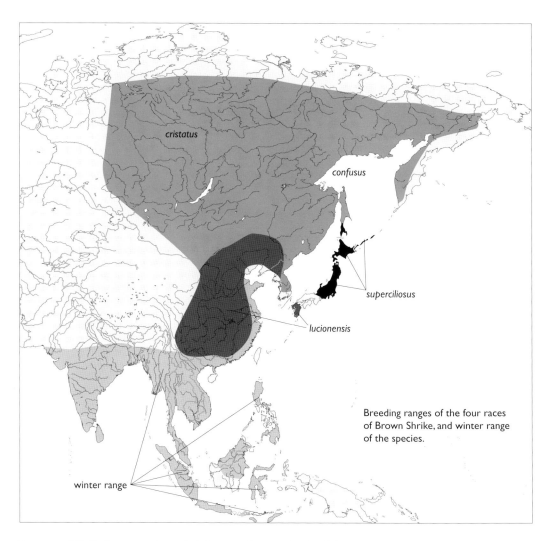

Breeding ranges of the four races of Brown Shrike, and winter range of the species.

Bare parts Bill black or, sometimes, dark brown with a bluish-grey base in adult females; in young birds, bill blue-grey or grey-brown with black or dark brown tip. Legs black or plumbeous. Iris brown or dark brown.

MEASUREMENTS Wing 84-90; tail 77-89 (mean c. 84); bill (to skull) 19-21; tarsus 24.5-26.5. Weight 30-38 on Mongolian breeding grounds, 21-35 in winter in India.

DISTRIBUTION AND STATUS The breeding range lies entirely in the eastern Palearctic where this shrike can be regarded as the ecological counterpart of the Red-backed Shrike, widely distributed in western Eurasia. The vast range extends from the eastern parts of western Siberia (approximately from the middle Ob area at c. 81°E) and the Russian Altai, north-eastwards to the north of the Kamchatka peninsula, east to the Korean peninsula, Sakhalin and the Japanese islands, and south-east over the central Altai and northern Mongolia, to the eastern and south-eastern provinces of China south to northern Guangdong. The southern boundary of the breeding range roughly follows the

Tropic of Cancer at 23°28'N whereas the northern limits lie beyond the Arctic Circle not far from 70°N. This latter latitude is nearly reached in the west of the range, just south of the Taymyr peninsula, in the Norilsk region. In China, the western boundary crosses north-east Gansu and northern and south-west Sichuan.

GEOGRAPHICAL VARIATION Four races are recognised. *Confusus* is not separable in the field from *cristatus.*

L. c. cristatus (north-west of range, from eastern Siberia to Kamchatka and south to the Russian Altai, north-west Mongolia and upper Amur and Zeya river basins; possibly also in northern Sakhalin). Described above.

L. c. confusus (Amur and Ussuri basins, Manchuria, Amurland north to about the middle Zeya river) Difficult to tell from *cristatus.* Upperparts paler and white frontal patch wider.

L. c. superciliosus (southern Sakhalin and Japan: Hokkaido south to south-central Honshu) Easily separable. Facial mask characterised by small narrow black line at base of rather long bill. Upperparts much more rufous and darker than in other races. Crown and rump much 'redder'. White frontal patch wider. Underparts more rufous (except on throat which remains white and contrasts with the rest).

L. c. lucionensis (Korea, parts of northern, eastern and south-east China, locally on Kyushu and possibly Tsushima, Japan) Easily separable. Bill as strong as in *superciliosus*. Upperparts much greyer than in other races; only rump and uppertail-coverts are markedly tinged rufous. Forecrown pale grey (not pure white), grading into pale ashy on top of crown.

HYBRIDS Only two or three hybrids between this species and the Red-backed Shrike are known. See also under Isabelline Shrike and Tiger Shrike.

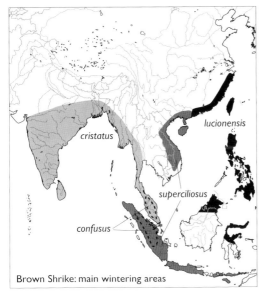

Brown Shrike: main wintering areas

MOVEMENTS Almost all the populations are migratory and spend the winter south of the breeding range, mainly north of the Equator. The race *lucionensis*, however, partly winters in its breeding area in southern Korea and in south-east China. The winter quarters and migration routes of the different subspecies somewhat overlap. Nominate *cristatus* is the Brown Shrike found in winter in the Indian subcontinent, roughly south and east of a line from Ahmednagar through the Surat Dangs (Gujarat), Mhow (Madhya Pradesh), Lucknow (Uttar Pradesh) and central Nepal. In the latter country it is fairly common in the east, but uncommon in the west. *Cristatus* is also common in Sri Lanka. Eastwards, it is an abundant winter visitor in Bangladesh and all over the plains of southern Burma; in Thailand it has been reported from all parts of the northern plateau, the south-eastern provinces (Chanthaburi) and the central plains (Kamphaeng Phet), and in China it is known from Yunnan province. More to the south, this race is an abundant winter

visitor to the Malay Peninsula, but is uncommon south of Selangor. This race also occurs on the islands of Langkawi and Lalang and further west, occasionally, in the Andaman and Nicobar islands. Presumably it also occurs in western Borneo. *Confusus*, difficult to separate from *cristatus*, can be seen on passage or in winter in various parts of Thailand: northern plateau (Chaiya Prakan), eastern plateau, southern portion of the central plains and peninsular provinces from Prachuap Khiri Khan to the extreme south. It probably also occurs in southern Burma (Tenasserim) and is widespread in the Malay Peninsula, particularly from Selangor to Singapore including the island of Pisang. Presumably this is also one of the races to be found in Sumatra, Java, Borneo and Bali. *Superciliosus* winters in south-east Yunnan and on Hainan, China; it also occurs in Vietnam and Laos. In the Malay Peninsula, it appears mainly to be a passage migrant wintering further south in Sumatra and the Sunda islands, Java, Bali, Sumba, Flores. *Lucionensis* winters in southern Korea and in south and south-east China in the provinces of Guangxi, Guangdong and Fujian; it also winters on Hainan and in Taiwan. This is the Brown Shrike sometimes referred to as the 'Philippine Red-tailed Shrike' as it is common and widespread in winter in that archipelago. It is also to be found in the northern parts of Borneo and Sulawesi, and is the common Brown Shrike of the Andaman and Nicobar islands with occasional records as far west as Sri Lanka.

The migration routes of the different races are only partly known. Nominate *cristatus*, the northern and western subspecies, migrates south in autumn on a broad front. Birds breeding west of c. 110°E apparently avoid arid Central Asia and migrate roughly through eastern Mongolia, the Chinese province of Gansu, eastern Tibet, Burma and Bangladesh; many birds probably then undertake westward or south-westward movements to reach their winter quarters in the Indian subcontinent. *Cristatus* birds from the eastern part of the range and some populations of *confusus* (Amurland) migrate south-westwards in autumn. They cross Manchuria in northern China and then, central and western China, south to Burma and Malaysia. Some birds, apparently mainly *confusus*, travel further south and reach their winter quarters in Sumatra and the Sunda islands. *Superciliosus*, the 'Japanese' Brown Shrike, moves south-westwards in autumn. At that time many birds turn up in the coastal areas of the Chinese province of Jiangsu, in the mouth of the Chang-jiang and also on the Zhoushan islands which seem to be an important migratory halt for these shrikes, which have flown at least 700 km over the sea. The birds continue their route south-westwards along the Chinese coast to Laos and Vietnam; their passage in the Chinese provinces of Fujian and Guangdong appears to be fast, as there are relatively few observations (but also presumably low observer coverage). By contrast *superciliosus* is conspicuous on Hainan and in the south-western parts of Yunnan, which are both also part of the winter quarters. Many birds remain in Vietnam, Laos, Cambodia, but others move further on, appearing in the Malay Peninsula and then reaching their winter quarters in

Sumatra or further east in the Sunda islands. The race *lucionensis* mainly moves south-eastwards in autumn, but migrants from the Korean peninsula apparently first fly south-westwards and reach the area of the mouth of the Chang-jiang or appear on one of the many offshore islands after a flight of c. 500km over the sea. *Lucionensis* is, then, widespread in the Chinese province of Fujian, where some birds overwinter. Many others fly over to Taiwan where they may stay or move down the Heng Chun peninsula and cross to Luzon in the Philippines. From Luzon, some birds take a south-westerly direction and reach Palawan or even northern Borneo; others remain on Luzon or move further south-east through Mindanao to northern Sulawesi. A vagrant has been found as far east as Manokwari in extreme north-eastern New Guinea. The birds wintering in the Andaman and Nicobar islands probably follow a quite different route which, starting in Yunnan, crosses north-west Laos, north-west Thailand and southern Burma. As far as is known, the different races take the same respective routes to fly back to their breeding grounds.

For all four subspecies, post-nuptial movements start at the end of July or in August, adults preceding young birds. The breeding areas are almost completely vacated by mid-September. Nominate *cristatus* passes through north-east Burma between 10 September and 29 October. It can be seen in the Indian subcontinent from August to mid-April, with a few stragglers staying on till early June. In Bangladesh, the extreme known dates are 6 September and 2 May. Few precise data exist for *superciliosus*, which passes through the Malay Peninsula between 22 September and 7 November and again in April. It is known to be present in its winter quarters, in Sumatra, between 19 September and the beginning of May. *Lucionensis* appears in Taiwan as early as August, and passage is strong in September; birds wintering in Taiwan start disappearing gradually from late March when passage birds, presumably from the Philippines, appear again and can be found until May. This is also the race generally identified in Hong Kong; it is often numerous there from the end of August until late October and again between mid-April and mid-May. The peak spring arrivals of the various races can be summarised as follows: last week of April and first week of May for *lucionensis*, second week of May for *superciliosus*, second and third week of May for *confusus* and 25 May to mid-June for *cristatus* (depending on latitude).

Among the observations of this shrike outside its normal range, there are two made in the extreme east of Kazakhstan in July and two in the western Palearctic: one at Sumburgh, Shetland, from 30 September to 2 October 1985, and one trapped at Falster, Denmark, on 15 October 1988. Two birds have also been seen in extreme north-east Russia respectively in early summer and mid-August. The Brown Shrike is also on the list of American birds with one seen on St Lawrence Island from 4 to 6 June 1977, one, presumably of the race *lucionensis*, on Shemya Island in the Aleutians on 10 October 1978, and one on Farallon Island, California.

MOULT The post-juvenile moult, involving mainly the body feathers, starts soon after fledging even before the flight and tail feathers have reached full length, but it is interrupted during migration and resumed on arrival in the winter quarters, where an almost complete moult takes place. Some juvenile inner primaries, some secondaries and primary-coverts are often retained.

The complete post-nuptial moult of the adults begins when the young are independent. It is uninterrupted and completed in the breeding season for the southern subspecies, *lucionensis* and *superciliosus*, whose wintering grounds are relatively close to the breeding areas, but also for birds of the race *confusus* nesting on Sakhalin and even for some *cristatus* birds which have not nested at all. Most individuals of *cristatus* and late-breeding *confusus*, however, complete their moult during migratory halts, apparently chiefly in southern China. Late breeders of the northern race *cristatus* and of *confusus* adopt another strategy: their post-nuptial moult starts on the breeding grounds with the renewal of the tertials, is then suspended during migration, and resumes again in the winter quarters when the primaries are renewed. For these northern and late-breeding birds there can be strong variations. Before migrating, some individuals may only change their body feathers and others their tail feathers. The Brown Shrike renews almost its entire plumage twice a year, with a prenuptial moult taking place in the winter quarters. This moult occurs in all four races. The Chinese subspecies *lucionensis*, for instance, after having completed a moult on its breeding grounds in September, begins a new one the following February in its winter range (mainly the Philippines); it is over at the beginning of May at the latest. This second moult tends, however, to be incomplete as a variable number of primaries and secondaries are retained. This is probably particularly the case for birds with a late post-breeding moult.

Another peculiarity of the Brown Shrike is that the primary moult of all races frequently starts not with P1, but with P3, P4, P5 or P6, from which focus it may proceed simultaneously in both directions.

VOICE The song is not very loud, rather similar to that of the Red-backed Shrike, but less rich and varied. However, it also contains many imitations. In the Gobian Altai it was heard throughout one night in late May. At the beginning of the breeding season, the display-flight is accompanied by calls sounding like *kriki-kriki-kriki tchf tchf*. A common call, heard throughout the year, is a harsh, loud *chr-r-ri*. In its winter quarters, the species is generally silent, but its harsh, noisy chattering calls can sometimes also attract attention, particularly at dusk. The song of the Brown Shrike has occasionally been heard prior to the return migration.

HABITAT The wide breeding range of this shrike includes several types of climate and vegetation zones, but everywhere the structure of the habitat is very similar to that favoured by the Red-backed Shrike (i.e. presence of bushes or small trees). Locally however, it may be more attracted to open forests and behave more as a 'woodland' shrike than the Eurasian species. It can ascend to at least 1,800m e.g. in the Russian Altai.

Nominate *cristatus*, the Siberian form, typically inhabits subtaiga and southern taiga subzones and the highest population densities are found at the edges of dense forest stands along steppe rivers, clear-cuts and burns. In mountains the species is only common in open, mixed forests; it is rather sparse in pine forests, but more regular where pine trees grow on or near *Sphagnum* peat bogs. It can be a common breeder on forest meadows as on the Yenisey floodplain and on overgrown hay-fields. It favours low, sparse or trampled vegetation and avoids dense forests and floodplain meadows with rank vegetation and high grasses. Further north, at c. 68°-69°N, this shrike even occurs, albeit at low densities, in forest tundra, willow and alder groves, open mixed forests of birch and spruce, and open larch and birch forests. Further south, nominate *cristatus* occurs in drier steppe-like areas such as in Transbaikalia, but favouring the most humid zones: river valleys well dotted with bushes and groves or the edges of lakes. Nominate *cristatus* as well as other races, particularly *superciliosus*, can also nest in agricultural land with scattered trees or even in parks.

HABITS Rather similar to those of the Red-backed Shrike. Males just back from migration are very demonstrative, perching on the highest trees and performing display-flights accompanied by typical calls (see Voice). Densities may be high and presumably vary with habitat quality. Precise figures exist concerning nominate *cristatus* for some Siberian habitats 14 pairs/km² in a mosaic landscape of meadows and birch; 28 pairs/km² on dark coniferous cuts and c. 80 pairs/km² on pine forest cuts. On overgrown taiga burns there were 7 pairs/km² and only one pair/km² in floodplains and peat bogs with pine trees. Where densities are high the average distance between occupied nests can be as little as 70m. In Siberia, the breeding territory of a pair covers less than 10 ha. The Brown Shrike is highly territorial all the year round. Small individual territories mapped for 25 winter visitors to Taiwan averaged only c. 0.25ha, but the duration of stay was apparently short, less than 12 days in most cases. Site-fidelity probably occurs in summer; it has been proved in ringed birds in various parts of the wintering grounds: Taiwan, Malaysia, Thailand. In the latter country, an individual returned for five successive years to the same garden in Bangkok.

The Brown Shrike, when looking for prey, generally perches between 1 and 3m from the ground and, mostly, a little less than 2m. When roosting, however, it appears to prefer perches situated 4 or 5m above the ground as has been observed in Malaysia. In a winter study in Taiwan, most foraging attempts (n = 1,322) were from a perch to the ground (89.1%); in 8% of cases the birds went for flying insects from the perch and in a few cases they pecked at prey while perched on a strong plant. In the same study c. 59.5% of the total foraging was done within 1.5m of the perch; the farthest distance covered was 22m when a shrike pounced on a prey on the opposite side of a canal from a high perch. Larders are regularly kept and are indispensable when larger prey items are caught.

FOOD The diet, mainly composed of insects like locusts, grasshoppers, crickets and beetles and of small vertebrates like passerines (including occasional nestlings), small rodents, lizards and frogs, has been studied in detail in a wintering area in Taiwan (location of larders of *lucionensis*) and in northern Japan (observation at two nests of *superciliosus*). In Taiwan, the records are, of course, largely biased towards the larger prey items: out of 222 victims c. 60% were frogs *Rana limnocharis*, and c. 34% small reptiles: *Eumeces chinensis*, *Takydromus stejnegeri*, Agamidae and Gekkonidae. There were also larger insects, particularly Orthoptera and Scarabaeidae; together they formed 3.2% of the impaled items. The remainder were earthworms, small rodents and birds. In Hokkaido 238 prey were identified during observations for seven days at two nests. The young were given caterpillars (33.1%), Orthoptera (24.1%), Arachnoidea (20.5%), Diptera (7.4%), adult Lepidoptera (5.9%), Coleoptera (4%), Dermaptera (2.4%), Hemiptera (1.7%) and one or two Odonata and Hymenoptera.

BREEDING At least in Siberia, males generally arrive a few days before females. Pair formation takes place as soon as the females arrive. The laying dates vary according to the geographical areas: at the beginning of May for *lucionensis* in south-east China, towards mid-May for *superciliosus* in Japan (even later in the north), at the end of May for *confusus* in Russian Amurland and only towards mid-June for *cristatus* in Siberia. Replacement clutches are frequent, and in all areas the breeding season extends until July. Nothing definite is known about possible normal second broods. The nest, built by both sexes, but mostly by the female, is finished in less than a week. It is hidden in a bush or tree and, at variable heights above the ground. *Cristatus* and *confusus* appear to be low nesters. Nests of the latter race are quite regularly found very near or even on the ground, in grass tussocks or amongst fallen leaves. In Russian Amurland, most nests of that subspecies are 0.5-1m above the ground, but with some nests placed in trees, in orchards for instance, up to a height of 3.5m. In Japan, *superciliosus* is said to nest 7-18m up in a tree, but six nests found in Hokkaido were at an average height of only c. 2m (0.9-6.2 m). In south-east China, the nests of *lucionensis* can also be a good height from the ground, on horizontal branches between 9 and 18m according to some sources (but few precise data and confirmation needed). The nests are relatively large cups mostly composed of small twigs, rootlets, dry leaves and grasses; bird feathers are also readily used. The construction has an outer diameter of 11.5-13cm and an average height of c. 12cm. The Brown Shrike lays 5-7 eggs in Russian Ussuriland (mean 6.12 for n = 12) and also in central Siberia. In Japan, clutches with 3-7 eggs have been found, but most nests contain (4) 5 or 6 eggs. Incubation, probably only or mostly by the female, lasts 13-15 days and the young leave the nest when 13-15 days old. They stay in a radius of c. 400m around the nest for at least another two weeks.

The species is locally parasitised by cuckoos; in eastern Russia by the Common Cuckoo *Cuculus canorus* and Indian Cuckoo *C. micropterus*, in Japan by the Common Cuckoo and Oriental Cuckoo *C. saturatus*.

REFERENCES Ali & Ripley (1972), Brazil (1991), Chalmers (1986), Cheng (1987), Chong (1938), Coates (1990), Cramp & Perrins (1993), Deignan (1945, 1963), Delacour & Jabouille (1931), Dement'ev & Gladkov (1968), Duckett (1988), Gore & Won (1971), Hume (1993), Inskipp & Inskipp (1991), Jahn (1942), Kozlova (1933), Kryukov (1995), La Touche (1925-1930), MacKinnon & Phillipps (1993), McClure (1974), van Marle & Voous (1988), Mauersberger & Portenko (1971), Medway (1970), Medway & Wells (1976), Neufeldt (1981), Olivier (1944), Panov (1983), Rogacheva (1992), Severinghaus (1991, 1996) Severinghaus & Liang (1995), Smythies (1960, 1986), Stresemann (1927), Stresemann & Stresemann (1971), Takagi & Ogawa (1995), Vorobiev (1954).

6   BURMESE SHRIKE
Lanius collurioides   Plate 1

Other name: Chestnut-backed Shrike

IDENTIFICATION Length 20-21cm. Somewhat smaller than the smallest races of Long-tailed Shrike, this little studied polytypic species is confined to South-East Asia. Adult males have a black forehead, lores and ear-coverts, and a dark ashy crown shading paler on nape and sides of neck. Mantle, scapulars, back and rump are as bright chestnut as in Red-backed Shrike. A white primary patch is generally conspicuous on the dark brown wings. The dark brown, relatively short (especially if compared with *schach*) tail is edged and slightly tipped white. The pale underparts are washed vinaceous-buff. Adult females are very similar to males, but can be distinguished at close quarters by their pale buff lores and nasal feathers. Juveniles have a greyish-brown crown and nape; otherwise their strongly vermiculated upperparts are pale rufous, and their chestnut-brown tail is bordered whitish. The off-white underparts are more variably washed warm buff, with narrow, wavy dark bars across breast and flanks.

The main confusion species is the Long-tailed Shrike with its various races; it is, however, slightly larger and longer-tailed, always has some orange-buff in its plumage including juveniles, and is not such a rich deep chestnut on its upperparts as the Burmese Shrike. Moreover, its tail is edged pale chestnut, not white.

DESCRIPTION *L. c. collurioides*
Adult male Facial mask black over anterior part of forehead (a few mm from base of bill), lores, eyes and ear-coverts. Crown dark ashy, becoming paler on nape (blacker facial mask can be distinguished at very close quarters). Upperparts bright chestnut from mantle to uppertail-coverts including scapulars. Wings dark brown with distinct white patch on primaries 4 to 9; wing-coverts, secondaries and tertials fringed warm buff. Tail black; two pairs of outer rectrices wholly white, the others tipped pale buff. Underparts off-

white, washed vinaceous-buff. Undertail almost wholly white when closed, except for black tips.
Adult female Very similar to male, but lores and nasal feathers pale buff; some juvenile-type barring may still be present on breast.
Juvenile Facial mask brown over lores, eyes and ear-coverts. Forehead, crown and nape greyish-brown barred blackish. Upperparts warm buff, with coarse barring from mantle to uppertail-coverts. Tail brown; two outer pairs of rectrices pale buff, the others tipped buff. Wings dark brown with primary patch already visible; primary coverts tipped buff; remiges tipped pale buff (primaries) or warm buff (secondaries and tertials). Underparts off-white, more or less washed buff and heavily vermiculated on breast and flanks. Undertail off-white.
Bare parts Bill horny brown, darker at tip and on culmen, flesh-coloured at base. Legs black. Iris reddish-brown.

MEASUREMENTS Wing 83-97; tail 92-102; bill (culmen) c. 14; tarsus c. 25. Weight: no data.

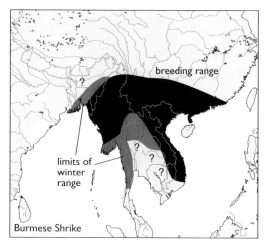

Burmese Shrike

DISTRIBUTION AND STATUS Confined to a limited breeding range in south-east Asia, the boundaries of which are still unclear. Its western limits may still lie in extreme eastern India (confirmation needed), where a nest was found in 1891 in northern Cachar District in Assam. Not known as a breeding bird in Bangladesh, this shrike is aptly named as it is locally widespread in Burma where it nests in the Chin Hills, the Shan States and the central and north-eastern parts (plains only) of the country. South-eastwards, its range extends to southern Vietnam where it is very common in the Lang Bian mountains in the Da Lat area. It very probably nests in parts of Laos and Cambodia and might even do so in northern and north-east Thailand, where it is generally considered a winter visitor only. East of Burma, the northern boundary crosses The Chinese border into Yunnan (western part, central Jingdong in central Yunnan and Xishuangbanna in the South), southern Guizhou and parts of Guangxi and Guangdong. There is no information about possible changes in distribution or abundance.

GEOGRAPHICAL VARIATION Slight. Two races are generally recognised.

  L. c. collurioides (whole breeding range except southern Vietnam) Described above. Individual variation exists. Some birds have, for instance, the head and hindneck paler grey and the mantle lighter chestnut; in some cases only the forehead is black and the rest of top of head grey.

  L. c. nigricapillus (southern Vietnam) Differs from nominate in the sooty-black colour of the head and hindneck, which fades to dark grey on the lower part of the neck, and in the richer chestnut of the mantle.

MOVEMENTS Some populations are migratory, others are resident or move only locally or altitudinally. Breeding and winter ranges largely overlap; the latter, however, lies somewhat more to the south and, perhaps, particularly to the south-east. The species is a passage migrant and probably a winter visitor to extreme eastern India: eastern Assam, Nagaland (?), and Manipur. It is also a rare visitor to south-east Bangladesh (no details of dates). Some birds winter in north-east Burma, but the species is apparently more common from December to March in the central and southern plains. After the breeding season, birds regularly appear as far south as Henzada, and some even reaching Amherst at c. 16°N. In winter, the species probably also occurs in Tenasserim, since in peninsular Thailand it is known as far south as Prachuap Khiri Khan just below 12°N. In Thailand, it regularly winters on the northern and eastern plateaus, but appears to be absent from the central and south-eastern provinces. Chinese birds are said to be resident (more information needed); this may also hold true for most eastern populations down to southern Vietnam where the Burmese Shrike, as in other parts of its range, is known for its altitudinal movements.

  In Burma, post-nuptial movements begin as early as June; from then on until August there is a constant stream of young birds and adults back to the dry plains to the south; the species is back in its breeding territories from March onwards. In north-east Thailand, in the Chiang Mai area, it is numerous between the beginning of July and mid-March; it is very rare (a few breeders?) or absent at other seasons.

  A vagrant has been noted in Hong Kong on 30 March 1988.

MOULT Little information. The post-juvenile moult and, more remarkably, post-nuptial moult are apparently completed between August and November, but details of the extent of these moults are lacking.

VOICE The song has been described as sweet and full. It includes harsh gratings as well as musical notes.

HABITAT This shrike lives in subtropical or tropical climates. It can be found from the plains, near sea-level, up to c. 1,800m in the Karenni Mountains in Burma and up to c. 2,400m on the high plateaus of southern Vietnam. It inhabits typical *Lanius* country such as scrubby open woodland, forest edges, secondary jungle, etc., including the edges of cultivated fields

or suitable gardens. It can often be seen along roads or highways.

HABITS Very little known. A confiding shrike, easy to approach and detect. Usually met with singly, but said to collect into noisy parties; this has probably something to do with pair and/or territory formation. Some site-fidelity appears to exist at least in winter and probably also in the breeding season; a wintering bird ringed in northern Thailand was trapped again in the same place twelve months later. Most prey is caught on the ground in typical *Lanius* fashion. To date, there are no records of larders.

FOOD Only insects such as grasshoppers have been recorded.

BREEDING In Burma, the breeding season extends from March to early June, most birds laying in April or the first part of May. In south-east China, fresh eggs have been found in the middle of June, but repeat clutches are probably common. Observations from southern Vietnam suggest a normal second brood (confirmation needed). The nest is usually built in a thorny bush, less often in a high, thin bush or low sapling. It is placed c. 2m above the ground (1.5-3.5m), made of grass, leaves, lichen and feathers, covered with cobweb and lined with fine grass. Some nests, particularly those hidden in bushes, are markedly larger than others. Clutch-size is 3-6, generally 5 (but few data).

REFERENCES Ali & Ripley (1972), Baker (1924), Brunel (1978), Cheng (1987), Deignan (1945, 1963), Delacour & Jabouille (1931), Etchécopar & Hüe (1983), Harvey (1989), La Touche (1925-1930), McClure (1974), Robson (1988), Smythies (1986), Wildash (1968).

7 EMIN'S SHRIKE
Lanius gubernator   Plate 11

Other name: Emin's Red-backed Shrike

IDENTIFICATION Length 14-15cm. A very poorly known species, confined to parts of western and central Africa. About the size of a House Sparrow *Passer domesticus*, it is the smallest *Lanius* shrike. Adult males have pale grey crown and nape and a chestnut back. They are thus rather similar to the somewhat larger adult male Red-backed Shrike, but their rump and uppertail-coverts are also chestnut, not blue-grey. A small white primary patch, very rare in *L. collurio*, is quite noticeable, particularly in flight, on the black-and-chestnut wings. The black tail is edged and tipped white and the underparts are tawny, except on throat and belly which are paler than the rest. Adult females differ little from males. They are, however, distinctly duller, the chestnut of the back being browner and the grey head tinged with a brownish wash; but they show no trace of barring. The juvenile is brownish, barred blackish above; its underparts are pale tawny, a diagnostic feature, barred blackish.

DESCRIPTION

Adult male Facial mask jet black over lores, eyes, ear-coverts and anterior part of forehead (2-3mm from base of bill). Forehead and area just above eyes whitish merging into mid-grey on crown. Nape and upper mantle also mid-grey. Upperparts from mantle to uppertail-coverts and including scapulars bright chestnut. Tail dark brown with middle feathers fringed rufous-chestnut, the others tipped and bordered white; outermost pair of rectrices with an entirely white outer web and much white on inner web, save for a dusky terminal patch. Wings dark brown; greater coverts, secondaries and tertials edged chestnut; white patch (up to c. 12mm long) across the five inner primaries. Underparts variably washed pale rufous, brighter on flanks. Chin, throat and approximate middle of belly white. Undertail greyish-brown edged and tipped whitish.
Adult female Duller than male. Facial mask dark brown, not extending over base of bill. Anterior part of forehead whitish-grey merging into mid-grey on crown. Nape and upper mantle also grey. Mantle and back browner. Rump and uppertail-coverts light rufous. Tail brown with outer web of outer pair of rectrices edged and tipped white. Wings as in male, but much duller and showing no or a very small white primary patch. Underparts variably washed light rufous, but throat whitish. Undertail as in male.
Juvenile Face mask as in adult female. Upperparts grey-brown heavily barred blackish with dull rufous tinges, particularly on rump and uppertail-coverts. Tail dark brown; outer pair of rectrices edged pale rufous. Wings brown; wing-coverts warm brown tipped white with black subterminal bar; secondaries and tertials narrowly edged warm brown and tipped whitish. Underparts off-white with heavy blackish barring particularly on breast and flanks; distinct rich buff tinges on breast and flanks. Undertail pale brown.
Bare parts Bill black, horn-brown in juvenile. Legs plumbeous. Iris brown.

MEASUREMENTS Wing of male 77-84, of female 78-84; tail of male 60-66, of female 64-67; bill 13-14; tarsus of male 23-25, of female 20-23. Weight: no data.

DISTRIBUTION AND STATUS Not usually common, this shrike occurs in West Africa, north of the Equator, from Ivory Coast (few records) eastwards to southern Sudan (rare) and northern Uganda. Definite proof of breeding only exists for Nigeria and Zaïre but the bird very probably nests in at least nine countries. It may have been overlooked to date in Togo, Benin and Burkina Faso.

GEOGRAPHICAL VARIATION None known. Monotypic.

MOVEMENTS Nothing is known about possible regular movements. Casual observations suggest that birds wander at least occasionally.

MOULT No information.

VOICE Few descriptions exist. In Nigeria calls were noted as various twitterings and whistles, together with low harsh *zut zut, chuz-zoo-wit*. A low *chark, chark* was

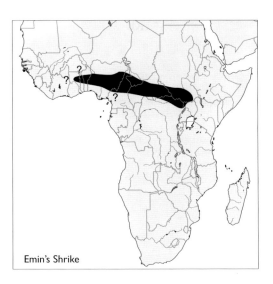

Emin's Shrike

also heard as a bird landed in a tree. As far as is known, no recording exists.

HABITAT In Ghana and Nigeria the species has been recorded in degraded Guinea savanna. In Nigeria it has also been seen in gallery forest. It seems to favour open, grass-covered woodland or forest clearings, but can also be found in old cultivated fields and abandoned village sites. In southern Sudan it is said to live in open bushed grassland within thicker woodland.

HABITS Very little is known. At least at certain times of the year, it may occur in small parties. Most records, however, refer to single birds or pairs. This shrike is generally easy to locate, perched on top of a shrub or on a telephone cable. It hunts in the usual shrike ways, taking most of its food from the ground but occasionally also catching insects on the wing.

FOOD So far only insects seem to have been recorded: beetles, grasshoppers, mantises.

BREEDING Apparently no nest or eggs have been described. In Nigeria adults have been seen with fledglings on 16 June. In north-east Zaïre, breeding occurs in March and April, at the beginning of the rains. Young in barred plumage were observed there in July; they seemed to have left the nest some weeks earlier.

REFERENCES Bannerman (1953), Cave & Macdonald (1955), Demey & Fishpool (1991), Grimes (1987), Lamarche (1981), Lippens & Wille (1976), Louette (1981), Malbrant (1952), Nikolaus (1987), Walsh (1968).

8   SOUSA'S SHRIKE
Lanius souzae   Plate 11

IDENTIFICATION Length c. 17.5cm. A small, poorly known, polytypic shrike (three races) from Central Africa, about the size of a Red-backed Shrike. It resembles the male of the latter, but is less vividly coloured with dull grey upperparts becoming browner on lower back and rump, both narrowly barred blackish. The russet-brown wings and the long, very narrow tail are also finely barred. The species shows a whitish supercilium and displays a generally conspicuous pale V formed by the scapulars. The underparts are almost completely dusky, only the throat being white. The sexes are similar except that females have a tawny patch on their flanks, rarely visible in the field. Juveniles, narrowly barred blackish, are even duller than adults; they are more uniform with no grey on their heads. Sousa's Shrike is unmistakable when seen well; much less conspicuous than other African *Lanius* shrikes, it is confined to open forested areas.

DESCRIPTION *L. s. souzae*
Adult male Facial mask jet black over lores and ear-coverts, passing just through eyes. Anterior part of forehead whitish merging into dark grey of crown and connected to a whitish, well-defined supercilium. Upperparts dark grey on nape and upper mantle becoming russet-brown on mantle and back. Scapulars pure white. Rump and uppertail-coverts grey to grey-brown. Tail long, narrow and dark brown with white fringes; basal half somewhat russet-brown finely barred black, the rest being darker and more uniform; outer pair of rectrices almost wholly white, and much white on inner webs of all other rectrices except two central pairs. Wings brown; wing-coverts, tertials and secondaries russet-brown finely vermiculated blackish. Underparts dusky on breast and upper belly, the rest being whiter particularly on chin and throat. Undertail almost wholly white.
Adult female Similar to male, but slightly duller, particularly on back. Flanks show distinct tawny patch.
Juvenile Facial mask brown. Supercilium whitish, already noticeable. Upperparts brown or russet-brown, densely but finely barred blackish. Scapulars whitish, barred blackish. Tail dark brown barred blackish and fringed pale buff; rectrices tipped buffish with black subterminal bars. Underparts off-white heavily barred, except on chin and throat. Undertail grey-brown.
Bare parts Bill and legs black. Iris brown.

MEASUREMENTS (*souzae*) Wing 81-90 and tail 76-90 for 25 birds from Angola measured by Benson (1950); bill 12.5-14; tarsus 19-23. Weight 21-30 (mean c. 26.5) for 23 birds weighed in Angola (da Rosa Pinto in Clancey 1970).

DISTRIBUTION AND STATUS The breeding distribution lies entirely south of the Equator; southwards it only penetrates marginally into southern Africa. It is found from central Congo in the west to western and southern Tanzania in the east. There is at least one record from extreme south-east Gabon, near Leconi.

Sousa's Shrike

In Congo, Sousa's Shrike occurs at least as far north as Djambala at 2°33'S. It is widespread in Zaïre south and south-east of Kinshasa, in the Kasai, Shaba and Katanga regions. In Rwanda, it is rare and restricted to an area lying upriver of the Rusumo Falls. In Tanzania, it is also uncommon and locally distributed; it is known in the south from Songea, and in the west from Mpanda to Kibondo and north to Lake Burigi at c. 2°S. It probably occurs in Burundi. Further south, it is well known in Angola and widespread in Zambia where it is, however, fairly local occurring throughout the Northern Province, west of the Muchinga Escarpment north to Mbala; it is also present in Western and Central Provinces south to Lusaka, Mumbwa and Chunga in the Kafue National Park; in North-Western Province it is widespread west to Balovale, and extends south in the Barotse Province to Luena River; finally it has been found in Mankoya between the rivers Lwazamba and Machili. In Malawi, the species occurs throughout, south to the Thyolo district. Sousa's Shrike also exists in some parts of northern Mozambique, particularly in the Tete District. Finally, the species is a rare vagrant (resident?) to the extreme north of both Namibia and Botswana where there were two records up to 1994 (M. Herremans pers. comm.); it has been seen along the Okavango and the Chobe rivers at c. 18°S. These points probably represent its southern limits in the western part of its range. So far, Sousa's Shrike has not been recorded in Zimbabwe, but it may well occur in the country's northern third.

This shrike is generally considered sparse and local. There are no data on possible changes in abundance or distribution.

GEOGRAPHICAL VARIATION Despite considerable individual variation, three races appear justified. The following paragraphs follow Clancey (1970). The respective ranges given here, however, warrant further research, particularly the boundaries between *souzae* and *tacitus*.

L. s. souzae (southern Congo, southern Zaïre,

Angola, except south-east) Described above.

L. s. burigi (north-west Tanzania, Rwanda and Burundi) Upperparts more brownish-grey, not so russet-brown on mantle and back as in nominate. No dusky vermiculations on lower back or uppertail-coverts. Wings and tail darker, much less rufous than in nominate. Wings less barred blackish. As a whole distinctly less vermiculated than *souzae*. Females have a larger and markedly deeper rufous area on their posterior flanks.

L. s. tacitus (south-east Angola, northern Namibia east to Zambia, Mozambique and the Katanga area in southern Zaïre) Mantle overlaid with drab or dull olive-brown. Wings as in *souzae*, but distinctly paler. Females have a reduced, paler and duller rusty wash on flanks. Appears to be distinctly smaller than *souzae*; wing-length of 25 males: 78-85 (mean 81.2) as against 84-91 (mean 86.6) for 25 males from Angola.

MOVEMENTS Little information. Generally regarded as strictly resident, Sousa's Shrike may in fact show some local migratory movements in certain parts of its breeding range in the dry season. The birds seen in southern Africa probably originate from further north. In Malawi it is thought that the species is migratory as it seems to be absent from certain parts of the country outside the breeding season.

MOULT Little information. The type of the race *burigi* is a male collected on 30 June with outer primaries in moult. Verheyen (1953) considers there to be a complete adult moult from March to May but bases his statement on very few specimens.

VOICE Rarely heard. The song has been described as a chattering whistling. Various calls have also been noted: a quiet *tzzer*, a low *tzzzzzick* (different transcription of *tzzer*?) of a wary bird near and on nest, a low grating chirp and a low chattering uttered at intervals by a female while an observer examined her nest.

HABITAT Confined to tropical savanna between the tropical rainforest lying north of its range and the drier subtropical steppe and desert which predominate just south of its range. Few details exist on the altitudinal range favoured by the species; in Malawi, Sousa's Shrike occurs between 750 and 1,800m, and in Zambia mostly between 1,000 and 1,800m. It is generally well segregated from other *Lanius* species as it is a woodland bird mainly found where the forest thins out. It may, however, also be encountered at the edges of well-wooded gardens. In part of its range it is virtually endemic to light miombo woodland (*Brachystegia*) with patches of short grass. In Rwanda it seems to be strictly confined to *Pericopsis* savanna whereas in Zambia it apparently occurs not only in miombo woodland but also in *Burkea* savanna and probably also in Mutemba woodland.

HABITS Little known. This shrike is not easy to detect in its relatively closed habitat. It has been regarded as shy, silent and, when disturbed, quick to slip away, to the upper branches of a tree where it disappears among the leaves. Some birds can, however, be very confiding

and easy to approach. Sousa's Shrike uses perches which grow under the woodland canopy; it usually sits 2-4m from the ground where it takes most of its prey by diving down in typical *Lanius* manner. No larder has been recorded to date.

FOOD Only arthropods have been recorded: insects and large spiders. Small vertebrates might occasionally be taken. In Malawi, an attack has been witnessed on a Violet-backed Sunbird *Anthreptes longuemarei*.

BREEDING In south-east Zaïre, breeding takes place at the start of the rainy season, and from mid-September to November. In Angola, occupied nests have been found in September and October. In Zambia and Malawi the species nests between September and December. The number of normal broods is unknown. The nest, placed in a tall shrub or the fork of a small tree, is generally well hidden in the foliage at a height of 3-6m from the ground. Two nests found near Lusaka (Zambia) were rather unusual as they were not situated in forks, but (a) on a horizontal branch, 2.5m from the trunk, and (b) on the intersection of two branches of a leafless tree. The nest is a fairly deep, thick, neatly built cup. Made mainly of small twigs and plant stems, it is mixed round the outside with greyish-coloured woolly plant-down and cobweb; it is also lined with a network of creeper tendrils or soft grass and may include some lichen. Its overall greyish appearance can make it quite inconspicuous on a lichen-covered fork or branch. Sousa's Shrike lays 2-3 eggs. The relatively modest data available suggest that most clutches have three eggs; clutches with four eggs are certainly exceptional. Incubation is probably by the female alone.

REFERENCES Benson (1950), Benson & Benson (1977), Benson & Irwin (1967), Benson *et al.* (1971), Britton (1980), Chapin (1950, 1954), Clancey (1970), Harris & Arnott (1988), Immelmann (1968), Lippens & Wille (1976), Medland (1991), da Rosa Pinto (1965), Sargeant (1993), Took (1966), Vande weghe (1981), Verheyen (1953), Vincent (1949), White (1946).

9   BAY-BACKED SHRIKE
Lanius vittatus   Plate 5

IDENTIFICATION Length c. 18cm. Confined to parts of Asia and particularly common in Pakistan and India, this is one of the smaller shrikes. Two races are generally recognised. The similar sexes resemble male Red-backed Shrikes insofar as their crown and nape are pale grey and their back and scapulars bright chestnut. A diagnostic broad black band crosses their forehead. The species also shows a distinct white primary patch on the black wings, a whitish rump and a rather long, black, graduated tail edged and tipped white. All these features are quite conspicuous in flight. A buffish wash appears here and there on the whitish underparts, the flanks being rusty. The brown, barred juveniles lack the black forehead; the primary patch is already visible, the tail rufous-brown.

DESCRIPTION *L. v. vittatus*

Adult male Facial mask black over lores, eyes and forehead (more than 1cm from base of bill). Crown and nape pale grey. Upper mantle dark grey merging into bright chestnut of mantle. Back and scapulars also bright chestnut. Rump and uppertail-coverts white. Tail long, slim, black and graduated (graduation c. 2cm); all rectrices, except central pair, tipped white and with much white at base; outer pair of rectrices almost wholly white. Wings black with conspicuous white primary patch. Underparts off-white with a distinct buffish wash; flanks and belly rusty. Undertail white.

Adult female Very similar to male and sexes generally not separable, but frontal band might be somewhat narrower. May occasionally be paler than male (this appears to be the rule in the race *nargianus*).

Juvenile Confusingly similar, when just out of the nest, to juvenile Red-backed Shrike; upperparts tend to be slightly paler and underparts perhaps less heavily barred (few birds examined). Birds moulting into first-winter plumage become mealy grey on the upperparts, which are tinged rufous on mantle; they also gradually lose their vermiculations. Wings dark brown; greater coverts and tertials pale rufous with whitish tips and dark contour lines; faint indication of a whitish wing-patch. Tail rufous-brown; outer pair of rectrices pale rufous. Undertail grey-brown.

Bare parts Bill relatively weak, dark horny-brown or black, somewhat paler at base of lower mandible in young birds. Legs horny-black or plumbeous, paler in young birds. Iris brown.

MEASUREMENTS (*vittatus*) Wing 82-90; tail 81-96 (usually under 90); bill (culmen) 13-15; tarsus 21-24. Weight 18-24 (mean c. 21) for birds from India.

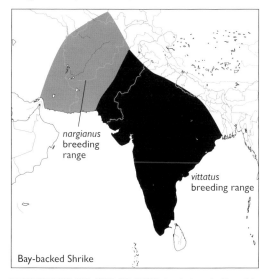

nargianus breeding range

vittatus breeding range

Bay-backed Shrike

DISTRIBUTION AND STATUS An Asian shrike with a rather restricted breeding range extending from south-east Iran east to West Bengal in India. In Iran it is known from Baluchistan, particularly from the Bampur and Iranshahr area; to the west its range probably extends at least as far as Bandar-e'Abbas. The species

may also occur in Khorasan (no confirmed breeding). In Turkmenistan it is confined to the south-east and more precisely to the Badchyzskij and Kushka areas. It seems to be local in Afghanistan, where it is not as common as the Long-tailed Shrike, but has been seen, among other places, near Lashkar Gah, Kandahar, Punjab and Kabul. It is a common bird in Pakistan throughout the Indus basin extending north to the main vale of Swat and the base of the Murree foothills, also nesting in the higher plateau regions and valleys of Baluchistan. The Bay-backed Shrike is widespread in all India from along the outer Himalayan ranges (including Chitral, Kashmir south of Pir Panjal Range, and Nepal terai) south throughout the peninsula to Kanniyakumari and from Rajasthan east to West Bengal; vagrant to Bhutan. It is absent from Sri Lanka. Occasional breeding may occur in Nepal.

GEOGRAPHICAL VARIATION Two races are recognised.

L. v. vittatus (Indus plains in western Pakistan, India) Described above.

L. v. nargianus (south-east Iran, southern Turkmenistan, Afghanistan, central and northern Baluchistan in eastern Pakistan) Intergrades with nominate race in Sind and north-west Punjab. Paler on upperparts in both sexes than nominate *vittatus*; averages larger: in 10 adult males (paratypes) wing 86-92 (mean 88.8), bill 17-20 (mean 18.5) as against 82-88 (mean 85.5) and 15.5-18 (mean 16.5) in 10 adult males from southern India (Vaurie 1955). Males and females are often separable (unlike *vittatus*), females being duller, greyer, with less striking colours on upperparts. Plumage variation between individuals, irrespective of sex, also seems to be higher than in nominate race.

MOVEMENTS The populations of the north-western part of the range (race *nargianus*) appear to be largely migratory, but little is known about the movements of birds from Iran and Afghanistan. Birds breeding in eastern Pakistan and India can be migrants or, in most cases, residents (allowing for local movements). Bay-backed Shrikes summering in Turkmenistan start leaving their breeding grounds from the beginning of August onwards; the last individuals are seen in mid-September or a little later, and the first are back in the last ten days of April. In Pakistan, populations from the higher plateau regions and valleys of Baluchistan leave at the beginning of October at the latest and the first birds reappear in the last week of March. It is thought that these shrikes winter along the Makran coastal area. In the same country, the nominate subspecies is largely sedentary in the Indus plains. This is also largely the case for Indian birds, except for those breeding in the north. In winter some birds occur outside the breeding range, in Nepal for instance, where this shrike is an uncommon winter visitor and passage migrant, keeping as a rule to low elevations, chiefly between 75 and 335m. In the western part of the range a few wintering birds have been recorded in the Gulf states and Oman (in all cases only one individual at a time): United Arab Emirates: at Sharjah on 10 April 1970, at Ras Al Khaimah where it stayed two weeks at the end of November 1972, at the zoological gardens of Al Ain on 23 February 1979; Saudi Arabia: in the Tihamah in April 1989; Oman: at Batinah on 29 April 1979.

MOULT The post-juvenile moult of Indian birds not only includes the body feathers but also all wing-coverts (except primary coverts), the tertials and a variable number of tail feathers. The moult from first-winter into first-summer plumage is poorly documented; it appears to vary individually. First-summer birds may not be distinguishable; they retain a variable number of unmoulted feathers. Adults undergo a complete moult immediately after breeding; in most cases this is already finished in the first or second week of August.

VOICE The song is a pleasant, loud warble which, as in other *Lanius* sp., is intermixed with excellent mimicry. A typical, rather scolding call, *chur-r* or *chee-urr*, is said to sound very like the squealing of a frog caught by a snake.

HABITAT A shrike of subtropical desert and subtropical savanna climates. It occurs from near sea-level up to about 1,800m in the outer Himalayan ranges. In Pakistan it ascends some of the higher hills up to c. 1,600m. In southern Turkmenistan, it can be found in hilly country at 600-800m (rarely up to 1,000m) on slopes well exposed to the south and protected from the influence of cold north winds. In Nepal, passage migrants have exceptionally been recorded at very high altitudes: 2,810m in April 1982 at Kagbeni and 3,965m in July 1988 north of Manang. It may be found almost anywhere where a few trees and bushes supply its requirements. Its preferred habitat appears to be intermediate between the dry semi-desert favoured by the race *lahtora* of the Southern Grey Shrike and the relatively more wooded, well-watered areas inhabited by the Long-tailed Shrike. It can, however, be largely sympatric with both these species, particularly the latter. The Bay-backed Shrike is mainly a tree nester. In Turkmenistan almost the entire known breeding population inhabits hilly pistachio woods *Pistacia vera*. In Pakistan the bird does not penetrate the Himalayan valleys, in sharp contrast to the Long-tailed Shrike, and particularly favours canal bank tree plantations or other such tree avenues. In India, it occurs in a variety of habitats: scanty desert scrub-jungle, thorny tree-jungle, waste or grazing land around villages, etc. In Kerala, south-west India, it frequents open scrub country interspersed with babul trees and thorny bushes. All over its breeding range it can be found in parks and gardens, even in large cities like Delhi.

HABITS Often conspicuous, relatively tame and easy to approach. Usually solitary or in isolated pairs, the Bay-backed Shrike is a typical *Lanius*, highly aggressive and quite territorial in both winter and summer. It drives away much bigger birds including congeners like the Long-tailed Shrike with which it is largely sympatric and, in the extreme west of its breeding range, the Lesser Grey Shrike, which often breeds in its vicinity.

Courtship behaviour is much like that of other *Lanius* shrikes. After pair formation and before breeding activities really start, the sexes keep in touch with soft calls. Both male and female also perform display-flights; those of the male recall Lesser Grey Shrike and become really impressive in the presence of an intruder, a rival male or another *Lanius*. It may then fly high up into the air in gliding curves with intermittent shallow wing-beats. Territory size of breeding pairs and of individuals appears 1-2ha; in very favourable habitats, densities can be quite high with a pair occasionally building about 50m from the nest of another pair, as near Quetta in Pakistan. In the same country along canal tree plantations, a pair can be found almost every 150-200m. In the Keoladeo Ghana National Park, at Bharatpur in northern India, the Bay-backed Shrike is a very common breeder with up to 25-30 pairs per km^2 in appropriate areas (Prakash Gole *in litt.*). Rather low densities are known from southern Turkmenistan; in the best-studied area during a three-year survey, only between 12 and 14 pairs were found to nest on 4km^2. In that country the distance between two neighbouring and occupied nests is generally at least 150m. In India, at the National Zoological Park in New Delhi, at least four pairs are known to breed in an area covering 107ha. The Bay-backed Shrike favours perches at an average height of c. 2-2.5m. Most prey is caught within a radius of 10m. Larders are regularly kept.

FOOD Comprises almost exclusively insects, mainly Coleoptera and Orthoptera. In Turkmenistan, 90% of prey brought to young in the nest were grasshoppers or crickets, the rest being composed of Lepidoptera, Diptera and Hymenoptera. Lizards, young mice and nestling birds are occasionally taken. During pair formation, when territoral activities are at their peak, this shrike may drive off all kinds of birds including small ones, but it has so far not been reported as attacking a full-grown passerine for food.

BREEDING In migrant populations, males generally arrive on the breeding grounds a few days before females. The breeding season is protracted and, overall, lasts from February to September, chiefly from February to April in southern India and from May to July elsewhere. In Pakistan, egg-laying may start in March, but in Turkmenistan, where the bird is not resident, it never begins before the first ten days of May. Repeat clutches are frequent and up to three attempts have been recorded. Normal second clutches are apparently common and probably occur throughout the breeding range. The same nest may be used, but a new one is built much more often. Very occasionally, successful pairs can have a normal third clutch (one definite record from Pakistan). The nest, built by both sexes in 6-8 days, is generally hidden at a moderate height, between 1.5-4m (range 0.9-10m) in a fork or crotch of a tree or in thorn bushes. Its outer diameter measures c. 10.5cm and its height c. 7cm; small nests have been recorded with an outer diameter of only 6.5cm, an overall height of 5cm and a depth of cup of c. 3cm. In Turkmenistan, the nests are almost exclusively built in pistachio trees at a height of 1-2.5m (mean 1.35 for n = 11). In the Punjab Salt Range most nests were found between 1.8 and 2.4m from the ground, but one was 6m high in a shisham *Dalbergia sissoo*. A great variety of trees can be chosen (mango, plum, orange, tamarind, toon, olive, etc.) and thorn trees such as *Acacia*, *Prosopis* or *Ziziphus* may be locally favoured. The nest of the Bay-backed Shrike is quite small and neat. The well-made cup can be lined with soft grass, rags, wool, tow and feathers, often with much cobweb on the exterior as binding material. A nest found in Sind (India) was very conspicuous and composed of little else than doves' feathers. Clutch-size varies from 3 to 5 eggs, but is usually 4. In south-east Turkmenistan 36 full clutches consisted of 3 (8.3%), 4 (69.4%) or 5 eggs (22.2%), mean 4.14. The female does most of the incubation, which lasts 14 or 15 days. The fledgling period has the same duration.

REFERENCES Ali (1969), Ali & Ripley (1972), Baker (1924), Desai & Malhotra (1986), Dement'ev & Gladkov (1968), Erard & Etchécopar (1970), Gallagher & Woodcock (1980), Inskipp & Inskipp (1991), Loskot *et al.* (1992), Panov (1983, 1991), Rahmani *et al.* (1994), Ramadan-Jaradi (1985), Reeb (1977), Richardson (1990), Roberts (1992), Vasic (1974), Waite (1948).

---

10   LONG-TAILED SHRIKE
Lanius schach   Plate 4

Other names: Black-headed Shrike, Rufous-backed Shrike, Schach Shrike, Dusky Shrike (melanistic variety of the nominate subspecies)

IDENTIFICATION Length 20-24cm. The size and structure of this polytypic (about nine races) Asian shrike recall that of the Great Grey Shrike. Its tail is, however, more graduated and relatively longer and its bill a little shorter. The race *erythronotus*, described here, occurs in the west of the species range and is a very rare vagrant to the western Palearctic. It is distinctly smaller, but very similar to the nominate subspecies which is confined to parts of China. In all plumages, including juvenile, *erythronotus* shows a characteristic rufous rump and a long, black, buff-sided tail. In the adults, a rather vivid orange-buff colour appears on the scapulars, lower back and uppertail-coverts. An orange-buff wash is also present on the flanks and undertail-coverts. The underparts are otherwise whitish. The dark brown wings show a generally small white patch at the base of the primaries. Seen face on, the species slightly resembles the Lesser Grey Shrike because of its pale grey head and mantle, and its black facial mask which narrowly joins over the forehead. The sexes are almost alike, the female being slightly paler. The juvenile is much duller, darker and heavily barred. This shrike is, in most cases, easy to identify. It can, however, be confused with the Grey-backed Shrike (see under that species). The ranges of both birds overlap in some areas, particularly in the Himalayan foothills in winter.

The Long-tailed Shrike is generally common, familiar and very conspicuous. It often perches high and draws attention to its presence by its harsh rasping cries.

DESCRIPTION *L. s. erythronotus*
Adult male Facial mask black over ear-coverts, eyes, lores and a few mm on forehead, just over base of bill. Supercilium thin, whitish, over broad black eye-stripe, extending over black line on forehead to form small whitish area. Upperparts pale grey from forehead to mantle, contrasting with the orange-buff of the lower back, scapulars, rump and uppertail-coverts. Tail long (up to 11cm), black and sharply graduated (graduation c. 3-4.5cm) with warm buff sides and tips. Wings black with small or very small white primary patch (sometimes absent); wing-coverts, inner secondaries and tertials fringed and tipped pale orange-buff. Underparts white on chin and breast, buff-white on belly and orange-buff on flanks and vent. Undertail greyish.
Adult female Very similar to male, sexes sometimes inseparable. Facial mask generally browner and more indistinct; black line on forehead smaller or absent. General plumage tends to be duller.
Juvenile Darker and duller than adults. Facial mask browner, less distinct; does not extend over eyes or base of bill. Upperparts brownish-grey, heavily barred; rump and uppertail-coverts with distinct orange-buff tinges. Tail light rufous-brown with darker central feathers. Wings with dark brown wing-coverts, secondaries and tertials edged buffish; no obvious primary patch. Underparts off-white, variably barred brown, particularly on flanks; orange-buff tinges on chest and flanks.
Bare parts Bill long, heavy and black (particularly in adult males during breeding season) or dark horn-brown (in females and young birds). Mandible with a flesh-coloured base in juveniles. Legs black in adults, dark brown in juveniles. Iris brown.

MEASUREMENTS (*erythronotus*) Wing of male 94-102, of female 93-99; tail of male 108-117, of female 102-112; bill (to skull) of male 20-22, of female 19-22; tarsus 27-31 for birds from Uzbekistan, Kyrgyzstan and Kazakhstan. Weight: 33-42 (mean c. 37) for birds from Kazakhstan and Afghanistan.

DISTRIBUTION AND STATUS The vast breeding range, centred on the Indian subcontinent and southern China, mainly covers the Oriental region. In the west, the species slightly penetrates the western Palearctic and in the south-east some populations nest in the Australasian region, north-east New Guinea. The western part of the breeding range extends north-west out of Afghanistan; it includes the Khorasan in north-east Iran (confirmation of survival there needed), south-east Turkmenistan, where the species is very local, eastern Uzbekistan and southern Kazakhstan. In the latter country, the Long-tailed Shrike reaches one of its northernmost points along the Syr-Darya river, where it has been reported from the Kzyl-Orda area and even from Kazalinsk at 45°46'N, a town about 100km east of the Aral Sea. A little further south and roughly along the Kazakhstan-Kyrgyzstan border, the northern boundary extends east as far as the Alma Ata

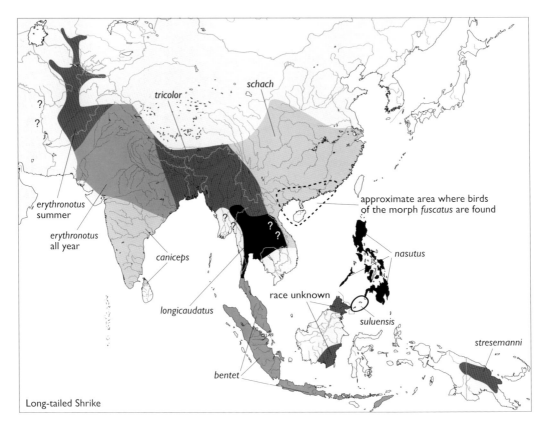

tricolor

schach

erythronotus
summer

erythronotus
all year

caniceps

longicaudatus

bentet

approximate area where birds
of the morph *fuscatus* are found

race unknown

suluensis

nasutus

stresemanni

Long-tailed Shrike

area. Southwards, the species is locally common in the mountains of western Kyrgyzstan and in Tajikistan except in the eastern Pamir. It is widespread and common in Afghanistan, except probably in the east and southeast. Its range is relatively well known in Pakistan where birds are common and widespread throughout the better watered parts of the Indus plains; they also nest in Baluchistan and the northern Himalayan region. The species is present throughout India, whereas in Sri Lanka it is confined to the north-west along the Jaffna peninsula and the offshore islands. It is also locally common in Bangladesh and Nepal as well as in south-east Tibet where it occurs, for instance, in the Lhasa area. Eastwards, the northern boundary crosses the Chinese province of Sichuan, then runs north-east to the province of Gansu at least as far north as Lanzhou at 36°03'N; from there it continues eastwards, mainly (exclusively?) south of the Huang (Yellow) river across southern Shaanxi, Shanxi and Shandong to the coast of the Yellow Sea. Near the north-eastern limits of its range, the Long-tailed Shrike has been recorded at Jinan at 36°40'N. It is thus widespread in China and quite common in Hong Kong; it also nests in Taiwan and Hainan. Further south, it is widespread all over South-East Asia – Burma, Thailand, Laos, Malay Peninsula – but appears to be absent, at least as a breeding bird, from extreme southern Cambodia and southern Vietnam. This shrike is also a fairly common resident virtually throughout the Philippines and in

the Greater and Lesser Sunda islands east to Timor. In Borneo, it is apparently a vagrant to the north and a local resident in the south-east. Finally, some populations occur as far east as eastern New Guinea: it occurs west to Telefomin and east to the Chirima valley and Woitape; it is also present in the Huon peninsula.

Few precise data exist for local status or population trends. Marked fluctuations were noted in *erythronotus* at the end of last century in southern Turkmenistan, which lies in the north-western part of the breeding range. In 1886, the species was still common in the orchards growing in the Ashkhabad area and even further west in Bakharden at 57°24'E. Towards 1900 the bird had already become very rare and today it only occurs occasionally. The same probably holds true for north-east Iran. The Long-tailed Shrike also disappeared from the Dushanbe area in Tajikistan at some time between 1949 and 1961. In the Malay Peninsula, evidence of local increases were recorded in the 1960s for *bentet*, but in Sumatra the same race was apparently much more numerous half a century ago. The race *tricolor* may have disappeared as a breeding bird from southern Burma. A population estimate exists for the town of Kabul (Afghanistan) for the 1980s: 1,000 to 1,500 breeding pairs on 120km²; the Long-tailed Shrike is one of the most numerous breeding birds in the area.

GEOGRAPHICAL VARIATION Many races have been described in the vast breeding area. The criteria used involve the colour of the upperparts and the size of the wing, the tail and the white wing-patch. However, there is complete intergradation of adjacent forms on the mainland and many individuals cannot be assigned satisfactorily to a given race. Nine races are recognised here, largely in accordance with Rand (1960) except that *tephronotus* is given specific status and *nigriceps* ignored as it has been shown to be intermediate between *tricolor* and *erythronotus* (Biswas 1950).

L. s. erythronotus (north-east Iran?, southern Turkmenistan, south-east Kazakhstan, southern Uzbekistan, Kyrgyzstan, Tajikistan, Afghanistan, Pakistan, northern and north-west India) Described above.

L. s. caniceps (western and southern India, Sri Lanka) Very like *erythronotus*, but somewhat darker on upperparts where rufous is generally restricted to rump and uppertail-coverts. Wings appear darker, blacker. Reminiscent of *L. tephronotus tephronotus*, but upperparts not so dark and tail black, not chestnut-brown. Resembles even more *L. t. lahulensis* (see under Grey-backed Shrike).

L. s. schach (eastern and southern China, Taiwan and Hainan) Markedly larger than *erythronotus* (wing 98-109; tail 128-145) with a very strong bill. Black band on forehead wider (up to about 2cm). Grey of upperparts somewhat darker and rufous definitely deeper, more 'chestnut'. Has a melanistic form called '*fuscatus*', described as follows: iron-grey upperparts from crown to upper mantle, a brownish-grey back, black wings (no white patch) and a black tail; forehead and ear-coverts black whereas chin, throat and upper breast are rather dark brown; rufous tinges may appear on mantle, scapulars, back and particularly rump; some birds may also show some rufous tinges on the dark grey underparts. This form is widespread in Hainan, Guangdong and south-eastern Fujian. Mixed pairs, normal *schach* and dusky birds, have been reported. Intermediate birds are frequently seen in Hong Kong.

L. s. tricolor (Nepal east to northern Burma and Yunnan in China, northern Laos and northern Thailand, where commoner in winter) Typical features: black cap (forehead, crown, nape), deep rufous, almost red-chestnut upperparts (small greyish area on upper mantle) and long tail.

L. s. longicaudatus (south-east and central Thailand) Similar to *tricolor*, but rufous on upperparts even deeper and tail much longer: 130-155 against 115-135. White primary patch generally larger.

L. s. nasutus (Philippines except Sulu Islands) Differs from *tricolor* in having the upper back grey, not chestnut, and paler rufous on rest of upperparts.

L. s. suluensis (Sulu archipelago, Philippines) Very similar to *nasutus*, but with a white-grey upper back, and upperparts somewhat lighter.

L. s. stresemanni (New Guinea) Very like *nasutus*, but with less grey on upper back and deeper rufous on rest of upperparts. White primary patch obvious.

L. s. bentet (Malay Peninsula, Sumatra, Java, South-east Borneo, Lesser Sunda islands, Timor) Extent of black on crown very variable. Colour of back fairly similar to that of *caniceps*. White wing-patch very inconspicuous or almost absent. Wings are rather short (as in *caniceps*) but tail longer than in any other race except *longicaudatus*. Birds from eastern Java, Bali and south-east Borneo are sometimes strikingly different from 'normal' *bentet*, with more black on upperparts. They might belong to a different race (see Smythies 1960 and recent discussion by Mees 1996).

MOVEMENTS Across its wide breeding range, the Long-tailed Shrike can be either resident or partly or entirely migratory. Local altitudinal movements are also known. The wintering area is smaller and lies entirely within the breeding range. The race *erythronotus* is a definite migrant in Central Asia. The birds from the north-western part of the range, from Kazakhstan, Turkmenistan and Afghanistan, are full migrants. In Pakistan, birds nesting in Baluchistan and the Himalayan regions are also migrants, whereas those from the more southerly parts such as the Indus plains, are resident. *Erythronotus* is widespread in winter in the Indian plains, south to Bombay and Hyderabad; in northern India it is then much more common than in summer; this is for instance quite noticeable in the Keoladeo Ghana National Park at Bharatpur. *Caniceps*, the race living in southern India, appears to be subject to local seasonal movements only. In the Himalayas, *tricolor* often winters within its breeding range, but at lower elevations, generally below 1,700m; Nepalese birds either remain to winter in the foothills or move south to India. In China, nominate *schach* is a resident or partial migrant. The races of the south-eastern part of the range are mainly, if not entirely, sedentary.

Routes taken by migrant *erythronotus* are not well known; in autumn south-east orientated movements probably occur on a broad front through both lowlands and mountains.

In the north-west of the range, movements begin in August, but peak in the second half of October. Observations become rare in October and are exceptional in November. The first birds are back on their breeding territories from early to mid-April with arrivals still recorded towards mid-May, and typically between 20-25 May in the mountains of Tajikistan. February records are known from temperate parts of Afghanistan.

Birds occasionally turn up outside their normal range. Two records are known from Japan: 23-24 March 1985, and 8-10 March 1987 (race unknown). To the west, the species has been found several times in Oman: in February 1983 and February 1984, from 31 December 1992 to 2 January 1993, from 21 January to 3 February 1994; in Israel, in the Negev Desert on 26 January 1983; in south-east Turkey, near Birecik on 24 September 1987. The only record for Europe is a bird seen in Hungary on 21 April 1979.

MOULT (*erythronotus*) A post-juvenile moult affecting head and body feathers, and possibly some wing-coverts and tertials, occurs soon after fledging. For birds of early broods it can be finished as early as the end of July; most juveniles are, however, moulting in the second part of August and some are still doing so at the start of October. The moult to first-summer plumage is not well documented. It is very variable in extent; some first-summer birds, after a complete moult, are indistinguishable from adults while others retain a varying amount of juvenile feathers including sometimes all flight feathers. The retained feathers are distinctly browner and more worn at tips. Adults have a complete post-breeding moult which starts with the body feathers. For migratory birds of the western part of the range, this moult is completed at the start of the autumn migration.

VOICE The song is a pleasant, somewhat metallic warble. It contains many imitations of calls and songs of other birds. Shrikes breeding in Baluchistan often mimic other species heard on their wintering territory. Mammals such as dogs may also be imitated. The song can be delivered without interruption for 5, 10 or even 15 minutes. At the beginning of the breeding season, single males are said to sing regularly at dusk and after sunrise. They also advertise their territory with a short harsh *rrrre*. The species commonly utters a repeated harsh *tchick* or a harsh buzzing *grennh*. The normal harsh grating notes have been compared to the squealing of a frog caught by a snake. The harsh scolding of angry birds is said to recall the distant rasping of Corncrakes *Crex crex*.

HABITAT The Long-tailed Shrike is a bird of warm climates. It occurs mainly in lowlands but breeds locally near the tree-limits in mountains. In Tajikistan, for instance, *erythronotus* usually nests up to 1,500m and sometimes up to 2,000m. In the Himalayas (Garhwal, Nepal, etc.), *tricolor* populations can be found between 3,000 and 4,300m. In Burma, the species probably breeds throughout the higher hills at any time of the year, but it avoids the plains, except for a large colony on the Putao plain (elevation 450m). In China, the nominate race breeds up to 3,050m. In New Guinea, *stresemanni* is widespread only in mid-mountain areas between 1,100 and 2,600m. In many areas, for instance in parts of India and Bangladesh, the species breeds in open, lightly wooded country with scrub, including occasionally evergreen forests and thin pine stands. It may thus appear as a scrub-jungle bird, but its association with cultivated country is obvious almost everywhere. It also favours cattle-grazed lands around villages. Very often, it seems tied to fairly tall trees and breeds in orchards, gardens, along roads and railways, etc. In Central Asia it colonised railroad villages as soon as trees began to grow in them. It can be found in parks within urban areas, for instance in Hong Kong. Well-watered country may be favoured: valleys of poplar-fringed rivers for *erythronotus* in Central Asia, reed-beds bordering cultivation for *bentet* in Sumatra, scrub-jungle near the sea for *caniceps* in Sri Lanka, paddyfields for *longicaudatus* in Thailand. The species avoids the very arid open-scrub desert tracts so much favoured by the race *lahtora* of Southern Grey Shrike.

HABITS The Long-tailed Shrike is generally quite conspicuous, with a reputation for being rather noisy and restless in the mornings and evenings. This highly territorial species is solitary in habits and very aggressive towards birds of the same species. It is particularly pugnacious, quarrelsome and noisy at courtship time when males pursue rivals and fly from one high vantage point to another. After nest-building, however, the birds become more skulking and rarely call, although they may still attack some but not all other species which come within a radius of c. 50m of the nest. The density is very variable and depends on quality of habitat. In *erythronotus*, and in well populated areas, the distance between occupied nests is generally at least 100-150m. In south-west Tajikistan, a very high density of 26 pairs has been found on 7ha of orchards and ornamental trees, and 4 pairs/km² were found at an elevation of 1,900m. In Kabul (Afghanistan) densities can be very high in green areas: for instance 6-7 pairs/ha in the former Russian embassy. Prey is caught in typical shrike manner. In India, the species is said to rob food from other birds even bigger than itself. A family of newly fledged shrikes has been reported to join together to kill fledgling House Sparrows *Passer domesticus* in China. Larders have often been reported, but the habit of impaling insects varies according to geographical area. Thus in Pakistan, only the Baluchistan summer breeding population is known to impale food on thorns.

FOOD This big shrike is a very opportunistic feeder. Ali and Ripley (1972) consider that it takes 'any small living creature that can be overpowered'. It catches a great variety of large insects and small mammals (mice, etc.), birds (including nestlings up to the size of Laughing Dove *Streptopelia senegalensis*), birds' eggs, fish, lizards, frogs (particularly in Sri Lanka), crabs, etc. It has occasionally been seen eating ripe fruit of neen *Melia* sp.

BREEDING As a rule, males of migrant *erythronotus* arrive in their breeding territories a few days before the females. Pair formation may, however, sometimes occur during migration stopovers. The breeding season is very protracted over the vast range. In the Indian plains, *erythronotus* starts laying at the end of March or in April; in Kashmir and the Himalayas, egg-laying only begins in May and fresh clutches are found into July. In Hong Kong, the breeding season of nominate *schach* extends from mid-March to the end of June. In Sri Lanka, fresh clutches of *caniceps* have been found between December and May. In the Malay Peninsula, eggs of *bentet* have been recorded in February, from June to September and in December. In Luzon, Philippines, *nasutus* breeds from March to June with peak intensity in April and May. Repeat clutches are frequent, but normal second clutches, more rarely even third ones, appear to be regular at least at lower elevations in India and Pakistan. In Central Asia, only one clutch seems to be the rule, but in Kabul some pairs manage to fledge two broods a season. The same nest may be used twice in succession. The Long-tailed Shrike is mainly a tree-nester with a preference for thorny trees such as acacias or, when available, conifers as in eastern Anhui, China. The height of the nest above ground varies with habitat and human presence. In Central Asia and India, it is generally placed 3-5m up (range 1.5-10, exceptionally 24m). In Kabul, where the birds are often disturbed or killed by people, the shrikes nest 4-12m above the ground. During a study in Luzon, 46 nests were found at heights of 0.75-3m (mean 1.7m) in low leafy trees in the open or along hedges. In the Malay Peninsula *bentet* typically nests amongst creepers or ferns at heights of 0.9-3.5m from the ground. The nest, built by both sexes in about 6-8 days, is a rather bulky and untidy affair. Its outer diameter can measure up to 18cm in nominate *schach* and its height c. 10-12cm. Thorny twigs are readily used and it can have bits of rag, cotton wool and other rubbish in its exterior wall, which may be chiefly composed of flowering grasses. It is usually lined with fine grass fibres and is quite neat in the interior cap. In India, *erythronotus* lays between 3 and 6 eggs, usually 4 or 5; very occasionally nests with 7 or 8 eggs have been found in Central Asia. In Anhui, China, nominate *schach* has 4-6 eggs. There appears to be a marked geographical variation (but more data are needed to confirm this) as in Sri Lanka *caniceps* is said to lay 4 eggs whereas *bentet* generally lays 3 eggs in the Malay Peninsula and *stresemanni* only 2 in New Guinea. Incubation takes 14-16 days in *erythronotus* and is undertaken mostly or exclusively by the female. The young stay in the nest for 15-17 days. If disturbed, they can leave the nest when 13 days old. They stay in their parents' territory for one or two months.

The Long-tailed Shrike is regularly parasitised by cuckoos. Definite records exist for India where parasitism by three species – Common Cuckoo *Cuculus canorus*, Common Hawk-Cuckoo *C. varius*, and Pied Cuckoo *Clamator jacobinus* – has been recorded.

REFERENCES Ali & Ripley (1972), Baker (1924), Biswas (1950), Caldwell & Caldwell (1931), Cheng (1987), Coates (1990), Cramp & Perrins (1993), Deignan (1963), Dement'ev & Gladkov (1968), Dunajewski (1939), Galushin (1996), Glutz von Blotzheim & Bauer (1993), Harvey (1989), Herklots (1974), Etchécopar & Hüe (1970), Inskipp & Inskipp (1991), La Touche (1925-1930), Lefranc (1993), Lu & Chang (1993), van Marle & Voous (1988), Medway & Wells (1976), Meyer de Schauensee (1984), Panov (1983), Paz (1987), Rabor (1936), Rand (1960), Rand & Gilliard (1967), Reeb (1977), Roberts (1992), Shirihai & Golan (1994), Smythies (1960, 1986), Stresemann (1923), Wait (1931), Wildash (1968).

11   GREY-BACKED SHRIKE
Lanius tephronotus   Plate 5

Other name: Tibetan Shrike

IDENTIFICATION Length c. 21-23cm. Polytypic (two races). This mainly eastern Palearctic, high-elevation shrike is about the same size as the smaller races of the Long-tailed Shrike, but its tail is less graduated and

a little shorter. In the breeding season, range and different ecological requirements largely separate it from the very similar *erythronotus* and *tricolor* races of Long-tailed Shrike. The diagnostic features of *tephronotus* adults (sexes alike) are a dark lead-grey back and a chestnut-brown, not black, tail. In the nominate race, rufous is confined to the rump and the uppertail-coverts. The wings are black with no (or an insignificant) white primary patch. In juvenile plumage, *tephronotus* is rather dark reddish-brown whereas young *schach*, including *erythronotus*, is lighter, more reddish-grey. Under good conditions nominate *tephronotus* can be easily separated from *schach*; however, the race *lahulensis* poses problems (see below).

DESCRIPTION *L. t. tephronotus*
Adult Sexes similar in plumage. Facial mask black over lores, eyes, ear-coverts and very slightly on forehead, just over base of bill. Supercilium whitish, very faint or even absent. Upperparts dark lead-grey from forehead to lower back, rufous on rump and uppertail-coverts. Tail chestnut-brown tipped buffish; external pair of rectrices light brown. Wings black with no or very small white primary patch; most wing-coverts, secondaries and tertials fringed pale rufous. Underparts washed rufous, particularly on flanks; chin, throat and upper breast off-white. Undertail brownish-grey.
Juvenile Facial mask dark brown, already well marked, particularly on ear-coverts. Upperparts dark brown with fine vermiculations on head and coarser barring on mantle and back; rump and uppertail-coverts light rufous barred blackish. Tail rufous-brown. Wings dark brown. Underparts off-white, heavily barred all over except on upper throat. Undertail as in adult.
Bare parts Bill black in adults, horn-brown in juveniles. Legs dull black. Iris brown.

MEASUREMENTS (*tephronotus*) Wing 95-108; tail 102-109; bill (from skull) 20-23; tarsus 28-30 (India). Weight: 39-54, females perhaps slightly heavier on average (India; Ali & Ripley 1972).

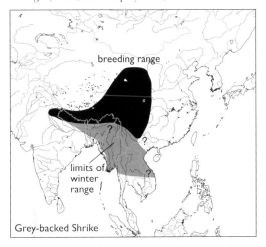

breeding range

limits of winter range

Grey-backed Shrike

DISTRIBUTION AND STATUS The range almost completely lies in the Palearctic region but includes the Himalayas. The species breeds from northern

Kashmir in India south-east through Himachal Pradesh, north-east Uttar Pradesh (?), Nepal, Sikkim, Bhutan and Arunachal Pradesh. The northern parts of its range lie in the mountainous areas of China from central and south-east Tibet (regions of Gyirong, Lhasa, Yadong, Nyalam, Bomi, Riwoqe and Zayu) north-east through south-east Qinghai to Gansu and Ningxia. From there, the limits progressively drop south-west through eastern Shaanxi, Sichuan, central Guizhou and south-east Yunnan. The northern limit appears to lie at c. 40°N in Gansu whereas the eastern boundary apparently passes just west of 110°E in Shaanxi.

GEOGRAPHICAL VARIATION Two races are recognised; however, *lahulensis* may be a stabilised hybrid population of Grey-backed and Long-tailed Shrikes (Panov 1983).

L. t. tephronotus (Nepal, Sikkim, Bhutan, Arunachal Pradesh and parts of China, including central and eastern Tibet) Described above.

L. t. lahulensis (northern India: northern Kashmir east to Ladakh in Kargil and Suru valleys and Himachal Pradesh near Lahul, Spiti, Kulu, etc. Also possibly western Tibet) Somewhat smaller than nominate (wing 93-103 against 95-108) with weaker, more slender bill. Upperparts paler grey with rufous extending up rump to hindmost scapulars. Usually a small but distinct white primary patch. Tail black as in Long-tailed Shrike. Looks very much like the race *caniceps* of that species (southern peninsular India and Sri Lanka) but distinctly darker on upperparts. The breeding ranges of *lahulensis* and *caniceps* do not overlap.

MOVEMENTS The species may be defined as a partial migrant. Most birds winter within their breeding range, but at lower elevations. Others spend the winter more to the south. The race *lahulensis*, in the western part of the range, appears to be mainly a resident or altitudinal migrant. Nominate *tephronotus* also descends to lower elevations or travels further south. In India, wintering birds regularly occur in the plains of Uttar Pradesh and Bihar, with stragglers reaching West Bengal. In Bangladesh the species is a local winter visitor, the first birds being recorded in mid-October and the last at the very beginning of May. In Nepal is mainly as an altitudinal migrant: summering chiefly between 2,745 and 4,575m, it winters between 275m and at least 2,560m with relatively few birds being seen below 365m; in the Kathmandu valley, most records are from October to March. In Burma, *tephronotus* is a winter visitor throughout, excluding Tenasserim. It is particularly common in the Kachim hills. The earliest and latest dates for the Myitkyina plains are 27 September and the first week of May, most birds having gone by mid-March. Chinese birds seem to winter chiefly within their breeding range, in the Red Basin of Sichuan for instance. At least some of the birds wintering in northern Thailand (Chiang Rai, Chaiya Prakan, Chiang Mai, Phrae) might, however, come from China. Other countries of South-East Asia where the Grey-backed Shrike occurs in winter are Vietnam, Laos and Cambodia, but few details are available.

MOULT Few details. A complete post-nuptial moult generally begins in September and appears to be completed in December for Indian birds. Birds in their second calendar year possibly perform a complete moult in March-April (in Hellmich 1968 and Ali & Ripley 1972, but confirmation needed).

VOICE The song, rather similar to that of the Long-tailed Shrike, is a beautiful subdued musical soliloquy, sustained for several minutes and interspersed with expertly mimicked calls of other birds. Harsh grating cries are typical of the species, which can become particularly noisy towards sunset.

HABITAT A high-elevation shrike which well merits its other common name of Tibetan Shrike. It nests up to at least 4,500m in Nepal and Yunnan (China). In Nepal, breeders become common from 2,700m upwards. In northern India, *lahulensis* breeds between 2,700 and 3,300m. The species needs forest clearings, plateau plains or mountain meadows dotted with small trees or fair-sized bushes. Open scrub at high altitudes, in the form of low thorny bushes for instance, may also be favoured: in southern Tibet, the species prefers the presence of *Rosa*, *Ribes*, *Berberis* or *Hippophaë salicifolia* bushes. The structure of its habitat is very similar to that of the Red-backed Shrike in Eurasia. In winter the species can be found at lower altitudes in valleys and plains. It can then be seen near human habitations, around hill cultivation and clearings, although in general it seems somewhat less tolerant of people than the Long-tailed Shrike (but see Habits).

HABITS The Grey-backed is less conspicuous than the Long-tailed Shrike, but like other *Lanius* it perches upright on exposed bushtops, telegraph wires, etc. It can be quite confiding but is highly territorial at all times of the year, occurring singly or in widely separated pairs. In Burma, a few wintering birds have been observed gathering at dusk to roost. Larders appear to be regular.

FOOD Very similar to that of other shrikes, particularly Long-tailed. Most prey items are insects: crickets, grasshoppers, beetles, caterpillars, etc. Small vertebrates are also taken: lizards, frogs, birds (particularly sickly or young ones), small rodents, etc.

BREEDING Migrant birds are back in their breeding territories from the beginning of May, but non-migrants may maintain their territories throughout the year. In Tibet, the breeding season is principally from the middle of May to the end of June. Eggs have been found there between the beginning of May and mid-August and it is possible, but not yet proven, that normal second broods can be raised even at these elevations. The nest is hidden in a small tree or bush (thorny ones such as *Berberis* sp. appearing to be favoured) at a height of generally c. 2m (1.5-8m). The tree or bush in which it is built can be in scrub-jungle, in a row of trees alongside a stream or irrigation canal, or more or less isolated. The bulky, rather untidy nest has an outer diameter of 13-20cm and an overall height of c. 8.5cm; it is almost invariably made of twigs and grass, the former often very thorny. It may have a good deal of sheep's wool or goats' hair matted in with the other material, plus all sorts of oddments when it is built near a village, such as scraps of rag. The number of eggs laid varies from 4 to 6. Incubation and fledgling periods are not known, but should be similar to those of Long-tailed Shrike.

REFERENCES Ali & Ripley (1972), Baker (1924), Biswas (1950, 1962), Cheng (1987), Deignan (1945, 1963), Delacour & Jabouille (1931), Dunajewski (1939), Harvey (1989), Hellmich (1968), Inskipp & Inskipp (1991), Mayr (1947), Meyer de Schauensee (1984), Olivier (1944), Rand & Fleming (1957), Roberts (1992), Smythies (1986), Stresemann *et al.* (1937), Vaurie (1972).

12   MOUNTAIN SHRIKE
Lanius validirostris   Plate 5

Other names: Strong-billed Shrike, Grey-capped Shrike

IDENTIFICATION Length c. 22.5cm. A rather large, little-known species with three races, all endemic to the Philippines, with a characteristic strong, heavy bill. The sexes are alike and very similar to the Grey-backed Shrike with their dark grey upperparts and dark brown wings and tail. The underparts are mainly grey-white except on the flanks, which are rufous. The only confusion species is the Long-tailed Shrike, represented in the Philippines by the race *nasutus*. It is about the same size as Mountain Shrike, but with a shallower bill and a longer, more graduated tail; its adults have a black, not grey, crown and some rufous on the lower back. The juveniles of both species are very similar, but the crown of Long-tailed is much more obviously mottled than that of Mountain.

DESCRIPTION *L. v. validirostris*
Adult male Facial mask black over lores, eyes and ear-coverts. Supercilium white, thin, but generally well marked, starting above the lores and extending well beyond the eyes. Forehead whitish over base of bill, grading into grey towards crown. Upperparts dark grey from forehead to uppertail-coverts. Rump and uppertail-coverts at least sometimes with faint traces of rufous. Tail dark brown, relatively short. Wings dark brown (no primary patch) fringed pale buff. Underparts grey-white, but with variable extent of rufous on flanks, undertail-coverts, vent and, to a lesser extent, breast; throat grey-white with very faint black markings on sides. Undertail white.
Adult female Similar to male, but averages slightly smaller (see Measurements). Underparts perhaps slightly browner.
Juvenile Not examined; supposed to be very similar to juvenile Grey-backed Shrike.
Bare parts Bill black. Legs dark brown. Iris dark brown.

MEASUREMENTS (*validirostris*) Wing 86-94 (mean 89.3) for 12 males and 85-88 (mean 86.5) for 6 females; tail 94-102 (mean 96.8) for 12 males and 91-93 (mean 92.0) for 6 females; bill (culmen) 17-19.5; tarsus c. 26. Weight: no data.

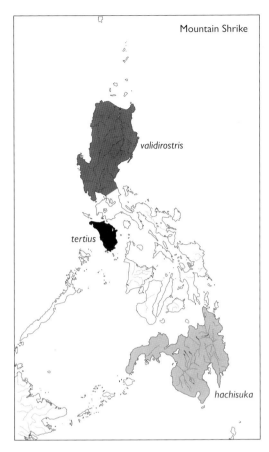

Mountain Shrike

validirostris

tertius

hachisuka

DISTRIBUTION AND STATUS Inhabits three of the major Philippine islands. In Luzon, it is confined to the Cordillera Central and Sierra Madre which run through the northern part of the island. It also occurs on Mindoro and on the large southern island, Mindanao. In the latter area, it is known from Mt Apo, Mt Malindang, Mt Katanglad and Civolig, Misamis Oriental. It is said to be common in appropiate habitats in Luzon. On Mt Cetaceo, in the Sierra Madre, it has been described as very common at 1,400-1,650m.

GEOGRAPHICAL VARIATION Three races are recognised, one for each inhabited island. The differences are slight and concern the colour of the underparts and the size. The race *tertius* is only known from the type series.
   L. v. validirostris (northern Luzon) Described above.
   L. v. tertius (Mindoro) Differs from nominate and the following race in being much smaller: wing-length of type: 83 and of female: 81; tail length of type: 90 (Salomonsen 1953). Its flanks and undertail-coverts are much deeper and darker cinnamon-rufous; its breast and abdomen are washed with pale rusty.
   L. v. hachisuka (Mindanao) Differs from nominate in having underparts suffused with cinnamon-rufous from below the throat over the whole

117

undersurface; this colour is richer and slightly darker than the flank colour of *validirostris*. It is rather similar in coloration to *tertius*, but distinctly larger.

MOVEMENTS Probably strictly resident; may undertake local altitudinal movements, but no information.

MOULT No information.

VOICE Song said to be similar to that of the Bull-headed Shrike. More information needed.

HABITAT Lives in a tropical region, but occurs at high elevations generally between 1,200-2,400m. It frequents open second growth, clearings and forest edges in oak and pine woods. It may also be found in scrubby grassland.

HABITS Little information.

FOOD Little information. The stomachs of seven birds collected in Luzon contained only insects, chiefly small and medium-sized beetles: Cerambycidae, Curculionidae, Brenthidae, Scarabaeidae, Lucanidae, Chrysomelidae. Many of these insects are associated with wood and extremely hard-bodied; the thick bill is possibly adapted for taking such animals.

BREEDING Little information. A pair was feeding juveniles on 15 May on Mount Cetaceo.

REFERENCES Danielsen *et al.* (1994), Delacour & Mayr (1946), Dickinson *et al.* (1991), duPont (1971), Morioka & Sakane (1979), Ripley (1949), Salomonsen (1953).

13 LESSER GREY SHRIKE
Lanius minor   Plate 6

IDENTIFICATION Length c. 20cm. A Eurasian shrike, generally considered polytypic (two races), intermediate in size between Woodchat and Great Grey. It looks very much like the latter species with its blue-grey upperparts and black wings with distinct white primary patch. Both sexes show a large black facial mask extending to the forehead, sometimes partially or even wholly grey in the generally slightly duller female, and their breast and flanks are washed pinkish. Young birds do not show these characters and are paler than adults (see also Description).

In its Eurasian breeding range, the only confusion species are the Great Grey and the Southern Grey Shrikes. Unlike the Lesser Grey Shrike, *excubitor* often has a fairly obvious white supercilium along the upper border of its facial mask and the white on its scapulars is very distinctly broader. Nominate *meridionalis*, confined to the Iberian peninsula and the south of France, can be particularly confusing as its underparts are also pinkish and it also displays a markedly smaller, white wing-patch on its otherwise black wings. It may be necessary to check structural features, especially when confronted with young birds. The Lesser Grey Shrike has a relatively short tail, long wings and a long primary extension. Its bill is rather 'finch-like', short and deep. It has thus a characteristic compact, stubby

profile, quite different from that of the longer-tailed (c. 2.5cm more) and longer-billed Southern Grey and Great Grey Shrikes. When perched, the Lesser Grey Shrike often adopts a more erect stance. It hovers more regularly than *excubitor* and *meridionalis* and its flight is less undulating, less 'woodpecker-like'. When seen in flight, its long pointed wings are fairly obvious. In the Middle East and in north-east Africa the main confusion species is the Southern Grey Shrike with several races (see under that species). The Lesser Grey Shrike is a passage migrant in East Africa, where there is a slight risk of confusion with the Grey-backed Fiscal, whose adults also have a broad black band on their foreheads but are about a third bigger with a much longer and diagnostically patterned tail.

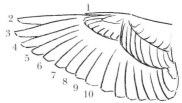

Lesser Grey Shrike *L. minor*

Great Grey Shrike *L. excubitor*

Wing outlines of Lesser Grey Shrike and Great Grey Shrike. Note differences in wing-shape and wing formula. In *minor* the first primary is very short, hardly as long as the longest primary covert; in *excubitor* it is distinctly longer. In *minor* the second primary is as long or almost so as the fourth primary which is not the case in *excubitor*, which has a distinctly rounder wing.

DESCRIPTION *L. m. minor*
Adult male Facial mask black over lores, eyes, ear-coverts and forehead up to 10-15mm from base of bill (so extending sometimes even to forecrown). Upperparts from crown to lower back ashy grey-blue, becoming slightly paler on rump and uppertail-coverts. Scapulars faintly whitish on outside. Tail black, fringed and tipped white except on central pair; T5 and T6 mainly or wholly white. Wings black with conspicuous, white patch on base of primaries; tertials, inner secondaries and fresh primaries tipped white. Underparts white, washed pinkish (mauve-pink) on breast and flanks. Undertail white.
Adult female Similar to male, generally somewhat duller (variable). Facial mask greyer or browner, particularly on forehead. Upperparts greyer, not so blue. Underparts paler, less pink in tone.
Juvenile Facial mask dusky brown, limited to lores and ear-coverts. Forehead whitish. Upperparts from crown

to mantle grey-brown; crown finely barred dark grey-brown; back with coarser bars and rump with few, faint bars. Scapulars grey-brown with pale edges. Tail as in adult, but duller with less white on outer tail feathers. Wings also duller with pale buff tips on flight feathers. Underparts off-white, rather faintly barred and only on sides of breast, flanks (sometimes) and undertail-coverts. Undertail white.

Bare parts Bill rather short, deep (somewhat bullfinch-like) and black or dark plumbeous-grey in adults, flesh-grey in juveniles. Legs plumbeous-grey or black-ish. Iris brown or dark brown.

MEASUREMENTS (*minor*) Wing 111-125 (usually 115-120); tail 84-94; bill (to skull) 19-23; tarsus 24-27. Weight 42-55 (mean c. 46).

DISTRIBUTION AND STATUS The breeding range is mainly limited to warmer parts of Eurasia with Mediterranean or continental types of climate. It is something over 6,000km from west to east, that is from north-east Spain (Catalonia) to the upper stretches of the rivers Ob and Irtysh in the Altai region. From north to south, it is about 2,200km at most. It extends north to about 55°N in European Russia and to about 54°N in Siberia, where it reaches the towns of Novosibirsk and Omsk. The southern border, from west to east, roughly follows the northern coast of the Mediterranean, then crosses Syria, northern Iraq, northern Iran, north-east Afghanistan, Tajikistan and the northern fringes of the Tien Shan between China and Kazakhstan. The westernmost points reached by this species, now very rare in western Europe, lie in Spain where two areas are still regularly inhabited. One of these largely coincides with the Parque Nacional de los Aiguamolls de l'Empordà in Catalonia, near the town of Castello d'Empuriès; the other, much larger, embraces the lower courses of the Segre and Cinca rivers in the Ebro basin, roughly at 41°31'N and 0°21'E. About 100km north-east of the breeding area in the Parque Nacional lies one of the two last strongholds of the species in France, between the towns of Narbonne and Béziers; about 40km further north-east, the species also still regularly nests just west of Montpellier. Occasional nesting occurs elsewhere in the Languedoc-Roussillon region and in Provence. In Italy, the Lesser Grey Shrike is more widespread, but now also restricted, in relatively small numbers, to certain areas including Sicily (see detailed map in Meschini and Frugis 1993). In Austria, the Lesser Grey Shrike is confined to a tiny area near Lake Neusiedl and the Hungarian border; it is still fairly widespread in eastern European countries, in the Kiskunsag and Hortobagy areas in Hungary, in the Dobruja plain of Romania, etc.

The population trends for the last 150 years are relatively well known for western Europe. In the 19th century, the Lesser Grey Shrike was a fairly common bird in southern and central Europe. Its breeding range extended well into France, Germany and even the Benelux countries. Locally, it was regarded as the most numerous shrike, particularly in the 1880s. After World War I a marked contraction of range began. Two

rather modest increases occurred in the 1930s and 1960s. Since then, the decline has again been very sharp. The last regular breeding in Germany dates back to 1976 and the species has also disappeared from Belgium (1930), Luxembourg (1946) and Switzerland (1972). It has also become rare and localised in Italy and even more so in Austria (see above). In recent decades, the range has begun contracting in eastern Europe, particularly in Hungary, Poland and Slovakia. The Lesser Grey Shrike disappeared from the Czech Republic between 1985 and 1989; it was common throughout the country at the end of last century.

Recent estimates of breeding populations (in pairs) exist for some countries: Austria: 5-10 (1988), Belarus: 50-200 (1990), Bulgaria: 1,000-10,000 (1990), France c. 50 (1996), Greece: 2,000-3,000 (1990), Hungary: 5,000-8,000 (1990), Italy: 1,000-2,000 (1990), Lithuania: 10-20 (1985-1988), Moldova: 10,000-15,000 (1988), Poland: 10-50 (1988), Romania: 30,000-70,000 (1988), Russia: 10,000-100,000 (1988), Slovakia: 400-600 (1994), Slovenia: 20-30 (1988), Spain: 45-90 (1995), Turkey 10,000-100,000 (1988), Ukraine: 3,000-3,500 (1986).

GEOGRAPHICAL VARIATION Very slight, although two races are often recognised (e.g. Vaurie 1955). Recent Russian literature (e.g. Stepanyan 1978) and also Roselaar (1995) consider the species monotypic.

L. m. minor (western part of breeding range: from Spain to Russia and including southern areas: Italy, the Balkan peninsula and Turkey) Described above.

L. m. turanicus (eastern part of breeding range: Siberia east of the Ural Mountains, Iran and Central Asia) Adults hardly different from nominate *minor*, although perhaps slightly paler. Juvenile and first-year *turanicus* are somewhat more sandy-brown than the greyer *minor* (see Clancey 1980).

HYBRIDS Two adult hybrids between this species and the Red-backed Shrike were described in Germany in 1844 and another, also in Germany, in June 1969.

MOVEMENTS All populations are migratory. The Lesser Grey Shrike is a long-distance migrant which winters in southern Africa. The winter quarters mainly cover the extreme south of Angola, Namibia, Botswana, parts of southern Mozambique and South Africa (as far as Damaraland, Transvaal and Natal). Individual birds may, however, be seen outside that area in January or February. A few have even been observed at that time in western Africa (Gabon, etc.) or in the Arabian Peninsula. It is notable that the main wintering area is much smaller than the breeding range: about 1.5-1.75 million km² against some 8 million km². It chiefly lies in semi-arid areas within the 600mm isohyet (see Dowsett 1971).

European birds undertake a loop migration; in spring they pass more to the east than in autumn. The post-nuptial migration takes them towards Greece and its islands; they are then very common on the islands of the Aegean Sea and on Crete, but also further east on Cyprus. Africa is entered on a narrow front in Egypt, roughly between the border with Libya and the Suez

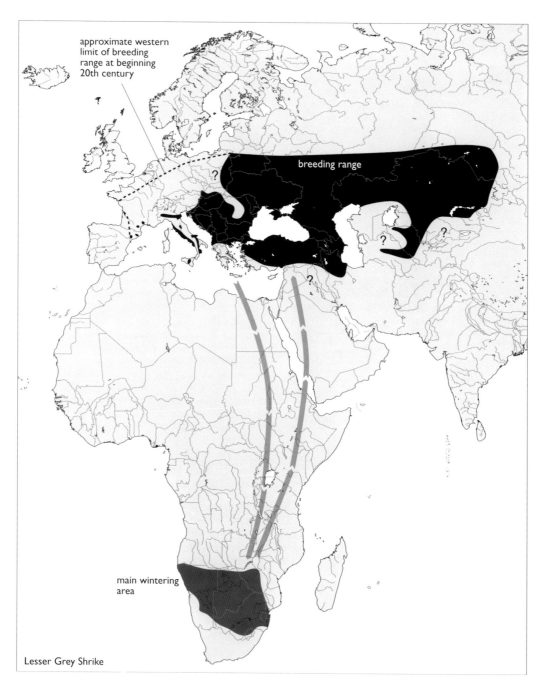

approximate western
limit of breeding
range at beginning
20th century

breeding range

main wintering
area

Lesser Grey Shrike

Canal. There are few observations to the west of Libya. The species is a common autumn migrant in northeast Sudan, Eritrea, eastern Chad and Zaïre although large forest areas are avoided. In spring, the birds head northwards on a more easterly route, the Rift Valley seeming to act as a huge corridor. Thus in Zimbabwe and Malawi the species can be numerous on passage and it is also then much commoner in Tanzania, Kenya and Ethiopia than in autumn. Sudan and Egypt are now almost completely avoided and the passage is strong on the Arabian Peninsula and continues towards the Levant and over Turkey, Cyprus, Greece (no observations at that time in Crete) into Europe. Birds of the east of the range travel, both ways, over Iran and the Arabian Peninsula. However, they might also follow looping routes in Africa as almost the only spring observations are from Somalia and almost the only autumn observations are from Sudan.

In Europe post-nuptial movements begin as early as the end of July or the start of August. They reach a peak towards the end of August and very few birds are seen in the breeding range after mid-September. Eastern birds also leave early and, in August, may be seen passing over high mountains up to 3,400m. High concentrations occur locally in August, as in Greece or Turkey. The first birds turn up in Egypt at the beginning of August and Lesser Grey Shrikes can be seen there until the beginning of October (late November). The earliest of the rare autumn migrants recorded in Kenya appeared on 15 October and the last was seen on 29 November. Zimbabwe is reached from the last ten days of October, but most birds arrive in mid-November. The same dates hold for other southern African countries. Spring migration starts towards the end of February. Almost all birds have disappeared from the winter quarters at the end of March, but a few may linger on, like the one seen in Zimbabwe on 1 May. Passage in East Africa is heavy all through April, but the first birds may appear there from the middle of March. In the Suez Canal area, there are normally no observations before mid-March; in Israel numbers are far smaller than in autumn with a passage period 12 April-18 June and a main peak in the middle of May. In Cyprus, early birds are seen at the end of March, but the passage peaks at the end of April and at the beginning of May. The first birds arrive on their European breeding grounds in the last ten days of April (earliest known date 15 April in Dalmatia) but most turn up towards mid-May.

Like the Woodchat, the Lesser Grey Shrike is a rare vagrant to north-west Europe. It rarely occurs in the Netherlands with only 12 observations between 1900 and 1968 and 22 between 1969 and 1987 when there was much heavier observer coverage. For Denmark, where the first bird was identified in 1828, only 36 observations were known up to 1990. The Lesser Grey Shrike is also rare in Sweden, with an average of two or three birds seen per year; at the end of the 1980s, there had been 120 records with 105 observations from May to July and only 15 from August to October; most shrikes were recorded in the southern third of the country, but four were found as far north as c. 64°N. In Norway, only two birds were known up to 1971. An average of two birds are seen per year in Finland where there were 41 records between 1960 and 1983. The Lesser Grey Shrike is a regular but rare vagrant to Great Britain with an average of three birds per year; there were 32 records before 1957 and 119 from 1958 to 1994. Most birds (60%) are seen in spring and particularly in the first ten days of June, with most observations coming from the south and east coasts and from the Shetland Islands. There are three records for Ireland. The Lesser Grey Shrike may also turn up in some African areas which normally lie outside its regular migration routes (see Dowsett 1971). A few observations are thus known from western Africa and even from North Africa, more particularly from Tunisia where a juvenile was collected on 2 July 1914 at Sfax (from a local brood?) and a bird was seen on 14 November 1993 near Menzel Bourguiba.

MOULT Very similar to that of the Red-backed Shrike. The post-juvenile moult, limited to head and body feathers, starts barely a week after fledging when tail and flight feathers are not yet fully grown yet. The post-juvenile moult is completed when the birds are 10-11 weeks old, that is in the second half of August or at the beginning of September. First-winter birds have brownish-grey upperparts which retain a highly variable amount of (and sometimes no) feathers with dark subterminal bars; their underparts are tinged cream. These birds undergo a complete moult in Africa and are then similar to adults. A few first-summer birds, back in spring on the Eurasian breeding grounds, have, however, been found with one or two unmoulted, worn and bleached secondaries and/or tertials. Adults can have a partial body-moult, sometimes involving one or more tertials, when still on the breeding grounds. It is probably suspended during autumn migration. A complete moult takes place in the winter quarters between mid-December and mid-March (early April).

VOICE The song, sometimes lasting 15 minutes or more, is a babbling chatter, generally rather weak (courtship song) except when given by unpaired males. It contains typical harsh shrike-like notes but also excellent mimicry of a variety of birds and even mammals (dogs for instance). It can be heard even in the southern Africa winter quarters in March and April, just before the start of migration. The most frequent and characteristic call is a *kerrib-kerrib* often used in territory defence including against humans. The warning call near the nest is *tscheck tscheck* similar to that of other shrikes. Attacks on enemies can be accompanied by loud grating *tr-tr-tr-trrr*.

HABITAT The primeval breeding habitat of the Lesser Grey Shrike was probably the thinly forested or open steppe dotted with copses and/or isolated trees. Thus in Europe the species may have been long confined to the steppe zones of the south-east. Forest clearance and fragmentation, combined with favourable climatic conditions, enabled it to colonise other areas. This shrike needs hot, dry, continental or Mediterranean summers and is primarily, even if not entirely, a bird of lowlands or hilly country. This is (or was) particularly true in western Europe. In Germany the species was reported nesting up to 460m; in Sicily pairs were found at an elevation of 570m and in Slovakia some populations nest on relatively steep south-facing slopes up to 850m. The last colonies known in France and Spain occur near sea-level. In Russia, in areas with hot summers, this shrike may be found in mountains up to 1,500m and in Kazakhstan even up to 2,200m. In August, eastern birds are sometimes recorded in mountains at elevations between 2,300 and 3,400m. The species has adapted well to cultivated areas dominated by non-intensive mixed farming. Foraging areas usually consist of grasslands, especially with low vegetation and large areas of bare soil (up to 90% of the territory surface for a few pairs in the south of France). They may include melon, beetroot, potato, tobacco fields and, particularly, vineyards, etc. In such cultivated steppe-like areas, trees may be rare, but they are always present as they are needed for the bird's nest, which is apparently very rarely built in a bush (only one possible record known for western Europe). The species uses lines of trees growing along roads, cart-tracks, ditches, etc. Orchards may also be favoured, provided the trees are well spaced (5-15 trees/ha). In Russia, the species may be found in shelter-belt woods crossing open landscapes. It sometimes occurs in parks. On passage, it may appear in less typical habitats.

Most of the southern African winter range is in semi-arid areas within the 600mm isohyet. In Botswana, Kalahari region is locally densely populated. There the Lesser Grey Shrike inhabits mainly dry acacia thornbush country. It also occurs in dry open mopane woodland *Colophospermum mopane* and in open acacia parkland.

HABITS The Lesser Grey Shrike generally perches conspicuously in very open or relatively open habitats. Where several pairs nest in a loose colony at the beginning of the breeding season, the characteristic display-flight attracts attention. The male ascends quite high with shallow wing-beats before gliding down with wings and tail fully spread. These flights, which can also take place after a potential nest-predator has been driven away, may be accompanied by the typical *kerrib-kerrib* calls and precede the song. The Lesser Grey Shrike is a relatively gregarious species. Pairs often nest close together, sometimes in neighbouring trees, even within 25m, but generally they are separated by 100-150m. In Spain, two occupied nests have been found in the same tree. Eight pairs have bred along 1km of road in Germany, seven pairs on 1km^2 in southern France, up to ten pairs per km^2 in Moldova, and four nests in a 1ha orchard in Slovakia. Solitary pairs are, however, no exceptions. In the wintering quarters too, the species may be found in loose groups of up to ten individuals, but most birds are solitary and territorial. Site-fidelity was proved when the species still nested in south-west Germany (Hantge 1957). From one year to the next, nearly one third of the adults, eight in all, were located between 0 and 3km from their previous year's territory. Young birds appear to be much less faithful to their natal site but, again in Germany, a one-year-old female was found nesting 200m from the nest where she was raised. On passage, a great number of these birds may be seen in the same area at the same time, but such gatherings are probably largely due to chance as the species is a solitary night migrant. During the breeding season, these shrikes take most of their food within 150m of the nest, but they will sometimes fly as far as 600m. What is remarkable in this species is that several adults may forage over the same field without apparent conflict. The hunting territories of adjacent pairs can thus partly overlap. In Slovakia the average size of the foraging territory was 3.3ha (range: 1.9-5.2ha for n = 12). Loose associations with other breeding birds are not rare, even sometimes with falcons nesting in the same tree: Kestrel *Falco tinnunculus* in Hungary, north-east Spain and southern France, Red-footed Falcon *F. vespertinus* in Hungary. Like other shrikes, *Lanius minor* uses the sit-and-wait foraging technique. It particularly likes to perch 2-4m high and uses a variety of lookouts: electric wires, fence-

posts, low branches of trees, agricultural machinery left in fields, scarecrows, etc. This steppe bird also very often hovers like a Kestrel, and much more so than any other European shrike: 10 to 30 seconds at a time and at a height generally of 2-6m. It may also hop on the ground like a wheatear *Oenanthe* sp., particularly in wet weather. Most insects are taken on the ground, but in fine weather many are also caught in the air, particularly rather big slow-flying ones like beetles *Melolontha*, etc. or bumble-bees *Bombus* sp. It often hunts well into dusk: attacks on small bats *Pipistrellus pipistrellus* have been reported in Kazakhstan. Impaling of prey is rare; very few insects have been found at larders in Europe, but small vertebrates, rarely taken, have of course to be impaled for dismemberment.

FOOD The Lesser Grey Shrike is almost exclusively insectivorous, much more so than the only slightly larger Great Grey Shrike. Beetles and grasshoppers are taken in great numbers. Bumble-bees and bugs (Hemiptera) often come next in importance. Not surprisingly, ground-dwelling Coleoptera and particularly Carabidae are favoured. Pellet analyses in Germany have shown that many Silphidae, Curculionidae and Scarabaeidae are also caught. In a central Slovakian study the nestling diet (identified prey = 346) was dominated by crickets (38%), grasshoppers (26.4%), beetles (19.2%) and caterpillars (14.2%, mainly Noctuidae); average body-length of prey was 22.7mm (see Kristin 1995). Snails, earthworms and small vertebrates (voles, particularly *Microtus arvalis*, small lizards, fish) are occasionally taken. Birds very rarely fall victim to this shrike. There are of course exceptions, exhausted migrants for instance like a Quail *Coturnix coturnix* in the United Arab Emirates which was seen being flushed out from some grass onto a road and then struck down. Fruit has also been recorded, particularly cherries and figs, but definite proof seems to be lacking.

BREEDING Males and females appear at practically the same time on the breeding territories, where pair formation, apparently very rapid, has been witnessed; nevertheless many observers think that it may also take place on migratory halts or even in the winter quarters. Laying may exceptionally begin at the end of April, but generally not before mid-May. In most areas and in most years, it peaks at the end of May and in the first two weeks of June. Replacement clutches are produced until the end of June. A second normal clutch is exceptional; it has been recorded once in France (outcome unknown) and possibly occurred in Poland. The Lesser Grey Shrike is a tree-nester. The nest, built by both sexes, is generally hidden at a good height (2.5-20m) in fruit-trees, poplars, acacias, elms, etc., very rarely in a conifer. It can be against the trunk, on a lateral branch or, often, in the crown. It has sometimes been found in an old nest of Carrion Crow *Corvus corone* or Magpie *Pica pica*. It is a rather loose structure with an outer diameter of c. 15cm and an overall height of c. 9cm. Made of twigs, rootlets, grass, etc., it contains hair and, sometimes, feathers; man-made materials such as string left in fields are readily taken. Nests regularly include green plant stems of aromatic species with flowers attached: *Artemisia, Anthemis, Gnaphalium, Mentha*, etc. Last century, a German birdwatcher even claimed that he could locate the nests by smell! Five and more often 6 eggs are laid in first attempts and usually 4 or 5 in replacements (range 3-9). No geographical variation in clutch-size is known. Incubation lasts 15-16 days and the fledging period normally 16-18 days. The young stay with the parents for at least another two weeks.

The species is very rarely parasitised by the Common Cuckoo *Cuculus canorus*; a record exists for north-east France of a a nest with three shrike's eggs and one cuckoo's.

REFERENCES Andrews (1995), Bara (1995), Bechet, *et al.* (1995), Chacon (1996), Clancey (1980b), Cramp & Perrins (1993), Delprat (1994), Dowsett (1971), Glutz von Blotzheim & Bauer (1993), Gorman (1996), Hantge (1957), Harris & Arnott (1988), Herremans (1994), Horvath (1959), Kristin (1991,1995), Lefranc (1978, 1993, 1995b), Meschini & Frugis (1993), Niehuis (1968), Panov (1983), Roselaar (1995), Shirihai (1995), Stepanyan (1978), Streich & Sargatal (1995), Tucker and Heath (1994), Western (1992).

---

14 LOGGERHEAD SHRIKE
Lanius ludovicianus   Plate 7

Other name: Migrant Shrike

IDENTIFICATION Length c. 22cm. A polytypic North American shrike, very similar to the Great Grey and Southern Grey Shrike (particularly its North African race *algeriensis*). Its upperparts are dark grey or 'deep mouse' grey. A narrow, dull white supercilium is often apparent just over the black facial mask. The latter, continuous across the base of the upper mandible, also slightly extends just above the eyes. These details, visible from a short distance only, are diagnostic. The underparts are usually entirely white, sometimes washed greyish, possibly more often in females, which might also, more regularly, show traces of vermiculation. The juvenile shows brownish-grey upperparts, is paler and fairly distinctly barred overall.

The confusion species is, of course, the Great Grey Shrike with its two very similar North American races *borealis* and *invictus*. Outside the breeding season it may be seen in Loggerhead country: almost all over the northern part of the States where the two species are sometimes found together in the same areas, occasionally even in such northern regions as Michigan and Ohio. The Great Grey Shrike is slightly larger with paler, more silvery upperparts. More important, and quite obvious with a little experience, its head appears longer and larger in proportion to body size. This is due to its longer, heavier and more strongly hooked bill. The white supercilium is often more conspicuous and the black facial mask narrower; it does not extend above the eyes and the feathering just above the bill is generally whitish, not black as in *ludovicianus*. The barring of the underparts can also be useful: as a rule

it is heavier, more distinct in *excubitor*, even in post-juvenile birds. Young Great Greys, brownish-looking and with heavily vermiculated breast and flanks, are easy to identify.

A slight risk of confusion exists with the Northern Mockingbird *Mimus polyglottos*, which is only slightly larger and shows an overall similar colour pattern; it has, however, a slimmer bill and a different head pattern with no well-defined facial mask. Particular caution is needed at a distance with birds in flight; the shrike has much darker wings and tail and a smaller white wing-patch.

DESCRIPTION *L. l. ludovicianus*
Adult male Facial mask black over base of bill (very thin line), lores, just over and under eyes and on ear-coverts. Supercilium dull white, narrow and poorly indicated. Upperparts slate-grey from forehead to lower back, becoming somewhat paler, more mid-grey on rump and uppertail-coverts; scapulars white, forming a conspicuous white V on back. Tail black, fringed white; rectrices tipped white except central pair; T6 with outer web completely white; outer web of T5 can also be entirely white. Wings black with a distinct white primary patch; the four inner primaries, secondaries and notably tertials are tipped white. Underparts off-white, sometimes washed pale or light grey on sides and flanks, breast showing occasionally faint, poorly defined vermiculations. Undertail white, tipped blackish.
Adult female Very similar to male. Underparts possibly more often washed with grey and more regularly showing traces of vermiculation. At least in certain areas, female slightly smaller and with browner primaries than male. A completely reliable method of determining sex in the field, based on external characters, does not appear to exist.
Juvenile Facial mask dark brown. Upperparts brownish-grey and finely vermiculated from forehead to nape; mantle and back rather olive-grey with generally faint, indistinct vermiculations; rump and uppertail-coverts light drab or clay colour, finely vermiculated. Scapulars buff-white and vermiculated. Tail black, fringed white and tipped cinnamon-buff. Wings black with white primary-patch already noticeable; four inner primaries with progressively broader, whitish tips; secondaries and tertials tipped whitish or cinnamon-buff; greater coverts distinctly tipped cinnamon-buff. Underparts brownish-grey on breast, sides and flanks, which are heavily vermiculated; chin, throat, part of belly and undertail-coverts off-white; dusky bars often appear on sides of throat. Undertail white.
Bare parts Bill long, thick and black in breeding adults, becoming rather dark brown in autumn; in young birds with various shades of brown and often a flesh colour at base of mandibles. Legs black. Iris brown.

MEASUREMENTS (*ludovicianus*) Wing 88-106 (mean c. 97); tail 86-104 (mean c. 96); tarsus c. 27; bill (culmen) 10.5-12.5. Weight: mean c. 56 for 129 Canadian birds presumably of race *excubitorides* (Collister and Wicklum 1996); mean c. 48 (range 35-58.5) for 105 birds from Florida possibly of race *miamensis* (Yosef 1996).

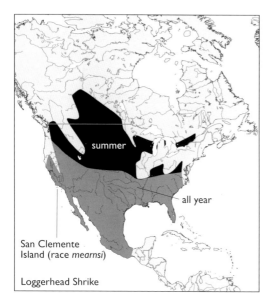

summer

all year

San Clemente
Island (race *mearnsi*)

Loggerhead Shrike

DISTRIBUTION AND STATUS The breeding range entirely lies in North America and includes some southern parts of Canada, almost the entire USA except the north-eastern states and some large unsuitable areas in the Rocky Mountains and further west in the Cascade Range. The species also nests in most of Mexico including Baja California. From west to east the northern limit lies at c. 48°N in Washington, where a rather isolated population occurs. Further east the limit runs through south-east Alberta, central Saskatchewan and south-west Manitoba. In Alberta in the 1950s the species nested as far north as Fairview at 56°04'N. Farther east the limit drops sharply south-east so that the Loggerhead Shrike has become very rare in Minnesota, Wisconsin, Michigan, Ohio, south-east Ontario and southern Quebec. In the north-eastern USA, breeding has become exceptional, but is still regular in North Carolina. From there the limit follows the Atlantic and Gulf coasts south and east to Mexico, crossing central Oaxaca, Guerrero, eastern Colima and south-west Jalisco, then turning north up the Pacific coast to Washington state. In the west, the range includes some California and Baja California islands.

The distribution and abundance of the Loggerhead Shrike have undergone significant changes over the last two hundred years. In the course of the 19th century, the species gradually expanded into the Great Lakes region, New England and eastern Canada. The populations were apparently at their highest level at the start of the 20th century and up to the 1920s when declines began to be obvious in the Great Lakes region, although the species was still doing well in Quebec where up to 1970 it seems to have extended its breeding range northwards. It even bred at Rimouski which lies at 48°26'N, c. 535km north-east of Montreal. However, anecdotal accounts from the 1940s reveal that the Loggerhead Shrike was then declining throughout the north-eastern portion of its breeding range. This negative trend was confirmed by the data of the

North American Breeding Bird Survey, set up in 1966. Between 1966 and 1993 the species declined at an average rate of 2.9% per year. Average rates of regional decline varied from 2.5% to 3.4% annually. These declines were prevalent in most states. It appears that only Texas, Colorado, Louisiana, Montana and South Dakota have stable nesting populations. In Ontario, the Loggerhead Shrike populations are now concentrated mainly near the southern edge of the Canadian Shield; it was estimated that there were fewer than 75 pairs in 1992. In Quebec, where previous populations probably totalled several thousand pairs, it was estimated that in 1993 there were at most 10 pairs. Further south, in Wisconsin, the shrike has been experiencing an alarming decline since the mid-1950s and in 1979 was added to the state's list of threatened species. In Michigan, only nine confirmed breeding pairs were found between 1983 and 1988; the map published in the 1991 atlas shows that the distribution pattern in the 1980s was similar to the historic one, but in drastically lower numbers. The atlas for Ohio was also published in 1991; the statewide population was estimated at 10-20 pairs. The Loggerhead Shrike has virtually disappeared from the other north-eastern states. Surprisingly, two nests were found in Pennsylvania in 1992; no nest had been recorded there since 1937. The atlas of New York state (1988) says that the shrike is one of the seven birds listed as endangered, although formerly it was a fairly common breeding species in western and central New York; the atlas only reveals three records, all in Orleans County. The Loggerhead Shrike has always been a rare breeder in Vermont; the 1985 atlas mentions a nesting pair in 1977 and another in 1978; no definite record exists for the period 1979-1983. Towards the end of last century, breeding took place even in Nova Scotia with a probable breeding record in 1942 and a confirmed one in 1969.

GEOGRAPHICAL VARIATION Complex. The classification of races is based on sometimes slight differences in coloration and morphometrics. The standard work was for a long time Miller (1931), who suggested that the wing-chord to tail-length ratio (WC:TL) was an important variable for the identification of subspecies. Rand (1960) lists ten of the eleven races recognised by Miller and adds *miamensis* from southern Florida, described in 1933. The differences, if any, between a few of the 'established' races are very slight indeed. The situation is all the more problematic because birds inside a resident population may show relatively large individual variations in both coloration and size. These points have already been stressed and the following paragraphs heavily draw on the revision in Phillips (1986). See also Haas (1987) and Collister and Wicklum (1996); the latter think that significant variation in WC:TL ratios within populations precludes its use in correctly identifying subspecies of Loggerhead Shrike. Eight races are listed below, but undoubtedly the subject needs further research.

L. l. ludovicianus (south-eastern USA from southern Louisiana and maybe adjacent Texas, eastwards and northwards, east of the Appalachians, to central-north Carolina and possibly central Virginia, south to central Florida) Described above. The contrast is stronger than in northern races between the dark upperparts, including rump, and the mainly white underparts. The bill is heavy.

L. l. migrans (now isolated populations in the north-east of the range in Michigan, southern Ontario and Quebec where very rare; otherwise from south-east Manitoba east to the Atlantic Coast and south to eastern Texas and central Louisiana north-east to western North Carolina and Virginia) May average slightly paler on upperparts than nominate, with a darker, greyer wash on underparts and a smaller bill. Included in *mexicanus* by Phillips (1986).

L. l. mexicanus (from eastern Washington in the north, south to southern California and Mexico and east to the Great Plains) Rather dark above, but colour of rump and uppertail-coverts variable; it may be mid-grey, pale grey or white. Underparts generally less white, more greyish than in nominate. Bill slender as in *excubitorides*. Includes *gambeli* and *nelsoni* (see Miller 1931, Phillips 1986).

L. l. excubitorides (the race of the Great Plains; from central Alberta and central Saskatchewan south to about Sonora in central California and to southern Texas, to about Corpus Christi; west to north-eastern Idaho) Upperparts distinctly paler grey than in other races, except the following; on average more white in plumage than in other northern subspecies on anterior part of forehead, above dark eye-patch (often a fairly prominent supercilium) and on lower rump and uppertail-coverts. Includes *nevadensis* and *sonoriensis* (see Miller 1931).

L. l. miamensis (southern Florida, except Keys; north to about Palm Beach and Fort Myers area) Upperparts paler than in any other race, at least in females. Averages smaller than *excubitorides*, but bill usually longer and heavier as in the darker *ludovicianus* (see Rand 1957 for further details).

L. l. anthonyi (islands off south-west California: Santa Rosa, Santa Cruz, Anacapa and Santa Catalina) Upperparts even darker than in nominate; scapulars with less white; rump and uppertail-coverts pale grey; less white on tail and primaries than in nominate.

L. l. mearnsi (San Clemente Island off south-west California) Upperparts even somewhat darker grey than in *anthonyi* and with equally little white in tail; rump area, however, whiter, less grey; scapulars as white as in *mexicanus*. Underparts generally paler than in *anthonyi*. Bill usually shorter than in mainland races and only slightly curved or hooked at tip. A recent genetic study has shown substantial genetic differentiation between this race and two other coastal southern Californian subspecies (Mundy and Woodruff 1996).

L. l. grinnelli (San Diego area in south-west California, south to at least 30°N and in Baja California except Gulf coast, desert and islands) The darkest of the Pacific mainland races, with very little or no white on anterior part of forehead and no or a very slight white supercilium; also has the least amount of white tipping on tail. Differs from *mexicanus* in darker grey back and less white in primaries, on tip of inner secondaries and on rump area, which is largely or entirely grey; the underparts are also darker, greyer particularly on breast and flanks.

MOVEMENTS A partial migrant, northern populations being largely migratory while southern ones are resident. It appears that birds nesting in areas with a relatively extended snow cover, 10-30 days per year, are forced to move south. The winter range lies mainly south of 40°N. Ringing recoveries indicate that populations east of the Rockies migrate partly or wholly to the south-eastern states for the winter; thus birds ringed in Alberta and Saskatchewan have been recovered in Missouri, Texas and Oklahoma (see map in Burnside 1987); the longest distance travelled by one of these birds was 2,554km. Not much is known about the movements of populations nesting west of the Rockies.

In autumn, migratory birds leave their breeding grounds between September and November; they are back between (early) mid-March and late April. In Ontario, birds can be seen until mid-September, occasionally until late December; they are back, as a rule, early in April (late February). In Wisconsin, nearly all the birds have left by 15 September; the earliest known arrival date in that state is 17 March, but birds generally only appear during a warm spell on or soon after 25 March, mainly between 5 and 15 April, and migration may still be in progress in May. In Michigan, the few remaining birds arrive by early April and depart from early August to late September. In Illinois, autumn migration apparently begins as early as July or August; birds may be seen until mid-October and the last exceptional observation comes from 17 November; for that state a few average spring arrival dates are as follows: 30 March near Chicago (seven years); 18 March at Urbana (20 years) and 21 March in Sangamon County (14 years).

Vagrants have been encountered outside the normal breeding and wintering ranges in Guatemala in December 1979, and on the islands of Grand Bahama, Great Exuma, Andros and, more surprisingly, in Bermuda.

MOULT The post-juvenile moult begins when the birds are about 40 days old, that is c. 20 days after fledging, when their rectrices are fully grown. It is a partial moult affecting the body feathers but sometimes also, unlike the Great Grey Shrike, a varying number of inner secondaries, outer primaries and even part or all of the rectrices. Moulting young birds can be found from late April (in the south of the range) to late November, but for a given individual it appears to last about three-and-a-half months (see Miller 1928 for details). Birds in their first-winter plumage are already very similar in coloration to older birds whatever the number of retained juvenile feathers; the most reliable criterion for identifying them are some retained, buff-tipped, inner primary-coverts. In February-March both these and adult birds undergo a very partial body moult, which has been considered as little more than sporadic feather replacements with, however, a 'freshening' of the normally white throat.

Adult shrikes, including first-summer birds, undergo a complete moult which may start immediately after the fledging of the young; the first primaries are generally lost as early as the beginning of July; most birds have probably changed all their feathers towards mid-October. The mean duration of the adult moult for an individual is apparently a little less than three months; it is thus somewhat more rapid than the post-juvenile moult.

VOICE The song consists of repeated double- and triple-note calls or trills, occasionally mixed with warbled notes which render it somewhat more melodic. The notes are varied in rhythm, pitch and quality. It is not unlike the songs of the Great Grey and Southern Grey Shrikes (more comparative studies needed) but apparently includes no mimicry. A common screech or call-note consists of from four to ten or more harsh forceful utterances of progressively diminishing intensity, the first notes slightly higher-pitched and shorter than the terminal notes. During courtship displays this screech may become more metallic. A sharp call which has been transcribed as *bzeek, bzeek* is heard when a possible conspecific intruder or a potential nest predator is in view; it can accompany an ensuing chase.

HABITAT Mainly a bird of temperate climates, but also occurring in subtropical and even desert climatic zones. Subarctic and harsh mountainous types of climate are largely avoided. The Loggerhead Shrike, as a rule, breeds in lowland plains or on gently sloping hills, although it may do so around farms in higher mountains; generally, however, it stays below an elevation of c. 2,000m (locally up to 2,800m in Mexico). It occurs in semi-open country with areas of short grass and bare soil dotted with fairly widely spaced, often spiny shrubs and low trees. It is thus found in various types of relatively flat landscapes showing a wide variety of plant associations. In many regions, its presence is correlated with agricultural land characterised by a high percentage of grazed pastures and grasslands rich in perches such as shrubs, fences and wires. It also readily nests in orchards, hedgerows bordering fields, marginal or abandoned farmland with scattered hawthorn shrubs, woodland edges, etc. Its habitat may comprise residential lawns, golf courses, cemeteries, mowed roadsides, etc. In the western United States, it is also associated with semi-arid sagebrush areas, desert scrub and pinyon-juniper woodlands. On San Clemente Island, the race *mearnsi* inhabits washes, ravines and mesas with either scattered tall bushes such as toyon and wild cherry or low thorny scrub and cactus patches.

A detailed study of nesting habitat in north-central California has shown that within 100m of shrike nests, short grass habitats such as pastures, hay fields and residential lawns predominated, comprising, on average, more than 80% of the area (see Gawlik and Bildstein 1990 for details). Another study of habitat in the Upper Midwest in Minnesota revealed that the Loggerhead Shrike nested in thirteen different tree species in the study area, the most frequently used being those that had a very shrubby or bushy growth form. Most nests were in sites between agricultural fields; 37% were located immediately adjacent to a crop field; 45% were located in grassland habitat and 18% in pastures. All of the 48 studied sites had more than 50% herbaceous ground cover and over half had more than 75% coverage.

HABITS Generally conspicuous, using a great variety of perches including utility lines and poles, often along highways. In certain types of habitat, and particularly during the breeding season, this shrike may, however, become relatively unobtrusive, for instance in landscapes dominated by sagebrush. In spring, its screeching calls betray its presence; they may accompany displays similar to those in Great Grey and Southern Grey Shrikes, when birds flutter their wings and spread their tail, often while uttering sounds reminiscent of the begging calls of fledglings. These displays are directed at possible intruders and mainly take place along territory borders. Territory defender and would-be intruder can be seen displaying at the same time; fights very rarely ensue as one of the birds generally gives way and flies off. This agonistic behaviour is not to be confused with a very similar kind of 'dance' performed by the male during pair formation. Females also indulge in wing-fluttering just before copulation and when, with head pointed up, they solicit males for food. At the beginning of the breeding season, erratic, zigzagging flights with vertical undulations and changes in pace can be observed, as well as occasional group-meetings as in the Great Grey Shrike in Europe. The territory size of a pair varies, presumably with the structure and general quality of the habitat, roughly between 6 and 20ha. On San Clemente Island, the endangered race *mearnsi* uses a large area, 34ha on average, during the breeding season; other large territories possibly occur in similar vegetation structures, particularly in desert scrub. Loggerhead Shrikes forage up to 250m or even 400m from their nest. There are no marked differences in size between breeding and winter territories. Densities are highly variable; neighbouring nests are at least 80m apart. This distance is generally greater, 150-800m even in well populated areas. Occasional 'colony' nesting was reported in the 1930s in Mississippi with for instance seven nests in thorn trees along an unused road; no two nests were more than 18m apart and it was less than 60m from the first to the last nest in a straight line down the road (see Bent 1950 for another example). Densities have been assessed during roadside surveys with for instance one pair per 10km in Texas, one pair per 7.7km in Minnesota, one pair per 2.4km in Missouri. In the south-western section of San Clemente Island where most nesting of the race *mearnsi* occurs, the overall density over a four-year study, from 1985 to 1988, varied between one pair per 4.3km and one pair per 11.6km.

Male and female of resident pairs either remain together and maintain the same territory throughout the year, or separate and occupy different, but often adjoining territories. The first strategy is the rule in Florida and the second apparently in California. Migrant individuals show a certain fidelity to the breeding site but the return rates appear to vary between geographic areas; the results of various studies also strongly suggest that males are much more site-faithful than females. In Missouri, 54% of ringed birds were back in their territories the following year; in Minnesota during a three-year study this percentage varied from 41% to 59% and in North Dakota it was only 28% (see Yosef 1996 for more data). Few migratory birds ringed as nestlings turn up near their natal site; a study in Alberta showed that they dispersed 7km on average between years.

Most prey is caught on the ground after a flight attack often less than 5-12m; the Loggerhead Shrike generally perches 2-10m from the ground but the perch-height varies of course with the structure of the habitat. On San Clemente Island, this height averages only c. 2m and is significantly lower than on the mainland where various habitats offer a greater choice of vantage points. In a study area in California, the mean perch-height during the breeding season was thus c. 7m. From time to time, this shrike hovers in order to locate possible victims; after an unsuccessful trip to the ground in pursuit of moving prey, it may hop about, inspecting and probing plants. Larders are regularly kept; much prey is, however, left uneaten. In a sagebrush habitat in south-west Idaho, impaling stations were often well protected in the interior of shrubs and averaged 0.44m off the ground; the mean distance from the nest was 28m (range 7 to 65m); prey was impaled on broken branch ends, branch forks or split branch stumps; it was not left there, but eaten or fed to the incubating female or nestlings.

FOOD The species is less dependent on small vertebrates than the Great Grey Shrike, and so its reputation is less 'bloodthirsty' than the latter. However, it takes a variety of mice, reptiles (particularly lizards), amphibians and small birds. Among the largest prey recorded are a desert massasauga rattlesnake *Sistrurus catenatus*, measuring 41cm and weighing at least 33g, and an adult Mourning Dove *Zenaidura macroura*; the latter, having been disturbed at its nest by the observer, was feigning injury when it was struck on the neck by an opportunistic shrike. Vertebrates are particularly taken in winter when arthropods are less available. The latter are, however, caught in great numbers all the year round. The insect orders most frequently taken are Coleoptera, Orthoptera and Hymenoptera. Isopods, arachnids and land snails also fall victim to this shrike as well as, occasionally, crayfish.

Relatively few detailed studies exist. Among them, that by Scott and Morrison (1990) on the threatened race *mearnsi* on San Clemente Island is of particular interest. A total of c. 6,500 items were identified in 715 pellets: the most numerous prey items were earwigs *Forficula* sp. 17.1%, ants 13.9%, crickets *Gryllus* sp. 13.1%, grasshoppers Acrididae 8.7% and side-blotched lizards *Uta stansburiana* 6.7%. Other

vertebrate prey items were Rock Wrens *Salpinctes obsoletus*, Orange-crowned Warblers *Vermivora celata*, House Finches *Carpodacus mexicanus* and mice *Mus musculus* and *Peromyscus maniculatus*. These vertebrate taxa were only 14.1% by prey number, but they probably composed the majority of prey biomass. The same probably holds true elsewhere, for instance in Florida where the summer diet, according to observations, comprises 6-10% amphibians (mainly frogs *Hyla cinerea*, etc.), and 8-13% reptiles (*Eumenes inexpectatus*, *Scincella lateralis*, *Anolis carolinensis*) (see Yosef and Grubb 1993 for details). Vertebrates are also fed to nestlings; they accounted for 4% of the 155 prey items visually identified and delivered to a nest in South Carolina (Gawlik *et al.*); in that study 59% of prey items were Orthoptera, 15% Lepidoptera, 10% Coleoptera and 8% arthropod larvae. The Loggerhead Shrike is not a typical scavenger, but will readily feed on carrion, for instance on the carcasses of birds killed by hawks or even occasionally on such big animals as a dead sheep. The food supplementation experiments made by some researchers (mostly using laboratory mice) show that it is quite willing to eat prey that it has not killed.

BREEDING In southern resident populations, where male and female remain together in winter, breeding begins at the end of winter or early in spring. A very early complete clutch was found near Savannah in Georgia on 15 February 1919. Available data suggest that clutches are laid later in mountainous areas and at higher latitudes (see Movements). Over the vast breeding range, fresh eggs may be found between mid-February and the beginning of July. Overall, the peak laying period lies between mid-March and mid-June. In the north-east of the range, Ontario and Quebec, egg-laying only commences from the end of April to early May. Replacement clutches are frequent, most pairs making at least a second attempt; up to five sets of eggs have been recorded for a single pair after four successive failures. Second normal broods occur, but their frequency is probably related to latitude and to local meteorological conditions in a given season. Not surprisingly, they appear to be much more common in southern populations; thus almost all pairs in south-central Florida attempt second broods whereas in South Carolina, as well as much further north in Minnesota, only about 10% of successful pairs renest a second time. Replacement clutches as well as second normal ones are laid in nests generally built a few hundred metres from the first. It is not yet clear whether the male or female chooses the nest site. They both gather nest material but the female generally does most, if not all, of the building, which takes c. 7-12 days. Materials from an old nest may be used; occasionally the shrike may even build on top of one of its own old nests or that of another species such as the Northern Mockingbird. Not infrequently, the nest can be placed inside an old Magpie's *Pica pica* nest in areas where both species occur together, as in south-west Idaho. Nesting sites are very variable, partly with geographical area. Both trees and bushes, preferably thorny ones which provide good cover, are selected. In grazed pasture habitats many nests are placed in hawthorn, red cedar, osage orange, etc. In Florida, they are also found in cabbage palms and blackberry. In the western states, in sagebrush country, the Logger-head Shrike mainly nests in sagebrush, bitterbrush and greasewood. On San Clemente Island the endangered race *mearnsi* hides its nests in various shrubs over two metres tall: lemonade berry, island cherry and toyon. The average nest height above the ground varies with the height of the trees and bushes present in a given habitat. In sagebrush country, in south-west Idaho, 162 nests were built at an average height of 0.79m (range 0.33-1.6m) in shrubs averaging 1.62m in height (range 0.89-2.97m). In other areas and habitats, the mean height found was 2m in Colorado, 2.3 on San Clemente Island, 3 in Oklahoma and Alabama, 3.2 in Missouri, 3.4 in Florida, 3.7 in Virginia and 4.4 in South Carolina (see detailed table in Woods and Cade 1996). Occasionally, nests have been found up to 15m above the ground. The nest is relatively bulky for the size of the bird, with an outer diameter of c. 15.5cm and a height of c. 11.5cm on average; it is usually made of thick twigs, firmly woven and lined with rootlets or fibres; it can be padded with cotton and occasionally with rags and paper. The inside also receives soft materials such as flowers, hairs, feathers, moss, etc. The Loggerhead Shrike mainly lays 5 or 6 eggs; such clutch-sizes account for more than 70% of all known historical records (range 1-9). As in the Great Grey Shrike, there appears to be a latitudinal cline as clutches found in the northern part of the range tend to be larger (see table in Yosef 1996). Interestingly, there appears to be no correlation at the same latitude between clutch-size and date of nest initiation and no significant difference in the clutch-size in first or second nests. Only the female incubates, for 15-17 days, and the young fledge when 16-20 days old.

The species is occasionally parasitised by the Brown-headed Cowbird *Molothrus ater*. Only three cases are known (two failures, one success), all from south-west Iowa. There was a remarkable age gap between the young shrikes and the cowbird, the incubation period of the latter species being only 11-12 days. In the successful case, mentioned above, apparently one young cowbird and three young shrikes fledged.

REFERENCES Andrle & Carrol (1988), Anderson (1976), Applegate (1977), Balda (1965), Bent (1950), Bildstein & Grubb (1980), Bohall-Wood (1987), Bohlen (1989), Brauning (1992), Brewer *et al.* (1991), Brooks & Temple (1990a,b), Bruce & Peterjohn (1991), Bull (1974), Burnside (1987), Cade & Woods (1994), Cadman (1985), Cadman *et al.* (1987), Chapman & Casto (1972), Collister (1994), Collister & Wicklum (1996), Craig (1978), Cuddy (1995), Ericsson (1981), Friedmann *et al.* (1950), Gawlik & Bildstein (1990, 1995), de Geus & Best (1991), Godfrey (1986), Haas (1987), Haas & Sloane (1989), Hunter *et al.* (1995), Johnsgard (1979), Kridel-baugh (1983), Laporte & Robert (1995), Laughlin & Kibbe (1985), Miller (1928, 1931), Morrison (1980, 1981) Morrison *et al.* (1995), Mundy & Woodruff (1996), Peter-john & Rice (1991), Peterjohn & Sauer (1995), Phillips (1986), Rand (1957, 1960), Robbins (1990), Scott & Morrison (1990), Semenchuck (1992), Slack (1975), Smith (1973a), Swanson (1927), Telfer (1992), Tufts (1986), Tyler (1992), Wilbur (1987), Woods (1993, 1995), Woods & Cade (1996), Yosef (1992b, 1996), Yosef & Grubb (1993, 1994), Yosef & Whitman (1992), Zimmerman (1955).

15   GREAT GREY SHRIKE
Lanius excubitor   Plates 7 & 8

Other names: Northern Shrike, Grey Shrike

IDENTIFICATION Length c. 24cm. The true shrike 'par excellence' with many races and a large breeding area stretching over the northern part of the Holarctic. About the size of a Starling *Sturnus vulgaris*, it was designated as the type of the genus *Lanius* (Swainson 1824, *Zool. Journ.* 1 p.294) of which it shows the characteristic features well: a rather long and hooked bill and a black facial mask. Its upperparts are mainly pale blue-grey and its underparts white. The longish tail and the round wings are black, but marked with white on outer tail feathers, tips of most of the flight feathers and wing-patch. In the nominate race, the latter may be limited to the base of the primaries or extend onto the secondaries. A white supercilium is variably present. The white scapulars appear as a well-defined white band between the black of the closed wings and the pale blue-grey mantle. The sexes are similar or almost so (see Description). Juveniles look very much like adults. They are, however, duller with brownish-grey upperparts and greyish-freckled underparts.

This shrike is generally conspicuous, but it can be remarkably elusive during the breeding season. When seen from a distance and when facing the observer, it has a definite 'snowball' appearance which makes it quite conspicuous. When it changes perches, it usually drops close to the ground, flies low and finally sweeps upwards again to a new lookout. A prolonged flight is typically undulating and somewhat recalls that of a woodpecker *Picus* sp.

The confusion species are the Southern Grey Shrike, the Lesser Grey Shrike, the Chinese Grey Shrike and the Loggerhead Shrike (see under those species).

DESCRIPTION *L. e. excubitor* (based on central European birds)
Adult male Facial mask black over lores, just over and under eyes and on most of ear-coverts. Supercilium narrow, white or whitish over eyes and almost to end of ear-coverts; sometimes inconspicuous or lacking. Anterior part of forehead just over base of upper mandible pale grey. Upperparts mid-grey with a slight bluish tinge from forehead to lower back; rump and uppertail-coverts somewhat paler grey. Scapulars white, forming a conspicuous V between the grey mantle and back and the black wings. Tail long, black and fringed white; rectrices with increasing white from central to outer pairs; outer pair sometimes completely white or with some black at base of inner web. Wings black with a very distinct white primary patch (c. 1cm long) and often with a second and smaller white wing-patch at

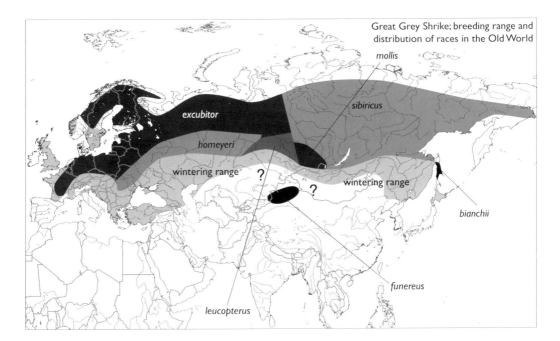

mollis

excubitor

sibiricus

homeyeri

wintering range ?

wintering range ?

bianchii

funereus

leucopterus

base of secondaries; white tips on primaries and particularly secondaries and tertials give the wing a narrow white trailing edge visible in flight; primary coverts and greater coverts black generally narrowly tipped whitish. Underparts pure white or off-white; occasionally, in fresh plumage, with a very subtle pinkish tinge on breast and flanks; undertail whitish with black band at base.

Adult female Very similar to male, but at least central European birds have, generally, less white in their plumage: white wing-patches slightly smaller; more grey tones in the white scapulars; whitish tips narrower on wing feathers. The underparts are also greyer in tone, not so pure white and sometimes with indications of vermiculations on upper breast (see Schön 1994a).

Juvenile Similar to adults, but facial mask dark brown and supercilium whitish, not well marked. Upperparts grey-brown with generally faint traces of vermiculations on nape, rump and uppertail-coverts. Underparts whitish, washed grey-brown on breast and flanks which are crossed by rather faint, narrow, dark brown vermiculations (not always visible on birds observed at a distance).

Bare parts Bill long and strong, black in adults, but with base tinged horn in males from around June to October and in females from around June to late January. Bill blue-grey in juveniles with pale base. Legs black. Iris dark brown.

MEASUREMENTS (*excubitor*; central European birds) Wing 107-121 (mean c. 114); tail 102-116 (mean c. 108); bill (to skull) 21.5-24.3 (mean c. 23); tarsus: 26-28.8. Weight: very variable, 48 (exhausted birds) - 81 (mean c. 67).

DISTRIBUTION AND STATUS A Holarctic shrike with nine races and a wide breeding range lying mainly in the taiga belt extending over the northern parts of the American continent and Eurasia. In the latter area the species is absent, as a breeding bird, from Iceland and the British Isles in the west and from the Kamchatka peninsula in the east (see map).

In the Old World, the species reaches its southwestern limits in France, with populations breeding at mid-altitudes in mountainous areas just north of the Mediterranean zone. The southernmost points lie on the relatively fresh and humid Causse Montbel (département de Lozère) near Châteauneuf-de-Randon at 44°39'N. Less than 30km further south, in much drier habitats, the range of the nominate race of the Southern Grey Shrike begins. From south-central France, the range of the Great Grey Shrike extends rather patchily north-east over central and eastern France, the Benelux countries, Germany and Denmark. Northwards still, it nests in most of Scandinavia except in south-east Norway, the southern third of Sweden and extreme southern Finland; the northern boundary lies just over 70°N in Finnmark (Norway) and at c. 68°N in the Kola peninsula; eastwards it roughly runs just north of the Arctic Circle and south of the estuaries of the rivers Pechora, Ob and Taz and finally reaches the Chukotsk peninsula giving onto the Bering Strait. From eastern France, the southern boundary of the breeding range runs east now avoiding Switzerland and, as a rule, extending north of the Alps and Carpathian Mountains, but with a distinct south-east extension in Romania, into Transylvania west of the Carpathians and into Moldova to the east. Further east, in Russia, the boundary roughly lies at c. 54°N and in western Siberia at c. 57°N. The precise limits are not well known in the eastern part of the range, but they lie further south and a race of the species breeds even in the Tien Shan range in south-east Kazakhstan and in north-west China in Xinjiang autonomous region, possibly as far south as c. 43°50 N. Another race breeds in southern Siberia and Mongolia and the species is also represented by a race breeding on Sakhalin and presumably some of the Kuril Islands even just south of 45°N.

In the New World, the Great Grey Shrike breeds from western Alaska to Labrador, in a relatively narrow belt. In Alaska it can be found north of the Brooks Range, at least 220km north of the last spruce stands and up to c. 70°N, as in Eurasia. From there its range extends east over north-west and southern Mackenzie, northern British Columbia (at least as far south as Dease Lake at 58°35'N), northern Alberta (presumably not south of Lake Athabasca), northern Saskatchewan, northern Manitoba (at least as far south as York Factory) and northern Ontario, where breeding was first proved in 1981 and where the species probably reaches its southern limits near Moosonee at 51°17'N. Further east, this shrike nests in central Quebec from La Grande Rivière in the west to the Schefferville region in the east and locally south to Cabbage Willows Bay; the northern limits appear to lie near Rivière aux Feuilles; the species is probably absent from the Ungava peninsula. Further east, the Great Grey Shrike nests in Labrador from the northern parts to Sandwich Bay in the south at c. 53°35'N.

The recent history of the Great Grey Shrike is relatively well known in Europe (nominate *excubitor*). In Fenno-Scandia, its breeding range was much more restricted at the beginning of this century. In Sweden, until the start of the 1950s, the southern limits lay at c. 62°20'N in Härjedalen and Angermanland. The range then gradually extended southwards with regular breeding down to 60°N; a few pairs were even found further south. The same trend was observed in Finland where the species was almost exclusively a northern breeder in the first half of the 20th century. The Finnish breeding population was estimated at c. 4,000 pairs in 1950 and at 6,000-8,000 pairs in the 1970s; at that time, the species nested almost as far south as the Gulf of Finland. About 15-20 years ago, the trend started to reverse with a decline in numbers detected in many areas, both in Sweden and Finland. In Denmark, as far as is known, the species only became established in 1927 when breeding occurred in western Jutland; at the end of the 1950s breeding was also recorded in northern Jutland, and in 1967 the population was estimated at roughly 200 pairs and in 1976 (atlas work) at 30-50 pairs. More recent estimates, for 1990 only mention 10-11 pairs. In west-central Europe, a definite downward trend has been evident since at least the beginning of the 1960s. The species has completely disappeared as a breeding bird from Switzerland, where the last nest was found in 1986 in the western part of Ajoie; up to 1960, it was still locally fairly common in many areas of the country. In Germany there were 1,900-2,300 pairs at the beginning of the 1990s, but the bird was much more common there 20-30 years ago. Good evidence for its catastrophic decline comes from Baden-Württemberg, in the south-west: in the 1960s it was still widespread over that whole region

with about 800-1,000 pairs; in 1973 there were c. 500 pairs, in 1979 c. 300 pairs, in 1983 c. 100 pairs and in 1992 only c. 50 pairs left and the downward trend was continuing. In France, the two successive atlases respectively for the periods 1970-1975 and 1985-1989 show a marked reduction in the breeding range. The species disappeared from large areas in the west, but also for instance from Burgundy in the centre and Alsace in the north-east. In the latter province there were still at least 200 pairs about 25 years ago; only c. 10 pairs are known nowadays. The stronghold of the species now lies mainly in mid-mountains (plateaus) in the south-central provinces of Limousin and Auvergne with perhaps up to 1,500 pairs in the latter region. Total estimates for the country in 1994 are a few thousand pairs. The species fares better in eastern Europe. In Poland, it is apparently more widespread today than at the beginning of the century. It is even locally common with stable populations in large grassy river valleys and a total breeding population of 4,000-4,500 pairs in 1992. It is also holding its own in the Czech Republic with c. 1,200 pairs in 1993, and in Slovakia with at least 500 pairs. Other recent estimates are as follows: Austria: 12-15 (1990), with almost all the remaining pairs in Niederösterreich, near the Czech border; Belarus: 600-1,200 (1990), Belgium: c. 200 (1994), Luxembourg: 50-100 (1993), Netherlands: 12-18 (1983, end of atlas work), Norway: 5,000-10,000 in the 1980s, Romania: 1,000-3,000 (1992, end of atlas work), Ukraine: 900-1,200 (1988). A rough estimate exists for Russia with between 100,000 and 1,000,000 pairs. In the western part of that country, the species has apparently spread northwards in the last 40 years, up to the Kola peninsula, Arkhangelsk region, the lower Pechora delta, and to the Arctic Circle in the Ob river valley. Further to the east the species expanded southwards to the Transbaikal region, southern Tuva Altai, the Volga delta and the Great Caucasus. In the New World, the present breeding population of Arctic Alaska, north of 68°N, has been estimated at c. 6,000 pairs (median number).

GEOGRAPHICAL VARIATION Nine races are listed here in accordance with standard works, for instance Vaurie (1959) for the Palearctic. The European Great Grey Shrikes from western Europe to the southern parts of western Siberia gradually become paler, and nominate *excubitor* is replaced by *homeyeri* which has more white in its plumage, almost always with a double wing-bar; birds living south-east of *homeyeri* in a relatively dry climate are even paler and have been named *leucopterus*. East of the range of nominate *excubitor*, typical adult *sibiricus* show yellow-brown tinges on upperparts and faint barring on underparts. These birds are very similar to the North American subspecies *borealis* and *invictus* which also always have one wing-bar. Great Grey Shrikes living in mountainous areas of Central Asia are dark birds, divided in two subspecies, *mollis* and *funereus*, with brown-grey, heavily barred underparts even in adults. The race *bianchii*, confined to Sakhalin and the southern Kuril Islands, is much paler, rather similar to the nominate.

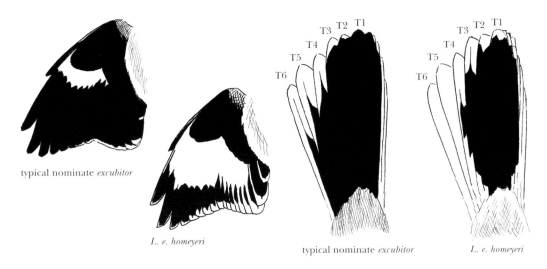

typical nominate *excubitor*

L. e. homeyeri

typical nominate *excubitor*

L. e. homeyeri

Wing and tail patterns of Great Grey Shrike. Note much more white in wings and tail in *homeyeri* than in *excubitor*.

Palearctic races:

L. e. excubitor (western and northern Europe east through Russia as far as Kaluga, Tula, Riazan, Nizni Novgorod, Kazan and Perm) Described above. Variable. Even inside the nominate race, two slightly different morphs are recognisable: one is rather pale with pale grey upperparts and few indications of barring on the underparts; these birds generally have more white in the wing with a wing-bar extending onto the secondaries; the other has darker upperparts and often a wing-bar confined to the base of the primaries; these birds may also show faint vermiculations on the underparts, even in adult males. There is no clear boundary between these two colour-phases, but individuals with two white bars appear to be more frequent in central-western Europe (birds from France and western Germany have sometimes been separated as *galliae*); in Scandinavia, they occur alongside birds with a single white bar (see Olivier 1944, Salomonsen 1949, Voous 1950, Beretz and Keve 1975).

L. e. homeyeri (Bulgaria, Romania; from Ukraine and south-east Russia east to the southern Urals and across western Siberia, north to c. 58°N) Upperparts paler grey than in nominate; forehead whitish, white supercilium generally conspicuous; uppertail-coverts and often also rump whitish not grey; tail pattern different with more white, even at base of central rectrices (c. 2cm). Wings also with more white and almost always with double wing-bar, forming one large white patch across primaries and secondaries. Rare individuals from contact zones with *excubitor* show only one white primary patch.

L. e. leucopterus (western Siberian steppes to the Yenisey) Very similar to *homeyeri*, but even paler; rump and uppertail-coverts white; wing with very large white area; may average slightly longer wing-length (see Vaurie 1959). Inhabits dry areas east and south of *homeyeri* with which it intergrades in contact zones.

L. e. sibiricus (Siberia, east of nominate to the Kolyma Basin, Anadyrland and the Chukotsk peninsula, south to the Lake Baikal area, Transbaikalia and northern Mongolia, northern Amurland and Kamchatka) Upperparts less grey than in nominate, variably tinged with ochre. Underparts vermiculated even in adult plumage.

L. e. bianchii (Sakhalin and southern Kurils) Similar to *sibiricus* but upperparts paler, greyer, less buffy. Underparts generally not so heavily vermiculated. A rather small insular form with wing-length averaging c. 111mm and tail c. 105mm.

L. e. mollis (Russian Altai and north-west Mongolia) Darker than *sibiricus* with smaller white wing-patch. Underparts more dingy and buffy and more heavily vermiculated. Intergrades with *sibiricus* in Khangai (north-west Mongolia).

L. e. funereus (Tien Shan range in Russian and Chinese Turkestan and perhaps the Dzungarian Ala Tau and the Tarbagatay) Similar to *mollis* but underparts distinctly darker, brownish-grey and more heavily vermiculated. This mountain bird appears to be the largest race with a wing-length averaging c. 121mm according to Panov (1983) against c. 112 for nominate *excubitor* and c. 118 for *mollis*, also a large race.

Nearctic races:

L. e. borealis (central and northern Quebec, northern Ontario) Upperparts as in nominate, but with pale or light grey lower rump and uppertail-coverts; supercilium prominent. Wings with white patch always limited to base of primaries. Underparts not so pure white, more pale smoke-grey particularly on breast and flanks; distinct narrow bands of dusky drab vermiculations almost all over, except on chin, throat and sometimes upper belly. Adult females are very similar to males, but in breeding plumage average slightly darker grey on head and back and may show slightly buffier under-parts; their white wing-patch is also less extend (all these characters are almost impossible to discern in the field). Juveniles are very different from juvenile *excubitor* as they have much browner, 'woodier' upperparts, darker, more heavily vermiculated underparts and browner flight feathers. The mean wing-length given by Miller (1931) is 113.2mm (very similar to *excubitor*). Other means given by same author: tail 113.2; bill 13.8; tarsus 25.9.

L. e. invictus (northern Alaska, Mackenzie and northern Manitoba south to extreme northern British Columbia and Alberta) Very similar to *borealis* and Asian *sibiricus*. Upperparts said to be slightly paler in dorsal area than in *borealis*; supercilium generally more prominent; lower rump and uppertail-coverts pure white (usually grey in *borealis*) and underparts on average less heavily vermiculated. Juveniles somewhat paler, not so dark as *borealis*. Intergradation with *borealis* probably occurs in northern Manitoba and Keewatin. *Invictus* might on average be slightly bigger (see Miller 1931, also Phillips 1986).

MOVEMENTS A partial migrant. In the Old World, only the movements of European birds are relatively well known. The extreme northern populations vacate their breeding areas completely or almost so, as a few birds prefer to stay, presumably near their breeding territories, up to at least 67°N in Norway and occasionally up to 68°21'N in the Kiruna or Abisko regions in Sweden. The normal wintering range, however, lies south of 60°N. Populations breeding in the south-western part of the range, in areas to some degree influenced by a relatively mild maritime climate (Germany, France) appear to have a larger percentage of sedentary birds than populations in central Europe enduring a more continental climate (Czech Republic, for instance). In the western Palearctic, individual shrikes can be either long-distance migrants, short-distance migrants, altitudinal migrants or residents. The wintering range includes almost all the breeding range, but also some areas beyond: southern Sweden, Great Britain, south-west France, etc., and even, occasionally, northern Spain and Ireland. The southern winter limit roughly extends from northern Spain to southern France and northern Italy. It then follows the Mediterranean coast from Slovenia to Turkey. The species probably never reaches North Africa, but odd birds have turned up on Corsica, Malta and Rhodes (recovery of a bird ringed in Finland). The range of eastern Palearctic birds also extends further south in winter; birds of the race *homeyeri* appear in the Balkans and regularly winter at least as far south as northern Iran or, further east, northern Pamir foothills. Some individuals of this race (or perhaps *leucopterus*?) have even been recorded near Gilgit and Quetta at 30°12'N in Pakistan and in the Srinagar region of extreme north-west India; this subspecies also winters in extreme north-west China, in the western parts of Xinjiang and apparently at least as far south as c. 40°N. The race *mollis*, a bird of mountainous areas

in southern Siberia and Mongolia, undertakes altitudinal movements, but also occurs further south in winter: in China, it is known from the northern provinces of Liaoning, Hebei and Gansu, with occasional records as far south as c. 35°N. This race is accidental in Japan where two records are known from Honshu and one from Kyushu, all before 1900 (collected specimens). *Sibiricus* also partly leaves its breeding range in winter and appears in southern parts of eastern Siberia, west to the Altai area and east as far south as Amurland in far-eastern Russia, Inner Mongolia and the north-eastern Chinese provinces of Liaoning and Hebei. The Sakhalin race *bianchii* seems to be mainly resident, but in winter birds appear on southern islands of the Kuril chain and also, regularly in small numbers, in northern Japan (Hokkaido), where they might even occasionally attempt to breed, as observations have been made in all months except September. From time to time, this race is also found further south, in Honshu. It is also a rare vagrant to Korea.

In the New World, most shrikes vacate their breeding areas; wintering birds may, however, be found as far north as southern or, occasionally, central Alaska. The regular winter range extends over the Canadian provinces and also over the northern part of the United States where, from west to east, the southern boundary runs through north-central California, northern Nevada, northern Arizona, central New Mexico and then north-eastwards over northern Texas (very rare), central Oklahoma, Kansas (very irregular), central (occasionally southern) Iowa and east to south-west Indiana, Pennsylvania, northern New York, Connecticut, Maryland and even northern Virginia where the species appears to reach its south-eastern limits. There are, however, some rare records from North Carolina. The Great Grey Shrike apparently reaches the southern limits of its North American winter range in New Mexico. Up to 1978, 129 individuals were recorded there in 131 winters; most records are concentrated in the north-west quadrant of the state, except for a few observations, verified by photographs or specimens, which were made in southern parts including one at Las Cruces at 32°18'N.

The migration routes of west European shrikes are relatively well known thanks to recoveries of ringed birds. Long-distance migrants breeding in Scandinavia move south to south-westwards in autumn with the exception of a very few birds which take a south-easterly direction (see map of recoveries in Zink 1975). Migrant shrikes from central Europe, Germany and formerly Switzerland also take a mainly south-westerly direction and winter somewhere in France or the north of Italy. The c. 75 Great Grey Shrikes which nowadays turn up annually in Britain all very probably come from Fenno-Scandia; not surprisingly, the majority of autumn records are from the east coast and particularly from Norfolk, south-east Yorkshire and the northern isles of Scotland. Later, in the cold season, the shrikes can also be seen as far to the west as Ireland (44 observations up to 1989).

Most migrant Great Grey Shrikes leave their breeding territories in September, but movements are already evident in August or even July, involving either early successful breeders or early failed breeders. In Béarn, in south-west France at the foot of the Pyrenees, where the species does not breed, birds can be seen there exceptionally in the first ten days of July; more shrikes appear in the first half of August, but the bulk of the wintering population, which numbers possibly between 130 and 170 individuals annually, arrives in September and early October. The origin of these birds is unknown; they leave the area, as a rule, between 15 February and 10 March. Another wintering area, lying outside the breeding range, has been studied in detail in south-east Sweden; most birds arrive there in late September or early October and generally leave at the end of March (mean spring departure in 14 years was 29 March) after a stay of c. 169 days. Throughout Britain, where the species is scarce in winter but observer coverage very high, very few birds have been seen in autumn before the last week of September; there is one record for July, one for August and two for the first part of September; most birds arrive in October, particularly in the last week; arrivals continue into November. Birds become rare from mid-March onwards. There are a few exceptional May records including a bird which stayed from 18 May to 8 July 1991 in east Suffolk; two June records come respectively from south Northumberland and north-east Yorkshire.

The timing of Great Grey Shrike migration in North America is about the same as in Europe; in a study area in south-west Idaho, the first autumn birds arrived rather late, on 9 November 1988 and 10 November 1989, and the latest spring dates in the same area were 24 March 1989 and 28 March 1990; so birds spend roughly 120 days in their winter quarters. In New Mexico, where the species is rare and at the southern boundary of its winter range, the earliest autumn record is 14 October and the latest spring record 22 March. The peak in records, as for many other regions, is December, but this is mainly due to the Christmas Bird Counts.

Birds occasionally occur outside their normal winter range; the race *homeyeri* has thus been recorded a few times in western Europe. This subspecies is, however, difficult to identify in the field and most reliable records concern trapped or killed shrikes. There are only five definite records for Germany, all before 1900; one for the Czech Republic on 25 October 1922; one for eastern France in April 1971 (now at the Natural History Museum at Tring in England), a few for Italy and one for southern Sweden on 30 September 1993.

MOULT Juveniles in central Europe undergo a partial moult between roughly the end of July and November. It affects all or almost all the head and body feathers and one, two or all tertials and sometimes T1. It does not involve the primary coverts or most outer greater coverts. First-winter birds are very similar to adults and particularly to adult females. They can, however, be recognised through to the following spring thanks to the pale brown tips still present on the unmoulted greater coverts; some body feathers may also remain unmoulted. Adults, including those of migrant populations, undergo a complete moult on the breeding grounds; it generally starts when the young have just fledged. Birds in central Europe start moulting at the end of June and all adult shrikes have changed their plumage in November or December. According to observations made on six captive birds in Germany, primaries are replaced on average in 95 days, secondaries and tertials in 97 days and tail-feathers in 68 days. Adults undergo a partial body moult between March and May when the central rectrices may also be replaced.

VOICE (based on nominate *excubitor*) Two types of song can be distinguished; the more frequent one, from October to March-April, is a repetition of single and/or double notes in short phrases *trrr-turit-trrr-turit* ... Single notes of this short song may constitute contact calls. It is mainly in the presence of a female, at courtship time, that the song changes into its second type, a relatively melodious, not very audible, warble also containing harsh noises and mimicry of other birds. A typical call is the loud drawn-out whistle, a kind of *prii* or *trrri* (other probable transcription: *kwiet*) which carries far and betrays the presence of the species; it indicates annoyance and/or aggressive intent. Very typical also, in the rather wide repertoire, are the unpleasant *kwäää* (other translation *grèè grèè*) calls, somewhat reminiscent of a Eurasian Jay *Garrulus glandarius*, and heard when adults with young out of the nest are being disturbed by observers or potential predators. Fluted *tli* appear to be typical nest-showing calls of the male. Rattle calls, *tr* sounds incorporating bill-snapping, are uttered during flight-attacks on possible nest-predators like Black-billed Magpies *Pica pica*. Both sexes, females more rarely, may sing in their winter territories even when far from the breeding range as for instance in Britain or the United States.

HABITAT The Great Grey Shrike suits its American name of Northern Shrike well, as it breeds in circumboreal regions of the Old and New World in subarctic and temperate climates. It is a typical but scarce bird of the taiga belt where it occurs in light pine or spruce forests opened up by storms, fires, insect activities or clear-fellings; locally it also occurs in open birch woods. It frequents the forest edges of bogs, probably still very similar to its primeval habitat. In many areas, Latvia, Lithuania, Estonia, parts of Russia, etc., it mainly if not exclusively nests in such landscapes, dominated by undeveloped bog systems. In Alaska, remarkably, its range extends at least 220km north of the last fingers of spruce forest: north of the Brooks Range the race *invictus* inhabits riparian shrub vegetation, mainly stands of feltleaf willow *Salix alaxensis* ranging from 1.5 to c. 4.5m in height and growing in irregular patches along the major river systems. In the south of its Palearctic breeding range this shrike can be found in a variety of habitats kept semi-open by non-intensive types of farming or, much less often, by forestry practices or storms affecting woodlands. Breeding territories are established in flat or gently sloping areas with good herbaceous cover and dotted on average every 30m with vertical structures which provide suitably varied perching-heights: bushes 1-5m high and trees up to 30m. Man-made structures like pylons, poles, fences and particularly electric wires are also readily used. Last, but certainly not least, optimal habitat, whether in summer or winter, is also optimal habitat for voles, by far the most important prey (see Food). In central-western Europe, the species used to be widespread in lowlands and hilly country. Nowadays, because of the intensification of agriculture, it has largely disappeared from these areas and its last strongholds are in relatively flat areas of mid-mountainous regions. In France for instance, the best populations are now found in the Massif Central, on the plateaus of Auvergne at altitudes between 600 and 1,000m with nesting recorded up to 1,300m; on the plateaus of the Jura Mountains, the Great Grey Shrike locally still finds suitable conditions roughly between 600 and 800m. In Germany, the species nests up to c. 800m in the Harz Mountains and up to c. 1,050m in the Black Forest. Typically a Great Grey Shrike breeding habitat is a contrast of densely wooded and very open areas; intermediate zones with c. 5-10 perches per ha are always present and cover about a quarter of the whole territory, as for example in a relatively thriving population breeding in grassy river valleys in the Vosges (eastern France). Almost all the nests are hidden in artificial spruce stands aged 20-50 years and each covering 0.5-3ha. The nests are placed at an average height of 12m and 1-2m from the tops of trees growing on the edge of plantations. The position of the nest enables the pair to have a clear view over most of its large territory, which covers at least a few tens of hectares (30-100ha in many cases). Foraging occurs up to several hundred metres from the nest in very open areas, particularly in pastures, but also in more closed habitats like small forest clearings, or fallow-land recolonised by scrub vegetation. Suitable perches are provided by isolated trees, small groves, bushes and also pylons, electric wires and fences. The area supports many voles. For a detailed habitat study in Germany, see Schön (1994e).

HABITS (based mainly on central European birds) The species well deserves its Latin name *excubitor* (sentinel) as it is generally conspicuous and often remains for long periods on the same perch. During the breeding season it is, however, more elusive with rather skulking habits when there are young in the nest. Almost throughout the year, but particularly in spring, a typical warning call sounding like a whistle and here transcribed as *prrii* helps advertise its presence (see Voice). It is used in the presence of possible rivals, or when the bird appears to be uneasy in some way or other. In winter and at the beginning of the breeding season, sometimes even in autumn, it is possible to witness impressive 'inspection flights', apparently only once a day, performed by males and possibly by both sexes. The birds involved gradually, in successive stages, fly upwards, often hover when they are between 30 and 100m from the ground, then glide down again, sometimes, at the appropriate time of year, towards a potential or actual mate. Another interesting behaviour is the group-meetings observed in long-term studies in eastern France and Germany particularly in spring, but also in early September (Schön 1994b). Up to six birds, but usually four, gather at border areas

between several territories; much calling ensues and the meeting can last 15 minutes to two hours. This kind of behaviour possibly facilitates future mate choice and also enables the birds to have a clear idea of territorial boundaries. It may also simply be due to the intrusions and disturbances caused by transgressors, particularly during pair formation. The highly territorial Great Grey Shrike needs to know its territory well. The territory of a pair covers 30-100ha probably depending on the quality of the habitat and particularly on the abundance of well-distributed perches and food. Males may occasionally fly up to 800m or more from the nest while the female is incubating, but they also spend long periods perched 10-25m from, and above, the nest; they can then be very conspicuous or on the contrary well hidden in foliage. Potential nest-predators are generally abundant; in a study in eastern France, it has been noted that the foraging territory of a pair tended to become smaller when there were young in the nest. The shrikes rarely moved more than 200m from the nest, as they often needed to defend the nest from Carrion Crows *Corvus corone*, Jays and Magpies and occasionally other birds including Grey Herons *Ardea cinerea*, Common Kestrels *Falco tinnunculus* and Red Squirrels *Sciurus vulgaris*. These attacks are accompanied by bill-snapping sounds *trtrtr-trtrtr*. When the young are out of the nest, but still clumsy or unable to fly far and fast the unpleasant, far-carrying, harsh *kwäää* alarm-calls are vigorously given (see Voice). Individual winter territories show a tendency to be larger on average than summer territories of pairs; in a study in south-west Germany, territories occupied all year round covered 68ha on average against 35ha for summer territories, and 52ha for individual winter territories (see detailed study by Schön 1994e). In Idaho, USA, the winter territories of six colour-ringed shrikes covered 216ha on average, but over one-half of the activity of each shrike was confined to a core area of approximately 50ha. Breeding densities in optimal areas, presumably in or after a good vole year, are close to one pair per 100ha in central-western Europe. They are often much lower: in the taiga belt the breeding territories are thinly distributed and large tracts of apparently suitable habitat remain unoccupied. Neighbouring occupied nests, in still well-populated areas, and in years of good densities, are separated by at least 300m according to observations in eastern France and on average by nearly 1,000m. In winter, the territories are also evenly distributed; in southern Sweden it has been estimated that there were 3.7 wintering individuals per 100km². Some Great Grey Shrikes, and particularly non-migratory birds from western-central Europe, probably spend all their life in a given territory provided it remains suitable. Winter site-fidelity in non-breeding areas has been proved several times, for instance in the Netherlands, southern Sweden and even Great Britain in the case of a somewhat aberrant individual relatively difficult to tell from a Lesser Grey Shrike (see Tucker 1942). This site-fidelity does not always occur, however, as has been shown by recoveries of ringed birds.

At least in parts of Finland, Germany and eastern

France, the species often nests in close proximity to Fieldfares *Turdus pilaris*. Occupied nests of the two species may be less than 10m apart. This association is probably based on mutual protection against predators; this does not prevent some degree of mutual aggression and at least one case is known where a fledgling Fieldfare fell victim to the shrike.

When looking for prey, the Great Grey Shrike spends long hours scanning the ground, perched on a variety of rather high vantage points, preferably between 3-8m (extremes 1-18m). It can stay in the same spot for up to half an hour or more, but generally changes perch much more often. Wintering shrikes, watched in southern Sweden, did so on average every 8.6 minutes and also on average covered a distance of 11.8km per day using 5.6 perches per km. The species also frequently hovers, particularly when the grass is high or when there is a scarcity of perches; most hovering is done at 3-8m and the bird often changes height after short normal flights. From time to time, in bad weather, this shrike can be seen hopping on the ground. That is where most prey is caught, as a rule, after a slanting or vertical drop or after a drop followed by a flight just above the ground; in good weather flying insects can be snatched after upward or direct flights. Passerines are generally taken by surprise while they are on a perch or on the ground; flying birds may, however, be pursued in a typical Sparrowhawk *Accipiter nisus* way and be taken from above, from the side or even from below. Occasionally, this shrike moves about the branches of trees or bushes with quivering wings and twisting movements of the tail in order to flush quarry into flight. The Great Grey Shrike regularly impales its victims or, in the case of small vertebrates, generally wedges them. Larders can be found anywhere in the territory, sometimes as far as 1,500m from an occupied nest, but there is usually at least one only 15-20m away. After a vole or much more rarely a bird has been caught, frequent flights between the butchering site and the nest can be observed; the small animals are generally hung up in a bush, small tree, etc., some 0.5-1.5m from the ground and 5-30m from the base of the tree in which the nest is hidden. Occasionally the prey is fixed in a suitable position, much higher up, almost level with the nest and only a few metres from it. Several victims can be found impaled in a given territory on the same day; a record comes from the Czech Republic where Stanclova (1983) counted 99 voles cached in a territory where a pair had seven nestlings. In Alaska (race *invictus*), the larders seen by Cade (1967) were always more than 100m from the nest.

FOOD Small vertebrates play a dominant role in the diet of this shrike, which spends the year round in subarctic or cold temperate climates where insects are scarce in winter. Among the vertebrates, small rodents and particularly voles *Microtus* sp. come first in importance. Wherever it occurs in the western Palearctic, the Common Vole *M. arvalis* figures greatly in the diet; between 9 and 12cm long, weighing c. 30g on average, it is an ideal size, rather slow and readily enters short grass. The Field Vole *M. agrestis* is also much taken, but probably more difficult to locate and to catch as it keeps more to higher vegetation, although it is the only common vole for birds wintering in southern Sweden or in Great Britain. *Microtus* species account for 66-90% of the total biomass of prey taken, mainly in winter months, based on stomach contents or pellet analyses, in eastern Austria, Finland, north-east Slovakia, south-east Sweden, Switzerland (Ajoie) and several parts of Germany. Interestingly, but not surprisingly, in Westphalia (Germany), where the Great Grey Shrike breeds in large forest clearings created by storms or by clear-felling, the commonest small vertebrate preyed on is the Bank Vole *Clethrionomys glareolus*, with 48% of the prey biomass. In other European territories where grassland is the main foraging habitat, the Bank Vole, a species mainly of woodlands but also of dense shrubs, is rarely taken. In Alaska, north of the Brooks Range, it is the Singing Vole *Microtus miurus* which is the most important prey species in the diet of breeding birds, representing more than 80% of the total biomass of prey species. In a study of the winter diet in south-west Idaho, small rodents also made up the bulk of the diet measured by biomass, with over 83%; most of them were voles *Microtus longicaudatus* and *M. pennsylvanicus*, although deermice *Peromyscus maniculatus*, harvest mice *Reithrodontomys megalotis* and a few wild house mice *Mus musculus* were also taken. The latter species is also very occasionally caught in Europe, as well as other species of mice like those of the genus *Apodemus*, which are very agile and largely nocturnal; in south-east Sweden, however, they make up to 11.5% of the winter prey. In the western Palearctic, at least eight species of shrew are listed as victims of the Great Grey Shrike, the commonest being the common shrew *Sorex araneus*, comprising 11% of the vertebrate prey in a study in Finland and 11.5% of the prey caught in winter in south-east Sweden. Shrews appear to be taken in relatively high numbers in poor vole years. The same holds true for passerines, which are otherwise not favoured as they are more difficult to catch than voles. They made up 6% of the biomass in a year-long study in Switzerland and 9% of the biomass in a winter study in Sweden. The species involved are mainly characteristic of open habitats and often ground-feeders. Birds are usually caught as inexperienced fledglings (very rarely as nestlings) and in severe winters when voles are protected by snow cover. Handicapped birds are always vulnerable targets: exhausted migrants, passerines entangled in mist-nests, etc. At the beginning of the breeding season, displaying male birds can be particularly vulnerable and pay a heavy price. This has been witnessed in Alaska where the shrikes, just back in late April or May, first subsist mainly on early-arriving flocks of Redpolls *Acanthis* sp., Snow Buntings *Plectrophenax nivalis* and Lapland Longspurs *Calcarius lapponicus*, then on displaying males of the same species and finally mainly on adult voles as the snow melts. Among other small vertebrates, frogs and lizards are regularly taken: in Finland, probably in relatively wet areas, bogs, etc., the common lizard *Lacerta vivipera* is a regular prey in the breeding season. In two different studies in that country it made up respectively 26.7% of the prey brought to the nests and 19.7% of the total numbers of vertebrates found in 900 pellets collected near 15 nests. slow worms *Anguis fragilis*, newts *Triturus alpestris* and fish sp. are rare or occasional prey. Among the largest and occasional vertebrate prey, the following have been recorded: moles *Talpa europaea*, a young rat *Rattus rattus*, a young hamster *Cricetus cricetus* and even young weasel *Mustela nivalis* and stoat *M. erminea*. Birds up to the size of a Song Thrush *Turdus philomelos* (exhausted migrants or otherwise handicapped birds) or even fledgling Fieldfares *Turdus pilaris* are occasionally found impaled. Arthropods are caught in almost every month of the year, but particularly in the breeding season when they appear to be necessary for young nestlings; however, they rarely represent more than 15% of the biomass of the prey even if, in number, they are by far the most important. The captured invertebrates are insects belonging to many orders: Coleoptera, Orthoptera, Hymenoptera, etc., generally in that order: among the Coleoptera, the genus *Carabus* or the family Carabidae often predominate (see for instance Bassin *et al.* 1981 for a study in Switzerland) followed by other families of ground-dwelling species: Elateridae, Scarabaeidae, Silphidae, Staphylinidae. Among the Hymenoptera, *Bombus* sp. are readily taken; together with wasps and grasshoppers they play a significant role in the diet of young shrikes throughout the summer in northern Alaska. Field crickets *Gryllus gryllus*, different species of Scarabaeidae, etc., and arachnids can be caught almost all the year round, even sometimes on the snow where they are very conspicuous. Invertebrate prey less than 5mm long are rarely taken; most (c. 75%) measure between 6 and 19mm and about 20% between 20 and 25mm. Worms (Lumbricidae) are not uncommonly caught, perhaps particularly in mild winters with low densities of voles. Snails and crayfish (Astacidae) occasionally fall victims to this shrike, which may also eat carrion as has been witnessed in Finland where a pair fed its week-old nestlings with the flesh of a young Mountain Hare *Lepus timidus* which had died not far from their nest.

BREEDING In migrant populations, pair formation takes place as soon as the birds are back in their breeding territories; observations from Germany strongly suggest that some pairs form towards the end of winter while the birds are still in their winter quarters including areas where the species does not nest (see Grünwald 1994). Once the pair is formed and before the nest is built, the two birds, male closely following female, can be seen on inspection tours anywhere in what is to become the territory. This can last for a few weeks depending partly on meteorological conditions. The beginning of egg-laying varies with latitude and with the migratory status of the birds involved. In west-central Europe, eastern France and Germany, it can very occasionally, in mild weather, start at the end of March, but the peak takes place around mid-April. In southern Finland, laying only starts at the end of April or, more generally, at the beginning of May; in Lapland the first eggs are laid even later, at the end of May or the beginning of June. In northern Alaska, laying occurs mainly in May, the earliest known start being on 5 May; most June clutches there appear to be sec-

ond attempts, except in the case of very late springs. Replacement clutches are common, but very few pairs make three attempts and some even give up once their first nest has been destroyed at a late stage. During a long-term study in eastern France, repeat nests were found between 5 and 1,150m from the original site. In the case of the greatest distance the pair had completely left its first territory. In Switzerland, the average distance between six first nests and six second attempts was 688m (extremes 50 and 1,300m). Normal second clutches are either extremely rare or non-existent; observations by Fischer (1994a), however, strongly suggest such a possibility in spring 1993 in Rheinland-Pfalz (Germany), with the first egg of the first clutch laid around 22 March and the first egg of the second, also successful clutch, laid around 26 May. The nest-site is chosen by the male and the nest is built by both sexes, the male being mainly a provider of materials. Building generally takes a good week, sometimes even two weeks or more if activities are interrupted by bad weather. The nest may be hidden in a large thorny bush, such as blackthorn *Prunus spinosa*, but much more often in a tree. In the taiga belt, but also in west-central Europe available, conifers are preferred. The typical position of nests in spruce plantations has already been described (see Habitat). In other trees, many nests are hidden in mistletoe *Viscum*, ivy or 'witches broom' tree growths. The nest-site is chosen according to local circumstances; it can be on a side branch of a large oak *Quercus* sp., or of an alder *Alnus* sp., in outer twigs of a fruit-tree, etc. In Alaska, north of the Brooks Range, most nests are placed in dense shrubs mainly composed of feltleaf willow *Salix alaxensis*. The height above the ground is variable; on average it is at c. 2m in a bush, c. 4m in a fruit tree and 8-15m in other trees like conifers, oaks, poplars, etc.; extreme heights have been recorded in Germany with a nest near the ground and another c. 38m high in a pine *Pinus* sp. The nest is rather bulky, untidy-looking, with an outer diameter averaging c. 20cm (even 25 in Alaska) and a height of c. 14cm (even 20 in Alaska); the foundation is made of twigs, moss, grasses, etc., and can also include man-made materials like plastic; rootlets, flowers, hair, feathers, etc., compose the lining. A few nests almost entirely made of feathers are known from eastern France and Germany. Where available, wool is also readily used. The Great Grey Shrike lays 4-7 eggs in west-central Europe and generally 6 in first attempts. In northern latitudes, nests with 7, 8 or even 9 eggs are much more common. In Alaska, 23 full-clutches had between 6 and 9 eggs (mean 7.6 and mode 8). In southern Finland, 15 early clutches had 7.13 eggs on average. Incubation, undertaken almost entirely by the female, lasts 17 days and the young stay in the nest 19-21 days. Once out of the nest, the juveniles remain with their parents for 4-5 weeks. According to Schön (1994c) the brood is 'divided' between the parents when the fledglings are about 10 days old. From then on, each parent looks after its own group. In certain areas in western Europe, the Great Grey Shrike was regularly parasitised by the Common Cuckoo *Cuculus canorus*. This happened in central-eastern France (Burgundy, Lorraine, Alsace), in south-western Germany and in Switzerland. No case has apparently been reported in the last 20 years or so, possibly because of the present rarity of the shrike in the regions mentioned. The shrike readily accepted the cuckoo's egg and the young cuckoo readily accepted the food, including morsels of voles, brought by the foster parents. In general the young cuckoo did not, or could not, evacuate the shrike's eggs; a case is known where three young shrikes and two young cuckoos were brought up together (Cuadon 1955, Ferry and Martinet 1974).

REFERENCES Ali & Ripley (1972), Atkinson (1993), Atkinson & Cade (1993), Bassin *et al.* (1981), Beretz & Keve (1975), Cade (1962, 1967), Cade & Swem (1995), Carlon (1994), Cheng (1987), Claudon (1955), Dement'ev & Gladkov (1968), Ferry & Martinet (1974), Fischer (1994a,b), Fraser & Ryan (1995), Glutz von Blotzheim & Bauer (1993), Godfrey (1986), Grünwald (1994), Hildén & Hildén (1996), Hölker (1993), Hromoda & Kristin (1996), Hubbard (1978), Kowalski (1993), Lefranc (1993, 1995a), Martorelli (1908), Miller (1931), Olivier (1944), Olsson (1981, 1984,a,b,c, 1985, 1986), Panov (1983, 1995), Phillips (1986), Rehsteiner (1995), Root (1988), Rothaupt (1991), Salomonsen (1949), Schön (1994a-f), Stanclova (1983), Straka (1991), Tucker (1942), Tucker & Heath (1994), Vaurie (1959), Voous (1950), Wagner (1994), Zink (1975).

16   SOUTHERN GREY SHRIKE
Lanius meridionalis   Plates 9 & 10

Taxonomic note: formerly treated as conspecific with Great Grey Shrike *L. excubitor.*

IDENTIFICATION Length c. 25cm. A polytypic species, distributed in a vast belt stretching over northern Africa, the Middle East and parts of Asia. The nominate race, very distinct, confined to the Iberian peninsula and southern France, is about the size and has the general appearance of the Great Grey Shrike. It is, however, easily distinguished from nominate *excubitor*, the only race with which it comes into contact, apparently only outside the breeding season. *Meridionalis* is much darker and generally, when low in bushes, more difficult to spot than the Great Grey Shrike. Its upperparts are lead-grey. When seen from a distance, its underparts also appear rather dark except for a pale throat. When watched at close range, a pinkish tinge is apparent on the breast, flanks and belly. A narrow white supercilium is prominent and strongly contrasts with both the black facial mask and the slaty-coloured crown. The white wing-patch is small and restricted to the base of the primaries. The sexes are alike. Juveniles are very similar to adults, but duller; their underparts may be greyish or already pinkish. Faint barring is only occasionally present on the sides of the breast.

Nominate *meridionalis* may be confused with the Lesser Grey Shrike in southern France and Catalonia (Spain). The latter also has pinkish underparts, but its structure is quite different (see under that species).

DESCRIPTION *L. m. meridionalis*
Adult male Facial mask black over lores, just over and under eyes and on ear-coverts. Supercilium very narrow, white, always conspicuous and sometimes extending slightly over bill. Upperparts dark plumbeous grey, becoming somewhat paler on rump and uppertail-coverts; scapulars with rather restricted white, contrasting sharply with dark back and wings. Tail black, fringed white; three outer pairs of rectrices tipped white; outer pair basally black with tip white for up to 55mm. Wings black with small white patch confined to base of primaries; secondaries narrowly tipped white; tertials with broader white tips. Underparts typically tinged vinous-pink; chin, sides of neck and vent white or whitish. Undertail white.
Adult female Indistinguishable from male; might on average have less white in plumage and more often show dusky bars on underparts (Olivier 1944).
Juvenile Similar to adults, but facial mask dark brown; lores partly whitish. Upperparts paler grey (brownish-grey). Underparts greyish or washed buffish-pink sometimes with faint dusky vermiculations; throat and sides of neck whitish.
Bare parts Bill and legs black. Iris dark brown.

MEASUREMENTS (*meridionalis*) Wing 102-112 (mean c. 107); distinctly smaller than in nominate *excubitor* which has 114 on average; tail 101-118; bill (to skull) 23-25; tarsus: 29.5-31. Weight: c. 70 ranging from 53 to 93 for 23 birds weighed in Spain (Cruz Sollis & Lope Rebollo 1985).

DISTRIBUTION AND STATUS From west to east, the distribution of this Saharo-Sindian arid zone species (see Harrison 1986) is rather patchy over parts of northern Africa, the Middle East, Central Asia and the northern part of the Indian subcontinent; about eleven races are involved. Isolated subspecies occur in extreme south-west Europe (nominate *meridionalis*), on the Canary Islands, and on Socotra. Isolated populations of desert races breed in suitable areas throughout the Sahara Desert. The south-western limits reached by breeders lie near Aleg at c. 17°N in Mauritania, and the southern boundary of the breeding range, which extends along the Sahel zone, roughly corresponds to a line drawn between that locality and Socotra in the Red Sea at c. 12°30'N. The western limits cross Tenerife, the westernmost Canary Island inhabited by this shrike at c. 16°35'W, whereas the northernmost points reached in Europe lie in the southern parts of the French départements of Lozère, Ardèche and Drôme, roughly at c. 44°30'N. Eastwards, an apparently isolated population of the race known as the 'Steppe Grey Shrike' breeds as far as about 107°E in the Chinese province of Ningxia.

Few data exist on the status and the recent history of the Southern Grey Shrike. It is common in Spain where the present breeding population has been estimated at 200,000 pairs at least; in France, there are now about 1,500 pairs (estimated range 1,050-2,050 pairs). The race in the Canary Islands totals between 1,000 and 1,500 pairs. Some 5,000-10,000 pairs of the race *aucheri* breed in the United Arab Emirates.

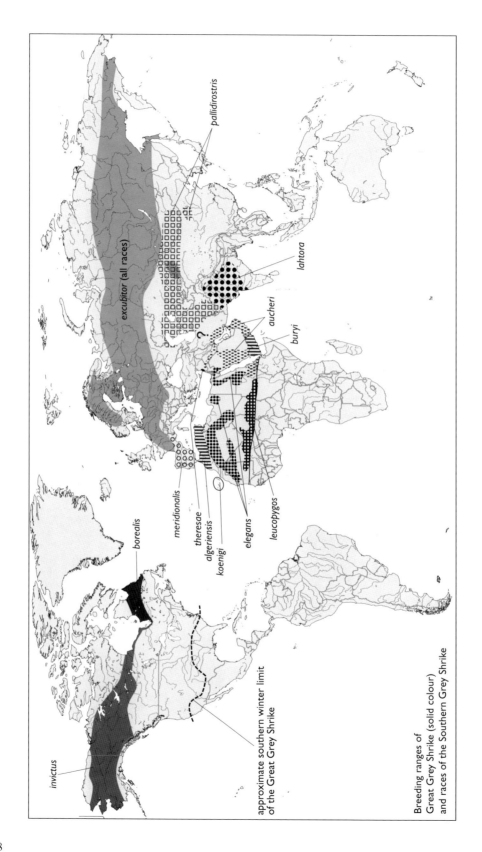

pallidirostris

excubitor (all races)

lahtora

aucheri

buryi

meridionalis

theresae

algeriensis

koenigi

elegans

leucopygos

borealis

invictus

approximate southern winter limit
of the Great Grey Shrike

Breeding ranges of
Great Grey Shrike (solid colour)
and races of the Southern Grey Shrike

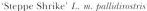

'Steppe Shrike' *L. m. pallidirostris*   Great Grey Shrike *L. e. excubitor*

Comparison of wing shapes of Great Grey Shrike (nominate *excubitor*) and Southern Grey Shrike (race *pallidirostris*). Note 2nd primary as long as (or longer) than 5th in *pallidirostris*, whereas it is shorter than 6th in *excubitor*.

GEOGRAPHICAL VARIATION Eleven races are listed below. This is in accordance with Vaurie (1959) for the Palearctic and Rand (1960) for the world, except that the race *theresae* proposed by Meinertzhagen (1953) is also included following Shirihai (1995). Variation is complex; birds of north-west Africa gradually become paler south-eastwards as arid conditions intensify (see Jany 1948). These strongly clinal changes are obvious when the races *koenigi*, *algeriensis*, *elegans* and *leucopygos* are considered in that order. The race *aucheri* from north-east Africa north-east to Iran is somewhat darker with less white in its plumage and slightly greyer underparts. More to the north-east *pallidirostris* is again very pale with underparts faintly tinged salmon-pink, and the Indian race *lahtora* shows white underparts. Typical birds of the different races are relatively easy to identify in the field. The observer may, however, be faced with intermediates as intergradation is common between various subspecies: *algeriensis* and *elegans*, *elegans* and *aucheri*, *aucheri* and *pallidirostris*, and probably *pallidirostris* and *lahtora*.

L. m. meridionalis (Iberian peninsula, southern France particularly the Languedoc-Roussillon region; eastwards more sparsely in the Provence–Côte d'Azur region as far as the areas lying north of Nice where scarce) Described above.

L. m. algeriensis (north-west Africa, along the Atlantic coast from western Mauritania and Rio de Oro to Morocco, thence to Tunisia, northern Tripolitania and Cyrenaica, inland to the northern borders of the Sahara) Similar to *meridionalis*, but upperparts very slightly paler; supercilium poorly indicated or lacking; throat often pale, contrasting with rest of rather dark underparts (typically tinged grey). Bill thicker than in other races.

L. m. koenigi (Canary Islands: La Graciosa, Lanzarote, Fuerteventura, Gran Canaria and Tenerife) Very similar in coloration to the darker populations of *algeriensis*, but smaller with shorter wings and tail; wing-length 97-105 (mean 101) in ten males, as against 106-114 (mean 109) in ten *alge-*

riensis (Vaurie 1959). Supercilium from base of bill to eye almost always present but less conspicuous than in nominate *meridionalis*. Bill proportionately more slender, longer and on average more strongly hooked.

L. m. elegans (in the desert, from Mauritania, northern and central Sahara, southern Tunisia, Libya to Egypt along the coast to the Sinai peninsula and southern Israel; along the Nile and the Red Sea coast south to about Port Sudan) Variable, but much paler above and below than *algeriensis*. White areas on the scapulars, wings and tail larger or even much larger; outer pair of rectrices generally completely white. Underparts pure white or almost so. Intergrades into *algeriensis* in the Maghreb where intermediate birds are sometimes recognised as *dodsoni*, and into *aucheri* in southern Israel.

L. m. leucopygos (southern Sahara in the Aïr east to about Dongola in northern Sudan, south to the valleys of the Blue and White Niles, Kordofan, Darfur, region of Lake Chad, northern Nigeria and west to Mali to about Tombouctou or beyond) Similar to *elegans*, but distinctly smaller; wing 94-104 (mean 100) and bill 19-23 (mean 21) in ten males, as against, respectively 105-111 (mean 107) and 22-25 (mean 23.5) in ten *elegans* (Vaurie 1959). Rump and uppertail-coverts even whiter, contrasting with pale grey of mantle and back, but underparts not so pure white, more creamy.

L. m. aucheri (west coast of the Red Sea from about Port Sudan south to Eritrea, northern Ethiopia and from Sinai and southern Israel north to Syria, Iraq and southern Iran; also in the Arabian Peninsula, but not Yemen) Difficult to tell from *elegans*. Upperparts generally similar or slightly darker with generally less white in the wings and tail; a narrow black band at the base of bill on the forehead is typical (narrower or lacking in *elegans*). Underparts not so pure white, but tinged to a variable extent with a greyish wash. In Iran intergrades into *pallidirostris* in southern Khorasan and possibly with

139

lahtora in the western part of Pakistan (see also *elegans*).

L. m. theresae (Galilee hills in northern Israel and possibly southern Lebanon) Close to *aucheri*, but marginally larger and saturated with darker grey over much of body plumage; white in tail and wing panel somewhat reduced compared to *aucheri*.

L. m. buryi (Yemen) Similar to *aucheri*, but upperparts distinctly darker, as slaty-grey as in *algeriensis* and with less white on scapulars. Underparts also darker, usually with a dark throat.

L. m. uncinatus (Socotra) Resembles *aucheri*, but with less white on scapulars and a longer bill on average.

L. m. lahtora (eastern Pakistan east to the Nepalese terai, Bihar and West Bengal in India and from the Himalayan foothills south through central India to Belgaum in southern Bombay and the Cuddapah district in Madras) Similar to *aucheri*, but with a distinct, relatively wide, black frontal band. Upperparts with more white; outer web of secondaries with much white; inner webs wholly white; two outer pairs of rectrices wholly white. Underparts whiter, not washed with greyish. Bill distinctly heavier on average.

L. m. pallidirostris 'Steppe Grey Shrike' (from the region north-east of Astrakhan on the lower Volga, east to the Zaisan Nor region, to Dzungaria and southern Mongolia in the Gobi to about 111°E, south to the Ala Shan, Aral/Caspian region, plains of Turkmenistan and north-east Iran; in Khorasan south to Seistan, Afghanistan and northern Pakistan) Differs from *aucheri* and *lahtora* by the absence of a black frontal band, duskier (sometimes even whitish) lores, a generally horn-coloured bill (black in a few adults) and usually faintly salmon-tinged underparts. Juveniles and first-winter birds are very distinct, and increasing numbers of them are being noted in western Europe. They can be identified relatively easily thanks to the following features which differ from first-winter Great Grey Shrikes: general pallor, typical head-pattern with rather pale lores (from greyish-buff to dark dusky brown), reduced dark brown mask behind the eye, and typical pale bill with a dark tip. As in adults, the underparts can be tinged with pale pinkish-buff in fresh plumage. It must also be remembered that *pallidirostris* is a Southern Grey Shrike with no white at the base of the secondaries (often present in the nominate race of the Great Grey Shrike and almost always so in its pale steppe race *homeyeri*).

MOVEMENTS Most populations are resident. Some populations of the race *pallidirostris* are, however, long-distance migrants. Small-scale movements, not yet clearly understood, have also been noted in various desert races and in nominate *meridionalis*. In winter in Cerdagne, southern France, the latter is absent from certain breeding territories in mid-mountain areas between 1,100 and 1,700m and is 'replaced' there by migrant Great Grey Shrikes (see Desaulnay 1982). Many *meridionalis* can be seen year round in the same spot, but others regularly appear in winter in areas

where the species is not known to breed, particularly in the Midi-Pyrénées and Aquitaine regions in south-west France. A few birds have even been found, also during winter months, as far north as the central-western départements of Vendée, Deux Sèvres and Indre et Loire. In Spain, a juvenile dispersion, probably not affecting all young birds, has been recorded: two nestlings ringed in the south-west were recovered respectively 170 days later 230km to the north-west and 155 days later 32km to the south-east. Nominate *meridionalis* regularly appears in September – November on Gibraltar and some birds might well turn up in North Africa; Ledant *et al.* (1981) mention three observations on the north coast of Algeria, but caution is needed as North African Southern Grey Shrikes may get reddish-tinted underparts following contact with wet sand (see Gloe 1996 for such a case on the Tunisian island of Djerba). Two vagrant nominate *meridionalis* have been found well north of their normal range: one on the German island of Heligoland before 1900 and one in southern Norway, near Klepp/Rogaland on 5 October 1984. There are also about 25 winter records from northern Italy, which lies just east of the breeding range; most records come from Liguria. This race is also a vagrant to Sicily and Malta.

In North Africa most populations appear to be strictly sedentary, but regular movements have been reported in certain areas. The race *elegans*, for instance, regularly winters in the lower Sénégal valley where it is not known to breed. In winter, the same race is also more common than in summer in the Tafilalt region in Morocco. Changing desert conditions possibly explain these movements. In Tunisia, northernmost populations of the race *algeriensis* seem, at least partly, to disperse to semi-desert areas outside the breeding season. Poorly documented movements have also been noted for the Sahel race *leucopygos*, possibly linked to severe droughts; this subspecies is a vagrant to The Gambia where at least five records are known between 16 December and 4 April; one bird was found as far south as Tono in northern Ghana in March and April 1982.

Definite but limited movements occur in the Middle East. In Israel some *aucheri* regularly turn up here and there in non-breeding areas, and there are signs of migration during August-October and March-April; in Jordan, too, this race and possibly also *elegans* is more widespread outside the breeding season. Movements are apparent in the Arabian Gulf states, particularly in the Eastern Province of Saudi Arabia in March-April and September-November. In the United Arab Emirates, the large resident breeding population of *aucheri* is augmented in winter by a substantial visiting population. The same holds true for Yemen where the resident populations of the dark race *buryi* are augmented in winter by migrants, presumably *aucheri*, from the north. *Pallidirostris*, as already mentioned above, is a special case. This Central Asian shrike is a partial long-distance migrant. Some populations are strictly sedentary; in southern Turkmenistan it has been estimated that about a third of the birds winter locally. Many Iranian birds probably also do so. Birds nesting further north, in Uzbekistan and Kazakhstan, are regular migrants. They winter south of the breeding range, possibly Iran, but some birds travel as far south-west as eastern Sudan, Eritrea, Ethiopia and northern Somalia. The southernmost point reached, presumably by a vagrant, lies 18 km south of Kibish, in the Ilemi triangle near the Kenya/Sudan border at c. 5°20'N 35°40'E. This exceptional observation was made on 17 February 1988, about 600km from the nearest regular wintering grounds in Sudan at c. 11°N (see Pearson 1989). Birds wintering in north-east Africa take a south-west direction in autumn and migrate over Iran, the Arabian Gulf, and the southern part of the Arabian Peninsula before flying over the Red Sea. A few birds may take a more westerly route as there is one confirmed observation in Israel, at Eilat on 20 November 1987, another (photographed by I. J. Andrews) in Jordan, near Aqaba on 10 October 1994, and one from Egypt, at Quseir on 20 February 1928. Movements of south-eastern populations are not well known, but apparently exist at least on a local scale in Pakistan; in winter, stragglers can be found in India: Sibi plains, Sind, Punjab and Rajasthan. Exceptionally, a vagrant was recorded in Brunei (Borneo) on 4 October 1990; this was the first record for south-east Asia (Mann and Diskin 1993).

Migrant *pallidirostris* nesting east of the Caspian Sea and in the Aral Sea area leave their breeding grounds towards mid-September; return movements are already apparent in the first ten days of March, but new arrivals are still appearing at the beginning of April.

MOULT As far as is known, moult is rather similar to that of the Great Grey Shrike. The partial juvenile moult starts soon after fledging; it mainly affects the body feathers, but often also some outer primaries; in some desert races, including *pallidirostris*, a variable number of secondaries and tail feathers may also be involved (see Cramp & Perrins 1993), but a clear separation of this moult from the moult to first-summer plumage appears impossible. Adults of nominate *meridionalis* undergo a complete post-breeding moult between late June and October, and a very partial, often weakly discernible head and body moult between February and April.

VOICE The differences in vocalisations between *excubitor* and *meridionalis* require further research. Things appear complicated because of the large ranges and many subspecies involved for both the Great Grey and Southern Grey Shrike. No significant differences are evident in the notes which make up the 'short song' of the two species.

Some calls appear different, however; the contact or excitement note of nominate *meridionalis* is softer, more fluted than the whistle of nominate *excubitor*. For differences in calls between nominate *excubitor* and the race *pallidirostris*, see sonograms in Panov (1983).

HABITAT As its name suggests, this shrike is a bird of warm, dry, southern areas of the northern hemisphere. Its breeds in mediterranean, desert and even, sometimes, (partly for race *lahtora*) tropical savanna types of climate. The habitat is always fairly open, dotted with thorny bushes where the nests are built, with or without large trees present.

In southern France, nominate *meridionalis* breeds in a variety of landscapes which can be briefly reviewed. It typically occurs in the open 'garrigue', scrubland dominated by *Quercus coccifera* growing on calcareous soils, including well-exposed and relatively rolling mountainous areas, generally below 1,000m (Col de Vence in the département of Hautes-Alpes). These areas, with their all-important patches of bare soil and low grassy vegetation, retain their suitability as long as they are grazed by sheep; the species also benefits from fires, frequent in the Mediterranean zone. In the Camargue, near sea-level, the Southern Grey Shrike is confined to sandy soils colonised by evergreen, prickly *Phyllirea* sp. bushes. In the neighbouring 'Crau sèche', the only French stony desert, it commonly nests in *Rubus* bushes growing against piles of stones which were gathered in the flat landscape by 1939-45 prisoners of war in order to prevent the landing of Allied airplanes. The species also occurs in less natural, extensively cultivated areas including vineyards, provided there are some trees, but above all, bushes and insect-rich dry pastures, fallow-lands and abandoned fields.

The North African races *algeriensis* and *elegans* inhabit desert-like areas typically characterised by sandy soils where thorny *Ziziphus* bushes grow in irregular patches; the Sahel race, *leucopygos*, as Bannerman (1953) puts it, makes its home in any desert in which there are small thorny trees and particularly *Acacia tortilis* or *Balanites* sp. The race *pallidirostris*, the 'Steppe Grey Shrike', occurs in a variety of arid landscapes and locally penetrates into the temperate zone. In Central Asia, Kazakhstan and Mongolia, this shrike is widespread in hilly, arid and sandy areas where bushes such as *Calligonum*, *Ammodendron* and *Tamarix*, etc., manage to grow. Locally this race, like those in North Africa, can be confined to oases near springs, or to bushes growing along temperate rivers. Occasionally, natural nesting sites are scarce; in that case, *pallidirostris* readily builds its nest on pylons when these are available. In southern Turkmenistan, it is one of the commonest birds in light pistachio *Pistacia vera* stands.

HABITS Nominate *meridionalis*, relatively dark even when facing the observer, is in general less obtrusive than the Great Grey Shrike, all the more so for inhabiting areas dotted with low, scrubby vegetation. However, it also seeks to display itself to other birds and so often perches conspicuously on the highest dry twigs of a bush and occasionally more than 5m above the ground on trees or wires. The bird has a deserved reputation for wariness and is difficult to approach. Locally, however, desert races can be remarkably tame and approached to within arm's length like several African shrikes. In southern Tunisia a pair of the race *elegans* was even known to perch on the terrace umbrellas of a hotel and take food items from around tables. At the beginning of the breeding season, the nominate race is very vocal and demonstrative particularly along territory boundaries. The song is mainly heard in the mornings and evenings, and typical harsh calls somewhat reminiscent of those of young shrikes begging for food are then also frequent. The latter

Southern Grey Shrike gathering wool for nest.

vocalisations, given when at least two birds (in most cases two males) are in visual contact, are accompanied by much wing shivering. Soft *hui, hui* calls, which serve for contact between two established or potential partners, are uttered by both males and females in very upright postures. Display-flights in shapes of circles, half-circles or 'eights', etc., all over the territory are common in the mornings at the end of winter or early in spring. Territory disputes and actual fights between neighbouring males appear to be much commoner than in the Great Grey Shrike.

The territory of nominate *meridionalis* is relatively small; it is sometimes only 10ha, and often between 15 and 25ha, both for individual birds observed in winter and for breeding pairs. In the Central Asian race *pallidirostris* and in North African *elegans,* breeding territories generally cover only about 10ha, but in the Negev Desert the race *aucheri* occupies much larger areas, averaging 62ha (range 53-77) in a three-year study of 31 pairs in all (see Yosef 1992). In southern France, nominate *meridionalis* was studied in some detail in 1994 and 1995 in an area of the Crau covering about 1,200ha. Each year there were 12 pairs, that is 1 pair per 100ha (Lepley 1995). In this relatively isolated population, the average distance between two neighbouring occupied nests was 938m in one year and 710m in the other (range 250-1,225). In a favourable habitat covering 4,000ha in north-west Spain, Hernandez (1994) also found c. 1 pair per 100ha. Densities can be extremely high locally in some desert races; in a date-palm grove in Algeria, up to five breeding pairs of the pale race *elegans* have been found in an area of about 4ha; all appeared to have newly fledged young (Parrot 1980). In winter, four individuals per ha have been recorded on Djerba in Tunisia with an estimated total population of c. 5,000 birds for that island in January 1992 (Gloe 1996). In southern Turkmenistan, there can be up to 10 pairs/km² of the race *pallidirostris* in pistachio stands.

A strong site-fidelity exists for an unknown, but probably high proportion of adult male Southern Grey Shrikes. They may even spend all their life in the same territory, as strongly suggested by observations of colour-ringed individuals of nominate *meridionalis* in Spain and France and of *aucheri* in Israel. Females, as shown by the same studies, soon disappear after the breeding season. They very rarely occupy the same territory the following spring. Contrary to what was once supposed (Dorka and Ullrich 1975) for nominate *meridionalis*, the pair does not stay together in winter and the pair-bond is not renewed in successive seasons.

The hunting techniques are similar to those of the Great Grey Shrike, but hovering appears to be much less frequent at least in nominate *meridionalis*. The preferred perching height is 2-3m as in the Red-backed Shrike; this is obviously due to the structure of the habitat. Small vertebrates are of course regularly impaled or wedged; arthropods are apparently less often stored than in the Great Grey Shrike, presumably because they are more numerous and, as a whole, much more available and accessible in warm areas. Yosef & Pinshow (1989) showed that in Israel mate selection by female *aucheri* was strongly affected by cache size and that reproductive success was increased in individuals with larger caches. In the same country, extraordinary nestling transfer was witnessed (see Introductory chapters).

FOOD Small vertebrates and particularly small reptiles, mainly lizards, play a significant part in the diet. Voles *Microtus* sp. are much smaller components of their diet than for the Great Grey Shrike as they are less frequent in desert-like habitats than in grasslands. Passerines are sometimes taken and arthropods are caught all year round. A detailed study of the food of nominate *meridionalis* has been carried out in the 'Crau sèche' (M. Lepley unpublished). It is based on 5,409 prey items identified in 257 pellets picked up between January and December. The remains of relatively few vertebrates were found and they represented only c. 21% of the total prey biomass. The only two small mammals were the Greater White-toothed Shrew *Crocidura russula* with 10.3% of the prey biomass in May and 2.4% in June, and the Wood Mouse *Apodemus sylvaticus* found only in November with c. 41% of the biomass. Birds were taken in April, June, July and December; in July, they represented 24.5% of the prey biomass. Small reptiles, *Podarcis muralis* and *Psammodromus hispanicus*, were taken in some numbers with up to 4% of the biomass in October. Amphibians were also among the victims with *Hyla meridionalis* representing c. 12% of the biomass in June and *Rana esculenta* c. 3% of the biomass also in June. Arthropods were caught in great numbers throughout the year with Arachnida representing 10.7% of the biomass, Crustacea (*Armadillidium vulgare*) 0.8%, Chilopoda (*Scolopendra cingulata*) 3.6% and insects 63.7%. Among the latter the most frequent groups taken were Coleoptera with 26.6% of the arthropod prey biomass, then Orthoptera with 12.9%, Lepidoptera 16.2% and Hymenoptera 4.7%, etc. What is known of the food of desert races confirms that small reptiles play a dominant role; apart from the lizards already mentioned for nominate *meridionalis,* at least the following species have been recorded: *Agama stellio, A. pallida, Chamaelo chamaeleon, Acanthodactylus boskianus, A. pardalis, Psammodromus algirus, Mesalina guttulata, Ptyodactylus hasselquisti oudrii, Chalcides bedriagae* and *Blanus cinereus* plus the small snakes *Coluber rogersi, C. rhodorhacis, Telescopus dhara.* In Oman, an individual of the race *aucheri* was even seen killing a young horned viper *Cerastes* sp. (see drawing in Glutz von Blotzheim & Bauer 1993 after photos by Erikson published in *Birds International* 1 (3) 1989). The remarkable thing is that the bird in question was seriously handicapped at the very start as it had somehow 'lost' two-thirds of its upper mandible. Small desert mammals like gerbil *Meriones crassus* and jerboa *Jaculus jaculus* are sometimes taken; so are passerines. A long list of insect families has been recorded; among these the Tenebrionidae, so frequent in desert sands, deserve special mention.

BREEDING For nominate *meridionalis,* the breeding season in Spain begins as early as mid-January, when females start to visit the territories of resident males. About a month can elapse between the first feeding of the female by the male and nest construction. In Spain, the first eggs are laid at the end of February; in March about 50% of full clutches are found. In southern France, by contrast, only a few pairs have been known to lay as early as the end of March; precise data for

about 80 nests show a marked peak between mid-April and May; fresh clutches are rare from mid-May, but found until the end of June. Replacement clutches are frequent and second normal broods are known from Spain, but not proved so far in France; the percentage of pairs undertaking such broods is not known. In the Crau, the average distance for two successive nests built by eight different pairs after a failure was 143m (25-300m). Other races of the Southern Grey Shrike regularly appear to raise two broods, for instance in North Africa where fresh eggs can be found between February and the end of June or even July. In the Negev Desert in Israel, second normal clutches are common, third ones are not rare, involving about 10% of the breeders, and occasional fourth attempts can take place; the breeding season extends from the end of January to August. The Central Asian race *pallidirostris* lays one normal clutch in the northern part of its range, but regularly two further south where the proportion of resident birds appears to approach 30%; in the northern part of the range, migrant males, as a rule, turn up a few days before the females and as early as mid-March. In southern France, nests of nominate *meridionalis* are generally placed at an average height barely more than 1m (range 0.3-2.2m in the Crau). They are generally hidden in a thorny bush or small prickly tree, mainly *Rubus* sp. or sometimes *Quercus ilex* in the Crau, *Phyllirea* sp. in the Camargue, *Juniperus oxycedrus, Pyrus amygdaliformis, Quercus coccifera,* etc. in the open 'garrigue'. Occasionally they are found in old Magpie *Pica pica* nests. In the Guadalquivir delta in Spain, the species chiefly nests low in *Halimium* sp. bushes, which can be 1.5m high. In the Iberian peninsula, nests have also been found between 1.3 and 5m up in *Quercus ilex* stands. The other races also typically nest low in bushes, for instance in *Ziziphus* sp. in North Africa, although in oases the nest of *elegans* can also be found rather high up in palm-trees. In Central Asia, *pallidirostris* often builds between 0.5 and 1.5m in bushes on sandy soils, particularly *Calligonum* and *Ammodendron* sp. Locally, its nest can be found in trees, for instance pistachios in southern Turkmenistan, at a height between 1.25 and 4.2m; occasionally, in areas with few shrubs, it is located on pylons. The nest of nominate *meridionalis* recalls a relatively bulky nest of Blackbird *Turdus merula* with an outer diameter averaging about 16.5cm and a height of c. 12.5cm. As a rule, it is smaller than that of the Great Grey Shrike. Made of locally available and often dry material, it may look 'old'; wool is readily used when possible, as are feathers. Nominate *meridionalis* lays (3) 4-7 eggs, most clutches having 5 or 6, whether in Spain or in southern France. In the latter country, 43 full clutches had 5.3 eggs on average; only one nest, a replacement clutch, had 3 eggs. The North African races lay between 3 and 7 eggs throughout the long breeding season, the average clutch-size being about 4.6 eggs (see Heim de Balsac & Mayaud 1962 for details). It is thus lower than in south-west Europe. In Israel, the local races also lay 3-7 eggs. In nominate *meridionalis,* incubation lasts 17-18 days and the young stay in the nest for 18-19 days. In Spain, the period of dependence has been estimated at 39 days.

REFERENCES Ali & Ripley (1972), Andrews (1995), Aspinall (1996), Bannerman (1953), Cheng (1987), Cramp & Perrins (1993), Cruz Sollis & Lope Rebollo (1985), Cruz Sollis *et al.* (1985-1990), Dement'ev & Gladkov (1968), Desaulnay (1982), Dohmann (1985), Dorka & Ullrich (1975), Eck (1990), Gloe (1996), Glutz von Blotzheim & Bauer (1993), Goodman & Meininger (1989), Harrison (1986), Heim de Balsac & Mayaud (1962), Hernandez (1993a,b, 1994), Hirschfeld (1995), Isenmann & Bouchet (1993), Jany (1948), Ledant *et al.* (1981), Lefranc (1993, 1995a), Lefranc & Lepley (1995), Lepley (1995), Meinertzhagen (1953), Moltoni (1970), Morel & Morel (1990), Olivier (1994), Pearson (1989), Panov (1983, 1995), Parrot (1980), Richardson (1990), Roberts (1992), Salvan (1969), Shirihai (1995), Smith (1955, 1957), Thomsen & Jacobsen (1979), Tucker & Heath (1994), Vaurie (1959), Vorobiev (1934), Yosef (1992a,b), Yosef & Pinshow (1988a,b, 1989).

17 CHINESE GREY SHRIKE
Lanius sphenocercus Plate 6

Other name: Chinese Great Grey Shrike

IDENTIFICATION Length c. 30cm. This is the largest *Lanius* shrike, with two distinct races confined to parts of eastern Asia. It looks very much like a big Great Grey Shrike with a prominent white supercilium, a large white wing-patch and a long and strongly graduated tail. The sexes are similar. Juveniles have greyish-brown upperparts and off-white underparts, tinged tawny. They are narrowly and transversely barred dark brown.

The only confusion species is the Great Grey Shrike. The differences in size and structure are good clues, particularly when confronted with young birds. *Sphenocercus* is markedly larger and has a longer tail (c. 4cm more). Moreover, the adults of that species have a grey not white rump. The races *mollis* and *sibiricus* of the Great Grey Shrike occur within the Chinese Grey's range (see description under Great Grey). *Pallidirostris*, a race of the Southern Grey Shrike, may occur in the west of the species's range, but in quite different habitats.

DESCRIPTION *L. s. sphenocercus*
Adult male Facial mask jet black over lores, eyes and ear-coverts. Supercilium white and broad (3-4mm behind eye), joining over base of bill to form a small white area on anterior part of forehead. Upperparts mid-grey from crown to uppertail-coverts. Scapulars white. Tail black, fringed white and graduated (graduation 3-4.5cm); three pairs of outer rectrices almost wholly white; T2 and T3 tipped broadly white; central pair almost wholly black save for tiny buff spots at end. Wings black, edged white; much white at base of primaries and at base of outer and inner webs of secondaries, which are broadly tipped white; wing-coverts almost completely black. Underparts off-white with sometimes pale buff or rosy wash (at least on museum specimens). Undertail white except for small black tip.

Adult female Similar to male as far as known; extent of white on wings variable, but apparently not sex-related.
Juvenile (not examined; description after Dement'ev and Gladkov 1968) Upperparts as in adults but ochre-tinged and indistinctly vermiculated. Flight feathers broadly fringed whitish-ochre; wing-coverts also with broad ochre tips. Underparts off-white, tinged ochre on breast.
Bare parts Bill long, strong, well hooked and black with a greyish base to lower mandible; horn-brownish in young birds with black confined to culmen. Legs black in adults, pale brownish in juveniles.

MEASUREMENTS (*sphenocercus*) Wing 118-124; tail 130-148 (mean c. 140, perhaps slightly longer on average in males); bill (culmen) 18-20; tarsus c. 30. Weight 80-100 (generally 90-100, but few data).

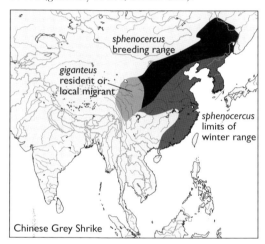
Chinese Grey Shrike

DISTRIBUTION AND STATUS The breeding area almost exclusively covers north-east and central China; however, the northern boundary lies just inside far-eastern Russia and reaches at least 50°N. The species probably also breeds in extreme north-east Korea. The limits are still unclear but the range extends from the Amur area in Russia south-west over China: Heilongjiang, then south to Hebei and Shandong and west through Shanxi and the Ordos desert in Inner Mongolia to Gansu and the Nan Shan and Koko Nor regions of eastern Qinghai, where it turns south to the Muli region of southern Sichuan. The southern limits lie at c. 28°N and the western at c. 98°E.

GEOGRAPHICAL VARIATION The distinct race *giganteus* is a high-mountain bird. Vaurie (1972) speculated whether it was not a distinct species.

L. s. sphenocercus (Amur region in far-eastern Russia, north-east and central China) Described above.
L. s. giganteus (eastern Nan Shan and eastern Tibet, south to upper Mekong) Distinctly larger than nominate with wings and tail at least 2cm longer; wing-length averages c. 140mm and tail-length c. 160mm in males, females slightly smaller. Upperparts darker with no trace of white on forehead and no white supercilium. Tail with less white on

outer rectrices. Wings with no white on outer webs of secondaries. Underparts not so white, rather pale lavender-grey. Juvenile *giganteus* has somewhat darker upperparts than nominate and is more distinctly tinged ochre, particularly on underparts.

MOVEMENTS The nominate race is a partial migrant. Breeding range and winter quarters somewhat overlap. The bulk of the latter apparently lies in south-east China, mostly north of the Chang-jiang and as far west as c. 105°E, in the provinces of Shanxi, Hebei, Henan and Hubei; the eastern and southern limits follow the coasts of Korea and China about as far south as Hong Kong, where up to 1986 there were only three records (4 November 1952; 1 November 1964 and 12 September 1976). The provinces of extreme south-east China where the species appears to be regular if rare are Jiangxi, Fujian and Guangdong. This shrike rarely crosses the sea; it is an accidental winter visitor to Japan, with only five records before 1953 and currently probably fewer than one individual on average per winter, most observations coming from the south-west. On Sado Island, the first Chinese Grey Shrike was observed in winter 1993. The race *giganteus* is probably mainly, if not exclusively, resident, only undertaking local and altitudinal movements. The migration routes of nominate *sphenocercus* are not well known, but most birds appear to travel south or south-west in autumn. A few may already turn up far from their breeding grounds at the end of June. Most birds in Russian Ussuriland depart between the end of August and October; a few may, however, spend the winter in the southern part of the area. The bulk of the breeding population is back in the second half of March. In Korea, where the bird is an uncommon winter visitor, there are a number of records for October-April, but most for November-December. The few birds observed in Japan occurred between 23 November and 21 March. In Hebei, China, *Lanius sphenocercus* is said to appear at the end of August and to leave in the latter part of March. Some details are known for the Beidaihe area: the shrike is found sparingly there in spring, but is seen more regularly in autumn when records go from 20 August to 16 November (after that date, Chinese Grey Shrikes may, however, be less rare than birdwatchers!). Further south, near Nanking, the bird has been seen between the beginning of December and March.

MOULT The post-juvenile moult takes place soon after fledging and only involves the body feathers. It is generally finished in the first ten days of September. Adults undergo a complete moult starting immediately after breeding as early as the end of June or July. It is over at the beginning of October and the birds may then show a faint pinkish wash on their breasts.

VOICE The song, rather similar to that of the Great Grey Shrike, is mainly a repetition of two relatively melodious notes, the second being higher in pitch. Often one only hears a prolonged version of that last sound, a kind of long *tschrii*. This loud song is occasionally interrupted by a long, hardly audible warble. A characteristic harsh, somewhat nasal alarm call has been transcribed as *tscheee*.

HABITAT Occurs in temperate types of climate. In far-eastern Russia, the nominate subspecies breeds from sea-level to an elevation of c. 200m. In China, it may nest up to 1,100m and in winter it can be found up to 1,800m in the Nan Shan foothills. The race *giganteus* is a high-elevation bird, breeding at roughly 3,000-5,000m. The structure of the habitat is very similar to that occupied by the Great Grey Shrike; in Amurland nominate *sphenocercus* favours broad river valleys, meadows and pastures dotted with bushes and scattered groups of trees. In China, it is said to occur also in open steppes and even in semi-deserts. The few birds seen in Japan were on cultivated plains, around open woodlands or on reclaimed land with grass and shrubs. In Tibet, *giganteus* breeds along or above the timberline, particularly in stunted vegetation stands, for instance rhododendron scrub.

HABITS Very similar to those of Great Grey Shrike. Generally very conspicuous and sometimes easy to approach, particularly the race *giganteus*, which is said to be very confiding. The abundance of this large shrike is low; in Russia, in central Amurland it varies between 0.11 and 0.34 pairs per km^2 and in the plains near Lake Khanka between 0.4 and 1 pairs per km^2. In the latter area, where good densities occur, occupied nests of neighbouring pairs are 1-2.5km apart. Territories do not overlap and appear to be relatively small, c. 4ha on average (2.3-5.8ha for four pairs studied in far-eastern Russia). Male and female hunt between 10 and 400m from the nest, though most of the time only 40-70m from it. Most prey is caught in low vegetation using the classic sit-and-wait technique. The Chinese Grey Shrike prefers to perch relatively high, 2-8m and generally 4-6m above the ground. It regularly flies from its perch and hovers for 10-30 seconds c. 5-6m above the ground. From time to time, it also catches insects in the air; slow-moving ones are caught in the usual flycatcher *Muscicapa* sp. way; others or birds can be pursued up to 100m in Sparrowhawk *Accipiter nisus* style. Larders are regularly kept.

FOOD The Chinese Grey Shrike is a very opportunistic feeder. Its diet is made up of arthropods, chiefly insects, and small vertebrates; vertebrates are preferred to invertebrates. A detailed study in Amurland during the breeding season, mainly based on pellet analyses, has shown the importance of the latter (Winter 1987). Out of a total of 2,813 prey, 455 (16%) were vertebrates composed of 13.63% amphibians, 34.29% birds and 52.53% small mammals. From their arrival back from their winter quarters until the first ten days of May, the shrikes fed almost exclusively on small rodents; birds were mainly taken between mid-May and mid-June and amphibians at the end of June and at the beginning of July when the frog *Rana amurensis* was numerous and easy to catch on its spawning grounds. Invertebrates played an important part in the diet from the end of April to June; most of them were Coleoptera (51.61%), then Orthoptera (24.98%) and Hymenoptera (18.62%). Remarkably, almost one arthropod out of four was a carabid beetle (24.09%); the most important single species was, however, an orthopteran:

the mole-cricket *Gryllotalpa africana* with 22.14% of all invertebrates taken. Some spiders were also taken (1.06%). Other observations show that lizards figure in the diet. There are few data on the food in winter, but rodents and, more rarely, birds are certainly regularly taken. However, one of the rare Chinese Grey Shrikes seen in Japan spent the winter apparently feeding mainly on mole-crickets.

BREEDING All available data come from far-eastern Russia and concern the nominate subspecies. Laying begins in the second half of April. The first eggs generally hatch towards the end of the first ten days of May in the Lake Khanka area, and about a week later near the northern limits of the breeding range at c. 49°N. Fledging mainly occurs between the start and end of June. Broods from late clutches can, however, leave the nest ãs late as mid-July. There is only one normal clutch, but replacement clutches are regular. The nest is built at a height of 1.2-5m above the ground in a variety of small trees, particularly willows *Salix* sp., oaks *Quercus mongolicus*, elms *Ulmus propinqua*, birches *Betula dahurica*, etc. It can be a sizeable structure very conspicuous from a distance or, on the contrary, appear small for the size of the bird. Its outer diameter can reach 26.5cm. Seven nests measured in Amurland had an average outer diameter of 21.5cm (19.5-23.8), a height of 14.9cm (12-17.5), an inner diameter of 10.8cm (10.2-11.9), and a depth of 8.4cm (7.4-9). The nest, made of twigs, rootlets, grass, dry and fresh leaves, is lined with dead vegetation, feathers and down. The clutch comprises 5-8 eggs. The mean clutch-size for 19 nests found in Amurland was 6.8. Incubation lasts 16-17 days and the young stay in the nest at least 20 days. Adults and their young appear to stay together for about two months.

REFERENCES Brazil (1991), Chalmers (1986), Cheng (1987), Chong (1938), Dement'ev & Gladkov (1968), Gore & Won (1971), Kondo (1993), La Touche (1925-1930), Meyer de Schauensee (1984), Panov (1983), Schäfer (1938), Shaw (1936), Sokolow & Vietinghoff-Scheel (1992), Stresemann *et al.* (1937), Vaurie (1972), Vorobiev (1954), Williams *et al.* (1992), Winter (1987).

18   GREY-BACKED FISCAL
Lanius excubitoroides   Plate 11

IDENTIFICATION Length c. 25cm. An African shrike (three races) which to the European or North American birdwatcher may superficially resemble a rather bulky, long-tailed Great Grey or Southern Grey Shrike with a black forehead. It has mid-grey upperparts, a whitish rump, dark wings with a white primary patch, very conspicuous in flight, and a long tail with a diagnostic white basal half and a black terminal half. Its underparts are white. Females are very similar to males, but show some dark chestnut on their flanks. In the field, this characteristic can only be seen during territorial displays or when the birds are preening. The juveniles, heavily barred, have grey-brown upperparts

becoming paler on rump; their dark brown wings already carry a white primary patch and their dark brown tail is fringed whitish at base.

The Grey-backed Fiscal, often quite tame, is a conspicuous bird, all the more so for being a cooperative breeder and therefore gregarious.

The confusion species are:
— Common Fiscal, smaller, slimmer, darker on its upperparts (back and mantle) and with very distinct white scapulars;
— Taita and Somali Fiscals, also smaller and both with a dark cap;
— Long-tailed Fiscal, slimmer, longer-tailed and also with a dark 'hood' on its head;
— the *leucopygos* race of Southern Grey Shrike, distinctly smaller, with paler upperparts and no black band on forehead (Sahel area);
— Lesser Grey Shrike, which may appear in *excubitoroides* country while on migration. Adults also have a black forehead, but their facial mask does not extend down to the nape. They also have a different structure with a much smaller tail, fringed white but with no white at base, and a shorter, deeper bill.

Grey-backed Fiscal. Note black band on forehead and typical tail pattern with basal half white, the rest black.

DESCRIPTION *L. e. excubitoroides*
Adult male Facial mask black over forehead (at least 1cm from base of bill), lores and ear-coverts; passes just above eyes and extends to base of nape and even, sometimes, to sides of upper mantle. Supercilium whitish, fairly obvious along facial mask from over middle of eye to end of ear-coverts. Upperparts mid-grey from crown to back, becoming somewhat paler on lower back. Rump and uppertail-coverts whitish. Tail black with white base and bordered white on almost whole length of basal half, long (up to c. 16cm) and graduated (graduation c. 3.5-4cm); all rectrices, except central pair, faintly tipped white and with much white at base (fresh plumage). Wings black with distinct white primary patch. Underparts white. Undertail white (most of basal half) and black.

Adult female Similar to male, but with a distinct chestnut patch on flanks (hidden by closed wings).
Juvenile Facial mask dark brown over lores, eyes and ear-coverts (not or very faintly on forehead). Supercilium whitish, discreet but present from over middle of eyes almost to end of ear-coverts. Upperparts grey-brown, heavily but finely barred blackish from forehead to lower back. Rump and uppertail-coverts buff-white also barred blackish. Tail dark brown with some white at base and slightly tipped buff. Wings dark brown with white primary patch; wing-coverts dark, slightly barred and edged buff. Flight feathers, particularly tertials, also variably tipped buff. Underparts off-white, rather faintly barred and almost only on breast and flanks. Undertail white (almost basal half) and dark brown, fringed and tipped pale buff.
Bare parts Bill and feet black. Iris brown.

MEASUREMENTS (*excubitoroides*) Wing 105-115 (120); tail 130-160; bill 16-17; tarsus 28-32. Weight: Kenyan males 47-63.5 (mean 55.5 for n = 42); Kenyan females 46.5-59 (mean c. 52 for n = 26).

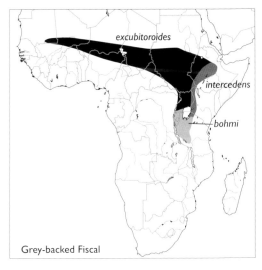

Grey-backed Fiscal

DISTRIBUTION AND STATUS The breeding distribution lies entirely south of the Sahara and is confined to central-eastern Africa. From west to east, it extends from south-east Mauritania to south-west Ethiopia and western Kenya (west of the Rift Valley); the eastern limits lie roughly at 37°E. The species has not been recorded in south-east Ethiopia or Somalia; it is thus absent from the Horn of Africa. In the west, the huge forest areas are avoided by this shrike which seems to be confined to the Sahel zone where it can be found alongside the *leucopygos* race of Southern Grey Shrike. In Mali, it is said not to occur south of 15°N. It may have been overlooked, so far, in north-east Burkina Faso and south-east Niger, but it probably does not inhabit the countries adjoining the Gulf of Guinea, except north-east Nigeria, just west of Lake Chad, and northern Cameroon where it has been met with at Yagoua and also 60km south of Maroua. In Chad, it is a characteristic but rare bird of the Sudanese zone. In

Sudan, it is widespread south of c. 12°N and from there its range extends south across extreme eastern Zaïre (Rift Valley), Uganda, Burundi and western Tanzania. The southern boundaries cross Tanzania near Lake Rukwa and the Usangu Flats at c. 8°30'S.

GEOGRAPHICAL VARIATION Three races are generally recognised. The differences are imperceptible in the field.

> *L. e. excubitoroides* (western part of the range east at least to Sudan) Described above.
> *L. e. intercedens* (central Ethiopia, north-west Uganda and western Kenya) Similar to nominate, but larger as reflected in wing-length: 116-126 against 105-115.
> *L. e. bohmi* (western Tanzania, Rwanda and south-west Uganda) Similar to *intercedens*, but with distinctly browner, more dusky-grey upperparts.

MOVEMENTS Little known. Most populations are probably resident. Reports of elaborate migrations in Kenya's Rift Valley appear to be wrong. Regular movements at least on a local scale may, however, exist in western parts of the range where the species inhabits typical Sahel areas. In Mauritania and Mali it is said to 'disappear' or to be very rare during the rains. Wanderers sometimes turn up in unexpected places like the bird seen at Mau Narok at c. 3,000m in Kenya.

MOULT No information.

VOICE The species has about half a dozen calls. Two distinct territorial ones have been described: in threat, a metallic monosyllable which can be transcribed as *kyoir-l*, and a display call, like a duetting chorus, uttered by defenders going for an intruder: *kyoir-l, kyoi, kyo-ooh*. Duetting Grey-backed Fiscals are only heard during territorial disputes, but these are very frequent in the breeding season. The male breeder often gives a brief song during nuptial feeding when the female utters a loud *pssh* just prior to being fed. The combination of the song (male) and *pssh* call are a good indicator of pending nesting activity. The birds also have a loud, harsh alarm call given, for instance, when a hawk is spotted (S. Zack pers. comm.).

HABITAT This shrike lives in a dry subtropical climate; in Kenya, where it occurs between 1,000-1,900m, its range lies entirely within the 500mm isohyet. It is common in bushed and wooded grassland as well as in open woodland, and can also be met with in gardens, parks or even cultivated areas if sufficiently well provided with relatively high trees. In a study area near Lake Naivasha, the Grey-backed Fiscal mainly nested in stands of yellow-barked acacia *Acacia xanthophloea* with an understorey of several perennial shrubs and Naivasha star grass *Cynodon plectostachyus*. Territories with a high perennial shrub-cover were of particular importance for both survivorship and the production of young (see Zack & Ligon 1985b), presumably because insect abundance in the dry season was higher there than in other areas. In the western part of its range, the species is mainly to be found in the thorn scrub of the Sahel zone.

HABITS A gregarious, cooperatively breeding species, easily located even when silent and often very tame.

147

Several birds can be seen together when feeding young at the nest and, throughout the year, during the territorial disputes described below and at prey concentrations when for instance ants *Dorylus* sp. or *Cossus* caterpillars emerge from the bases of acacias. At other times the individual birds are dispersed throughout their territories, at least during the day. At night, they tend to roost as a group on densely foliaged acacia branches. Groups can number up to 20 or more individuals; up to 16 breeding groups studied in Kenya numbered from two to eleven birds. Only one pair breeds per group, with all the other group members aiding in the rearing of young. Territories are relatively large; in a Ugandan study they varied from 9 to 34ha (n = 7). The larger ones occupied habitats of a poorer quality due to the effect of farming practices which tended to eliminate grass leys. Territorial display and encounters make the birds very conspicuous. Self-advertisement takes the form of perching in high positions or of boundary patrolling; rival family units can be seen engaged in territorial display, each one very noisily defending a corner of its own territory. The flight at an intruder is direct, with rapid wing-beats, changing to gliding flight when the defender approaches contact. The defenders often perch on tall trees and rock back and forth with outstretched wings and fanned tails. They frequently change perches. If necessary, the threat changes to a duetting accompanied by a sort of 'dancing' reminiscent of babbler *Turdoides* behaviour: the defenders, having alighted near the intruder, jump up and down, almost a foot into the air; to do this, they take off with rapid flapping and land with wings outstretched and tails fanned; they then gently wave their tails up and down. All the family, both adults and mature progeny, takes part in this 'dancing', which may last up to 30 minutes. Generally the intruder leaves before there is any physical fighting; the latter appears, however, to be fairly regular when territorial transgression by a mated pair of shrikes or a group takes place. Aerial battles between flocks also occur, with grappling in mid-air. In a close study of three adjacent territories in Kenya, the number and mean duration of rallies increased with the onset of the major rains, which signals the start of the breeding season; from April to August, c. 1.5 rallies were observed per hour. Site-fidelity is high in this mainly resident shrike, and young males, after having been helpers, can acquire breeding status within the natal territory. The favoured perch-height appears to be 2-4m. Prey is caught mainly on the ground, but also sometimes in the air; family parties can be seen catching flying ants. This confident shrike sometimes visits gardens where it readily perches near a busy gardener likely to disturb insects! Larders are apparently regular, but there is no detailed study.

FOOD The diet is mainly composed of a variety of rather large insects. Small vertebrates are also taken including, occasionally, birds. The species has been seen plundering Quelea nests *Quelea quelea*. In a study area in Kenya, Grey-backed Fiscals were captured in traps baited with large prey items such as small frogs and *Cossus* caterpillars.

BREEDING The timing of breeding is obviously linked with the rains and thus with insect abundance. In a study near Lake Naivasha (Kenya) nesting attempts were made almost throughout the year, but they generally followed increased rainfall and most successful nests were associated with the rains. The major breeding effort started in May and ended in November, after short rains. This general pattern roughly concords with schedules in other areas. In Uganda, the species is known to breed between May and July and again in October-December. In Ethiopia, fresh eggs have been found in April and June. The situation remains unclear in the western part of the range. Breeding has, however, been reported in February and March in Mauritania and Mali. A bird caught in Cameroon was in breeding condition in April. Breeding success was very low in the Kenyan study mentioned above, and replacement clutches are probably frequent. Before nest-building starts, the single mated pair appears to isolate itself from the other members of the flock; this is the time when the male feeds the female (see Voice). Nest-building is done primarily by the breeding female; her mate may carry nest material, but apparently does not engage in nest construction. Near Lake Naivasha, nests (n = 55) were exclusively found in yellow-barked acacias of all sizes; they were situated either on peripheral branches or against the trunk, at a height of 1-10m or more. The nest is compact, firmly constructed of grass stems, roots and bark fibre on a foundation of twigs, mainly of acacia, often with thorns protuding. Small feathers can be used for the lining. The nests are probably never re-used, but material can be taken from old ones as well as from those of other birds. The Grey-backed Fiscal lays 2-4 eggs (mean 2.82 for n = 17 in Kenya) and incubation, only performed by the female, lasts 13-15 days. The young stay in the nest about 20 days. The breeding male is the most active food provider of the incubating female and later of the nestlings. In Kenya it was found that male helpers help more than female helpers during both the egg-stage and when the chicks are in the nest. The juveniles are completely dependent on adults for food for at least two weeks after fledging. At about 50 days, however, they forage at rates and in ways similar to those of adults. They do not appear to join adult territorial disputes in the first six months of their lives; they interact with members of their natal groups for up to several years.

REFERENCES Banage (1969), Britton (1980), Brown & Britton (1980), Chapin (1954), Elgood (1994), Friedmann (1937), Jackson (1938), Lamarche (1981, 1988), Lewis & Pomeroy (1989), Louette (1981), Nikolaus (1987), Salvan (1969), Schouteden (1960), Urban & Brown (1971), Zack (1986a, 1995), Zack & Ligon (1985a,b), Zimmerman *et al.* (1996).

19   LONG-TAILED FISCAL
Lanius cabanisi   **Plate 12**

IDENTIFICATION Length 26-30cm. A large, pied and appropriately named East African shrike. Its upperparts are mainly dark, with crown, neck and sides of head black, upper back dusky grey and lower back grey. The very long tail, about 16cm, is also mainly black. So are the wings which, however, show a small white primary patch. The white rump and uppertail-coverts contrast with the rest of the upperparts and are very conspicuous when the bird is in flight. The underparts are pure white. The sexes are very similar, but females have a concealed chestnut patch on their flanks (hidden by closed wings). The juveniles are browner on the upperparts and off-white on the underparts. They are finely barred blackish all over. Their dark brown wings possess a white primary patch.

The Long-tailed Fiscal is rather conspicuous. Very sociable, it is often seen and heard in noisy parties.

Its long tail makes it almost unmistakable. It can hardly be confused with the Common Fiscal, whose tail is shorter and which shows white 'shoulder-patches'. There might be a slight risk of confusion with the Magpie Shrike which is, however, even larger and longer-tailed, and which, despite its white scapulars, is darker with almost completely dark underparts.

DESCRIPTION
Adult male Bill strong and heavy. Top and sides of head black; facial mask noticeable at very close quarters with lores, ear-coverts and base of neck black; forehead, crown, nape and upper mantle dark brown. Mantle and upper back mid-grey becoming pale grey on lower back. Rump and uppertail-coverts white or whitish; distinct barring on tips of uppertail-coverts often present even in adults. Tail dark brown very faintly tipped white (fresh plumage), long (about 16cm) and graduated (graduation c. 5.5-6.5cm). Wings dark brown with small primary patch; tertials and most secondaries very slightly tipped whitish (fresh plumage). Underparts pure white. Undertail black.
Adult female As male, but with a chestnut patch on flanks.
Juvenile Facial mask dark brown over lores, eyes and ear-coverts. Upperparts grey-brown, finely barred blackish from forehead to lower back. Rump and uppertail-coverts buff-white with heavy dark barring. Tail dark brown; rectrices with black subterminal bars and tiny buff tips. Wings dark brown with white primary patch; wing-coverts grey-brown barred blackish; tertials and some secondaries with subterminal bars. Underparts off-white with fairly heavy barring on breast and upper belly. Undertail dark brown.
Bare parts Bill and legs black. Iris dark brown.

MEASUREMENTS Wing 105-118; tail 150-180; bill 17-20; tarsus 28-32. Weight: no data.

DISTRIBUTION AND STATUS The breeding range is quite restricted and limited to parts of East Africa where the bird is common in suitable habitats. The Long-tailed Fiscal only occurs in three countries: Kenya, Tanzania and Somalia. In the latter it is widespread south of 3°N; in Kenya it is confined to the south, almost from the shores of Lake Victoria to the coast, with few observations north of the Equator. The western boundaries lie at approximately 34°50'E and the southern limits cross eastern Tanzania from Kilosa and Morogoro to Dar es Salaam at c. 6°30'S; most birds found south of c. 5°S may, however, be wanderers.

Long-tailed Fiscal

GEOGRAPHICAL VARIATION None known. Monotypic.

MOVEMENTS Little known. The birds appear to be mainly resident; wanderers have, however, apparently been recorded slightly south of the regular breeding range in Tanzania.

MOULT No information.

VOICE The species gives a variety of chattering, scolding cries, including a frequent harsh *chit-er-row*; it also utters a mellow whistle. The typical chorus given by the birds starts with a *cha cha raa*.

HABITAT The Long-tailed Fiscal replaces the Grey-backed Fiscal in drier, more open habitats. The two species are very largely allopatric. The Long-tailed Fiscal often lives in the same geographical areas as the Taita Fiscal, but in somewhat moister habitats. In Kenya, it occurs from sea-level near the coast to c. 1,600m in the southern and eastern peripheries of the highlands. It can be met with in vast, shrubby, nearly treeless savanna and also in cultivated areas or in patches of open woodland.

HABITS Little studied, but obviously very similar to those of the Grey-backed Fiscal. The Long-tailed Fiscal is also a cooperative breeder and shows similar territorial displays. During these displays the birds are very vocal; they pose with the body well up, the wings down or slightly open, and the long tail swinging in all directions, up and down, side to side, in a figure eight, then over the back and fanned. An interesting behaviour has been described in Tsavo (Kenya) between an individual shrike and a flock of Red-billed Buffalo

Weavers *Bubalornis niger*. The shrike benefited from the grasshoppers and other insects flushed at ground level by the foraging weavers, and followed them. The latter, in turn, took advantage of the anti-predator behaviour and alarm calls of the shrike. On one occasion when a predator approached, the weavers flew away for a time before re-associating again with the shrike; on another they simply 'froze' temporarily. Both species followed each other for one-and-a-half hours, but there was no 'leader' or 'follower', the two species playing both roles in turn. This behaviour has only been witnessed (or published) once, but may well be of regular occurrence. Prey is caught in the usual shrike manner and larders have been reported (confirmation needed).

FOOD Mainly insects and particularly Orthoptera and Coleoptera, but little information. Lizards, small snakes and young birds are taken when opportunity offers.

BREEDING No detailed study of this cooperative breeder has been published. Clutches have been found between December and May, particularly in the wet months of April, May and December, but also from August to October and particularly in the dry month of September. The nest is relatively large, built mainly of grass and rootlets, coarse ones for the exterior, finer ones for the lining; very often spider web is worked around the rim. It is hidden in a bush or thick tree, a few metres from the ground. The eggs are usually 3 in number, sometimes 4. Incubation lasts 13 or 14 days and the nestling period is 16 to 18 days.

REFERENCES Ash & Miskell (1983), Britton (1980), Brosset (1989), Brown & Britton (1980), Friedmann & Loveridge (1937), Jackson (1938), Lewis & Pomeroy (1989), Mackworth-Praed & Grant (1955), Olivier (1944;), van Someren (1956), Zimmerman *et al.* (1996).

20 TAITA FISCAL
Lanius dorsalis   **Plate 12**

IDENTIFICATION Length c. 21cm. A medium-sized, rather stocky, pied, and little-known East African species. Its black cap, which extends to the base of the upper mantle, and the black sides of its face contrast with the rest of the upperparts: pale grey mantle, back and rump and white scapulars. A white primary patch appears on the otherwise black wings. The relatively short tail is also black, fringed white. The underparts are pure white. Females only differ from males in having, at least sometimes, some chestnut streaks on the flanks. Juveniles are grey-brown, finely vermiculated on the upperparts which become paler on rump; their dark brown tail is fringed whitish. The off-white underparts are also heavily vermiculated.

The main confusion species by far is the Somali Fiscal (see under that species and also under Grey-backed Fiscal).

DESCRIPTION
Adult male Upperparts black from forehead to upper mantle including sides of head (lores and ear-coverts). Scapulars white. Lower mantle and back mid-grey becoming paler towards and on rump. Uppertail-coverts whitish. Tail black, relatively short and graduated (graduation c. 2-2.5cm); outer web of pair of outer rectrices fringed white; three outer pairs of rectrices broadly tipped white. Wings wholly black except for rather large white primary patch (c. 2cm long). Underparts white. Undertail dark brown with white spots towards end.

Adult female Similar to male, but with an unobtrusive chestnut patch on flanks.

Juvenile Facial mask dark brown over lores and ear-coverts. Upperparts grey-brown and finely vermiculated from forehead to lower back. Rump and upper-tail-coverts pale buff, also barred blackish. Tail dark brown fringed whitish; rectrices tipped pale buff, the three inner with black subterminal bars. Wings black; wing-coverts, tertials and some secondaries fringed and tipped pale buff with black subterminal bars. Undertail as in adult.

Bare parts Bill black. Legs black. Iris brown.

MEASUREMENTS Wing 98-103; tail 90-100; bill c. 17; tarsus 25-28. Weight: no data.

Taita Fiscal

DISTRIBUTION AND STATUS The Taita Fiscal is confined to East Africa. Its rather restricted range partly overlaps that of the Somali Fiscal and involves six countries, particularly Kenya. In that country, the species is almost completely absent only from the highlands (and adjacent moist, subhumid/humid areas) and from a coastal strip running from about Malindi to the Kenya/Tanzania border. In Somalia, it is widespread and fairly common in the south and west below 7°N and west of c. 47°E. The northern limits are not well defined, but cross southern Ethiopia where *L. dorsalis* is locally frequent. It is also fairly common but very localised in Sudan, where it is confined to the extreme south-east. In Uganda it is only known from the north-east from Moroto to Kidepo valley, and in northern Tanzania it breeds from the lowlands of Kilimanjaro to the drier parts of the Serengeti plains, including Ndutu, Lake Eyasi and Lake Natron.

GEOGRAPHICAL VARIATION None known. Monotypic.

MOVEMENTS Very few data. In Kenya, local movements may exist but are poorly documented. A 'great movement' has been witnessed on the Juba river, in Somalia, from Kismayu to the Garre-Lewin country during May, June and the first half of July (probably a post-nuptial migration). Presumed wanderers have been spotted outside the normal range of the species, for instance at Dar es Salaam (Tanzania) or in unsuitable habitats, like the bird seen in humid country near Kericho in Kenya.

MOULT No information.

VOICE Different types of call have been recorded: a low chuckling, a flute-like whistle, and a typical harsh grating *Lanius* alarm. The song has been described as a quaint mixture of *chwaaa pikereek chrrrr yook pikerchik... skyaaa*.

HABITAT The Taita Fiscal inhabits dry, open bush and open woodland from sea-level up to at least 1,500m. In Kenya, it may be locally sympatric with the less common and very similar Somali Fiscal, but the latter usually occurs in even more arid and very sparsely bushed habitats. The highlands and adjacent moist subhumid/humid areas, so much favoured by the Common Fiscal, are avoided. The Taita Fiscal is also rarely in direct contact with the Long-tailed Fiscal. Both species may be met with in the lowland scrub of southeast Kenya, but the Long-tailed is generally to be found in somewhat moister situations.

HABITS Little information. Has a reputation of sometimes being shy and difficult to approach. Probably, like *somalicus*, impales some of its prey, but no information.

FOOD Mainly composed of insects. The species also takes spiders and small vertebrates; the greater part of a small rat has been found in a stomach of a bird collected in Kenya.

BREEDING Few data, but the breeding season appears to be protracted and in Kenya coincides with the rains: March to May (June) and December-January. The nest, typical of shrikes, is made of twigs and grass, and hidden in a thorn bush. The full clutch comprises 3 or 4 eggs. Number of regular clutches, duration of incubation and fledging period are not known.

REFERENCES Ash & Miskell (1983), Brown & Britton (1980), Friedmann (1937), Lewis & Pomeroy (1989), Mackworth-Praed & Grant (1955), Nikolaus (1987), Olivier (1944), Urban & Brown (1971), Zimmerman *et al.* (1996).

21   SOMALI FISCAL
Lanius somalicus   Plate 12

IDENTIFICATION Length c. 20cm. Monotypic. A pied, East African shrike about the size of the Lesser Grey Shrike. In fact it is very similar to the Taita Fiscal both in built and in colour with, however, a little more white in its plumage. Like the Taita Fiscal, it shows a black cap extending to the upper mantle, a grey mantle, back and rump, white scapulars, a black tail fringed white, black wings with a white primary patch and pure white underparts. The diagnostic features are: rather broad white tips to the secondaries (wholly black in Taita), tail broadly fringed white with the two outer pairs of rectrices almost wholly white (only outer web of outer pair of rectrices wholly white in Taita), and a wholly white undertail when tail closed (black with white spots in Taita). The sexes are very similar, females having the axillaries duller black. Juveniles are grey-brown and heavily barred, particularly on upperparts. Their dark brown wings show a white primary patch and their secondaries and tertials are distinctly tipped white.

DESCRIPTION
Adult male Upperparts black from forehead to upper mantle including sides of head (lores, ear-coverts). Scapulars white. Lower mantle and back mid-grey. Rump and uppertail-coverts sometimes with some grey feathers, but mainly white (grey in *L. dorsalis*). Tail black; two outer pairs of rectrices almost wholly white; other tail feathers broadly tipped white except two central pairs. Wings black, except for a large primary patch (c. 3cm long) and diagnostic, fairly broad, white tips to tertials and secondaries. Underparts white. Undertail wholly white when tail closed.
Adult female Very similar to male, but with axillaries brownish ashy-grey, not black. Lacks traces of chestnut streaks on flanks, unlike adult female *dorsalis*.
Juvenile Facial mask dark brown over lores and ear-coverts. Upperparts greyish-brown from forehead to lower back. Rump and uppertail-coverts pale buff. Tail dark brown, fringed and tipped pale buff. Wings dark brown with a white primary patch and diagnostic white tips to tertials and secondaries. Underparts off-white with vermiculations limited to breast and flanks. Undertail almost wholly white as in adults.
Bare parts Bill black. Legs dark horn. Iris brown.

MEASUREMENTS Wing 94-108; tail 94-106; bill c. 16; tarsus c. 26. Weight: no data.

DISTRIBUTION AND STATUS The breeding range lies almost exclusively in the Horn of Africa. As its name suggests, the species is common and widespread in Somalia, particularly in the north-west; from 5°N south to 1°N it is confined to a narrow coastal strip. The Somali Fiscal is fairly common in southern and southeast Ethiopia; the northern boundaries remain unclear, but seem to be close to 11°N and to pass through Danakil country. In Kenya, this shrike is rather thinly distributed and confined to the north-west; its absence from the apparently suitable north-east is curious; as far as is known, the southern boundary reaches Kapedo at about 1°N. Only four records are known from Sudan, all in the extreme south-east. Breeding has not been proved there, nor in Djibouti where a bird was seen on 14 March 1984.

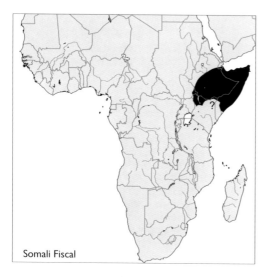
Somali Fiscal

GEOGRAPHICAL VARIATION None known. Monotypic.

MOVEMENTS Generally regarded as strictly resident. Birds do, however, occur outside their normal breeding range. Wanderers have been recorded in Kenya as far south as the northern periphery of the highlands and even in atypically high, moist country at elevations of c. 1,500m. The few observations from extreme south-east Sudan and Djibouti also probably refer to wanderers.

MOULT No information.

VOICE The song is made up of short phrases, rather complicated and variable, of which a common form is *bur-er-er* followed by a quick *lit-it-it.* A low churring alarm note has also been recorded.

HABITAT Frequents very arid and sparsely bushed habitats. In some areas, north of Marsabit in Kenya for instance, it is sympatric with the Taita Fiscal, but as a rule the latter species inhabits more thickly bushed plains and is less tolerant of very arid conditions. The Somali Fiscal breeds between 400 and 1,000m in Kenya. In Somalia, it is distributed from sea-level to about 1,950m at the top of Mount Wagar. It can, however, be regarded mainly as a bird of open grass plains and semi-desert tracts. In Ethiopia this shrike is found in acacia short-grass savanna (perhaps from sea-level to about 2,000 m), in thorn bush (*Acacia-Commiphora*) below 900m, and in semi-desert savanna (*Acacia-Chrysopogon*) below 1,200m.

HABITS Very little is known. Most records are of solitary birds or pairs. It has a reputation of being rather a weak flier, never going very far. A typical *Lanius* shrike which likes perching on the topmost twig of a bush or on the outermost branch of a sparsely foliaged thorn tree from which it can get an uninterrupted view of everything passing. It also favours artificial perches, particularly telegraph wires. In the breeding season, it darts out to attack any species up to the size of a Raven *Corvus* sp. which happens to pass anywhere near its nest. It catches its prey in the usual shrike manner and appears to keep larders regularly.

FOOD Large insects such as beetles, grasshoppers, mantises, etc. Small birds have occasionally been found impaled.

BREEDING The breeding season is protracted. In Ethiopia, nests with eggs have been found in March, from May to August and in November. In Somalia, egg-laying begins from mid-April near the coast, sometimes even earlier (February); it seems to start later in the interior, at higher elevations. In Kenya, clutches (few data) have been recorded in May and November. Like the Taita Fiscal, the Somali Fiscal tends to breed mainly in the wettest months when food is likely to be plentiful in arid thorn-bush habitats. The nest is invariably built in a small bush, generally 1-1.5m from the ground. Rather shallow, it is composed of thorn twigs, fibrous material, etc. The full clutch contains 4 or less often 3 eggs. Number of regular clutches, duration of incubation and fledging period are not known.

REFERENCES Archer & Godman (1961), Ash & Miskell (1983), Brown & Britton (1980), Clarke (1985), Friedmann (1937), Jackson (1938), Lewis & Pomeroy (1989), Mackworth-Praed & Grant (1955), Nikolaus (1987), Urban & Brown (1971), Welch & Welch (1984).

22   MACKINNON'S SHRIKE
Lanius mackinnoni   Plate 13

Other name: Mackinnon's Fiscal

IDENTIFICATION Length 20-21cm. This pied, monotypic shrike from Central Africa resembles a Great Grey or Southern Grey Shrike. Seen in good conditions, it is easy to identify. Its sooty-grey head and mantle contrast with the conspicuous white supercilium, striking white scapulars wholly black wings. It is paler on the lower back and rump. The black tail is fringed and broadly tipped white. The white underparts are variably washed pale buff. Females differ from males in having a distinct patch of chestnut on the flanks. Juveniles have heavily barred grey-brown upperparts, with scapulars already distinctly whitish and underparts off-white variably washed buff.

The main confusion species in both range and habitat types is the Common Fiscal. The latter is slimmer with black upperparts. In areas where Mackinnon's Shrike occurs, the Common Fiscal never shows a striking white supercilium, but always a white primary patch even in young birds. See also Grey-backed Fiscal and Lesser Grey Shrike.

DESCRIPTION
Adult male Facial mask black through lores, eyes and ear-coverts. Supercilium white or creamy, fairly broad (2-3mm), extending well beyond eye (about 1cm) and

over lores before joining a small whitish area on anterior part of forehead. Upperparts dark sooty-grey from forehead to lower back, paler on rump and uppertail-coverts. Scapulars white. Tail black, graduated (graduation c. 4-4.5cm); rectrices tipped broadly white, except central pair. Wings wholly dark brown. Underparts off-white, usually faintly washed pale buff. Undertail dark brown tipped white.

Adult female Similar to male, but with a fairly large, distinct patch of chestnut on flanks (hidden by closed wings).

Juvenile Facial mask dark brown over lores and ear-coverts. Supercilium whitish, already conspicuous. Anterior part of forehead whitish. Upperparts grey-brown, heavily barred from forehead to uppertail-coverts. Tail dark brown; all rectrices tipped pale buff, with a dark subterminal bar. Scapulars whitish, tipped pale buff with a dark subterminal bar. Underparts off-white, variably washed buff and vermiculated, particularly on breast and flanks. Undertail as in adult.

Bare parts Bill black. Legs black. Iris dark brown.

MEASUREMENTS Wing 82-92; tail 92-115; bill 15-17; tarsus 22-25. Weight: no data.

Mackinnon's Shrike

DISTRIBUTION AND STATUS A rather curious distribution, confined to Central Africa around the huge rainforest areas of Congo and Zaïre. The western limits appear to lie at c. 9°E on the Obudu Plateau in Nigeria. From there, the range extends in a belt running slightly south-eastwards along the northern edge of the Lower Guinea forest and crossing southern Cameroon, northern Congo and northern Zaïre to south-west Uganda and extreme western Kenya. The eastern limits lie roughly at c. 35°50'E. In Kenya, this shrike only nests west of the Rift Valley. Along the northern edge of the rainforest the belt appears to be surprisingly narrow, perhaps only c. 80 km wide. In these areas, the northern limits seem to lie at c. 3°N; there are no records from the Central African Republic. In the west, the species occurs in a strip south from south-east Nigeria across south-west Cameroon,

Equatorial Guinea, Gabon, southern Congo and north-west Angola. Mackinnon's Shrike nests at least as far south as Quiculungo at c. 8°30'S. An extension southwards also exists in the eastern part of the range from south-west Uganda and western Kenya (few observations north of 1°N) through Rwanda, Burundi and north-east Tanzania. In this area, the southern limit appears to lie in western Zaïre and Burundi where the species reaches at least 4°S.

GEOGRAPHICAL VARIATION None known. Monotypic.

MOVEMENTS Appears to be strictly resident. Juveniles probably undertake local movements.

MOULT No information.

VOICE The relatively sweet, varied song includes good mimicry of other birds, particularly of bulbuls Pycnonotidae. Among the calls, there is a low musical *chickarea* and a low churr while young are being fed. A prolonged low alarm whistle has also been recorded.

HABITAT The breeding range lies in a tropical rainy climate and the species can be found from almost sea-level, as in Mayumba in Gabon, up to at least 2,200m as on the central Kivu volcanoes in Zaïre or in western Kenya. Mackinnon's Shrike avoids dense forest, but neither is it a bird of savannas. In parts of its range, it shows rather similar habitat preferences to the Common Fiscal, but the latter occurs in more open habitats, whereas *mackinnoni* is a forest-edge species favouring moist, subhumid and humid areas. It needs bushes to hide its nest in. Partial to clearings and wooded and bushed grassland, it benefits from deforestation and can be very common in second-growth bush, and in farms and gardens of small towns and villages. In Gabon, it mainly occupies such habitats.

HABITS Little studied. Can be unobtrusive in its relatively closed habitat, especially if compared with the Common Fiscal. Territory size is 1-6ha according to the prevalence of bushes. It seldom perches high and like other *Lanius* shrikes it takes its prey mainly from the ground, but also sometimes in the air or from foliage. Larders are regularly kept. Locally in Gabon prey is impaled on *Citrus* spines.

FOOD All kinds of insects, chiefly Orthoptera, Coleoptera, Hemiptera, winged termites, ants, etc. Small vertebrates are regularly taken: geckos, frogs and small passerines, whose nestlings have been found impaled.

BREEDING In the western part of its range (Gabon), displays, copulations and occupied nests have been observed between August and April, with fledged young still being fed by their parents at the end of May. In Cameroon, breeding has been proved between September and April. In the east breeding takes place between February and August and is centred on the long rains, with peaks in the pre- and early rains period. At any given point in the year this shrike is likely to be found breeding somewhere in its range. Second normal broods are probably quite regular in a season; in Gabon a pair bred successfully in December and then again the following April. The nest is built in a thick, generally thorny bush, or in a small tree, 1-3m above the ground. It is rather bulky and made of coarse dry grass, shreds of bark, weed-stalks and lined with finer fibres. Mackinnon's Shrike lays 2 or, less often, 3 eggs.

REFERENCES Bannerman (1953), Britton (1980), Brosset & Erard (1986), Chapin (1954), Elgood (1994), Gaugris *et al.* (1981), Germain *et al.* (1973), Hall & Moreau (1970), Jackson (1938), Lewis & Pomeroy (1989), Louette (1981), Mackworth-Praed & Grant (1973), Schouteden (1960), Zimmerman *et al.* (1996).

23   COMMON FISCAL
Lanius collaris   Plate 13

Other names: Common Fiscal Shrike, Fiscal Shrike, Long-tailed Pied Shrike

IDENTIFICATION Length 21-23cm. By far the most common *Lanius* shrike of sub-Saharan Africa. It is a medium-sized, slim, mainly black-and-white bird with a long graduated tail. Nominate *collaris*, which breeds in southern Africa, has grey-black upperparts with a grey rump. Its whitish underparts are characterised by fairly obvious greyish freckling, which can give it a 'dirty' appearance. Otherwise, as in all the other races, the notable features are a white V on the back, formed by the folded scapulars, a rather small white primary patch, and white tips to most of the tail feathers. Females are slightly duller than males, with chestnut on their flanks. Juveniles are quite distinct, ash-brown above with dirty brown scapulars, and light grey below with fine vermiculations. The secondaries and tail feathers are edged buff. This shrike, which is generally common and easy to spot in all types of country, including towns, is readily identifiable if seen well (see Grey-backed Fiscal).

DESCRIPTION *L. c. collaris*
Adult male Upperparts blackish-brown with a grey gloss from forehead to lower back including sides of face. At very close range the blacker ear-coverts can be distinguished in this race. Scapulars white. Rump and uppertail-coverts grey, sometimes rather whitish. Tail black, long (up to 11.5cm), thin and graduated (graduation 4-6cm); all except central pair of rectrices with some white; outermost pair almost wholly white. Wings blackish-brown with small but distinct white primary patch. Underparts off-white, usually finely vermiculated with grey from breast to lower belly. Undertail mainly white, tipped black.
Adult female As male, but upperparts duller, browner. Some chestnut on flanks (apparently not a constant feature).
Juvenile Facial mask dark brown. Upperparts brownish from forehead to lower back, finely and heavily barred blackish. Rump and uppertail-coverts lighter, more buffy, also finely barred. Tail brownish, fringed and tipped pale buff. Scapulars whitish, already well defined. Wings dark brown with white primary patch; wing-coverts, tertials and secondaries fringed warm

buff. Underparts white on chin and middle of belly, the rest off-white finely barred dusky. Some chestnut on flanks up to about 18 months even for young males. Undertail barred whitish and brown.
Bare parts Bill and legs black. Iris brown or purplish-brown.

MEASUREMENTS (*collaris*) Wing 93-103 (mean 98.9, n = 14); tail 100-113; bill (culmen) 16-25; tarsus 25-30. Weight 34.7-50 (mean 41.8 for 34 males) and 34.9-43 (mean = 37.6 for 5 females).

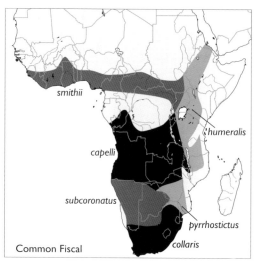

Common Fiscal

DISTRIBUTION AND STATUS The breeding range covers almost all the Afrotropical region. North of the Equator, the species occurs in a vast belt running from Sierra Leone in the west to mid-Ethiopia and Eritrea in the east. The northern boundaries seem generally to lie south of c. 10°N but in Mauritania the species has been seen as far north as c. 15°N in the Guidimaka area (vagrants?), in Mali at c. 13°30'N near San and Tominian, and in Niger at c. 12°N. In Eritrea, in the east of its range, this shrike may even occur as far north as 16°N, but it is absent from most of the Horn of Africa; eastern limits pass through central Kenya and roughly coincide with 38°E. The Common Fiscal largely avoids the major forest areas of West and Central Africa; however, an isolated population exists from southern Gabon to lower Congo. The species is widespread south of the Equator down to Cape Agulhas in South Africa. It can be locally frequent in suitable habitats as for instance in parts of Ethiopia, central-eastern Kenya, Zambia and particularly in southern Africa, where recent atlas work has shown that it is present virtually throughout Natal, Orange Free State, Transvaal and Southwestern Cape; in that last area it was actually the most frequently reported bird species during the atlas period. In certain areas it is much more patchily distributed, as in Mozambique. Apart from large forest areas, it is also absent from vast desert zones such as those occurring in central Botswana or, locally, along the coast of southern Angola. There is no detailed published information about population trends.

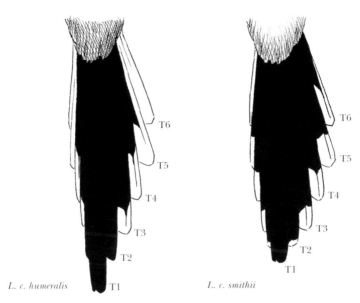

L. c. humeralis   *L. c. smithii*

Comparison of tails of two races of the Common Fiscal. Note strongly graduated tails. The East African race *humeralis* **has distinctly more white in the tail than the West African race** *smithii*.

GEOGRAPHICAL VARIATION Variation mainly involves the intensity on the upperparts, presence or absence of a white supercilium, extent of sexual dimorphism and amount of white in the tail. Many races have been described; some are easily identifiable in the field if the birds are seen well, notably *smithii*, *humeralis* and *subcoronatus*, while others are more subtle and a few subject to controversy. The following list is based on White's revised checklist (1962), with additional comments.

L. c. collaris (southern Africa: Cape Province to Orange River and Transvaal) Described above.

L. c. smithii (the 'West African Fiscal': from Sierra Leone to central Cameroon and east to southern Sudan) Bill weaker than in nominate. Upperparts black with distinct bluish gloss; rump grey. Tail with outer rectrices having basal half black. Tertials and some secondaries generally distinctly tipped white (1-2mm). Underparts almost pure white; chestnut patch on flanks very faintly marked and most often absent in adult females.

L. c. humeralis (the 'East African Fiscal': Eritrea, Ethiopia, southern Sudan east of Nile, Kenya, parts of Tanzania and northern Mozambique) Upperparts dull black, not so glossy as in previous race; rump generally paler (variable). Tail whiter, with outer pair of rectrices almost wholly white. Underparts not so pure white as in *smithii*; chestnut patch generally well marked on flanks of females.

L. c. capelli (western Uganda, eastern and southern Zaïre west to Kinshasa, Angola, Zambia and Malawi) Similar to *humeralis*, but extent of white on tail variable; often much basal black on outer rectrices, at least on inner web. Chestnut patch on flanks of females very faint or, often, absent.

L. c. pyrrhostictus (southern Africa: Natal, southern Mozambique, eastern and northern Transvaal,

southern Zimbabwe) Upperparts slightly greyer, less black than in *humeralis*. Underparts often greyish, not pure white; chestnut patch on flanks of females.

Clancey (1980a) synonymises this race with *collaris*, but distinguishes *predator* described by himself. *Predator* is said to inhabit the coastal regions of Transkei to Natal and Zululand, eastern and northern Transvaal, the Zimbabwe plateau and the southern high interior of Mozambique. It is very similar to *humeralis*, but with more sooty upperparts, a darker grey rump and consistently broader rectrices and a shorter tail: 100-105 as against 112-125 (see Clancey 1953).

L. c. subcoronatus (the 'South-West African Fiscal': Namibia, Botswana and south-west Angola) Similar to *pyrrhostictus*, but with a thin, distinct white supercilium from base of forehead (shows distinct white frontal band) and extending well beyond eye (c. 1cm). Lower rump and uppertail-coverts generally whiter than in *pyrrhostictus*, contrasting with greyer rump and back. Underparts often whiter with distinct chestnut patch on flanks of females.

Clancey (1955) proposed a new race *aridicolus*, very closely allied to *subcoronatus* and said to live in the dune and fog zone of the Namib of Namibia from at least Walvis Bay north to western Kaokoveld. Compared to *subcoronatus* it is judged to be paler and greyer dorsally, with the underparts purer silky-white.

All these southern African races broadly intergrade with contiguous subspecies.

MOVEMENTS Mainly resident. In Kenya, some degree of movement of non-breeding birds into semi-arid areas during the rains has been suspected. In Botswana, too, there are indications of local, regular movements. Odd birds turn up in areas where they are not expected; thus the species is a rare winter vagrant to the Kruger National Park in Natal and the race *subcoronatus* has occasionally been spotted near Pretoria and Johannesburg, well outside its normal range.

MOULT In Kenya, young *humeralis* begin to moult when they are about three months of age. This post-juvenile moult takes about a month, after which the birds are indistinguishable from adults. In the same region, almost all adults undergo a complete moult between August and December; there is no overlap with breeding. In Ghana, in a study of the race *smithii*, the first signs of post-juvenile moult were visible in the field when the young were between 8-12 weeks old. This moult was completed usually 5-7 months after fledging. The moult of adults appeared to take place from September to November when breeding activity was low. In southern Africa, adults and juvenile *collaris* have a complete moult between the end of December and March, whereas a partial body-moult appears to take place throughout the year.

VOICE The vocalisations of nominate *collaris* have been studied by Harris (1995), which see for details and sonograms. Common contact calls at short range are a single *tch* or a repeated *ktch* note, used all year round. A double *ktch-ktch* call is most often used by unpaired males and usually turns into a song. Whistles are also frequently heard; with the previous sound they often form part of a song sequence. A loud *terj* call is used in territorial advertisement by both sexes, particularly by unpaired males. A quiet *tjutju* is also used by these males to attract passing females. The passage of a raptor results in a dash for cover accompanied by a distinct *sqwark* alarm call (see also Habits).

HABITAT Absent from densely forested areas, but widespread over almost all remaining parts of Afro-tropical Africa in equatorial or subtropical climates in a vast range of open savanna habitats in the lowlands and highlands. In East Africa, the race *humeralis* is common in mountainous areas; in Kenya it has been recorded from 500 to 3,350m and in Ethiopia, where it is often also frequent at high elevations, it is rarely seen below 1,200m. In these countries, the Common Fiscal is predominantly a shrike of moister areas; it can even be found in the bushy margins of marshes. Likewise in West Africa the race *smithii* rarely occurs along the borders of the desert; its numbers soon thin out when the *Acacia* savanna gives way to the semi-arid belt. The race *subcoronatus* of south-west Africa is, however, a bird of fairly arid areas with few bushes including the dry coastal deserts of Namibia and south-west Angola. The Common Fiscal has adapted well to cultivated land and gardens in both rural and urban environments. It is for instance a common sight in the suburbs, if not the centre, of such large towns as Nairobi, Addis Ababa, Accra, etc. It favours areas of open short grassland with scattered trees, and readily uses man-made structures as perches such as fences, telephone-wires, scarecrows, etc.

HABITS A very bold, confiding and conspicuous shrike, generally easy to approach even to within a few metres. The Common Fiscal is quite vocal; the typical territorial advertisement call of nominate *collaris*, *terj-terj*, is often repeated by neighbouring birds, and can betray their presence as can the *kee* or *keer* alarm calls given when an intruder enters the territory or when potential predators are present. At the beginning of the breeding season and in the presence of a female, unpaired males perch conspicuously, utter *tjutju* calls and fluff out their white scapulars. Songs are also then heard and zigzag display-flights are common particularly after courtship feeding. Once the pair is formed, mutual feeding can apparently occur and duetting songs are characteristic: the territory is defended throughout the year and the pair maintains contact through *tch* calls. The density can be high with breeding territories often barely more than 1ha. In relatively dry or otherwise less favourable areas, they can, however, cover up to 13 or even, exceptionally, 18ha. Site-fidelity is high in this mainly resident shrike; ringed males have been seen in their territories for up to five years. Divorces and inter-territory movements are, however, not rare; in a Kenyan study they were even surprisingly frequent with birds moving up to 1,250m (see Zack 1986 for details) This shrike pugnaciously defends its territory against conspecifics and potential predators. In Transvaal, a bird even contrived to kill a Common Egg-eater *Dasypeltris scabra*: the snake, which measured 53cm and weighed 33g, was found dead, hanging from the shrike's nest; it had swallowed three eggs and the nest was empty. In a Ghanaian study, the Common Fiscal was found to be highly intolerant of the Senegal Kingfisher *Halcyon senegalensis*: individuals of the latter were violently attacked until they moved away. They were the only other common perch-and-pounce hunters of similar size in the shrikes' habitat, and this ecological similarity might explain the problems between the two species. When hunting, the Common Fiscal favours perches at 3-5m (range 1-10m). Most prey-items are caught on the ground within a radius of 15m, sometimes up to 25m or more; in habitats with relatively few perches, the species sometimes hovers; it also catches insects in the air, for instance termites during hatches. Other hunting techniques are much less frequent: plunge-diving to tadpoles like a kingfisher and wing-flashing in order to flush prey while hopping on the ground. In Ghana, young birds were frequently seen feeding on the ground like babblers *Turdoides* sp. This shrike can become very tame, hunting in gardens near bird-tables or birdbaths, killing cage-birds on verandahs and taking food scraps from dog bowls or plates once people have left the tables. Larders are used very regularly, but perhaps less so in the southern part of the range.

FOOD Insects form the bulk of the diet, but small vertebrates are also regularly taken: rodents, passerines (including nestlings), frogs, lizards, snakes. Among the bird victims recorded are guineafowl chicks up to 30 g and an adult Speckled Mousebird *Colius striatus*. Scavenging behaviour is probably not rare; it has been noted in a garden in Zimbabwe, where two birds fed on a large piece of chicken which had been thrown away. This shrike also eats seeds and food scraps (bread, porridge, etc.). A study in Ghana (Macdonald 1980) confirmed that almost all the prey-items are insects of a wide variety: Orthoptera, Coleoptera, Lepidoptera, Odonata, Isoptera (flying termites) and Hymenoptera (ants). One millipede (Diplopoda) was also noted. In size the insects ranged from 5 (probably beetles or ants) to over 30mm (crickets). Few vertebrates were taken: three small frogs (Anura), one skink (probably *Mabuya blandingi*, 60mm long), two rainbow lizards *Agama agama* (130 and 160mm long), two fledgling Bronze Mannikins *Lonchura cucullata* and one unidentified estrildid.

BREEDING Most Common Fiscals, particularly those living in relatively arid areas, breed in the rains. Nominate *collaris* and other southern African races breed almost all year round, except in February; most eggs are, however, laid between August and December (in 96% of 1,147 records). There are records for every month of the year for the East African race *humeralis*; in Kenya the wet April-May and November-December periods are especially well represented. During a study involving 19 nests near Lake Nakuru (Kenya), breeding attempts were triggered in March after the first substantial rains of the year, which lasted until July with a peak in May. Nest-building occurred in all months between March and August, with successful nestings taking place only in May and August. A few nests were again built during minor rains in November and December. A long-term study in southern Ghana showed that the race *smithii* also laid eggs in every month except November (dates calculated for 104 pairs) but least frequently between September and December. Replacement clutches are very common, but second normal broods appear to be usual throughout the range, and third normal broods are probably not rare. In the Ghanaian study mentioned above, it has been calculated that the mean interval between successive successful breeding cycles was 3.7 months and that each pair reared on average 2.2 successful broods per year during the main breeding season of eight months; because of a very high nest-failure rate it has been estimated that each pair probably began more than 13 clutches in a season (Macdonald 1980). The nest site is perhaps chosen by the female in spite of some nest-displaying by the male during pair formation; it is generally in a thorn tree against the trunk or in a fork on a lateral branch. The same nest can be used several times in the same season or rebuilt in another season; but material from old nests is often taken to make new ones. The nest may be built in a very short time, 2-5 days by both sexes, but the female does most of the gathering and weaving. In southern Africa, nearly 79% of 789 nests were placed at a height of 1-3m; the highest nest reported was estimated at 15m. The nest is rather bulky and includes a wide range of materials: small twigs, fine grass, flowerheads, rootlets, moss, feathers and, often, man-made objects like string, pieces of paper, etc. In southern Africa, its outer diameter averages 13cm (range 10-18), and its height 9.5cm (range 6.5-12) (see Cooper 1971a). The Common

Fiscal lays between 1 and, exceptionally, 6 eggs. In southern Africa, over 50% of 904 clutches had 4 eggs and c. 30% had 3 eggs. In southern Ghana, 15 full clutches had between 1 and 3 eggs, nine having 3 eggs. In Kenya, 12 full clutches also had between 1 and 3 eggs, but the modal clutch-size was 3. These data strongly suggest that the average clutch-size is larger in southern Africa than near the Equator. Incubation is done by the female alone for c. 15 days and the young stay in the nest for 17-18 days. They begin to attempt to feed themselves three weeks after fledging and become independent about two weeks later when aged 50 days or so. Juveniles remain in the parental territory for rather a long time, about four months in southern Africa, up to five months in East Africa and 5-7 months in West Africa. In Ghana it has frequently been observed that offspring from two or sometimes three previous broods may be present on the territory simultaneously; despite this, no part is taken by older immatures in the feeding or defence of younger ones, either in or out of the nest.

In southern Africa, the Jacobin Cuckoo *Clamator jacobinus* has been found to have parasitised nests in 13 cases out of 1,147.

REFERENCES Benson & Benson (1977), Brown & Britton (1980), Bruderer (1991), Brunel & Thiollay (1969), Clancey (1953, 1955, 1976, 1980a), Cooper (1971a,b), Dittami & Knauer (1986), Douglas (1992), Elgood (1994), Grimes (1987), Harris (1995), Harris & Arnott (1988), Hockey (1989), Kemp (1974), Lamarche (1981), Louette (1981), Macdonald (1980), Maclean (1993), Maclean & Maclean (1976), Marshall (1990), Marshall & Cooper (1969), Rand *et al.* (1959), van Someren (1956), Steyn (1976), Vincent (1935), White (1962), Zack (1986b).

24   NEWTON'S FISCAL
Lanius newtoni   Plate 13

Other common name: São Tomé Fiscal

IDENTIFICATION Length c. 19cm. A very rare species, confined to open primary forests of São Tomé in the Gulf of Guinea. It is very similar to the Common Fiscal and particularly to its West African race *smithii*. It differs from that subspecies in having a black not a grey rump and in lacking a white patch on the wing. Recent observations of live birds confirm that the underparts are rather yellow in adults. This colour is not seen in museum specimens. The sexes are alike. Juveniles are certainly very similar to those of the Common Fiscal, but show some fawn-yellow tinges on the breast. No other shrike occurs on São Tomé, but there have been a few records of vagrant Lesser Grey Shrikes.

DESCRIPTION
Adult Sexes similar in plumage as far as is known. Upperparts, including sides of head (lores, ear-coverts), glossy black from forehead to rump; some brownish tones on mantle and back (females?). Uppertail-coverts

grey. Tail black and graduated; three outer pairs of rectrices fringed white towards tips. Wings black with distinctly white-tipped tertials and, sometimes, a very narrow white band on primaries. Underparts white in museum specimens, but at least sometimes pale yellow or washed yellowish in living birds. Undertail blackish with distinct white spots towards extremity. As a whole, less white in tail than in races of *collaris*.

Juvenile Upperparts said to be greyish, washed brown and breast washed buff (de Naurois 1988). A young bird seen on 22 August already had a black bill and showed a thin, buffish supercilium, not extending far behind the black eye, which appeared large in the brown face. Its upperparts were brown, slightly greyer on the head; the scapulars formed a tawny V, quite visible on the back; the wings were brown with buff-tipped wing-coverts; the tail was dark brown and the entire underparts were tawny-orange. A juvenile seen on 13 January had brown, finely vermiculated upperparts and tawny-yellowish barred underparts; its throat was yellowish and its bill horn-brown (P. Christy pers. comm.).

Bare parts Bill black in adults and smaller than in the Common Fiscal; horn-brown in young birds. Feet dark brown or black in adults. Iris dark brown.

MEASUREMENTS Wing 91.5-96 for ten males (mean c. 93) and 87-96 for five females (mean 89.5); tail 110-117.5 for ten males (mean c. 114) and 100-115 for two females; bill (culmen) 13-14.5 for seven males (mean 13.8) and 12-13 for four females (mean 12.5); tarsus 23-26 for 14 adults (all measurements taken from museum skins: see de Naurois 1988). Weight: no data.

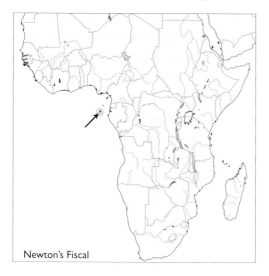

Newton's Fiscal

DISTRIBUTION AND STATUS Newton's Fiscal is endemic to the island of São Tomé which lies in the Gulf of Guinea, 255km off the coast of Gabon. The island is 857km² in area; together with the island of Príncipe, which covers 139km², it forms the Democratic Republic of São Tomé and Príncipe. These islands hold three endemic genera and 26 endemic species of birds. Their importance for conservation has been stressed in a survey of threatened Afrotropical forest birds by Collar

and Stuart (1985); these authors ranked the forests of south-western São Tomé, where Newton's Fiscal occurs, second in a list of 75 in terms of conservation value to birds. Up to 1991, the 22 known observations of this very rare bird almost exclusively came from areas along Rio Xufexufe and Rio Quija.

The species was discovered in 1888 by Francisco Newton, who collected for the Lisbon Museum. It was described by Barboza du Bocage in 1891. The shrike was found again in 1928 by Correia, who collected 13 specimens including one in the centre-east of the island, near the Io Grande river. Despite several surveys, there were no subsequent records until July 1990 when the species was relocated by a University of East Anglia/International Council for Bird Preservation expedition. It was again seen in August 1991, only c. 1km in a direct line from the 1990 sighting, and between March 1994 and January 1996 several individuals were seen and heard by P. Christy (pers. comm.) not only in the south-west but also in the central areas of São Tomé. It is difficult to estimate the range and status of so rare and inconspicuous a bird as Newton's Fiscal. The UEA/ICBP expedition considers that its population is likely to number in the hundreds.

GEOGRAPHICAL VARIATION None. Newton's Fiscal is regarded by some as a subspecies of the Common Fiscal.

MOVEMENTS No information exists about possible local movements.

MOULT No information.

VOICE A bird observed and trapped in July 1990 was heard to emit a low squawk on several occasions; it made a scolding churring sound while being handled. In 1994, P. Christy heard two types of song, one made up of about ten well-separated, fluted, far-carrying notes transcribed as *tiu tiu tiu tiu*, and the other more rapid, composed of long series of *tsink-tsink-tsink-tsink* notes somewhat metallic in tone. A young bird was also seen and heard singing a repeated three- or four-note *tieu-tieu-tieu*, similar to that of an adult, but more nasal. Singing birds were heard in December, January and August; one on 25 August 1995 gave a series of 250 notes without interruption.

HABITAT Remarkably, all observations of this shrike have been made in virgin forest below c. 700m. Newton's Fiscal seems to be strictly confined to undisturbed lowland primary rainforest. It is apparently a mid- to low-storey species and particularly difficult to see, which is very peculiar for a *Lanius* shrike. The closed-canopy forests where it lives have an open undergrowth strewn with many stones and boulders.

HABITS Very little is known. The few recent records mention quiet and unobtrusive birds, 'probably often skulking in low bushes'. The bird observed in 1990 was seen foraging on the rocks of a stream, hopping between boulders and searching for food items. The shrike spotted in 1991 was in closed-canopy primary forest and initially seen as it flew from the ground, where it had been feeding, to perch on a small sapling about two metres high. It had a very upright stance and remained motionless for several minutes before hopping down to the ground to feed. The birds seen under the canopy by P. Christy were generally perched 3-5m from the ground. At least a few of them were easily approachable.

FOOD A bird has been seen feeding on small beetles; another tried to catch a passing flying insect.

BREEDING Little information available. Two males in breeding condition in November/December and two females showing traces of juvenile plumage in the same months (Collar and Stuart 1985). Juveniles reported in January and August (P. Christy pres. comm.).

REFERENCES Atkinson *et al.* (1991, 1994), Bocage (1904), Collar *et al.* (1994), Collar & Stuart (1985), Collar & Andrew (1988), de Naurois (1988), Peet & Atkinson (1994), Sargeant (1994).

25 UHEHE FISCAL
Lanius marwitzi   Plate 13

IDENTIFICATION Length c. 20cm. A slim, long-tailed, pied, very little known shrike confined to the highlands of south-central Tanzania. Very similar to the Common Fiscal particularly to the race *subcoronatus*, as it shows the same type of white supercilium and frontal band. There is, however, hardly a risk of confusion as *subcoronatus* only occurs in south-west Africa; moreover, the Uhehe Fiscal has distinctly darker, blacker (less brown) upperparts and a grey not white or whitish rump.

The main confusion species is the race *humeralis* of Common Fiscal, which occurs in the same geographical area, but at lower elevations. It lacks the white supercilium and frontal band, so conspicuous in adult Uhehe Fiscals.These features are already discernible in juvenile *marwitzi*.

DESCRIPTION
Adult Sexes similar as far as is known. Upperparts dull black from forehead to back including ear-coverts. Supercilium white and distinct, covering lores and merging into white frontal band; also extends well behind eye (c. 1cm). Scapulars white. Lower back (sometimes), rump and uppertail-coverts dark grey. Tail black, thin, long and graduated (graduation up to at least 6.5cm); outer pair of rectrices almost wholly white; all tail feathers, except two central pairs, with large white spots. Wings black with a rather small white primary patch. Underparts off-white with some buffish wash. Undertail wholly white when tail closed, except at its apex which is blackish.
Juvenile Very similar to juvenile *collaris*, but perhaps slightly darker with lighter areas on scapulars, rump and uppertail-coverts. Traces of a whitish supercilium already visible.
Bare parts Bill and feet black. Iris dark brown.

MEASUREMENTS (few data) Wings 90-95.

DISTRIBUTION AND STATUS Confined to eastern and southern Tanzania, from Mpwapwa and the Ukagurus to Njombe, Mount Rungwe and Tukuyu.

Uhehe Fiscal

GEOGRAPHICAL VARIATION None. The Uhehe Fiscal is sometimes regarded as a subspecies of the Common Fiscal.

MOVEMENTS No information. Some local, altitudinal movements appear possible.

MOULT No information.

VOICE As far as known similar to that of the Common Fiscal. More information needed.

HABITAT A high-elevation bird, apparently only found in bush country above 1,500m, perhaps generally in less anthropogenic habitats than the Common Fiscal.

HABITS As far as known similar to those of the Common Fiscal. Apparently rather silent and shy.

FOOD No details.

BREEDING No information.

REFERENCES Britton (1980), Friedmann & Loveridge (1937), Mackworth-Praed & Grant (1955), White 1962.

26 WOODCHAT SHRIKE
Lanius senator   Plate 14

IDENTIFICATION Length c. 18cm. Confined to the south-western Palearctic, this polytypic shrike (three races) is slightly larger and bigger-headed than the Red-backed Shrike. The adults are pied except for their rufous crown and hindneck; this latter characteristic, reflected in the bird's name in many languages, makes it unmistakable. The pure white underparts stand out at long range; the upperparts are black (male) or dark brown (female) except for the white scapulars, rump, uppertail-coverts and primary patch. From a distance and in flight, confusion is possible with the slimmer Masked Shrike which may occur alongside the

159

Woodchat in extreme south-east Europe, some parts of the Middle East and the African wintering areas. Masked Shrike also has a pied appearance with white 'shoulders' and primary patch. Its head pattern is, however, quite different and its rump is black, not white.

The young *senator* resembles a young Red-backed Shrike, but its upperparts are whiter and greyer. Scapulars, rump and uppertail-coverts appear pale buff or white; these differences are quite conspicuous, particularly in flight. Confusion with immature Masked Shrike is more likely. Woodchat is, however, somewhat bulkier, shorter-tailed and browner, not so dark grey; moreover, it shows a whitish contrasting area on the rump, and lacks a pale supercilium accentuating the dark ear-coverts. From about September the difference is even stronger as the young Masked Shrike then starts to show a whitish forehead typical of the adult plumage but absent in Woodchat.

DESCRIPTION *L. s. senator*

Adult male Facial mask black over forehead, just around eyes and on ear-coverts; even extends onto base of neck. Anterior part of forehead pale cream with varying amount of black. Supercilium whitish, short, just behind upper rear corner of eyes, sometimes inconspicuous. Crown and upper mantle rufous-chestnut (fresh plumage) or rufous-cinnamon. Scapulars white, forming a striking V on back. Upperparts from mid-mantle to lower back black or dark brown, often with greyish tinges on lower back. Rump and uppertail-coverts white. Tail black, fringed white; only central pair of rectrices completely black; external pair completely white or, more frequently, with some black towards base of inner web. Wings dark brown with a broad white primary patch; secondaries and tertials narrowly tipped white; greater coverts, secondaries and tertials fringed pale buff (fresh plumage). Underparts white, washed cream-buff when plumage fresh. Undertail greyish.

Adult female Similar to male, but generally duller, particularly on upperparts which are somewhat browner (variable; most are very easy to tell from males, a few are not). Facial mask generally mottled brown-buff, particularly on forehead. Underparts may be rather lightly barred blackish on sides of cheeks, breast and flanks (this character is, however, very occasionally present in males).

Second calendar year adults can be recognised at close quarters in spring and even in autumn, as they retain some juvenile feathers (some inner primaries, outer secondaries and generally all primary coverts). The old feathers and particularly the primaries are much more abraded than the new. Males are easy to age as the contrast between new black feathers and old brown ones is obvious. In females, however, the difference in coloration between new and old feathers is often much slighter. Second-year adults may also show a few barred juvenile body feathers.

Juvenile Facial mask brownish over ear-coverts; lores with a mixture of brown and whitish feathers. Upperparts from forehead to lower back rufous-buff, soon bleaching to whitish-grey, each feather with a dark brown subterminal bar and whitish tip. Scapulars whitish; feathers tinged buff and edged by rather broad dark brown subterminal bars and white tips. Rump and uppertail-coverts pale rufous-buff and heavily barred, contrasting with the darker upperparts and tail. Tail dark brown fringed whitish; outer web of pair of outer rectrices buff-white; inner web with some brown; other rectrices dark, with a fine black subterminal bar and very narrow pale buff tips. Wings browner than in adults with an already distinct whitish-buff primary patch; flight feathers fringed warm brown and tipped pale buff; primary coverts tipped pale buff; greater coverts rather broadly edged warm brown and tipped pale buff. Underparts pale buff-white with grey-brown barrings on chin, cheeks, belly and flanks. Undertail pale buff-white with a darker area in the middle.

Bare parts Bill black in adults with lower mandible somewhat greyer; dark grey in juveniles with lower mandible paler. Legs black. Iris dark brown.

MEASUREMENTS (*senator*) Wing 96-103 (mean c. 100) for birds of western Europe, Iberia excluded; 92-97 (mean c. 95) for birds from Iberia and the Maghreb, sometimes regarded as distinct race *rutilans*; tail 74-82 (mean c. 78), shorter in Iberian and North African birds: 69-77 (mean c. 73.5); bill 17.5-20; tarsus 23-25.5. Weight: 21-59; on breeding grounds in western Europe: mean c. 36; spring migrants in the Maghreb: mean c. 30.

DISTRIBUTION AND STATUS The breeding range is limited almost entirely to the south-western Palearctic and mainly involves the Mediterranean region except for Egypt. Isolated breeding populations occur in the north-west and eastern parts of the range. The species regularly occurs in northern parts of the Maghreb; in Morocco mainly north of the Atlas Mountains (Anti-Atlas and High Atlas); in Algeria it nests as far south as the first Saharan oases, for instance at Laghouat and Beskra, while in Tunisia its southern limits seem to extend beyond Gafsa and Gabès, which lies just south of 34°N. More to the east the bird is mainly a coastal species: in Libya it nests between Sabratah and Misratah and an isolated breeding area exists much further east (c. 32°40'N 21°00'E) in the Djebel Al-Akhdar. Almost all the Mediterranean islands are occupied, whatever their size, but the species is a rare breeder in Cyprus where there were only four definite proofs of breeding up to 1993. The Woodchat is still locally common in European countries with a mediterranean or sub-mediterranean type of climate: in Spain (except in the northern areas of Asturias and parts of Galicia), southern France (particularly common in Languedoc-Roussillon), Italy, the southern parts of former Yugoslavia, Greece (particularly common in Thrace), and south-west Bulgaria. It is rare in south-east Romania (Dobruja). Its distribution extends into temperate zones where it becomes very patchy. In western Europe and particularly in France it lies within the July isotherm of 19°C. In that country the species does not breed west of a line drawn between the towns of Nantes and Charleville-Mézières. It no longer nests regularly in the Benelux countries (but in 1995 two pairs bred in Belgium near the French border at Torgny and Lamorteau, the latter site being reoccupied in 1996; these were the first nesting records since

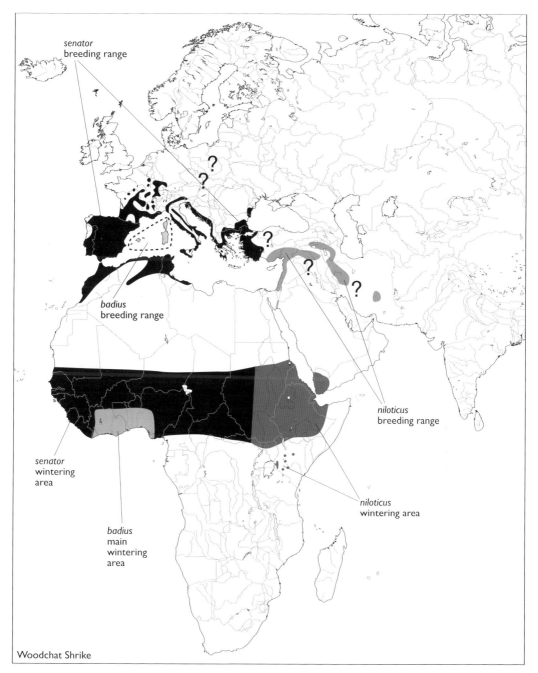

senator
breeding range

badius
breeding range

niloticus
breeding range

senator
wintering
area

niloticus
wintering area

badius
main
wintering
area

Woodchat Shrike

1982: M. Ameels pers. comm.) and is now found in very few areas in southern Germany and Switzerland. More to the east, it last bred in Austria in 1982 and in Hungary in 1981; in Poland and the Czech Republic very few areas are occupied and the bird has become very rare. In Turkey, the Woodchat nests in the western and southern third of the country with a few additional breeding sites much further east in the Kars area. It is particularly common in western Anatolia and between the Ceyhan and upper Firat rivers. To the

north-east, the breeding range extends into Georgia, Armenia and Azerbaijan. In the Levant, the species is locally common in western Syria (particularly in the Anti-Lebanon foothills and Damascus area), in Lebanon, in the north and centre of Israel and in western Jordan where it breeds in the Rift Margin highlands from Umm Qays south to Ash-Shawbak. The breeding range is not well known in Iraq, but this shrike appears to nest at least in the mountainous regions of Dahuk. The Woodchat also nests in north-west Iran

161

and on the south slopes of the Zagros Mountains down to the Fars area. Breeders also occur somewhat further east, but few data exist. The eastern limits are in the province of Kerman at c. 58°E.

In western and central Europe, the range of the nominate race has contracted markedly towards the south since the end of the 19th century and particularly in the last 30-40 years. Its fluctuations have been fairly similar to those of the Lesser Grey Shrike, but less dramatic. The last relatively good periods for the species occurred in the 1930s and 1950s, but cannot compare with the excellent situation in the 19th century when birds bred as far north as Grodno (53°41'N) in Belarus, and Kiev (50°26'N) in the Ukraine. A few nests of this shrike were found in the Netherlands in the 1850s and 1860s (last breeding records in 1896 and 1910), and it was then fairly widespread in Poland and locally common in Hungary. In 1856, the species appears to have nested on the Isle of Wight in the United Kingdom, and in the 1870s it still nested regularly in the 'Père Lachaise', a famous cemetery in the centre of Paris. Some population estimates reflect the recent decline in some countries. In Germany there were at least 500 pairs by the 1950s, c. 250 by the 1970s, c. 50 in 1984 and c. 30 by the 1990s. In Switzerland there were still c. 110 pairs at the end of the 1970s, but only c. 30 in 1995. In Luxembourg, where the population reportedly fluctuated between 150 and 750 pairs in the 1950s, no nest has been found since 1987. Recent estimates exist for some European countries; not surprisingly the highest figures come from Spain: 390,000-860,000 pairs (1989), Portugal: 10,000-100,000 (1989), Greece: 5,000-20,000 (1976), France: 6,000-12,700 (1994), Italy 5,000-10,000 (1976). Between 1986 and 1991 it was also estimated that there were 5,000-50,000 pairs in Turkey, and in the 1970s–1980s at least a few thousand pairs in Israel.

GEOGRAPHICAL VARIATION The three races recognised by Vaurie (1959) are relatively easy to distinguish in the field. A few more subtle races have been proposed.

L. s. senator (North Africa and Europe from Spain to western Turkey) Described above. The shrikes from North Africa and Spain are sometimes given the name *rutilans*. They are smaller on average (see Measurements), but this variation appears to be largely clinal. Birds from Sicily are said to be darker with more reddish-brown underparts. They might be separable as *hensii* (Clancey 1948). Birds breeding in Montenegro, Macedonia, Greece and western Turkey may show some of the characteristics of the race *niloticus*.

L. s. badius (western Mediterranean islands: Balearics, Corsica, Sardinia and Capraia) Forehead with less black than in other races: width of black at centre 5-8mm (mean 6.5) in males against 8-14mm (mean 10.2) for *senator* (Vaurie 1955). White primary patch absent or much reduced. Bill slightly heavier (not appreciable in the field).

L. s. niloticus (eastern Turkey, Levant east to Iran) White primary patch larger than in *senator*, extending 17-21mm beyond primary coverts in closed

wing of adult male against 10-16mm for nominate race (Vaurie 1955). Tail with more white at base, up to 25-35mm in Iran. Underparts whiter, flanks with a restricted amount of buff or pink. These characteristics are discernible in immatures, which also show greyer upperparts than *senator*.

HYBRIDS Six mixed *L. senator/L. collurio* pairs were found in France between 1985 and 1996 in Aisne (1985), Vosges and Alpes Maritimes (1988), Bas-Rhin (1990), Dordogne (1993) and Corsica (1996). In all cases the male was *collurio* and the female *senator*. Apart from two exceptions (Bas-Rhin and Corsica), the observations took place in areas where the Woodchat is now very rare and has long since stopped breeding. Three pairs (Alpes Maritimes, Bas-Rhin and Corsica) managed to produce young (see photos in Lefranc *et al.* 1989). In the field, the juveniles could easily have been taken for young *collurio*; they had no trace of a whitish primary patch and the feathers of their scapulars and rump were only very slightly paler than the rest. At least one record of a mixed pair, a male Red-backed Shrike feeding a female Woodchat, has also been made in Germany. However, a drawing in Panov (1983) shows a male Woodchat displaying in front of a female Red-backed Shrike, based on observations made in Transcaucasia.

Records of adult hybrids are very rare, but at least three such birds have been observed recently in France: one near Bordeaux (Gironde) in late July 1994, one near Valenciennes (Nord) in late June 1995 and one near Sables d'Olonnes (Vendée) on 14 August 1995. The bird seen near Valenciennes is illustrated on plate 11 based on photos and drawings made in the field.

MOVEMENTS All populations are migratory. The wintering area is a vast belt running across the African continent just south of the Sahara and largely north of the huge forest areas, roughly between 15°N and 5°N in the west and between 13°N and 2°N in the east. Some birds may, however, winter in Saharan oases in Algeria. The three definite races have different winter quarters. Nominate *senator* is found from southern Mauritania and Senegal east to Darfur in Sudan; to the south it reaches north-east Zaïre and Uganda; *niloticus* occurs from Sudan to Eritrea with a few populations also wintering in the south-west Arabian Peninsula; *badius* appears to be mainly confined to the southern seaboard countries of West Africa: Liberia (scarce), Ghana, Togo, southern Nigeria and probably Cameroon, reaching at least 9°50'N. Migration is on a broad front; the Mediterranean may be crossed almost anywhere, but particularly at its two extremities. In autumn, shrikes from central Europe (Germany, Switzerland, France) take a WSW or SW direction towards the Iberian peninsula and the western coast of Morocco and Mauritania. Birds from Italy may first adopt a south-easterly direction before heading south in Africa. It is possible that the Woodchats from the western Mediterranean islands (race *badius*) fly straight south to their winter quarters. Passage is strong in autumn and spring in the Levant (mainly race *niloticus*). In spring, migrant Woodchats appear in good numbers in countries where they are relatively scarce in autumn: Tunisia, Libya, Egypt and also Sicily, Crete and Cyprus. Possible non-stop flights in autumn may partly explain this, but direct observations and ringing results strongly suggest that at least some western populations make an anticlockwise loop-migration and return via routes that lie hundreds of kilometres to the east of those they take going south. In autumn, the dry coasts of the southern Mediterranean are largely but not completely avoided.

The autumn migration of this long-distance migrant begins in the second half of July, exceptionally even earlier for unsuccessful breeding pairs. Local post-breeding dispersal may also occur: in Israel such pre-migration movements take place from June in a radius of 50km from the breeding sites. A bird ringed in the Bouches-du-Rhône (France) in spring was already in the south of Spain on 31 July, and birds have been recorded in Senegal as early as mid-July. Most birds, however, leave their breeding sites at the beginning of August; stragglers, particularly young birds, can be observed fairly regularly until mid-September, exceptionally even until mid-October. Arrivals in the winter quarters peak after mid-August in Senegal, in September-October in Mali, and at the beginning of November in southern Niger and Chad. Return movements begin in February, for some birds even in January, and peak in March and April when many birds cross the Sahara. A few stragglers may lag behind and birds of the nominate race may sometimes still be observed in Senegal in mid-May. There is an exceptional record from 6 July in Togo. Normally the first *senator* arrive in North Africa at the end of February and in Europe at the beginning of April, sometimes at the end of March as in Portugal, Spain, Sicily, Malta, Cyprus, south-west Turkey, etc. Arrivals on the breeding grounds generally peak in the second half of April and at the beginning of May, but they are very protracted and in the east of France, for instance, late-comers may still turn up at the end of May or even in early June. Vanguards of birds of the eastern race *niloticus* appear in Israel between 25 January and mid-February, with the main influx between the last week of March and mid-April, while passage of the nominate race, which represents about 10% of the country's total numbers, seems to be generally later. Rearguards may still be noted in deserts in the first three weeks of June. Birds of the race *badius* regularly 'overshoot' and occur along the French Mediterranean coast in spring.

The Woodchat Shrike is a rare vagrant to the countries of north-west Europe. In the Netherlands, 23 birds were found during the Atlas years 1978-83 between April and September, with nine birds in May and seven in September; the subspecies *badius* was definitely identified for the first time on 6 June 1993 following a possible observation in June 1983. The species rarely occurs in Denmark, with 17 records between 1963 and 1977, mostly in May (10 records). The Woodchat also rarely turns up in Norway and Sweden; in the latter country, 31 observations were made between 1950 and 1986 with zero to four birds per year, all in the southern quarter of the country. This shrike is a rare but regular vagrant to the British Isles; during 1958-90 there were 480 records, of which c. 48% were of adults in spring, 23% adults in autumn and c. 29% immatures in autumn. The best year was 1988 with 27 records; the pattern shows a predominance of records on the south coast and in East Anglia, but there are records from most east coast counties all the way to Shetland, and most inland counties south of a line from the Severn to the Wash have single records; within the period 1958-90 there were 50 records in Wales and 28 in Ireland. The earliest shrike was recorded on 17 March 1990 (with six other exceptionally early records in the same month and year) and a very late bird was seen on 8 November 1978.

MOULT Juveniles undergo a partial moult soon after fledging; it begins when they are about four weeks old and affects the head and body feathers as well as some lesser and median wing-coverts. The extent of this moult is very variable and some young birds leave their natal areas in autumn with only a limited amount of new feathers. In the winter quarters, this moult is resumed (October) November and February (March) leading to first-summer plumage. It is almost complete except that the primary coverts and generally a few inner primaries and outer secondaries remain unmoulted (see Gargallo and Clarabuch 1995). Adults of nominate *senator* undergo a partial moult just after breeding when body feathers, plus one, two or, rarely, all tertials and sometimes a few rectrices, particularly the outer pair, are renewed; it is followed by a complete moult in the winter quarters between (October) November and January. Birds in their second calendar year moult up to four innermost primaries and, rarely, some outermost secondaries when still in their breeding territories; moult is then suspended and only resumed in the winter quarters.

Remarkably, the eastern race *niloticus* generally undergoes a complete moult before starting the autumn migration.

VOICE The song is more regular and, particularly in unpaired males, often louder than in other western Palearctic *Lanius*. It may occasionally be heard in the winter quarters. It is a warble containing both musical and harsh notes and a lot of good mimicry. The female may also sing and duets have been heard. The easiest call to transcribe, common to other *Lanius*, is a rattling bill-snapping *trr trr trr* given when attacking rivals or possible nest-predators. A short *crex* is typical and *gek gek gek* calls are also often heard, becoming more extended when the caller is excited. The common contact call appears to be a *kwikwik*.

HABITAT The species favours a Mediterranean type of climate and breeds in warm, open or semi-open areas. Some North African birds (*senator*) and some of the eastern populations (*niloticus*) nest in habitats which probably resemble original ones: very open grassy scrublands dotted with higher bushes or trees (for instance *Argania* in the Sous valley in Morocco) and growing on dry steppes or in semi-deserts. As a rule, the Woodchat is confined to lowlands, plains or hills up to 600-900m, but in the southern parts of its

Woodchat Shrike, in 'worried' pose.

range, on well-exposed slopes, it may occur at higher elevations; in Maghreb it regularly nests up to 1,200m and breeding has even been proved at 1,650m on Mount Hermon in Israel and at c. 1,900m in the High Atlas in Morocco. In western Europe, this shrike has been found breeding up to 1,100m in the warmer parts of the Massif Central in France, and exceptionally at 1,240m in the Wallis Mountains in Switzerland. The Woodchat favours areas with scattered trees, tracts of bare soil and alternate low and high plant cover. In southern Europe, it can be met with in very open oak forests *Quercus ilex* or *Q. suber* as in Spain (grazed dehesas are favourite habitats) or in open pine forests *Pinus* sp. as in both Spain and Greece. In the south of France it is common in open scrubland, where shrubs and trees cover 5-20% of the surface (rough or open pastures) leaving large patches of low, discontinuous herb layer (under 30cm in height composed mainly of lavender and wild thyme). The species also nests in a variety of plantations, particularly olive groves, and may be found on roadside trees. In the north of its breeding range it is a typical bird of old traditional orchards particularly when sheep or cattle are present. In such habitats, hunting occurs mainly in areas with short vegetation, on average 7cm in height. The Woodchat also nests in suitable city parks; in France for instance it was known, last century, in the centre of Paris; in the 1950s it still nested within the limits of Strasbourg, a large town in the north-east, and today it may still be found on the outskirts of such big southern towns as Marseilles and Nîmes.

In its African winter quarters, it is found in dry *Acacia* savanna; the structure of these light woodlands often recalls that of the traditional orchards inhabited in the breeding area. The species also occurs in rather flat, cultivated country dotted with trees.

HABITS The Woodchat Shrike is relatively conspicuous and easy to approach, up to a distance of 10-20m. During the breeding season, the male surveys its territory from well-exposed perches such as bare twigs. However, it also spends much time in trees, where it can be remarkably inconspicuous. Unpaired males are

nevertheless noisy. Duets probably contribute to the maintenance of the pair-bond. A tendency to nest in small groups undoubtedly exists, but is less pronounced than in the Lesser Grey Shrike. The density is highly variable: up to 3 or 4 pairs per 10ha in good habitats, for instance in the south of Europe, Maghreb or Central Asia; two neighbouring nests may be only 50(30)m from each other, but even in favourable habitats they are generally separated by c. 200m. The density in temperate zones is often low, c. 1 pair per km² in well-populated areas. It can, however, be locally high when two or more pairs nest close together in small 'oases' (generally orchards around villages) in areas which have otherwise largely become unsuitable because of the intensification of agriculture. The territory size is very variable; for 24 pairs studied in south-west Germany in 1966-1968 it was 8ha on average; it is generally much smaller in more southerly areas, which presumably provide habitats of a better quality with more available insect food. In Corsica the territories are said to vary between 4 and 5ha and the average size of the territory of four pairs closely studied in Spain was only 2.2ha. The size of the territory may also change with time. Thus in Germany during the breeding phase a male used a territory of less than 1ha; later, when the chicks were c. 1 week old, it foraged over an area of c. 3ha whereas its mate used another feeding territory nearby. Site-fidelity is particularly pronounced in males. In a five-year study in Alsace, north-east France, between 26 and 66% of the adults were back in the same general area in the subsequent year; most males were even found in exactly the same territory. However, the same study showed that partner-fidelity is very rare, while fidelity to the natal area varied between 2 and 32% from one year to the next (see Bersuder & Koenig 1995 for details). Loose associations with other breeding birds have been noted. In the north of its breeding range, the Woodchat sometimes nests close to the Fieldfare *Turdus pilaris,* particularly in orchards; in southern France a remarkable nesting association seems to exist with the Orphean Warbler *Sylvia hortensis*: occupied nests of both species have been found in the same bushes in the open dry grasslands of the 'garrigue'. This association may be an anti-predator device; it recalls that apparent in certain areas of eastern Europe involving Red-backed Shrike and Barred Warbler *S. nisoria*. The Woodchat perches between 1 and 5m high when hunting. The typical *Lanius* perch-and-pounce technique enables it to catch between 65 and 80% of its victims on the ground; in fine weather many flying insects are also caught in the air. This shrike hovers only occasionally; it has been seen doing so over a pool, trying to catch water-insects. In bad weather it may hop on the ground in search of small invertebrates. Impaling of prey is very irregular. No impaled vertebrate or invertebrate was found during a three-year study in south-west Germany (major work on the species by Ulrich 1971). In Corsica impaling is relatively rare, but apparently more frequent than in the Red-backed Shrike. Monitoring of 25 territories in north-west Spain showed food-storing in four of them (16%).

Woodchat Shrike drinking.

FOOD Mainly consists of insects, principally Coleoptera (Carabidae, Elateridae, Scarabaeidae, etc.) and Orthoptera (Gryllidae, Tettigoniidae, Gryllotalpidae, etc.). In central Europe, beetles generally dominate the diet at the beginning of the breeding season, but grasshoppers later play a more important part. Many insects of other orders are also taken, but generally less frequently: Hymenoptera (including ants), Lepidoptera (adults and larvae), Hemiptera, Diptera, Odonata, etc. (roughly in that order). Spiders are regularly taken, as are earthworms and sometimes snails in rainy weather. Small vertebrates are occasionally caught: voles, mice, lizards, frogs. Bird nests may be plundered and small passerines killed, particularly young ones or exhausted migrants. An adult male 'specialising' in killing small vertebrates has been recorded in Germany in two successive years (probably the same individual), but other studies failed to record anything other than arthropods. In a German study 62% of 50 measured prey-items were 6-15mm long. Plant material has also been noted: mulberries *Morus* sp. in Crete and berries of *Prunus mahaleb* in the south of France.

BREEDING In Europe males and females generally appear together in their breeding territory and are apparently already paired. Pair formation probably therefore takes place at migration halts when males defend temporary territories in the Mediterranean area, or even in the winter quarters. It can also occur, very quickly, just after arrival. In Israel, males (*niloticus*) are reported to precede females by an average of ten days. Unpaired males are very demonstrative, sing a lot and disturb already established pairs. The laying period begins at the end of April in the Maghreb, Spain and the western Mediterranean islands, in early May in Greece, and generally between 10 May and early June in central Europe and France. Replacement clutches are frequent and started until around mid-July. At least in temperate Europe few pairs start second replacement clutches, and only when the first fails at an early stage (during laying or at the start of incubation). As a rule there is only one normal clutch in Europe, but normal second clutches probably occur in North Africa. They have been proved in the Levant: in Israel c. 20% of the population is double-brooded. The nest-site is chosen by the male, who also starts to build; the female begins to help one or two days later and the construction is completed generally in 4-6 days, but up to two weeks have been recorded. The nest is generally placed in a tree, between 3-5m (extremes 2-20 m), but in the Mediterranean region also frequently in a dense or spiny bush like *Juniperus* sp, Christ's thorn *Paliurus* or even bramble *Rubus* sp, etc.; in the Languedoc-Roussillon region (France) most nests are c. 2m above ground (extremes 1-10m). Nest-trees are frequently oaks, poplars, pines, etc. and, particularly in temperate areas, fruit-trees. In south-west Germany for instance, 56 out of 102 nests were in apple, 44 in pear, one in cherry and one in plum. The nest is typically placed towards the end of a thick horizontal branch, but it can also be in the fork of a trunk, on an angled branch or in outer twigs. It looks very much like the nest of the Lesser Grey Shrike, but is stronger, not so loosely built. Its outer diameter averages c. 14cm and its height c. 7cm. Much plant material is used including fresh flowers. Rootlets, moss, wool, hair, cobweb and lichen are also incorporated in varying degrees. Feathers and small pieces of string are more rarely used. The Woodchat lays 4-8 eggs, generally 5 or 6 throughout its range, with replacement or late clutches having often 4 or 5 eggs. A geographical variation appears to exist, as in Armenia the race *niloticus* has 7-egg clutches (34%) much more often than the nominate race in Europe or North Africa (1-5%); a clutch containing 9 eggs is known from Georgia. Incubation lasts 14-16 days and the young stay in the nest for 15-18 days. After fledging, they continue to be fed by their parents for 4-6 weeks.

REFERENCES Andrews (1995), Bersuder & Koenig (1995), Bonaccorsi & Isenmann (1994), Clancey (1948), Clement (1995), Cramp & Perrins (1993), Gargallo & Clarabuch (1995), Glutz von Blotzheim & Bauer (1993), Hernandez (1993a,b,c, 1994), Isenmann (1996), Isenmann & Fradet (1995), Kowalski (1993), Lefranc (1993), Lefranc *et al.* (1989), Panov (1983), Roselaar (1995), Schaub (1995, 1996), Shirihai (1995), Svensson (1992), Tucker & Heath (1994), Ullrich (1971, 1974), Vaurie (1955, 1959).

27   MASKED SHRIKE
Lanius nubicus   Plate 14

Other name: Nubian Shrike

IDENTIFICATION Length c. 17cm. A small monotypic shrike confined to the south-east of the western Palearctic and particularly to the eastern Mediterranean area. It is about the same size as Red-backed Shrike but slimmer, more delicately built with a finer bill and a dark tail which appears longer and narrower. The latter superficially suggests a Pied Wagtail *Motacilla alba*, all the more so because its flight is lighter than other European shrikes. The pied appearance and particularly the dark upperparts and large white wing panels are reminiscent of Woodchat, but Masked Shrike shows a white forehead extended behind the eye by a prominent white supercilium. On the other hand, breast and flanks are rufous and rump dark, not white. Adult females are similar to males, but distinctly duller. Juveniles may be confused with young Woodchats, but are much slimmer and not so large-headed; moreover, they are greyer with a dark rump and already display show of a pale forehead and supercilium.

DESCRIPTION
Adult male Facial mask black, rather narrow, over lores, eyes and ear-coverts. Supercilium white, broad (c. 5mm behind eye), joining white of forehead (c. 10mm from base of bill). Crown to uppertail-coverts black with a bluish gloss. Scapulars white; may be washed buff. Tail black, fringed white; two pairs of outer rectrices almost wholly white. Wings dark brown with conspicuous white primary patch; wing-coverts, secondaries and tertials fringed pale buff (fresh plumage). Underparts off-white, washed pale orange-buff almost all over, except on throat and chin; flanks distinctly rufous. Undertail white.
Adult female Similar to male, but duller. Facial mask browner, not so jet black. Supercilium often less broad. Crown and nape dark brown. Mantle, back and uppertail-coverts brown. Scapulars white, frequently washed buff. Tail dark brown. Wings dark brown, not so black as in male, with a distinct white primary patch; wing-coverts, secondaries and tertials fringed pale buff. Underparts as in male, but somewhat duller. Undertail white.

Juvenile Facial mask brown over lores, eyes, and ear-coverts. Supercilium whitish. Forehead also whitish. Upperparts grey-brown, heavily barred from forehead to uppertail-coverts. Scapulars whitish (white feathers with a dark brown subterminal bar edged buff). Tail dark brown fringed white and very slightly tipped buff. Wings brown with distinct white primary patch; wing-coverts, secondaries and particularly tertials fringed and tipped pale buff. Underparts off-white, heavily barred dark brown with faint buff wash. Undertail white.
Bare parts Bill slender, black in males, rather dark brown or plumbeous-black in females. Legs black or dark brown. Iris brown or dark brown.

MEASUREMENTS Wing 87-95 (mean c. 91); tail 82-92 (mean c. 86.5); bill (to skull) 17-20; tarsus 22-23.5. Weight 15-30, usually c. 20-23 (relatively few data).

DISTRIBUTION AND STATUS A shrike with a rather small breeding range mainly centred on the eastern Mediterranean area, from the Balkans to Israel and with some populations further east, as far as Iran. The species probably still occurs in southern Macedonia (part of former Yugoslavia). In Greece, where some recent observations come from Lake Kerkini and even from Mikra Prespa, it is mainly found in Thrace, in the north-east of the country, and particularly from Kavala to Alexandroupolis (Avas valley). It also inhabits the Rhodope mountains more to the north, and nests at least on the following islands: Thasos, Samothrace, Lesbos, Chios, Samos, Paros and Kos. Some pairs breed in south-west Bulgaria, in the Kresna Gorge and probably also elsewhere. In Turkey, the Masked Shrike is restricted to Thrace, western Anatolia and the southern coastlands; it also occurs, apparently in very limited numbers, in the mountain valleys of the south-east and at the northern fringes of central Anatolia. Good populations exist in suitable habitats all over Cyprus. The bird is quite common in north-west Syria, particularly along the coast in the Ras al Basit and Kassab area and as far south as Tartus. It also occurs around Damascus and in the Barada valley up to Az Zabadani in the Anti-Lebanon on the Syria/Lebanon border. Its occurrence in the east of the country has not been established. Few details are available for Iraq, but the Masked Shrike certainly nests here and there in the north of the country, e.g. near Samarra and also south of Baghdad, e.g. in the Al-Amarah area. The picture remains confused as the bird is common as a passage migrant. More to the east, breeding occurs in Iran at least from the Zagros Mountains to Fars, possibly also north of Tehran along the Caspian Sea coast (Chalus area) and even patchily in the east where a bird was collected near Birjand on 24 May. A few birds seen in southern Turkmenistan may represent a small breeding population that might even extend into north-east Afghanistan. In Lebanon, the Masked Shrike is widespread and it also nests, presumably in small numbers, in north-east Jordan, particularly in the northern highlands from Jarash south to the Amman National Park. A few may also breed at Petra, in the Rift Valley, and in the Rum Desert. In the north and centre of Israel the species

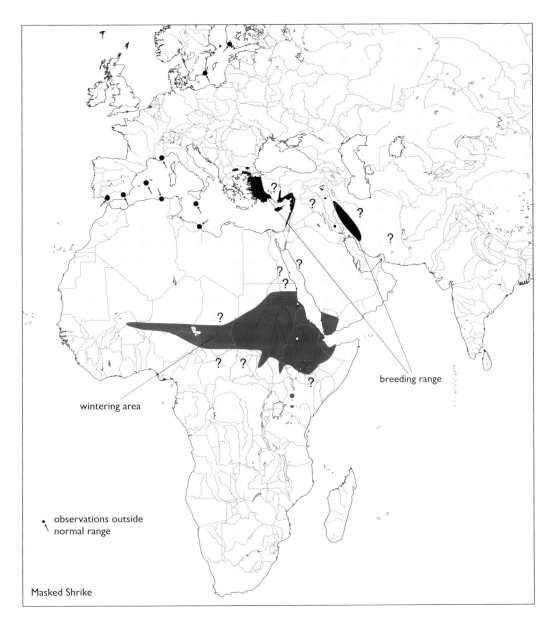

breeding range

wintering area

- observations outside
↙ normal range

Masked Shrike

reaches the southern limits of its breeding range. It nests on northern Golan, on Mount Hermon, in most of Galilee and in the Carmel; it is also present in some areas of Shomron and in the Judean Hills, and small numbers breed in valleys and plains of northern and western Israel. It might have bred in the Hejaz in north-western Saudi Arabia.

Some recent rough population estimates exist for certain countries, with 5,000-50,000 pairs in Turkey, 600-2,000 in Greece, 2,000-4,000 in Cyprus and 50-100 in Bulgaria. In the latter country breeding was first proved in 1976, but the species may previously have been overlooked. In Israel, the Masked Shrike declined greatly in the late 1950s and 1960s, apparently because

of the widespread use of pesticides; in the 1970s and 1980s, populations were estimated at a few thousand breeding pairs.

GEOGRAPHICAL VARIATION None known. Monotypic.

MOVEMENTS All populations are migratory and mainly winter in sub-Saharan Africa, particularly in the eastern part of the continent and rarely south of 10°N. The main wintering area lies in Ethiopia, Sudan and eastern Chad. In this area the northern boundary, very roughly, appears to lie at c. 14°30'N.

There are few records from northern Kenya; the Masked Shrike was annual at Lake Baringo from 1982

167

to 1991 and individuals also turned up at Lake Kanyaboli in November 1969 and at Lake Naivasha in March 1994. Somalia is also almost completely avoided, except in the north-west where some birds are occasionally found west of 46°E. The winter range extends eastwards to the extreme south-west of the Arabian Peninsula where the species is a localised winter visitor to the Tihamah foothills in Yemen and Saudi Arabia; it can even be locally numerous, as in the Muhayle-Khamis Al Bahr area. Remarkably, at least a few birds occasionally overwinter further north in the Gulf area, where two were seen during the winter 1988-89 in Abu Dhabi (United Arab Emirates). Others had already been seen in the Dhahran area in the winters 1972-73 and 1973-74, and a male stayed in the Manama Gardens in Bahrain from 30 November 1991 to at least 1 February 1992. Westwards the winter range extends to northern Cameroon, northern Nigeria, southern Niger (rare) and even eastern Mali. In both seasons birds are believed to pass through the eastern Mediterranean. Curiously, however, the Masked Shrike is a much commoner migrant in spring than in autumn in countries like Egypt, Jordan and Israel. It is also in spring that a few observations have been made in Libya and even one in Algeria. This suggests a clockwise loop migration but more data are needed on autumn movements, which might be on a narrower front or less conspicuous because of overflying.

According to observations from Cyprus and Israel, local post-breeding dispersal already begins in the second half of July and sometimes even in June. In Egypt, a migrant has been recorded as early as 29 July, but the autumn passage does not really start before the second week of August and appears to peak in the first half of September. At that time the Masked Shrike is very common outside its breeding range in parts of Iraq, Israel, the Arabian Peninsula, Egypt, etc. Stragglers are not uncommon in Egypt and even Turkey until mid-October. Observations in the breeding range are exceptional in November and December (one in Israel on 9 December and one in Baghdad on 19 December). Spring movements may occur in the winter quarters as early as the end of January, but the main exodus falls between mid-February and the end of March. In Egypt, where a few birds may winter in the extreme south, the main passage is between mid-March and late April. In the Arabian Peninsula, the passage is between late February and early May; it peaks in April. Most birds are back in their breeding territories at some time in April, but arrivals are very protracted. In Cyprus, birds may turn up as early as mid-March. In Jordan the first birds are seen at the end of March; peak passage occurs there in April, but the last spring bird at a non-breeding site was seen on 1 June. In Israel, in non-breeding areas, late birds have been seen between 27 May and 17 June. A few birds may summer in the winter quarters; breeding has even been suspected in Sudan.

Vagrants appear from time to time outside their breeding and wintering areas or normal migration routes. Birds have been seen as far west as Libya: two or three, 30km west of Misrath on 28 March 1966;

Algeria: one near Skikda on 6 April 1958; Malta: one near Lunzjita, Gozo, on 20 October 1985; France: one near Nice on 18 April 1961; Spain: three at Coto Doñana in May 1956, one in the Sierra Cazorla on 1 May 1962 and one at Puerto Pollensa, Mallorca, on 26 April 1991. Very few *nubicus* have been found in northern countries: Finland: one on 23 October 1983; Sweden: one caught at Ottenby on 1 October 1984.

MOULT The post-juvenile moult mainly involves the head and body feathers, but also the lesser and median coverts and sometimes one or two tertials. It starts on the breeding grounds a few weeks after fledging but, if not finished there, is suspended during migration and resumed in the winter quarters where it intergrades with the moult into first-summer plumage. The latter varies in extent; it might occasionally be complete, but generally some juvenile feathers are retained including some inner or all primaries, outer secondaries and often all primary coverts. These feathers are distinctly browner than the new black ones, and first-summer birds, watched in good condition, can be easily recognised irrespective of sex; the contrast between old and new feathers is, however, less well marked in the duller, browner females. Adults have a complete post-breeding moult which starts on the breeding grounds; it may be completed before autumn departure, but is generally suspended and resumed in the winter quarters between October and December.

VOICE The song is a warble and its phrases, which can last for a minute or longer, have been compared to those of several Old World warblers (particularly *Hippolais* sp.). One of the commonest calls is a kind of *keer keer keer*. Other sounds are reminiscent of other *Lanius* sp., particularly the *krrr krrr* given in alarm. The Masked Shrike has occasionally been heard singing in winter in various countries: Sudan, Eritrea, Yemen. Calls appear to be frequent in the winter range (see Habits).

HABITAT The Masked Shrike breeds in areas having a warm Mediterranean climate and winters in hot areas characterised by a dry subtropical steppe climate. More than any other western Palearctic shrike it can be found in relatively wooded country even on well-exposed mountain slopes up to 2,000m as in the Aladag in Turkey. It nests in a variety of open forests with thick tree-tops, often dominated by oak *Quercus* sp., pine *Pinus* sp. or even juniper *Juniperus* sp. It also occurs in semi-wooded and less natural habitats such as citrus and olive groves and cemeteries rather densely planted with cypresses (Turkey). Locally, it can be seen in more open habitats, for instance in cultivated land dotted with old trees. On Mount Hermon in Israel it nests mainly in cherry and apple orchards up to 1,000 (1,450)m.

Outside its breeding range, the species is also much attracted by terrain with a rather high tree cover. Low, hot acacia country is typical habitat in East Africa, but the species also favours other thin open forests including riverine woodland, and can be met with in open, relatively tall *Eucalyptus* plantations. It may also occur in gardens or holiday resorts well provided with trees as is the case near Lake Langano in Ethiopia.

HABITS The Masked Shrike is less often seen at the tops of trees than other European shrikes, except at the onset of the breeding season when males, new territory holders, advertise themselves by perching conspicuously. Later, the birds generally perch on inside or lower branches 2 to 6m from the ground, although they sometimes use electric wires. In the breeding season, pairs are generally solitary, but concentrations can occur locally and in very favourable habitats . The highest density reported comes from the north of Iraq (Kurdistan), where at least 10 pairs nested along an 800m fringe of open oak *Quercus* sp. forest. In Greece, 6 pairs were found in old olive groves covering a little more than 1km². In Israel, in the Carmel and environs, about 500 pairs were estimated in an area of approximately 220km², that is about 2.3 pairs per km². On migration, concentrations may occur, perhaps more so than in other migrating shrikes: in Israel more than 100 have occasionally been seen on peak days at favoured staging sites. The territory of a pair appears to be small: 2–5ha (pers. obs. in Cyprus). In Africa, wintering birds are solitary, apparently sedentary, and also highly territorial; territories do not appear to exceed 3ha. Three birds encountered during a trip to Ethiopia were all extremely noisy at the approach of observers. Small temporary territories less than 0.5ha are also held by birds at migration stopovers for a few hours or days. In spring, such territories are held for a shorter duration than in autumn. This shrike can be quite confiding and catch insects at the observer's feet. It may follow a gardener as he disturbs insects. Before dropping on ground prey, it may hover briefly. A bird watched in winter in Ethiopia regularly used to do so; it also used to emit angry, short, harsh *krek krek krek* calls before swooping on its victims. Flying insects can be taken after a flycatcher-like aerial chase. Vertebrate and invertebrate prey are regularly impaled.

FOOD The Masked Shrike catches many grasshoppers and beetles. Other insects commonly taken include dragonflies and moths. Small vertebrates are taken occasionally: lizards and even small passerines. The latter probably consist exclusively of exhausted migrants or otherwise handicapped birds. Proven victims include Lesser Whitethroats *Sylvia curruca* and, more surprisingly, a Little Swift *Apus affinis*. Nestlings may also be taken. The species has also been seen attacking Barn Swallow *Hirundo rustica*, Redstart *Phoenicurus phoenicurus*, Blackcap *Sylvia atricapilla* and Willow Warbler *Phylloscopus trochilus*.

BREEDING As a rule, males appear to arrive a few days ahead of females on the breeding grounds. Pair formation is rapid and little is known about courtship behaviour. Laying starts in mid-April with a peak in most areas at the beginning of May. It starts a few weeks later in mountainous areas than near sea-level, for instance in Cyprus or Turkey. At higher elevations, fresh eggs may still be found at the end of June. Repeat clutches are frequent and normal second broods are probably at least occasional as in Israel. The nest is built by both sexes in a dense, often thorny bush or,

more often, in a tree against the trunk in a fork or towards the end of a lateral branch. Made of rootlets, twigs, plant stems, moss, adorned with lichen and lined with wool, hair or man-made material, it is very carefully built and somewhat resembles a large nest of Chaffinch *Fringilla coelebs*. For a shrike, however, it is relatively small with an outer diameter of 11.5-15.5cm and an overall height of c. 6-7cm. Material from a destroyed nest may be used to construct a new one. Between 3 and 7 eggs are laid, most clutches having 4-6. Repeat clutches on average probably have fewer eggs than normal ones. Incubation lasts 15 days. The fledging period, based on observations in Israel, is rather long: 18-20 days. The young and their parents can be seen in a radius of up to 800m from the nest for at least 3-4 weeks.

REFERENCES Andrews (1995), Baumgart (1995), Chappuis (1970), Cramp & Perrins (1993), Flint & Stewart (1992), Hirschfeld (1995), Inbar (1995), Jennings (1981), Lefranc (1993), Panov (1983), Richardson (1990), Roselaar (1995), Shirihai (1995), Tucker and Heath (1994), Vatev *et al.* (1980), Zimmerman *et al.* (1996), Zink (1975).

28   YELLOW-BILLED SHRIKE
Corvinella corvina   Plate 15

Other names: Long-tailed Shrike

IDENTIFICATION Length c. 32cm. An unmistakable, giant, polytypic (three races) brown shrike of western, central and eastern Africa. Both its common names are appropriate as it is characterised by a strong yellow bill and a very long blackish-brown graduated tail. Its fawn-brown mantle is broadly streaked black and an orange-buff patch is very conspicuous, especially in flight, on the blackish-brown wings. The underparts are washed pale buff with narrow black streaks mainly confined to the lower throat and chest. The sexes are almost alike, but adult females have a distinct maroon patch on their flanks; in adult males the patch also exists, but is more rufous. These marks, hidden by the closed wings, are, however, visible during displays, territorial disputes or when the birds are preening. Juveniles are similar to adults, even showing a yellow bill, but are barred and mottled blackish above and below (not streaked), superficially resembling giant juvenile Red-backed Shrikes.

The Yellow-billed Shrike is a cooperative breeder; it is thus very sociable and often noisy. Loud grating calls often attract the observer's attention and its general habits may sometimes recall those of *Turdoides* babblers.

DESCRIPTION *C. c. corvina*
Adult male Facial mask dark brown over lores, eyes and ear-coverts. Supercilium pale buff, broad (c. 3-4mm), very noticeable. Upperparts fawn-brown and heavily streaked blackish from forehead to lower back. Scapulars paler, forming a fairly distinct large V on back; feathers pale buff with black subterminal bars.

Rump and uppertail-coverts somewhat paler than rest of upperparts and generally less heavily streaked. Tail dark brown, long (up to c. 18.5cm) and graduated (graduation c. 6-8.5cm). Wings dark brown with a well-marked (c. 5.5cm long) orange-buff patch at base of all primaries, on outer and inner webs; greater wing-coverts, tertials and secondaries dark brown fringed buff and bordered by black subterminal lines in fresh plumage. Underparts pale buff with narrow black streaks; a patch of colour between cinnamon and cinnamon-rufous is visible on the flanks.

Adult female Very similar to male, but the colour patch on the flanks is deep maroon.

Juvenile Facial mask dark brown over lores, eyes and ear-coverts. Pale buff supercilium already well defined. Upperparts fawn-brown from forehead to uppertail-coverts, paler on scapulars and rump, heavily covered with black barring (not streaks as in adults). Tail dark brown, tipped and fringed pale buff with black sub-terminal bars. Wings dark brown with orange-buff primary patch; primary coverts dark brown fringed buff; greater wing-coverts fringed warm buff with sub-terminal lines; tertials and secondaries fringed warm buff (almost orange-buff at base of primaries). Underparts pale buff, heavily barred except on chin and throat.

Bare parts Bill yellow, even in juveniles. Legs dark green. Iris dark brown.

MEASUREMENTS (*corvina*) Wing 118-130; tail 160-185; bill 15-19; tarsus 28-32. Weight 58-80 (mean 65.4 for eleven birds caught in Ghana).

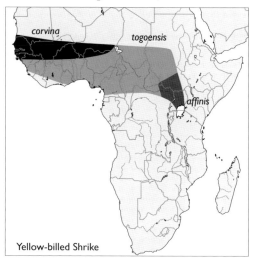

Yellow-billed Shrike

DISTRIBUTION AND STATUS The breeding range extends in a wide belt crossing the African continent just south of the Sahara, but generally, except in the extreme east, north of the Equator. The species is absent from the Horn of Africa. In the west, it is present in almost all the countries bordering the Atlantic from Mauritania to Cameroon. In Senegal, it is widespread south of 15°30'N, but a few populations also occur further north, in southern Mauritania along the Senegal river in the Guidimaka, a triangular-shaped

area between Senegal and Mali. In Mali, this shrike also occurs at least as far north as 15°N, but it is more regular south of 14°N. The same latitude is probably also reached in Burkina Faso, where the species is locally common in parks in Ouagadougou at 12°22'N. Further east, it occurs in southern Niger, northern Nigeria and as far north as c. 16°N in Chad. The northern boundary then crosses Sudan at c. 14°N, although birds are much more regular south of 12°N. From about mid-Sudan the limits drop sharply south-east towards the common borders of Sudan, Uganda and Kenya. The south-eastern limit of the species lies at 35°50'E. From west to east, the southern limits run across eastern Guinea, northern Sierra Leone and through the middle of Ivory Coast, the species only being found north of Bouaki (no observations so far from Liberia). Further east, however, birds reach coastal areas, for instance on the Accra plains in Ghana (although apparently absent in the south-west) and near Ibadan, Abeokuta and even, occasionally, near Lagos in Nigeria. In Cameroon, the southern boundary lies at least as far south as 4°N, as the species is present on the Benué plain. The limits then cross south-east Central African Republic before running through northern Zaïre, where birds are rather locally distributed in the savannas of the upper Uele, northern Uganda and western Kenya. In the latter country, some populations may be found just south of the Equator.

GEOGRAPHICAL VARIATION Three races are listed here. A few others have been described, particularly *caliginosa*; *chapini* and the latter which is very similar to *affinis* but perhaps slightly greyer and more heavily streaked (this bird is confined to southern Sudan and the extreme north of Zaïre).

   C. c. corvina (Senegal, Gambia east to Niger) Described above.

   C. c. togoensis (southern part of range from Guinea and Sierra Leone east across Nigeria, Central African Republic, and southern Chad to central Sudan) Very similar to nominate, but upperparts more heavily streaked.

   C. c. affinis (eastern part of range: south-east Sudan, extreme north-east Zaïre, northern Uganda and western Kenya) Upperparts distinctly more greyish-brown, less reddish than in the two preceding races. Orange-buff patch on primaries more restricted.

MOVEMENTS Definite movements exist even if they are not well documented. They mainly involve birds in the northern breeding range, particularly the Sahel zone. In southern Mauritania the species is reportedly migratory and flocks up to 150-200 individuals have been observed. In Mali it is common on the Bani river roughly between 13°N and 14°N, but apparently only between October to May. It might breed somewhat further north in the rainy season. In Chad, the species is present as far north as 16°N during the rains; it moves gradually further south with the advancement of the dry season in November and December. Birds breeding in Darfur (Sudan) also seem to retire somewhat southwards at the approach of the dry season. At least local movements have also been recorded in Kenya. All these movements are on a local scale involving a clear modest shift of range southwards in the dry season. Southern populations appear to be less migratory. In the dry season in Ivory Coast, however, some birds appear as far south as Toumodi at 6°33'N, whereas the normal breeding range extends north of Bouaké at 7°41'N. A population studied for several years at Legon, in Ghana, was strictly resident and this appears to be the case for all the birds inhabiting the Accra plains.

MOULT Little information. In a study conducted in Ghana, most adults had begun a complete moult in August when the breeding season was virtually over. During the post-juvenile moult both sexes had a small faint cinnamon-rufous patch on their flanks. In young birds, in their eleventh or twelfth week, the sexually dimorphic colours on the flanks are sufficiently developed to allow separation of the sexes in the field (see Grimes 1979a).

VOICE A very vocal species. There is a constantly repeated *scis scis* which has given the bird the local name of Scissor-bird in Uganda. A common shrill call has been written *may we-may we wait-may we*. The species also gives various rippling and parrot-like calls when moving in a group. See also Habits.

HABITAT In the northern part of its range, the Yellow-billed Shrike occurs in the dry steppe climate of the Sahel zone where it inhabits arid *Acacia* savannas. Many birds breeding in that area spend the dry season, roughly extending from October to June, somewhat further south (see Movements). The species also inhabits less arid areas in the Sudan zone and, even closer to the Equator, the Guinea savanna where rain may fall from March to December. *Acacia* stands are favoured almost everywhere, but this species occupies other types of woodland, for instance *Pterocarpus lucens* stands in Mali. It occurs in riverine forests, well-wooded parks, gardens and cultivated areas. In western Kenya, populations exist between 500-1,000m in arid or semi-arid country; others can be found at elevations up to 2,200m in areas with more than 1,000mm rainfall.

HABITS A gregarious species living in groups throughout the year and often very noisy. Eighteen breeding groups studied in Ghana (see papers by Grimes) numbered on average twelve members (range 6-25). There is only one breeding pair per group; all the other birds help to defend the territory, warn against predators and feed the incubating or brooding female, nestlings and fledglings. Normally, all the members of a group are dispersed over a territory, but they roost in the same tree at night and meet at the nest, at sources of abundant food, or during disputes with another group. In Grimes's study the average territory size was 16.5ha (for n = 18; range 10.5 - 27 ha). There was no correlation between this value and the number in the group; a group of six birds, for instance, inhabited an area covering 15ha, whereas one of 25 had a territory of 17ha. Disputes are frequent along common borders

and generally take place in tall trees. They start when one or more birds trespass into the territory of another group or when members of two groups come close together. Displays generally start with one or two birds moving by hops and short flights to a well-exposed section of a tree uttering a distinctive warbling note (sonogram in Grimes 1980). This note soon attracts other members, who join in; the increasing noise may even encourage the incubating females to leave their nests. During a display, birds of a group hop to and fro between branches, or bow towards their nearest neighbours; they also puff out their body feathers and frequently rub their bills on branches or move their tails slowly up and down or from side to side. Fights can occur and pairs of fighting birds sometimes fall locked together only to separate just before reaching the ground. Rallies often last 10-15 minutes. Potential predators, including human beings, may be greeted by loud harsh alarm calls; once a bird starts uttering them, other members quickly appear and join in the calling. Breeding-status females can be vocal during nest-building, incubation or brooding; they are then given food by the breeding male or by helpers. Young birds remain in a group for some years before dispersing, sometimes in parties of the same sex, the females moving on average further than the males. Most prey is caught on the ground by birds swooping from a perch or pouncing after a low, short flight over a feeding area. Insects such as winged termites are also taken in flight. In bad weather, the Yellow-billed Shrike can be seen feeding on the ground and turning over the litter, even pulling worms from earth in typical Blackbird *Turdus merula* fashion.

FOOD Mainly insects, including large ants, termites, grasshoppers, green mantids and caterpillars. Spiders, slugs and worms are also caught and, occasionally, small vertebrates like frogs.

BREEDING The breeding season of this cooperative shrike is protracted, but it appears to vary markedly throughout the range according to the timing and duration of rainfall. In northern Senegal, near Richard-Toll, the species mainly nests during the Sahel rains, from the end of June to August. More to the south, in Gambia, most nests are again found during the rains from July to October. In Kenya, breeding takes place at least in January, February and April. In southern Ghana and southern Nigeria, in more humid zones, nesting occurs almost throughout the year except in November and rarely in December. During a long-term study at Legon, Ghana, most clutches were laid at the beginning of the rains, between February and April; nesting continued through the main rainy season and ceased in most years in August. Many nests are destroyed, and replacement clutches are frequent. Second and even third normal clutches also occur in a season; the clutch following a successful breeding is laid while the fledglings are still being cared for by other members of the group. In the Ghanaian study it was also noted that some groups built or partly built several nests in quick succession before eggs were laid; this was apparently the case when there was more than one female competing for breeding status in a group. The nest is built by the breeding pair with the help of at least some other members of the group; it may take up to four weeks to complete. After a failure a new nest can, however, be built in less than a week. In Ghana 20 species of tree were used for 115 nests located in five years. The most frequently selected trees were *Fagara zanthoxyloides* and *Bambusa vulgaris* (26 nests each). The nests were generally well concealed in foliage at heights between 1.5 and 10m, 60% of them being placed at 3-6m. The same trees were often used in consecutive seasons and sometimes even in the same breeding season. The nest, rather a substantial structure, is made of small sticks and twigs and lined with roots and fibres. It usually receives 3-5 eggs (range 2-6), normally only incubated by the breeding female for 15-18 days. The breeding-status female may occasionally, and for a short time, be ousted from her nest by one of the helpers (even males). This can particularly occur during the early stages of incubation. The nestling period is 18-20 days. The young are brooded by the breeding female for about a week. During that time she normally receives all food from the breeding male and helpers, and distributes it to the nestlings. Later, all the birds help directly, but in a very irregular way. When the young leave the nest, they are unable to fly. They are closely attended by members of the group, who guide them into cover when necessary; they become independent only seven weeks after hatching. By the tenth week they are well integrated into the group, even taking part in communal displays. Young aged 14 weeks were seen feeding fledglings and 24-week-old young were observed feeding nestlings.

During a five-year study in Ghana, only one case of nest parasitism, by African Cuckoo *Cuculus gularis*, was discovered in over 160 nests that were checked.

REFERENCES Bannerman (1953), Britton (1980), Brown & Britton (1980), Brunel & Thiollay (1969), Chapin (1954), Elgood (1994), Gore (1990), Grimes (1979a,b, 1980, 1987), Jackson (1938), Lamarche (1981, 1988), Lewis & Pomeroy (1989), Louette (1981), Lynes (1925), Mackworth-Praed & Grant (1973), Morel & Morel (1990), Nikolaus (1987), Salvan (1969), Schouteden (1960), Thonnérieux *et al.* (1989).

29   MAGPIE SHRIKE
Corvinella melanoleuca   Plate 15

Other names: Long-tailed Shrike

IDENTIFICATION Length 40-50cm. A large, polytypic (at least two races), long-tailed, black-and-white species with populations in central-east and southern Africa. It is mainly glossy black. A white V formed by the scapulars is, however, very conspicuous on the back. White also appears in the wing as a primary patch, at the tips of the secondaries, and on the rump. The pied appearance is particularly striking in flight. The sexes are very similar, but a large white patch on the flanks

characterises the adult female. Young birds are duller, rather dark brown with typical brownish barring on the upperparts and whitish barring on the underparts.

Like the Yellow-billed Shrike, this species is conspicuous and often met with in noisy family parties, the birds flying in single file from one vantage point to another. Their flight is straight, relatively fast and never of long duration; it ends with an upward swoop to a new perch.

DESCRIPTION *C. m. melanoleuca*
Adult male Upperparts glossy black from forehead to lower mantle, including sides of head (lores and ear-coverts). Scapulars white. Rump white. Uppertail-coverts glossy black. Tail black, pointed, very long (up to c. 35cm) and strongly graduated (graduation up to c. 24cm). Wings black with distinct white primary patch; some greater coverts faintly tipped white; wing feathers tipped white, tertials tipped broadly white. Underparts with a dark brownish gloss on chin, throat and breast, blacker on belly and flanks. Undertail white.
Adult female Very similar to male, but with a large white patch on flanks which joins white on rump.
Juvenile Upperparts dark brown; the dark feathers, tipped brownish, give a vermiculated appearance. Scapulars and rump whitish with feathers fringed buff. Uppertail-coverts dark brown fringed lighter brownish. Tail black, very slightly tipped buff. Wings dark brown with buff tips to wing-coverts and pale buff tips to wing feathers, particularly visible on tertials and inner secondaries. Underparts dark brown, vermiculated whitish (dark brown feathers tipped whitish). Undertail dark brown.
Bare parts Bill and legs black. Iris brown.

MEASUREMENTS (*melanoleuca*) Wing 122-143 (mean 134 for n = 42); tail 215-340; culmen 16.5-20; tarsus 31-35.5. Weight 55-97 (mean 82.3 for 22 males and 82.4 for twelve females).

DISTRIBUTION AND STATUS The breeding range lies entirely south of the Equator and involves both

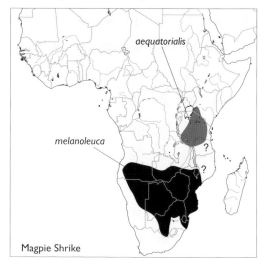

Magpie Shrike

extreme eastern and southern Africa. The northern limits are in Kenya where the species is very localised and only occurs between Magadi and the Masai Mara Game Reserve (near Siana Springs), which lies at approximately 1°15'S. From Kenya the range extends south through Tanzania and Mozambique. In northern Tanzania, the species is present on the south-east shore of Lake Victoria, in the Serengeti, near Lake Manyara and in Tarangire National Park; it also ranges widely in the interior and is found in the Mpanda, Rukwa, Usangu, Njombe and Ruaha National Park areas. It appears to be absent from southern Tanzania and northern Mozambique, but it is a rare non-breeding visitor to Malawi probably involving post-breeding dispersal from Zambia, although a small nesting population in the south cannot be ruled out. Between roughly 15 and 30°S the species is generally widespread across the continent, from southern Angola and northeast Namibia in the west to southern Mozambique and South Africa in the east. The dry south-west is, however, avoided. In Zambia, this shrike inhabits Southern Province and the lower Kafue basin from the Musa river southwards. It is widespread in Zimbabwe except in the north-east. In southern Mozambique it is restricted to the south and south-west of Sul do Save where it is local. It is well distributed in Transvaal except in the southern third where observations are rare in the west and non-existent in the east, the Escarpment and Highveld hosting occasional vagrants; the species is very common in the Kruger National Park, particularly in the south. Further south-westwards, the Magpie Shrike is only sparingly recorded in Orange Free State where most regular observations are from the Hoopstad district and the Koppies-Edenville area. Eastwards, in Natal, the species occurs in the extreme north-east, from Zululand northwards. The south-western boundaries are well known in Botswana; a recent atlas has shown that the species was fairly to very common in almost all regions except the desert of the south-west. In Angola, the northern boundary, as far as is known, crosses Quilenges, Capelongo and the Cuando-Cubango area.

GEOGRAPHICAL VARIATION Two races are currently admitted and quite distinct. Two more subtle forms have also been described.

   C. m. melanoleuca (southern Africa, south of the Zambezi river) Described above. Birds from southern Angola (*angolensis*) have been given subspecific status by Meise (1957) mainly on account of their short tail, which is said not to exceed 280mm. Another race (*expressa*) has been proposed mainly on the basis of differences in wing-length for birds living in Natal, Swaziland, southern Mozambique, northern Transvaal and southern Zimbabwe (see Clancey 1961).

   C. m. aequatorialis (eastern Africa, north of the Zambezi river) Similar to nominate, but tends to be blacker on chin, throat and breast, not so brownish-dark. Tail markedly shorter, not over 260mm.

MOVEMENTS Mainly strictly resident but possible and definite vagrants have been noted in various parts of the breeding range. Locally there might even be some regular movements in the dry season; they have been suspected in Zambia as an explanation of several birds seen together in the middle Zambezi valley at 27°40'E.

MOULT No information.

VOICE Often noisy. A sweet loud call has been transcribed as *needle-boom-needle-boom... come here, come here*, the first phrases being high-pitched, the '*needle*' being particularly stressed, and the second mainly being uttered while in flight. Harsh *chack chack* scolding alarm calls are frequent. Duets are not rare in the breeding season: the male utters a low-pitched *teelooo* and the female follows with a similar but higher-pitched note.

HABITAT The species inhabits a tropical savanna or steppe climate, mainly in areas with rainfall from November to April. Dry desert zones are avoided. In Kenya, at the northernmost point of its breeding range, the Magpie Shrike occurs up to 1,800m in semi-arid subhumid and intermediate 250-1,000mm rainfall zones. It is a typical bird of open park-like savanna with rather tall *Acacia* and areas of bare ground or close-grazed grass. Other woodland may also be favoured, particularly along river banks, but only where thorny bush occurs as in the case of the mopane habitat in Kruger National Park (Transvaal). In Botswana, at the south-west limits of the range, the species is commonest in moist areas and river valleys but it also occurs in semi-desert conditions well away from water.

HABITS The Magpie Shrike is a gregarious species which can be found in noisy parties of up to a dozen individuals, sometimes in company of other species such as larger weavers *Dinemellia*. Its social organisation is less well known than that of the Yellow-billed Shrike, but it is also a cooperative breeder, with pairs usually nesting in association with probably very few helpers. Displays with much body-bowing, wing-raising, tail-flicking and whistles are also common, but still little studied in detail. They occur along territory boundaries and are directed at intruders from another group. Similar displays may, however, also take place between members of the same group and be interpreted as greeting. A group can have a home range of at least several tens of hectares, but the breeding territory is rather small, c. 3ha; certain members of the group are apparently excluded from it. In the breeding season the female may call from the nest and then be fed by the male. Duets are then frequent (see Voice). The Magpie Shrike usually perches in an elevated position to scan the ground below, where most prey is caught; more rarely, insects are also taken in the air.

FOOD All kinds of insects, but also small vertebrates like reptiles and mice, and occasionally fruit.

BREEDING The season largely corresponds with the rains. In southern Africa, for nominate *melanoleuca*, breeding takes place from October to March in Zambia and Zululand, August to February (mainly October-November) in Transvaal and Zimbabwe, November to February in Botswana. In eastern Africa, for the race *aequatorialis*, there are records from January to April. Replacement clutches are frequent, but two normal broods can be reared in a season. Only the breeding pair appears to build the bulky nest which, is typically placed at a height of 2-10m above the ground in an acacia or other thorn tree, and well protected by numerous long spines. It is rather large and composed of dead, often thorny, sticks and twigs, fine rootlets and dry grass, and lined with finer rootlets and stems of creepers. The clutch comprises 2-6 eggs, usually 3-5 (mean 3.3 for n = 55 in southern Africa). The incubation period is unrecorded. The young stay in the nest for at least 15 days; when they fledge their tails are much shorter than those of adults.

REFERENCES Benson & Benson (1977), Benson *et al.* (1971), Britton (1980), Brown & Britton (1980), Clancey (1961, 1971, 1980a), Cyrus & Robson (1980), Earlé & Grobler (1987), Hall & Moreau (1970), Harris & Arnott (1988), Jackson (1938), Kemp (1974), Lewis & Pomeroy (1989), Mackworth-Praed & Grant (1955, 1963), Maclean (1993), Nichol (1964), Penry (1994), Priest (1936), Sclater (1901), Tarboton *et al.* (1987), Vincent (1949), Zimmerman *et al.* (1996).

30   WHITE-RUMPED SHRIKE
Eurocephalus rueppelli   Plate 16

Other common name: Northern White-crowned Shrike

IDENTIFICATION Length 19-21cm. A common, widespread, probably monotypic, but little-studied East African shrike of dry thornbush. The sexes are similar. This big, heavy bird has a powerful bill and brown upperparts except for the forehead, crown and rump which are white. The underparts are also white with, however, distinct pale brown patches on sides of breast and flanks. A dark facial mask is obvious; it extends from the lores under and just over the eyes, and then largely over the ear-coverts and onto the sides of the neck. Juveniles are similar, but their crown is brown and their underparts variably washed brownish.

The White-rumped Shrike is often seen in small groups, three, four or more individuals; it perches conspicuously and is easily approachable. Its butterfly-like flight interspersed with glides on stiff wings is characteristic and helps identification at long range. One of the two possible confusion species, roughly the same size, is the White-headed Buffalo Weaver *Dinemellia dinemelli*, generally widespread in the same areas but with white wing-patches and red rump. The White-crowned Starling *Spreo albicapillus* also bears a resemblance to this shrike but its upperparts, tail and wings are shining olive-green, not brown; in flight it shows a distinct white patch in the secondaries; it is confined to parts of Ethiopia, Somalia and arid bush in north-central Kenya.

DESCRIPTION
Adult Sexes similar in plumage. Black line from lores passes just above and below eyes and links up with a large black patch covering ear-coverts, sides of cheeks

and sides of nape forming an almost closed dark collar. Forehead, crown and nape white or creamy-white. Upperparts light brown on mantle becoming darker on scapulars and back. Rump and uppertail-coverts white. Tail dark brown; rectrices with narrow pale fringes. Wings dark brown; inner webs of primaries and secondaries paler than outer webs; wing feathers and wing-coverts very narrowly fringed pale. Underparts off-white with distinct brown patches on sides of breast and flanks. Undertail grey-brown.

Juvenile Similar to adults, but different head pattern with a dark crown and a large dark brown area resembling a 'submoustachial stripe' near the eye; it contrasts with the white on chin, throat, sides of cheeks and sides of nape. Upperparts also more uniform brown from forehead to lower back (crown may appear somewhat darker); each feather with pale fringes (fresh plumage). Rump and uppertail-coverts white. Tail as in adults. Wings dark brown; flight feathers and particularly wing-coverts distinctly fringed and tipped pale buff. Underparts more or less as in adults, heavily washed brown. Undertail as in adults.

Bare parts Bill black in adults, paler in young birds. Legs dark grey or brown. Iris brown.

MEASUREMENTS Wing 118-134; tail 86-103; bill (culmen) 16-18; tarsus 21-23.5 (based on 41 specimens from Ethiopia and Kenya, birds regarded as race *erlangeri* having wings 131 on average for n = 14 against 123.5 for 'nominate' for n = 27; see Friedmann 1937). Weight: no data.

White-rumped Shrike

DISTRIBUTION AND STATUS The breeding range is restricted to five East African countries. Its northwestern point lies in south-east Sudan at around 6°N 31°E. North-eastwards, the northern boundary crosses Ethiopia, very roughly just east of the Omo and Awash rivers and south-east of Djibouti. In north-west Somalia, the species is a common resident to 46°E and south of 8°N; it also appears to be particularly common in the south-west along the Juba River. The White-rumped Shrike is widespread in north-east Uganda and virtually throughout Kenya, but is absent from the Lake Victoria basin in the west, the coastal lowlands south of Malindi in the south-east, and many humid areas of the highlands. The species is common in Tanzania except in the north-west. The southern limits are reached at c. 10°S. Odd birds appear in Malawi and possibly northern Mozambique.

GEOGRAPHICAL VARIATION Zedlitz (1915) recognised five subspecies based on differences in colour of mantle and underparts. Of these, Sclater and Mackworth-Praed (1918), with difficulty, maintained three. Later, Macdonald (1940) came to regard the White-rumped Shrike as monotypic, since specimens compared month by month throughout the range were not separable geographically. He was followed by Rand (1960) and White (1962). Examination of four trays of birds at the Natural History Museum (England) confirms that there is little difference when birds at equal stages of moult and wear are compared. Fresh-plumaged birds have paler and worn birds darker upperparts. Moreover, as stated by Macdonald, the extent and tone of brown on the underparts varies throughout the species and is too unstable a character on which to base races. The same can apparently be said of size although this requires further study (see Measurements).

MOVEMENTS Mainly strictly resident; as far as is known only very local movements exist.

MOULT No information.

VOICE A sociable and noisy species; its sharp staccato calls have been transcribed as *kak-kak* or *kek-kek* and other common vocalisations as *weeyer-wook, weeyer-wook*. Notes given in series have been 'translated' as *chrrk, wirk-wirk, yerk-yerk, wuk-wuk* or *yerk-yerk-yerk-yerk*. Juveniles utter a sharp piercing *skeet*.

HABITAT A tree-dwelling species favouring dry thorn-bush country and open woodland. In Kenya, it can be met with up to 2,200m, but mainly below 1,400m, and avoiding many of the rather humid areas of the highlands and the moist west. The White-rumped Shrike is a typical inhabitant of *Acacia* or *Commiphora* woodlands; in Somalia it has been recorded on the plateau, in the open acacia-aloe country near old *kharias* (tribal encampments) or in the high mimosa trees bordering dry watercourses or *tugs*. It can be found in gardens or parkland near human habitations.

HABITS A generally conspicuous species as it moves in small, noisy, restless groups, often perching relatively high in trees. It is not shy and easily approachable. The White-rumped Shrike is fairly gregarious, although its social organisation is not well known. Moreau and Moreau (1939) recorded a case of an incubating bird surrounded by three others a few inches away. Some degree of cooperative breeding undoubtedly occurs, but such behaviour is apparently not regular as definite single pairs have also been observed. Two or more females may sometimes share a nest which may then receive as many as seven eggs. The hunting methods are similar to those of *Lanius* shrikes, but the White-rumped Shrike perhaps shows a tendency to take a higher proportion of its food in the air. It perches 3-4m up and catches most of its food in a 10m radius (see Lack 1985). When on bare ground it hops about energetically after insects.

FOOD Mainly insectivorous, but few details. The most common insect groups taken are beetles, grasshoppers and butterflies. The wings of the latter are snipped off and not eaten. Berries have also been recorded.

BREEDING Clutches are started in relatively ill-defined seasons but mainly in the rains, with May and November peaks in areas with two rainy seasons. Eggs have been found from February to August and in October-December. The protracted breeding season suggests that this shrike is double-brooded. The nest is a very neat, compactly built grass cup, rather small for the size of the bird, about 7.5cm in internal and 12cm in external diameter. The whole of the outside, and particularly round the rim, is covered with a thick coating of cobweb, which gives it a grey felted appearance; from a distance it may be mistaken for clay. Typically, nests are moulded onto horizontal acacia forks, 4-6m from the ground; 3-4 eggs are laid (range 2-5; exceptionally, possibly due to two females, 6 or 7).

REFERENCES Archer & Godman (1961), Ash & Miskell (1983), Brown & Britton (1980), Erlanger (1905), Friedmann (1937), Lack (1985), Lewis & Pomeroy (1989), Macdonald (1940), Mackworth-Praed & Grant (1955), Moreau & Moreau (1939), Nikolaus (1987), Rand (1960), Sclater & Mackworth-Praed (1918), Urban & Brown (1971), White (1962), Zedlitz (1915), Zimmerman *et al.* (1996).

31   WHITE-CROWNED SHRIKE
Eurocephalus anguitimens   Plate 16

Other name: Southern White-crowned Shrike

IDENTIFICATION Length c. 24cm. A large, stocky shrike with two races, locally common in dry, wooded areas of the southern third of Africa. The sexes are similar. The species is unmistakable with its powerful black bill and snowy-white forehead and crown contrasting with ashy-brown upperparts and darker tail and wings. A large dark facial mask extends from the lores just over and under the eyes to the ear-coverts and sides of neck. The throat and breast are white, whereas belly and flanks are washed ashy-brown. Juveniles have almost completely ashy brown underparts except for the throat, sides of face and nape, which are white; they also differ from adults in having a mottled, faintly barred, brownish crown.

The White-crowned Shrike is often seen in small noisy groups; its flight is very characteristic, somewhat parrot-like, with fluttering wing-beats interrupted by glides in which the wings are 'stiffly' held in a shallow V above the back.

DESCRIPTION *E. a. anguitimens*
Adult Black line from lores passes just above and below eyes and links up with a large black patch covering

ear-coverts, sides of throat and sides of nape. Forehead, crown and nape white. Upperparts ashy-brown from mantle to uppertail-coverts including scapulars. Tail dark brown; rectrices very narrowly tipped and fringed pale (fresh plumage). Wings dark brown; wing feathers darker than wing-coverts; all flight-feathers narrowly fringed and tipped pale. Underparts off-white from chin to mid-belly, tinged buff on upper breast; lower belly, lower flanks and vent ashy-brown. Undertail grey-brown.

Juvenile Similar to adults, but crown greyer, mottled and faintly barred. Flight feathers and wing-coverts fringed and tipped buff or pale buff. Underparts washed ashy-brown all over except on chin, throat and sides of nape, which are white.

Bare parts Bill black in adults, pale in juveniles. Legs dark brown, rather greyish in young birds. Iris brown.

MEASUREMENTS Wing 132-145 (mean c. 138); tail 99-109; bill (culmen from base) 23-37; tarsus c. 26. Weight 56-84 (mean c. 69).

White-crowned Shrike

DISTRIBUTION AND STATUS A southern African species occurring in dry country, very roughly from 14°S in south-west Angola, south of Lobito, and 28°55'S in the Kalahari Desert in south-west Botswana. From south-west Angola the range extends south over north-ern Namibia and south-east over northern and central Botswana, southern Zambia, the central plateau of Zim-babwe, western, northern and eastern Transvaal, north-east Swaziland and immediately adjacent south-ern Mozambique.

In suitable habitats, the species is generally wide-spread even if rather localised.

GEOGRAPHICAL VARIATION Rand (1960) and White (1962) considered the species monotypic. In 1965, Clancey proposed a new race, *niveus*.

    E. a. anguitimens (western part of the breeding range) Described above.

    E. a. niveus (Zambia, in the eastern districts, Mash-onaland and the midlands, south to the north-east and eastern Transvaal, north-east Swaziland and adjacent districts of Sul do Save in Mozambique)

Same size as nominate. Main difference reported-ly the paler feathers of the mantle and scapulars, which are broadly tipped and fringed with off-white; this gives the back a snowy appearance, which is apparently not due to bleaching or wear. For further details, see Clancey (1965).

MOVEMENTS Mainly resident, although movements may occur on a local scale, particularly in cooler win-ter months; indeed, according to Clancey (1965), the species is markedly nomadic and rather irruptive. Odd birds occasionally turn up slightly outside their nor-mal range with for instance two birds noted in northern Natal during atlas work (see Cyrus and Robson 1980).

MOULT No information.

VOICE A contact call accompanies birds on the move; it is a squeak, *kaee kaee* or *pep-pep*, uttered rapidly five or six times; Priest (1936) likened it to the noise of a baby's rubber bath toy. It may become harsher in the case of individual birds which have lost contact with the group and sound like *k-kaeek-k-kaeek*. A rather stuttering *kida-kida-kida* call may be a greeting used when one bird approaches another.

HABITAT The White-crowned Shrike is an open wood-land or open parkland bird. Its needs fairly tall deciduous, thorny trees and sparse ground cover, and is often found fairly close to a big river; in the drier west it is even mainly to be found in riverine bush but also occurs in semi-desert thorn savannas on Kalahari sands. Dry, low-lying areas are favoured. In Natal the species is thus absent from the Highveld and Escarp-ment, but widespread in the Bushveld and Lowland regions. The species nests in light forest country, par-ticularly in patches of *Acacia* or *Brachystegia* trees bordering such patches. It can, however, sometimes be found outside thorny woodland strips in suitably structured village gardens.

HABITS A noisy shrike, generally conspicuous. A few birds are often seen together indulging in group-calling, which probably has a territorial function or serves as a greeting display (see Voice). As the birds perch conspicuously, their vocalisations may be accom-panied by much tail-flicking and wing-shivering; they express threat by adopting a horizontal position with neck- and crown-feathers raised. Groups of this gre-garious species are usually composed of 3-6 individuals, but up to 20 have been recorded together outside the breeding season when a given group, possibly led by one dominant individual, may roam over an area cov-ering c. 200ha. These social shrikes may appear rather shy or, in other places, quite tame. They attack poten-tial predators such as raptors vigorously, but are not pugnacious to other birds. The company of species such as *Tockus* hornbills may even be favoured as those birds, when hopping on the ground, disturb insects which are then captured by the shrikes. The latter may also be much attracted by injured members of their own community: Sir Andrew Smith, who described the species in 1836, noticed that when such a shrike chanced to fall wounded, its companions continued hovering about and approaching it, until it was removed; this behaviour enabled a concealed collector to kill up to twelve in succession without moving from his hiding place (see Sclater 1901). The White-crowned Shrike's social organisation, apparently based on dominance relationships, is not yet well known. It is, however, obviously in some degree a cooperative breeder. Definite, 'real' pairs occur, but often up to five adults can be observed at the same nest. Helpers may take a share in nest-building and even in incubation. The White-crowned Shrike spends much time on high perches scanning the ground where most food is picked up. Insects are also gleaned from leaves and branches or caught in the air. Ginn (1974) observed a brooding female who had the unusual habit of dropping on any prey that she happened to see immediately below the nest; she would then grab the prey and return to the nest to feed the chicks. Another unusual behaviour concerned a pair of shrikes which, near their nest, were seriously pestered by two Icterine Warblers *Hippolais icterina*; when the shrikes were away, the Palearctic migrants regularly fed their three young (see Williams 1989).

FOOD The staple diet is large insects; in Zimbabwe this shrike has the reputation of being a great caterpillar eater. It also takes millipedes and has occasionally been seen eating cherry-like fruit.

BREEDING The breeding season stretches from September to February, but most clutches are started between October and December. There is apparently only one normal brood. The nest is built by both sexes, sometimes aided by one or two helpers, in 3-4 weeks. It is typically placed on the lateral bough of an acacia, sometimes in another deciduous tree, frequently at the farthest extremity. It can be at any height, but mainly 4-6m (range 2-18m). The construction is a very neat, strong, perpendicular-sided cup made of fine yellow grass-stems, tightly packed down. The whole is plastered in profusion with an even covering of cobweb which gives the nest a smooth silvery-grey finish that matches the usually lichen-covered branch on which it is placed. Hair and feathers are sometimes used for the inner lining. This very compact structure, measuring up to c. 12.5cm across and c. 7.5cm high, may be repaired and reused. The White-crowned Shrike mainly lays 3-4 eggs (range 2-6); clutches of 10 eggs have occasionally been reported and are presumably due to two females. Incubation, almost exclusively assumed by the female but occasionally, for short periods, by helpers, takes about 20 days. It is not known how long chicks stay in the nest.

REFERENCES Clancey (1965), Cyrus & Robson (1980), Ginn (1974), Harris & Arnott (1988), Irwin (1981), Kemp (1974), Mackworth-Praed & Grant (1963), Maclean (1993), Penry (1994), Priest (1936), Sclater (1901), Tarboton *et al.* (1987), Vincent (1949), Williams (1989).

BIBLIOGRAPHY

Alerstam, T. 1990. *Bird Migration*. Cambridge University Press, Cambridge.

Ali, S. 1969. *Birds of Kerala*. Oxford University Press, Madras.

Ali, S. and Ripley, S.D. 1972. *Handbook of the Birds of India and Pakistan*. Vol. 5. Oxford University Press, Bombay.

Alström, P., Colston, P. and Lewington, I. 1991. *A Field Guide to the Rare Birds of Britain and Europe*. Collins, London.

American Ornithologists' Union. 1983. *Check-list of North American Birds*, 6th ed. AOU.

Anderson, R.M. 1976. Shrikes feed on prey remains left by hawks. *Condor* 78: 269.

Anderson, W.L. and Duzan R.E. 1978. DDE residues and eggshell thinning in Loggerhead Shrikes. *Wilson Bull*. 90: 215-220.

Andrews, I.J. 1995. *The Birds of the Hashemite Kingdom of Jordan*. Published privately, Musselburgh.

Andrle, R.F. and Carrol, J. R. (eds) 1988. *The Atlas of Breeding Birds in New York State*. Cornell University Press, New York.

Applegate, R.D. 1977. Possible ecological role of food caches of Loggerhead Shrike. *Auk* 94: 391-392.

Archer, G. and Godman, E.M. 1961. *The Birds of British Somaliland and the Gulf of Aden*. Oliver and Boyd, Edinburgh and London.

Ash, J.S. 1970. Observations on a decreasing population of Red-backed Shrikes. *British Birds* 63: 185-205 and 225-239.

Ash, J.S and Miskell, J.E. 1983. Birds of Somalia. *Scopus* Spec. Supp. no. 1.

Aspinall, S. 1996. *Status and Conservation of the Breeding Birds of the United Arab Emirates*. National Avian Research Center, Abu Dhabi.

Atkinson, E.C. 1993. Winter territories and night roosts of Northern Shrikes in Idaho. *Condor* 95: 515-527.

Atkinson, E.C. 1995. Northern Shrikes (*Lanius excubitor*) wintering in North America; a Christmas Bird Count analysis of trends, cycles and interspecific interactions. *In* Shrikes (Laniidae) of the world: biology and conservation (R. Yosedf and F.E. Lohrer, eds). *Proc. West. Found. Vert. Zool.* 6: 39-44.

Atkinson, E.C. and Cade, T.J. 1993. Winter foraging and diet composition of Northern Shrikes in Idaho. *Condor* 95: 528-538.

Atkinson, P., Peet, N. and Alexander, J. 1991. The status and conservation of the endemic bird species of São Tomé and Príncipe, West Africa. *Bird Conserv. Intern.* 1: 255-282.

Atkinson, P.M., Dutton, J.S., Peet, N.B. and Sequeira, V.A.S. 1994. *A study of the birds, small nammals, turtles and medicinal plants of São Tomé with notes on Príncipe*. BirdLife International Study Report no. 56, Cambridge.

Austin, O. and Kuroda, N. 1953. The birds of Japan. Their status and distribution. *Bull. Mus. Comp. Zool.* 109: 279-637.

Bailly, J.B. 1853. *Ornithologie de la Savoie*. J.B. Clarey, Paris.

Baker, E.C.S. 1924. *The Fauna of British India*. Vol. II. Taylor and Francis, London.

Balda, R.P. 1965. Loggerhead Shrike kills Mourning Dove. *Condor* 67: 359.

Banage, W.B. 1969. Territorial behaviour and population in the Grey-back Fiscal Shrike. *Uganda J.* 33: 201-208.

Bannerman, D.A. 1953. *The Birds of West and Equatorial Africa*. Vol. 1. Oliver and Boyd, Edinburgh and London.

Bara, T. 1995. La population de Pies-grièches à poitrine rose (*Lanius minor*) de la basse plaine de l'Aude en 1994.

Alauda 63: 191-198.

Barthel, P.H. 1992. Bemerkenswerte Beobachtungen. *Limicola* 6: 301-314.

Bassin, P., Huber, C. and Zuber, M. 1981. Beitrag zur Ernährung des Raubwürgers (*Lanius excubitor*) in der Nordwestschweiz (Ajoie, Kanton Jura). *Jahrb. Naturh. Mus. Bern* 8: 217-230.

Baumgart, W. 1995. *Die Vögel Syriens*. Max Kasparek, Heidelberg.

Baumgart, W. and Stephan, B. 1987. Vögel Syriens. *Mitt. Zool. Mus. Berlin* 63. Suppl. Ann. Orn. 11: 57-95.

Bayle, P. 1994. Massacre de migrateurs à Chios. Encore la tradition...! *L'Oiseau Mag.* no.35: 22-24.

Bechet, A., Isenmann P. and Mauffrey, J.F. 1995. Un deuxième site de nidification de la Pie-grièche à poitrine rose en Languedoc. *Alauda* 63: 243-244.

Bechet, G. and Moes, M. 1992. Zur Population und Ökologie des Neuntöters (*Lanius collurio*) im Raum Junglinster. *Regulus Wiss. Ber.* no. 10: 2-17.

Benson, C.W. 1950. The races of *Lanius souzae* Bocage. *Auk* 67: 394-395.

Benson, C.W. and Benson, F.M. 1977. *The Birds of Malawi*. Montfort Press, Limbe.

Benson, C.W. , Brooke, R.K., Dowsett, R.J. and Irwin, M.P.S. 1971. *Birds of Zambia*. Collins, London.

Benson, C.W. and Irwin, M.P.S. 1967. *A Contribution to the Ornithology of Zambia*. National Museum of Zambia, Oxford University Press, London.

Bent, A.C. 1950. *Life Histories of North American Wagtails, Shrikes, Vireos, and their Allies*. U.S. Nat. Mus. Bull. 197. Smithsonian Institution, Washington.

Beretz, P. and Keve, A. 1975. Der Raubwürger in Ungarn. *Zool. Abh. Mus. Tierk. Dresden* 33: 151-161.

Bersuder, D. and Koenig, P. 1995. *Biologie d'une Population de Pies-grièches à Tête Rousse (Lanius senator) dans le Bas-Rhin*. Compte-rendu CRBPO. Centre d'Etudes Ornithologiques d'Alsace.

Beven, G. and England, M.D. 1969. The impaling of prey by shrikes. *British Birds* 62: 192-199.

Bildstein, K.L. and Grubb, T.C. 1980. Spatial distributions of American Kestrels and Loggerhead Shrikes wintering sympatrically in eastern Texas. *J. Raptor Res.* 14: 90-91.

Biswas, B. 1950. On the shrike *Lanius tephronotus* (Vigors), with remarks on the *erythronotus* and *tricolor* groups of *Lanius schach* Linné, and their hybrids. *J. Bombay Nat. Hist. Soc.* 49: 444-455.

Biswas, B. 1962. Further notes on the shrikes *Lanius tephronotus* and *Lanius schach*. *Ibis* 104: 112-115.

Blase, B. 1960. Die Lautäusserungen des Neuntöters *Lanius collurio*. Freilandbeobachtungen und Kaspar Hauser-Versuche. *Z. Tierpsychol.* 17: 293-344.

Bocage, J.V.B 1904. Contribution à la faune des quatre isles du Golfe de Guinée. 4. Ile de São Tomé. *J. Acad. Sci. Lisboa* 7: 65-96.

Bock, W.J. and Farrand, J. 1980. The number of species and genera of recent birds: a contribution to comparative systematics. *Amer. Mus. Novit.* 2073.

Bohall-Wood, P. 1987. Abundance, habitat use, and perch use of Loggerhead Shrikes in north-central Florida. *Wilson Bull.* 99: 82-86.

Bohlen, H.D. 1989. *The Birds of Illinois*. Indiana University Press, Bloomington.

Bonaccorsi, G. and Isenmann, P. 1994. Biologie de la reproduction et nourriture de la Pie-grièche à tête rousse *Lanius senator badius* et de la Pie-grièche écorcheur *Lanius collurio* en Corse (France). *Alauda* 62: 269-274.

Brandl, R., Lübcke, W. and Mann, W. 1986. Habitatwahl beim Neuntöter (*Lanius collurio*). *J. Ornithologie* 127: 69-78.

Brauning, D.W. (ed) 1992. *Atlas of Breeding Birds in Pennsylvania*. University of Pittsburgh Press, Pittsburgh.

Brazil, M.A. 1991. *The Birds of Japan*. Christopher Helm, London.

Brewer, R., Peak, G.A.M. and Adams, R.J. Jr. 1991. *The Atlas of Breeding Birds of Michigan*. Michigan State University Press, East Lansing.

Britton, P.L. 1980. *Birds of East Africa*. East African Natural History Society, Nairobi.

Brosset, A. 1989. Un cas d'association à bénéfice mutuel, celui de la Pie-grièche *Lanius cabanisi* avec les Bubalornis *Bubalornis niger*. *Rev. Ecol. (Terre et Vie)* 44: 103-105.

Brosset, A. and Erard, C. 1986. *Les Oiseaux des Régions Forestières du Nord-Est du Gabon*. Vol. 1. Suppl. 3. Terre et Vie, Soc. Nat. Prot. Nature, Paris.

Brooks, B.L. and Temple, S.A. 1990a. Habitat availability and suitability for Loggerhead Shrikes in the upper midwest. *Amer. Midl. Nat.* 123: 75-83.

Brooks, B.L. and Temple, S.A. 1990b. Dynamics of a Loggerhead Shrike population in Minnesota. *Wilson Bull.* 102: 441-450.

Brown, L.H. and Britton, P.L. 1980. *The Breeding Seasons of East African Birds*. East African Natural History Society, Nairobi.

Bruderer, B. 1991. Common Egg-eater *Dasypeltis scabra* killed at Fiscal Shrike *Lanius collaris* nest. *Ostrich* 62: 76-77.

Bruderer, B. 1994. Habitat and niche of migrant Red-backed Shrike in southern Africa. *J. Ornithologie* 135: 474-475.

Bruderer, B. and Bruderer, H. 1993. Distribution and habitat preference of Red-backed Shrikes *Lanius collurio* in southern Africa. *Ostrich* 64: 141-147.

Bruderer, B. and Bruderer, H. 1994. Numbers of Red-backed Shrikes *Lanius collurio* in different habitats of South Africa. *Bull. Brit.Orn.Club* 114: 192-202.

Brunel, J. 1978. Les oiseaux de la région du Lang-Bian, massif montagneux de la chaîne annamitique. *L'Oiseau et la R.F.O.* 48: 159-180.

Brunel, J. and Thiollay, J.M. 1969. Liste préliminaire des oiseaux de Côte d'Ivoire. *Alauda* 37: 315-337.

Bull, J. 1974. *Birds of New York State*. Cornell University Press, Ithaca and London.

Burnside, F.L. 1987. Long-distance movements by Loggerhead Shrikes. *J. Field Ornithology* 58: 62-65.

Burton, J.F. 1995. *Birds and Climate Change*. Christopher Helm, London.

Busbee, E.L. 1977. The effects of dieldrin on the behavior of young Loggerhead Shrikes. *Auk* 94: 28-35.

Cade, T.J. 1962. Wing movements, hunting, and displays of the Northern Shrike. *Wilson Bull.* 74: 386-408.

Cade, T.J. 1967. Ecological and behavioral aspects of predation by the Northern Shrike. *Living Bird* 6: 43-86.

Cade, T.J. 1992. Hand-reared Loggerhead Shrikes breed in captivity. *Condor* 94: 1027-1029.

Cade, T.J. 1995. Shrikes as predators. *In* Shrikes (Laniidae) of the world: biology and conservation (R. Yosef and F.E. Lohrer, eds). *Proc. West. Found. Vert. Zool* 6: 1-5.

Cade, T.J. and Swem, T. 1995. Ecology of Northern Shrikes nesting in Arctic Alaska. *In* Shrikes (Laniidae) of the world: biology and conservation (R. Yosef and F.E. Lohrer, eds). *Proc. West. Found. Vert. Zool.* 6: 204-214.

Cade, T.J. and Woods, C.P. 1994. Changes in distribution and abundance of Loggerhead Shrikes. *J. Ornithologie* 135: 288 (Proc. 21st Int. Orn. Cong., Vienna).

Cadman, M.D. 1985. *Status Report on the Loggerhead Shrike in Canada*. Cosewi, Ottawa.

Cadman, M.D., Eagles, P.F.J. and Helleiner, F.M. 1987. *Atlas of the Breeding Birds of Ontario*. University of Waterloo Press, Waterloo.

Caldwell, H.R. and Caldwell, J.C. 1931. *South China Birds*. Hester May, Vanderburgh, Shanghai.

Canadian Wildlife Service. 1992. *National Recovery Plan for the Loggerhead Shrike*. Final Draft, December 1992. Can. Wild. Serv./Envir. Canada. 31 pages.

Capello, M.A., Ebels, E.B. and Mahu W.R.L. 1994. Izabelklauwier op Texel in oktober 1993. *Dutch Birding* 16: 226-229.

Carlon, J. 1994. La Pie-grièche grise *Lanius excubitor* sur le versant nord des Pyrénées occidentales. Contribution à son écologie. *La Marie-Blanque* 3: 1-20.

Carlson, A. 1985. Prey detection in the Red-backed Shrike (*Lanius collurio*): an experimental study. *Anim. Behav.* 33: 1243-1249.

Carlson, A. 1989. Courtship feeding and clutch size in Red-backed Shrikes (*Lanius collurio*). *Amer. Nat.* 133: 454-457.

Castan, R. 1960. Les migrations pré- et post-nuptiales des Pies-grièches à tête rousse *Lanius senator senator* et *Lanius senator badius* dans le Sud Tunisien (Région de Gabès). *Alauda* 28: 129-142.

Cave, F.O. and MacDonald, J.D. 1955. *Birds of the Sudan*. Oliver and Boyd, Edinburgh.

Chacon, G. 1996. El alcaudón chico en la ribera del Cinca. *Quercus* 120: 32-33.

Chalmers, M.L. 1986. *Annotated Checklist of the Birds of Hong Kong*. Hong Kong Bird Watching Society, Hong Kong.

Chapin, J.P. 1950. Sousa's Shrike in Tanganyika Territory. *Auk* 67: 241-242.

Chapin, J.P. 1954. The birds of the Belgian Congo. *Bull. Amer. Mus. Nat. Hist.* 75B.

Chapman, B.R. and Casto, S.D. 1972. Additional vertebrate prey of the Loggerhead Shrike. *Wilson Bull.* 84: 496-497.

Chappuis, C. 1970. La vallée d'Avas en Thrace. *Nos Oiseaux* 30: 256-263.

Cheke, R.A. and Walsh, J.F. 1996. *The Birds of Togo*. BOU Check-list no. 14. Tring, Herts.

Cheng Tso-hsin 1987. *A Synopsis of the Avifauna of China*. Paul Parey, Hamburg and Berlin, and Science Press, Peking.

Chiba, H. 1990. First breeding record of the Bull-headed Shrike from the Ogasawara Islands. *Jap. of Ornithology* 38: 150-151 (in Japanese, English summary).

Chong, L.T. 1938. Birds of Nanking. *Contr. Biol. Lab. Sc. Soc. China* 12 Zool. Ser. 9: 258-269 (Laniidae).

Clancey, P.A. 1948. A new race of the Woodchat Shrike (*Lanius senator L.*) from the island of Sicily. *Bull. Brit.Orn.Club* 68: 90-92.

Clancey, P.A. 1953. Miscellaneous taxonomic notes on African birds 3. *Durban Mus. Novit.* 4: 57-64.

Clancey, P.A. 1955. A new geographical race of the Fiscal Shrike *Lanius collaris* Linnaeus from the deserts of South-West Africa and Angola. *Bull. Brit.Orn.Club* 75: 32-33.

Clancey, P.A. 1961. Geographical variation in the South African populations of the Magpie-Shrike *Lanius melanoleucus* Jardine. *Bull. Brit.Orn.Club* 81: 52-54.

Clancey, P.A. 1964. *The Birds of Natal and Zululand*. Oliver and Boyd, Edinburgh.

Clancey, P.A. 1965. Variation in the White-crowned Shrike *Eurocephalus anguitimens* Smith, 1836. *Arnoldia* 1: 1-3.

Clancey, P.A. 1970. Miscellaneous taxonomic notes on African birds 28. *Durban Mus. Novit.* 8: 325-351.

Clancey, P.A. 1971. A handlist of the birds of southern Moçambique. *Mem. Inst. Invest. cient. Moçamb.* 11. Sér. A. 1-167.

Clancey, P.A. 1973. The status and characters of the races of the Red-backed Shrike, wintering in the South African sub-region. *Bull. Brit. Orn. Club* 93: 92-96.

Clancey, P.A. 1976. Intergradation between two subspecies of the Fiscal Shrike. *Ostrich* 47: 145.

Clancey, P.A. (ed) 1980a. *Checklist of Southern African Birds.* Southern African Ornithological Society, Johannesburg.

Clancey, P.A. 1980b. On the Lesser Grey Shrike *Lanius minor* in southern Africa. *Durban Mus. Novit.* 12: 161-165.

Clarke, G. 1985. Bird observations from northwest Somalia. *Scopus* 9: 24-42.

Claudon, A. 1995. Le Coucou gris *Cuculus canorus canorus* Linné en Alsace. *Bull. Soc. Hist. Nat. Colmar* 46: 41-57.

Clement, P. 1995. Identification pitfalls and assessment problems. 17 Woodchat Shrike *Lanius senator. British Birds* 88: 291-295.

Clement, P. and Worfolk, T. 1995. Southern and eastern Great Grey Shrikes in northwest Europe. *Birding World* 8: 300-309.

Clinning, C. 1989. *Southern African Bird Names Explained.* Southern African Ornithological Society, Johannesburg.

Coates, B.J. 1990. *The Birds of Papua New Guinea.* Vol. 2. Passerines. Dove Publications, Alderley.

Collar, N.J. and Andrew, P. 1988. *Birds to Watch: the ICBP Checklist of Threatened Birds.* International Council for Bird Preservation (Technical Publication 8), Cambridge.

Collar, N.J., Crosby, M.J. and Stattersfield, A.J. 1994. *Birds to Watch 2: the World List of Threatened Birds.* BirdLife International, Cambridge.

Collar, N.J. and Stuart, S.N. 1985. *Threatened Birds of Africa and Related Islands.* ICPB/IUCN Red Data Book, Cambridge.

Collister, D.M. 1994. Breeding ecology and habitat preservation of the Loggerhead Shrike in south-eastern Alberta. Master's thesis. University of Calgary, Calgary.

Collister, D.M. and Wicklum, D.D. 1996. Intraspecific variation in Loggerhead Shrikes: sexual dimorphism and implication for subspecies classification. *Auk* 113: 221-223.

Cooper, J. 1971a. The breeding of the Fiscal Shrike in southern Africa. *Ostrich* 42: 166-174.

Cooper, J. 1971b. Post-nesting development in the Fiscal Shrike. *Ostrich* 42: 175-178.

Craig, R.B. 1978. An analysis of the predatory behaviour of the Loggerhead Shrike. *Auk* 95: 221-234.

Cramp, S. and Perrins, C.M. (eds) 1993. *The Birds of the Western Palearctic.* Vol. 7. Oxford University Press, Oxford.

Crespon, J. 1840. *Ornithologie du Gard et des Pays circonvoisins.* Castel, Montpellier.

Crick, H. 1990. Poisoned prey in the heart of Africa. *New Scientist* 24 November 1990: 39-42.

Cruz Solis, C. de la, and Lope Rebollo, F. de 1985. Reproduction de la Pie-grièche méridionale *Lanius excubitor meridionalis* dans le sud-ouest de la péninsule Ibérique. *Gerfaut* 75: 199-209.

Cruz Solis, C. de la, Lope Rebollo, F. de, and da Silva, E. 1990. Sobre la territorialidad del Alcaudón Real (*Lanius excubitor meridionalis* Temm.). *Actas VII Jornadas Orn. Españolas, Murcia 1985* (publ. 1990) 315-327.

Cuddy, D. 1995. Protection and restoration of breeding habitat for the Loggerhead Shrike (*Lanius ludovicianus*) in Ontario, Canada. *In* Shrikes (Laniidae) of the world: biology and conservation (R. Yosef and F.E. Lohrer, eds). *Proc. West. Found. Vert. Zool.* 6: 283-286.

Cyrus, D. and Robson, N. 1980. *Bird Atlas of Natal.* University of Natal Press, Pietermaritzburg.

Danielsen, F, *et al.* 1994. *Conservation of Biological Diversity in the Sierra Madre Mountains of Isabela and southern Cagayan Provinces, The Philippines.* DENR-BirdLife International, Manila and DOF, Copenhagen.

Davis, D.E. 1937. A cycle in Northern Shrike emigrations. *Auk* 54: 43-49.

Dean, A.R. 1982. Field characters of Isabelline and Brown Shrikes. *British Birds* 75: 395-406.

Deignan, H.G. 1945. *The Birds of Northern Thailand.* U.S. Nat. Mus., Smithonian Institution, Washington.

Deignan, H.G. 1963. *Checklist of the Birds of Thailand.* Mus. Nat. Hist. Smithonian Institution, Washington.

Delacour, J. and Jabouille, P. 1931. *Les Oiseaux de l'Indochine Française.* Tome 4. Exposition Coloniale Internationale, Paris.

Delacour, J. and Mayr, E. 1946. *Birds of the Philippines.* Macmillan, New York.

Delprat, B. 1994. Observation d'une Pie-grièche à poitrine rose en Tunisie. *Alauda* 62: 133.

Dement'ev, G.P. and Gladkov, N.A. 1968. *Birds of the Soviet Union.* Vol. 6. Israel Program for Scientific Translation, Jerusalem.

Demey, R. and Fishpool, L.D.C. 1991. Additions and annotations to the avifauna of Côte d'Ivoire. *Malimbus* 12: 61-86.

Desai, J.H. and Malhotra, A.K. 1986. Breeding biology of Baybacked Shrike (*Lanius vittatus*) at National Zoological Park, New Delhi. *J. Bombay Nat. Hist. Soc.* 83: 200-202.

Desaulnay, P. 1982. Statut et répartition de la Pie-grièche grise dans les régions Sud-Ouest, Midi-Pyrénées et Languedoc-Roussillon. *Bull. A.R.O.M.P.* no. 6: 2-4.

De Smet, G. and BAHC 1994. Izabelklauwier te Heist in september 1989. *Dutch Birding* 16: 229-231.

Dickinson, E.C., Kennedy, R.S. and Parkes, K.C. 1991. *The Birds of the Philippines.* BOU Checklist no. 12. Tring, Herts.

Dittami, J.P. and Knauer, B. 1986. Seasonal organization of breeding and molting in the Fiscal Shrike. *J. Ornithologie* 127: 79-84.

Dohmann, M. 1985. Morphologische Unterschiede und Verhaltensdifferenzierungen bei verschiedenen Raubwürger-Rassen. Spiegeln solche Unterschiede erkennbar die Entwicklungsgeschichte von *L. excubitor* wieder? Diss. Universität Tübingen.

Dorka, V. 1975. Zum "Faust"-Gebrauch beim Raubwürger *Lanius excubitor* (Laniidae) und Weissscheitelwürger *Eurocephalus anguitimens* (Prionopinae) *Anz. orn. Ges. Bayern* 14: 314-319.

Dorka, V. and Ullrich, B. 1975. Haben die Rassen des Raubwürgers *Lanius e. excubitor* und *Lanius e. meridionalis* unterschiedliche Paarbindungsmodi? *Anz. orn. Ges. Bayern* 14: 115-140.

Dorst, J. 1971. *La Vie des Oiseaux.* Bordas, Paris and Montreal.

Douglas, R. 1992. Homing instinct in the Fiscal Shrike *Lanius collaris? Mirafra* 9: 31.

Dowsett, R.J. 1971. The Lesser Grey Shrike in Africa. *Ostrich* 42: 259-270.

Dowsett, R.J. and Dowsett-Lemaire, F. (eds.) 1993. *A Contribution to the Distribution and Taxonomy of Afrotropical and Malagasy Birds.* Tauraco Research Report no. 5. Tauraco Press, Jupille, Liège.

Duckett, J.E. 1988. The Brown Shrike (*Lanius cristatus*) *Malay Nat.* 41: 6-8.

Dunajewski, A. 1939. Gliederung und Verbreitung des Formenkreises *Lanius schach* L. *J. Ornithologie* 87: 28-53.

DuPont, J.E. 1971. *Philippine Birds.* Delaware Museum. Greenville, Delaware.

Dymond, J.N., Fraser, P.A. and Gantlett, S.J.M. 1989. *Rare Birds in Britain and Ireland*. T. & A.D. Poyser, Calton.

Earlé, R.A. and Grobler, N.J. 1987. *First Atlas of Bird Distribution in the Orange Free State*. National Museum, Bloemfontein.

Eck, S. 1990. Die Systematische stellung von *Lanius excubitor meridionalis* Temminck. *Zool. Abh. Ber. Mus., Tierk, Dresden*. 46: 57-61.

Elgood, J.H. 1994. *The Birds of Nigeria*. BOU Checklist no. 4. (2nd ed.) Tring, Herts.

Ellenberg, H. 1986. Warum gehen die Neuntöter (*Lanius collurio*) in Mitteleuropa im Bestand zurück? *Corax* 12: 34-46.

Erard, C. and Etchécopar, R.-D. 1970. Contribution à l'étude des oiseaux d'Iran. *Mém. Mus. Nat. Hist. Nat.* Serie A. Vol. 66.

Erlanger, C. Freiherr von. 1905. Beiträge zur Vogelfauna Nordostafrikas. *J. Ornithologie* 53: 670-756.

Ericsson, S. 1981. Loggerhead Shrike in Guatemala in December 1979. *Dutch Birding* 3: 27-28.

Etchécopar, R.D. and Hüe, F. 1983. *Les Oiseaux de Chine, de Mongolie et de Corée*. Passereaux. Boubée, Paris.

Farner, D.S., King, J.R. and Parkes, K.C. 1985. *Avian Biology*. Vol. 8. Academic Press, Orlando.

Ferry, C. and Martinet, M. 1974. Le parasitisme de la Pie-grièche grise (*Lanius excubitor*) par le Coucou. A propos d'un nouveau cas. *Jean-Le-Blanc* 13: 11-17.

Fischer, K. 1994a. Zweite Jahresbrut beim Raubwürger (*Lanius excubitor*) *Fauna Flora Rheinland-Pfalz* 7: 483-484.

Fischer, K. 1994b. Zur Winterverbreitung des Raubwürgers (*Lanius excubitor*) im Westerwald. *Fauna Flora Rheinland-Pfalz* 7: 607-612.

Flickinger, E.L. 1995. Loggerhead Shrike fatalities on a highway in Texas. *In* Shrikes (Laniidae) of the world: biology and conservation (R. Yosef and F.E. Lohrer, eds). *Proc. West. Found. Vert. Zool.* 6: 67-69.

Flint, P. and Stewart, P. 1992. *The Birds of Cyprus*. BOU Checklist no. 6 (2nd ed.). Tring, Herts.

Fornasari, L., Bottoni, L., Schwabl, H. and Massa, R. 1992. Testosterone in the breeding cycle of the male Red-backed Shrike *Lanius collurio*. *Ethol. Ecol. and Evolution* 4: 193-196.

Fraser, P. and Ryan, J. 1995. Status of the Great Grey Shrike in Britain and Ireland. *British Birds* 88: 478-484.

Fraticelli, F. and Sorace, A. 1992. Prima osservazione di Averla Isabellina, *Lanius isabellinus*, in Italia. *Riv. ital. Orn.* 62: 183-184.

Friedmann, H. 1937. Birds collected by the Childs Frick Expedition to Ethiopia and Kenya Colony. Pt 2. Passeres. *Smithsonian Inst. United States Nat. Mus. Bull.* 153.

Friedmann, H. and Loveridge, A. 1937. Notes on the ornithology of Tropical East Africa. *Bull. Mus. Comp. Zool.* vol.81. Cambridge, Mass, USA.

Friedmann, H. , Griscom, L. and Moore, R.T. 1950. *Distributional Check-list of the Birds of Mexico*, part I. Cooper Orn. Club, Berkeley.

Gallagher, M. and Woodcock, M.W. 1980. *The Birds of Oman*. Quartet Books, London, Melbourne, New York.

Galushin, V.M. 1996. The Long-tailed Shrike (*Lanius schach*) in Kabul, Afghanistan. *Abstracts 2nd International Shrike Symposium*, 17-23 March 1996, Eilat (eds R. Yosef, T. Cade, F.E. Lohrer).

Gargallo, G. and Clarabuch, O. 1995. Moult and ageing in passerines. *Ringing and Migration* 16: 178-189.

Gaugris, Y., Prigogine, A. and Vande weghe, J.-P. 1981. Additions et corrections à l'avifaune du Burundi. *Gerfaut* 71:

3-39.

Gawlik, D.E. 1993. Seasonal habitat use and abundance of Loggerhead Shrikes in South Carolina. *J. Wildl. Mgmt.* 57: 352-357.

Gawlik, D.E. and Bildstein, K.L. 1990. Reproductive success and nesting habitat of Loggerhead Shrikes in north-central South Carolina. *Wilson Bull.* 102: 37-48.

Gawlik, D.E. and Bildstein, K.L. 1995. Differential habitat use by sympatric Loggerhead Shrikes and American Kestrels in South Carolina. *In* Shrikes (Laniidae) of the world: biology and conservation (R. Yosef and F.E. Lohrer, eds). *Proc. West. Found. Vert. Zool.* 6: 163-166.

Gawlik, D.E., Papp, J. and Bildstein, K.L. 1991. Nestling diet and prey-delivery rates of Loggerhead Shrikes (*Lanius ludovicianus*) in North-central South Carolina. *Chat* 55: 1-5.

Germain, M., Dragesco, J., Roux, F. and Garcin, H. 1973. Contribution à l'ornithologie du Sud-Cameroun. II Passeriformes. *L'Oiseau et R.F.O.* 43: 212-259.

de Geus, D.W. and Best, L.B. 1991. Brown-headed Cowbirds parasitize Loggerhead Shrikes: first records for family Laniidae. *Wilson Bull.* 103: 504-506.

Ginn, H.G. and Melville, D.S. 1983. *Moult in Birds*. B.T.O. Guide 19. Tring, Herts.

Ginn, P. 1974. *Bird Safari*. Longman, Rhodesia.

Giraudoux, P., Degauquier, R., Jones, P.J., Weigel, J. and Isenmann, P. 1988. Avifaune du Niger: état des connaissances en 1986. *Malimbus* 10: 1-140.

Gloe, P. 1996. Beobachtungen an Grauwürgern (*Lanius excubitor*). *Orn. Mitt.* 48: 98-101.

Glutz von Blotzheim, U.N., Bauer, K.M. and Bezzel, E. 1971. *Handbuch der Vögel Mitteleuropas. Band 4: Falconiformes*. Akademische Verlagsges., Frankfurt am Main.

Glutz von Blotzheim, U.N. and Bauer, K.M. 1982. *Handbuch der Vögel Mitteleuropas. Band 8/III: Charadriiformes*. Aula, Wiesbaden.

Glutz von Blotzheim, U.N. and Bauer, K.M. 1993. *Handbuch der Vögel Mitteleuropas. Band 13/II: Passeriformes (4. Teil), Sittidae-Laniidae*. Aula, Wiesbaden.

Godfrey, W.E. 1986. *The Birds of Canada*. Revised Edition. National Museum of Natural Sciences, Ottawa.

Goodman, S.M. and Meininger, P.L. 1989. *The Birds of Egypt*. Oxford University Press, Oxford.

Gore, M.E.J. 1990. *The Birds of the Gambia*. BOU Checklist no. 3. Tring, Herts.

Gore, M.E.J. and Won, P.O. 1971. *The Birds of Korea*. Royal Asiatic Society, Seoul.

Gorman, G. 1996. *The Birds of Hungary*. Christopher Helm, London.

Gotch, A.F. 1981. *Birds. Their Latin names explained*. Blandford, Poole.

Grant, C.H.B. and Mackworth-Praed, C.W. 1952. On the relationship of the European and African Great Grey Shrikes. *Bull. Brit. Orn. Club.* 72: 94.

Grimes, L.G. 1979a. Sexual dimorphism in the Yellow-billed Shrike *Corvinella corvina* and in other African shrikes (subfamily Laniinae). *Bull. Brit. Orn. Club* 99: 33-36.

Grimes, L.G. 1979b. The Yellow-billed Shrike *Corvinella corvina*: an abnormal host of the Yellow-billed Cuckoo *Cuculus gularis*. *Bull. Brit. Orn. Club* 99: 36-38.

Grimes, L.G. 1980. Observations of group behaviour and breeding biology of the Yellow-billed Shrike *Corvinella corvina*. *Ibis* 122: 166-192.

Grimes, L.G. 1987. *The Birds of Ghana*. BOU Checklist no. 9. Tring, Herts.

Grisser, P. 1995. Premiers éléments sur l'évolution d'un peuplement de Pies-grièches *Lanius* sp. en Dordogne. *Alauda* 63: 89-100.

Grünwald, H. 1986a. Mitteilungen zur Sommernahrung des Raubwürgers (*Lanius excubitor*) im Sauerland (1982/83 und 1983/84). *Charadrius* 20: 36-44.

Grünwald, H. 1986b. Zum winterlichen Kleinvogelfang des Raubwürgers (*Lanius excubitor*) im nördlichen Sauerland. *Charadrius* 22: 91-95.

Grünwald, H. 1994. Beobachtungen zur Paarbildung des Raubwürgers (*Lanius e. excubitor* L.) in einem Winterhabitat des nördlichen Sauerlandes. *Charadrius* 30: 36-43.

Gwinner, E. 1961. Über die Entstachelungshandlung des Neuntöters. *Vogelwarte* 21: 36-47.

Haas, C.A. 1987. Eastern subspecies of the Loggerhead Shrike: the need for measurements of live birds. *North Amer. Bird Bander* 12: 99-102.

Haas, C.A. and Ogawa, I. 1995. Population trends of Bull-headed and Brown Shrikes in Hokkaido, Japan. *In* Shrikes (Laniidae) of the world: biology and conservation (R. Yosef and F.E. Lohrer, eds). *Proc. West. Found. Vert. Zool.* 6: 72-75.

Haas, C.A. and Sloane, S. 1989. Low return rates of migratory Loggerhead Shrikes: winter mortality or low site fidelity? *Wilson Bull.* 101: 458-460.

Hall, B.P. and Moreau, R.E. 1970. *An Atlas of Speciation in African Passerine Birds*. British Museum (Natural History), London.

Hantge, E. 1957. Zur Brutbiologie des Schwarzstirnwürgers (*Lanius minor*). *Vogelwelt* 78: 137-146.

Harris, A. 1994. Woodchat Shrike pursuing Hoopoe. *British Birds* 87: 42.

Harris, T. 1995. Species recognition in the southern African population of the Fiscal Shrike (*Lanius collaris*). *In* Shrikes (Laniidae) of the world: biology and conservation (R. Yosef and F.E. Lohrer, eds). *Proc. West. Found Vert. Zool.* 6: 11-21.

Harris, T. and Arnott, G. 1988. *Shrikes of Southern Africa*. Struik, Winchester.

Harrison, C. 1982. *An Atlas of the Birds of the Western Palearctic*. Collins, London.

Harrison, C.J.O. 1986. The Saharo-Sindian arid zone birds. *Sandgrouse* 7: 64-67.

Hartert, E. and Steinbacher, F. 1934. *Die Vögel der paläarktischen Fauna*. Ergänzungsband, Heft 3. Friedlander und Sohn, Berlin.

Harvey, W.G. 1989. *Birds in Bangladesh*. University Press, Dhaka.

Hazevoet, C.J. 1994. Species concepts and systematics. *Dutch Birding* 16: 111-116.

Heim de Balsac, H. and Mayaud, N. 1962. *Les Oiseaux du Nord-Ouest de l'Afrique*. Lechevalier, Paris.

Hellmich, W. 1968. *Khumbu Himal*. Vol. 2. Universitäts Verlag,Wagner Ges., Innsbrück and München.

Herklots, G.A.C. 1974. *Hong Kong Birds* 2nd ed. South China Morning Post, Hong Kong.

Hernandez, A. 1993a. Estudio comparado sobre la biología de la reproducción de tres especies simpátricas de alcaudones (real *Lanius excubitor*, dorsirrojo *L. collurio* y común *L. senator*). *Doñana, Acta Vertebrata* 20: 179-250.

Hernandez, A. 1993b. Dieta de los pollos de tres especies simpátricas de alcaudones (*Lanius sp.*): variaciones con la edad, estacionales e interespécificas. *Donana, Acta Vertebrata* 20: 145-163.

Hernandez, A. 1993c. Almacenamiento de alimento por el Alcaudón común *Lanius senator* en el noroeste de España. *Butll. GCA* 10: 67-71.

Hernandez, A. 1994. Selección de habitat en tres especies sim-

pátricas de alcaudones (real *Lanius excubitor* L., dorsirrojo *Lanius collurio* L. y común *Lanius senator* L.): segregación interespecífica. *Ecología* 8: 395-413.

Hernandez, A. 1995. Selective predation by Northern Shrikes on small mammals in a natural environment. *J. Field Ornithology* 66: 236-246.

Hernandez, A., Purroy, F.J. and Salgado, J.M. 1993. Variacion estacional, solapamiento interespecifico y seleccion en la dieta de tres especies simpatricas de Alcaudones (*Lanius* spp.) *Ardeola* 40: 143-154.

Hernandez, A. and Sagado, J.M. 1993. Almacenamiento de presas por el Alcaudón real *Lanius excubitor* en la Serena (Badajoz) y la Sierra de Cabo de Gata (Almeria). *Butll. GCA* 10: 63-65.

Herremans, M. 1994. Different habitat of male and female Red-backed Shrike *Lanius collurio* and Lesser Grey Shrike *Lanius minor* in the Kalahari. *J. Ornithologie* 135: 291. (Proc. 21st Int. Orn. Congr., Vienna).

Herremans, M. and Herremans-Tonnoeyr, D. 1995. Non-breeding site-fidelity of Red-backed Shrikes *Lanius collurio* in Botswana. *Ostrich* 66: 145-147.

Hildén, O. and Hildén, M. 1996. Wide fluctuations in the Finnish population of the Great Grey Shrike *Lanius excubitor* during recent decades. *Ornis Fennica* 73: 35-38.

Hirschfeld, E. 1995. *Birds in Bahrain, a Study of their Migration Pattern 1990-92*. Hobby, Dubai.

Hockey, P. A.R. 1989. *Atlas of the Birds of the Southwestern Cape*. Cape Bird Club, Cape Town.

Holaň, V. 1993. Population density and breeding biology of the Red-backed Shrike (*Lanius collurio*) in north-east Moravia. *Sylvia* 29: 3-11 (in Czech, English summary).

Holaň, V. 1994. Notes on migration and nesting of the Red-backed Shrike (*Lanius collurio*). *Sylvia* 30: 152-154 (in Czech, English summary).

Hölker, M. 1993a. Untersuchungen zum Bruthabitat des Raubwürgers (*Lanius excubitor*) in Südostwestfalen. *Ökol. Vögel (Ecol. Birds)* 15: 99-113.

Hölker, M. 1993b. Untersuchungen zur Brutbiologie des Raubwürgers (*Lanius excubitor*) in Südostwestfalen. *Vogelwelt* 114: 86-98.

Hölzinger, J. (ed) 1987. *Artenschutzsymposium Neuntöter*. Beih. Veröff. Naturschutz Landschaftspflege Bad.-Württ vol. 48. Karlsruhe.

Hollom, P.A.D., Porter, R.F., Christensen, S. and Willis, I. 1988. *Birds of the Middle East and North Africa*. T. & A.D. Poyser, Calton.

Horvath, L. 1959. The life history of the Lesser Grey Shrike in Hungary. *Acta Zoologica* 4: 319-332.

Hromoda, M. and Kristin, A. 1996. Changes in the food of the Great Grey Shrike. *Biologia, Bratislava* 51: 227-233.

Hubbard, J.P. 1978. The status of the Northern Shrike in New Mexico. *Western Birds* 9: 159-168.

Hugues, A. 1932. Les Pies-grièches et leur chasse autrefois. *L'Oiseau et la R.F.O.* 4: 648-655.

Hume, R.A. 1993. Brown Shrike in Shetland: new to Britain and Ireland. *British Birds* 86: 600-603.

Hunter, S., Brauning, D., Chambers, R.E. and Kennell, A.L. 1995. Status of the Loggerhead Shrike in Pennsylvania. *In* Shrikes (Laniidae) of the world: biology and conservation (R. Yosef and F.E. Lohrer, eds). *Proc. West. Found. Vert. Zool.* 6: 78-80.

Immelmann, K. 1968. *Lanius souzae* near the Spitzkkopje, South West Africa. *Ostrich* 39: 41.

Inbar, R. 1995. Shrikes nesting on Mount Hermon, Israel. *In* Shrikes (Laniidae) of the world: biology and conservation (R. Yosef and F.E. Lohrer, eds). *Proc. West. Found.*

Vert. Zool. 6: 215-217.

Inskipp, C. and Inskipp, T. 1991.2nd ed. *A Guide to the Birds of Nepal*. Christopher Helm, London.

Institut Français de l'Environnement. 1996. Régression des milieux naturels: 25% des prairies ont disparu depuis 1970. *Données de l'Envt. Milieu no. 25*. Orléans.

Irwin, M.P.S. 1981. *Birds of Zimbabwe*. Quest Publishing, Salisbury.

Isenmann, P. 1996. Habitats et traits d'histoire naturelle de la Pie-grièche à tête rousse *Lanius senator*: quels remèdes pour une espèce menacée dans le midi de la France? Unpublished report.

Isenmann, P. and Bouchet, M.A. 1993. L'aire de distribution française et le statut taxonomique de la Pie-grièche méridionale *Lanius excubitor meridionalis*. *Alauda* 61: 223-227.

Isenmann, P. and Fradet, G. 1995. Is the nesting association between the Orphean Warbler (*Sylvia hortensis*) and Woodchat Shrike (*Lanius senator*) an anti-predator oriented mutualism? *J. Ornithologie* 136: 288-291.

Jackson, F.J. 1938. *The Birds of Kenya Colony and the Uganda Protectorate*. Gurney and Jackson, London and Edinburgh.

Jahn, H. 1942. Zur Oekologie und Biologie der Vögel Japans. *J. Ornithologie* 90: 7-302.

Jakober, H. and Stauber, W. 1980a. Flügellängen und Gewichte einer südwestdeutschen Population des Neuntöters unter Berücksichtigung der geschlechtsspezifischen Arbeitsteilung während der Brutperiode. *Vogelwarte* 30: 198-208.

Jakober, H. and Stauber, W. 1980b. Der Neuntöter als Kuckuckswirt in Baden-Württemberg. *Ökol. Vögel (Ecol. Birds)* 2: 37-41.

Jakober, H. and Stauber, W. 1987. Zur Populationsdynamik des Neuntöters (*Lanius collurio*). *Beih. Veröff. Naturschutz Landschaftspflege Bad-Württ*. 48: 71-78 (Artenschutzsymposium Neuntöter).

Jakober, H. and Stauber, W. 1989. Beeinflussen Bruterfolg und Alter die Ortstreue des Neuntöters? *Vogelwarte* 35: 32-36.

Jakober, H. and Stauber, W. 1994. Kopulation und Partnerwachung beim Neuntöter *Lanius collurio*. *J Ornithologie* 135: 535-547.

Jany, E. 1948. L'influence de l'humidité du climat sur la coloration du plumage chez les Pies-grièches grises de l'Afrique du Nord (*Lanius excubitor*). *L'Oiseau et R.F.O.* 18: 117-132.

Jennings, M.C. 1981. *The Birds of Saudi Arabia: a Check -list*. Published privately. Cambridge.

Johnsgard, P.A. 1979. *Birds of the Great Plains. Breeding Species and their Distribution*. University of Nebraska Press, Lincoln and London.

Johnson, A. 1940. Incubation behavior of *Lanius ludovicianus* in North Dakota. *Wilson Bull*. 52: 35-36.

Kalela, O. 1949. Changes in geographic ranges in the avifauna of northern and central Europe in relation to recent changes in climate. *Bird Banding* 20: 77-103.

Kemp, A.C. 1974. *The Distribution and Status of the Birds of the Kruger National Park*. N.P. Board of Trustees, Pretoria.

Kéry, M., Schaub, M. and Bolliger, J. 1996. Densité remarquable de Pies-grièches grises (*Lanius excubitor*) hivernantes dans le bassin du Drugeon (Doubs, France). *Nos Oiseaux* 43: 453-465.

Kondo, K. 1993. The first record of the Chinese Great Grey Shrike. *Strix* 12: 248-251.

Korodi-Gal, J. 1969. Beiträge zur Kenntnis der Brutbiologie und Brutnahrung des Neuntöters (*Lanius collurio*). *Zool. Abh. Mus. Tierk. Dresden* 30: 57-82.

Kowalski, H. 1993. Bestandssituation der Würger *Laniidae* in

Deutschland zu Anfang der 1990er Jahre. *Limicola* 7: 130-139.

Kozlova, E.V. 1933. On the birds of south-west Transbaikalia, northern Mongolia and central Gobi, part V. *Ibis* (13)3: 301-329.

Kridelbaugh, A.L. 1983. Nesting ecology of the Loggerhead Shrike in central Missouri. *Wilson Bull*. 95: 303-308.

Kristin, A. 1991. Brutbestand und Brutbiologie des Schwarzstirnwürgers (*Lanius minor* L.) in der Mittelslowakei (Tschechoslowakei). *Orn. Mitt*. 43: 131-133.

Kristin, A. 1995. Why the Lesser Grey Shrike survives in Slovakia: food and habitat preferences, breeding biology. *Folia Zoologica* 44: 325-334.

Kryukov, A.P. 1995. Systematics of small Palearctic shrikes of the "*cristatus* group". *In* Shrikes (Laniidae) of the world: biology and conservation (R. Yosef and F.E Lohrer, eds). *Proc. West. Found. Vert. Zool*. 6: 22-25.

Lack, P. 1985. The ecology of the land-birds of Tsavo East National Park, Kenya. *Scopus* 9: 2-23.

Lamarche, B. 1981. Liste commentée des oiseaux du Mali. Pt 2: Passereaux. *Malimbus* 3: 73-102.

Lamarche, B. 1988. Liste commentée des oiseaux de Mauritanie. *Etudes Sahar. et Ouest-Afr*. 1: 1-162.

Laporte, P. and Robert, M. 1995. The decline and current status of the Loggerhead Shrike in Québec. *In* Shrikes (Laniidae) of the world: biology and conservation (R. Yosef and F.E. Lohrer, eds). *Proc. West. Found. Vert. Zool*. 6: 85-87.

La Touche, J.D.D. 1925-1930. *A Handbook of the Birds of Eastern China*. Vol. 1. Taylor and Francis, London.

Laughlin, S.B. and Kibbe, D.P. 1985. *The Atlas of Breeding Birds of Vermont*. Vermont Inst. Nat. Sci., Hanover.

Ledant, J.P., Jacob, J.P., Jacobs, P., Malher, F., Ochando, B. and Roché, J. 1981. Mise à jour de l'avifaune Algérienne. *Gerfaut* 71: 295-398.

Lefranc, N. 1978. La Pie-grièche à poitrine rose (*Lanius minor*) en France. *Alauda* 46: 193-208.

Lefranc, N. 1979. Contribution à l'écologie de la Pie-grièche écorcheur *Lanius collurio* dans les Vosges moyennes. *L'Oiseau et la R.F.O.* 49: 245-298.

Lefranc, N. 1980. Biologie et fluctuations des populations de Laniidés en Europe occidentale. *L'Oiseau et R.F.O.* 50: 89-116.

Lefranc, N. 1993. *Les Pies-grièches d'Europe, d'Afrique du Nord et du Moyen-Orient*. Delachaux et Niestlé, Lausanne and Paris.

Lefranc, N. 1995a. Le complexe Pie-grièche grise/Pie-grièche méridionale *Lanius (e.) excubitor/L. (e.) meridionalis*: des "groupes" aux espèces. *Ornithos* 2: 107-109.

Lefranc, N. 1995b. Decline and current status of the Lesser Grey Shrike (*Lanius minor*) in western Europe. *In* Shrikes (Laniidae) of the world: biology and conservation (R. Yosef and F.E. Lohrer, eds). *Proc. West. Found. Vert. Zool*. 6: 93-97.

Lefranc, N. 1997. Shrikes and the farmed landscape in France. *In Farming and Birds in Europe* (D.J. Pain and M.W. Pienkowski, eds). Academic Press, London.

Lefranc, N., Boët, M. and Boët, M. 1989. Observations de couples mixtes *Lanius senator/Lanius collurio* en France. Brève synthèse des cas d'hybridation connus chez les Laniidés d'Europe. *Alauda* 57: 109-118.

Lefranc, N. and Lepley, M. 1995. Recensement de la Pie-grièche méridionale *Lanius meridionalis* en Crau sèche. *Faune de Provence (C.E.E.P.)* 16: 87-88.

Lepley, M. 1995. Alimentation et Reproduction de la Pie-grièche méridionale *Lanius meridionalis* en Crau sèche

(Bouches-du-Rhône). Diplôme EPHE, Montpellier.

Lewis, A. and Pomeroy, D. 1989. *A Bird Atlas of Kenya*. A.A. Balkema, Rotterdam.

Lierath, W. 1954. Beitag zur Ernährungsbiologie des Schwarzstirnwürgers *Lanius minor*. *Orn. Mitt.* 6: 1-3.

Lippens, L. and Wille, H. 1976. *Les Oiseaux du Zaïre*. Lannoo, Tielt.

Lorek, G. 1995a. Breeding status of the Great Grey Shrike in Poland. *In* Shrikes (Laniidae) of the world: biology and conservation (R. Yosef and F.E. Lohrer, eds). *Proc. West. Found. Vert. Zool.* 6: 98-104.

Lorek, G. 1995b. Copulation behavior, mixed reproductive strategy, and mate guarding in the Great Grey Shrike. *In* Shrikes (Laniidae) of the world: biology and conservation (R. Yosef and F.E. Lohrer, eds). *Proc. West. Found. Vert. Zool.* 6: 218-227.

Lorek, G. 1996. Great Grey Shrike eating Red-backed Shrike. *British Birds* 89: 456-457.

Lorenz, K. and Saint Paul, U. 1968. Die Entwicklung des Spiessens und Klemmens bei den drei Würgerarten *Lanius collurio, L. senator* und *L. excubitor*. *J. Ornithologie* 109: 137-156.

Loskot, W.M., Sokolow [=Sokolov], E.P. and Vietinghoff-Scheel, E.V. 1991. *Lanius tigrinus* Drapiez. In *Atlas der Verbreitung Palaearktischer Vögel*. Lief. 17. (H. Dathe and W.M. Loskot, eds.) Akademie Verlag, Berlin.

Loskot, W.M., Sokolow [=Sokolov], E.P. and Vietinghoff-Scheel, E.V. 1992. *Lanius vittatus* Valenciennes. In *Atlas der Verbreitung Palaearktischer Vögel*. Lief. 18. (H. Dathe and W.M. Loskot, eds.) Akademie Verlag, Berlin.

Louette, M. 1981. *The Birds of Cameroon: an Annotated Checklist*. Paleis der Academiën, Brussels.

Lu Changhu and Chang Jiachuan. 1993. Breeding behaviour of the Long-tailed Shrike. *Yesheng Dongwu (Chinese Wildlife)* 4: 19-21 (in Chinese).

Lynes, H. 1925. On the birds of north and central Darfur. *Ibis* 12(1): 71-131.

Macdonald, J.D. 1940. Notes on African birds. *Bull. Brit. Orn. Club.* 60: 71-72.

Macdonald, M.A. 1980. The ecology of the Fiscal Shrike in Ghana, and a comparison with studies from southern Africa. *Ostrich* 51: 65-74.

MacKinnon, J. and Phillipps, K. 1993. *A Field Guide to the Birds of Borneo, Sumatra, Java and Bali*. Oxford University Press, Oxford.

Mackworth-Praed, C.W. and Grant, C.H.B. 1955. *Birds of Eastern and North Eastern Africa*. Vol. 2. Longmans, London and New York.

Mackworth-Praed, C.W. and Grant, C.H.B. 1963. *Birds of the Southern Third of Africa*. Vol. 2. Longmans, London and New York.

Mackworth-Praed, C.W. and Grant, C.H.B. 1973. *Birds of West Central and Western Africa*. Vol. 2. Longmans, London and New York.

Maclean, G.L. 1993. *Roberts' Birds of Southern Africa*. 6th ed. J. Voelcker Bird Book Fund, Cape Town.

Maclean, G.L. and Maclean, C.M. 1976. Extent of overlap in two races of the Fiscal Shrike. *Ostrich* 47: 66.

Madon, P. 1934. Notes sur le régime des Pies-grièches. *Alauda* 6: 337-354.

Malbrant, R. 1952. *Faune du Centre Africain Français*. Lechevalier, Paris.

Mann, C.F. and Diskin, D.A. 1993. Northern Shrike *Lanius excubitor*, a species new to Borneo and South-East Asia. *Forktail* 8: 153-154.

Mann, W. 1983. Zur Ernährung des Neuntöters in Abhängig-

keit vom Insektenangebot auf verschiedenen Dauergrunlandtypen. *Vogelkdl. Hefte Edertal* 9: 5-41.

Mansfeld, K. 1958. Zur Ernährung des Rotrückenwürgers (*L. collurio* L.) besonders hinsichtlich der Nestlingsnahrung, der Vertilgung von Nutz-und Schadinsekten und seines Einflusses auf den Singvogelbestand. *Beitr. Vogelkde* 6: 270-292.

Marchant, J.H. 1992. Recent trends in breeding populations of some common trans-Saharan migrant birds in northern Europe. *Ibis* 134 suppl. 1: 113-119.

van Marle, J.G. and Voous, K.H. 1988. *The Birds of Sumatra*. BOU Checklist no. 10. Tring, Herts.

Marshall, B. 1990. Scavenging behaviour of the Fiscal Shrike. *Honeyguide* 36: 194.

Marshall, B.E. and Cooper, J. 1969. Observations on the breeding biology of the Fiscal Shrike. *Ostrich* 40: 141-149.

Martorelli, G. 1908. Il *Lanius homeyeri* Cabanis in Italia.. *Atti Soc. Ital. Sc. Nat.* 46: 257-270.

Massa, R., Bottoni, L. and Fornasari, L. 1993. Site fidelity and population structure of the Red-backed Shrike *Lanius collurio* in northern Italy. *Ringing and Migration* 14: 129-132.

Mauersberger, G. and Portenko, L.A. 1971. *Lanius collurio* L., *Lanius isabellinus* Hemprich & Ehrenberg und *Lanius cristatus* L. In *Atlas der Vergbreitung Palaearktischer Vögel*. Lief. 3. (E. Stresemann and L.A. Portenko, eds.) Akademie Verlag, Berlin.

Mayr, E. 1947. Le nom correct de la Pie-grièche du Thibet. *L'Oiseau et R.F.O.* 17 (NS): 4-8.

McClure, H.E. 1974. *Migration and Survival of the Birds of Asia*. Applied Sci. Res. Corporation of Thailand, Bangkok.

McCulloch, M.N., Tucker, G.M. and Baillie, S.R. 1992. The hunting of migratory birds in Europe: a ringing recovery analysis. *Ibis* 134, suppl. 1: 3-6.

Medland; R.D. 1991. Souza's Shrike attacking Violet-backed Sunbird. *Nyala* 15: 49.

Medway, Lord 1970. A ringing study of the migratory Brown Shrike in West Malaysia. *Ibis* 112: 184-198.

Medway, Lord and Wells, D.R. 1976. *The Birds of the Malay Peninsula*. Vol. 5. H.F. & G. Witherby, London.

Mees, G.F. 1996. *Geographical Variation in Birds of Java*. Nuttall Orn. Club, Cambridge, Massachusetts.

Meise, W. 1957. Über neue Hühner, Specht-und Singvogelrassen von Angola. *Abh. Verh. Naturw. Ver. Hamburg.* 2: 63-83.

Meinertzhagen, R. 1953. New geographical race of shrike *Lanius excubitor* Linnaeus. *Bull. Brit. Orn. Club.* 73: 72.

Meschini, E. and Frugis, S. 1993. Atlante degli Uccelli nidificanti in Itaia. *Suppl. alle Ricerche di Biologia della Selvaggina*. Vol 20, no. 1.

Meyer de Schauensee, R. 1984. *The Birds of China*. Oxford University Press, Oxford.

Miller, A.H. 1928. The molts of the Loggerhead Shrike *Lanius ludovicianus* Linnaeus. *Univ. Calif. Publ. Zool.* 30: 393-417.

Miller, A.H. 1931. Systematic revision and natural history of the American shrikes (*Lanius*). *Univ. Calif. Publ. Zool.* 38: 11-242.

Moes, M. 1993. Habitatnutzung beim Neuntöter (*Lanius collurio*). *Regulus Wiss. Ber.* no. 12: 1-26.

Moltoni, E. 1970. Altra Averla meridionale *Lanius excubitor meridionalis* Temminck presa in Liguria. *Riv. Ital. Orn.* 40: 1-4.

Monroe, Jr., B.L. 1992. The new DNA-DNA avian classification. What's it all about ? *British Birds* 85: 53-61.

Moore, H.J. and Boswell, C. 1957. *Field Observations on the Birds of Iraq*, part III. Iraq Nat. Hist. Mus., Ar-Rabita Press, Baghdad.

Moreau, R.E. 1972. *The Palaearctic-African Bird Migration Systems*. Academic Press, London and New York.

Moreau, R.E. and Moreau, W.M. 1939. Observations on some East African birds. *Ibis* (14)3: 296-323.

Morel, G.J. and Morel, M.Y. 1990. *Les Oiseaux de Sénégambie*. ORSTOM, Paris.

Morioka, H. and Sakane, T. 1979. Breeding avifaunas of Mt. Puguis, northern Luzon and Baracatan, Mindanao, Philippines (Part 1). *Bull. Nat. Sci. Mus. Ser. A. (Zool.)* 5: 65-74.

Morony, J.J., Bock, W.J. and Farrand, J. Jr. 1975. *Reference List of the Birds of the World*. American Museum of Natural History, New York.

Morrison, M.L. 1979. Loggerhead Shrike eggshell thickness in California and Florida. *Wilson Bull.* 91: 468-469.

Morrison, M.L. 1980. Seasonal aspects of the predatory behavior of Loggerhead Shrikes. *Condor* 82: 296-300.

Morrison, M.L. 1981. Population trends of the Loggerhead Shrike in the United States. *Amer. Birds* 35: 754-757.

Morrison, M.L., Kuehler, C.M., Scott, T.A., Lieberman, A.A., Everett, W.T., Phillips, R.B., Koehler, C.E., Aigner, P.A., Winchell, C. and Burr, T. 1995. San Clemente Loggerhead Shrike: recovery plan for an endangered species. *In* Shrikes (Laniidae) of the world: biology and conservation (R. Yosef and F.E. Lohrer, eds). *Proc. West. Found. Vert. Zool.* 6: 293-295.

Mundy, N.I. and Woodruff, D.S. 1996. Conservation genetics of the endangered San Clemente Loggerhead Shrike (*Lanius ludovicianus mearnsi*). Abstract *2nd Int. Shrike Symposium* 17-23 March 1996, Eilat (eds R. Yosef, T. Cade, F.E. Lohrer).

de Naurois, R. 1988. Note sur la Pie-grièche *Lanius newtoni* (Bocage 1891), endémique de l'île de São Tomé (Golfe de Guinée) *Cyanopica* 4: 251-259.

Neufeldt, I.A. 1981. Die Mauser der sibirischen Rotschwanzwürger (*Lanius cristatus* Linnaeus) im Brutgebiet. *Zool. Abh. Mus. Tierk. Dresden* 37: 67-84.

Newton, I. 1995. Relationship between breeding and wintering ranges in Palaearctic-African migrants. *Ibis* 137: 241-249.

Neufeldt, I.A. 1978. On the postnuptial moult in the Brown Shrike *Lanius cristatus*. In Sistematika, morfologija i biologija ptic. *Trudy Zool. Inst. Akad, Nauk SSR* 68: 176-227. (in Russian).

Neuschulz, F. 1988. Zur Synökie von Sperbergrasmücke (*Sylvia nisoria*) und Neuntöter (*Lanius collurio*) *Lüchow-Dannenberger Orn. Jber.* 11.

Nichol, W. 1964. Two males and one female of Long-tailed Shrike *Corvinella melanoleucus* attending to the same nest. *Ostrich* 35: 68-69.

Niehuis, M. 1968. Die Bestandsentwicklung des Schwarzstirnwürgers *Lanius minor* in Deutschland unter besonderer Berücksichtigung des Nahetals und Rheinhessen. *Mainzer Naturwissensch. Archiv* 7: 185-224.

Nielsen, B.P. 1981. Taxonomy of shrikes. *British Birds* 74: 534-535.

van Nieuwenhuyse, D. 1992. Evolution du statut de la Pie-grièche écorcheur *Lanius collurio* dans la région de Virton (Lorraine belge). *Aves* 29: 216-220.

van Nieuwenhuyse, D. 1996. Propositions pour la conservation de la Pie-grièche écorcheur *Lanius collurio*. *Alauda* 64 45-55.

van Nieuwenhuyse, D., Nollet, F. and Coussens, P. 1995. Digital method for recording and analyzing territory use and activity budget of the Red-backed Shrike (*Lanius collu-*

rio). *In* Shrikes (Laniidae) of the world: biology and conservation (R. Yosef and F.E. Lohrer, eds) *Proc. West. Found. Vert. Zool.* 6: 268-275.

van Nieuwenhuyse, D. and Vandekerkhove, K. 1992. Caractéristiques et typologie des territoires de la Pie-grièche écorcheur *Lanius collurio* en Lorraine belge. *Aves* 29: 137-154.

Nikolaus, G. 1987. *Distribution Atlas of Sudan's Birds with Notes on Habitat and Status*. Bonner Zool. Monograph. no. 25. Zool. Forschungsinstitut und Museum A. Koenig, Bonn.

Ogawa, I. 1977. Pellet analysis of the Bull-headed Shrike *Lanius bucephalus* and the seasonal change of food habits. *Tori* 26: 63-75 (in Japanese, English summary).

Olivier, G. 1944. *Monographie des Pies-grièches du genre Lanius*. Lecerf, Rouen.

Olson, S.L. 1989. Preliminary systematic notes on some old passerines. *Riv. Ital. Orn.* 59: 183-195.

Olsson, V. 1980. Recent changes in the distribution of the Great Grey Shrike *Lanius excubitor* in Sweden. *Fauna och Flora* 75: 247-255.

Olsson, V. 1981. Migration and wintering area of the Great Grey Shrike *Lanius excubitor*. *Vår Fågelvärld* 40: 447-454 (in Swedish, English summary).

Olsson, V. 1984a. The winter habits of the Great Grey Shrike *Lanius excubitor*. I Habitat. *Vår Fågelvärld* 43: 113-124 (in Swedish, detailed English summary).

Olsson, V. 1984b. The winter habits of the Great Grey Shrike *Lanius excubitor*. II Territory. *Vår Fågelvärld* 43: 199-210 (in Swedish, detailed English summary).

Olsson, V. 1984c. The winter habits of the Great Grey Shrike *Lanius excubitor*. III Hunting methods. *Vår Fågelvärld* 43: 405-414 (in Swedish, detailed English summary).

Olsson, V. 1985. The winter habits of the Great Grey Shrike *Lanius excubitor*. IV Handling of prey. *Vår Fågelvärld* 44: 269-283 (in Swedish, detailed English summary).

Olsson, V. 1986. The winter habits of the Great Grey Shrike *Lanius excubitor*. V Choice of prey. *Vår Fågelvärld* 45: 19-31 (in Swedish, detailed English summary).

Olsson, V. 1995a. The Red-backed Shrike *Lanius collurio* in southeastern Sweden: habitat and territory. *Ornis Svecica* 5: 31-41.

Olsson, V. 1995b. The Red-backed Shrike *Lanius collurio* in southeastern Sweden: breeding biology. *Ornis Svecica* 5: 101-110.

Pain, D.J. and Pienkowski, M.W. (eds). 1997. *Farming and Birds in Europe: the Common Agricultural Policy and its Implications for Bird Conservation*. Academic Press, San Diego and London.

Panov, E.N. 1983. *Die Würger der Paläarktis*. Neue Brehm Bucherei. Ziemsen, Wittenberg Lutherstadt.

Panov [=Panow], E.N. 1995. Superspecies of shrikes in the former USSR. *In* Shrikes (Laniidae) of the world: biology and conservation (R. Yosef and F.E. Lohrer, eds) *Proc. West. Found. Vert. Zool.* 6: 26-33.

Parrot, J. 1980. Frugivory by Great Grey Shrikes *Lanius excubitor*. *Ibis* 122: 532-533.

Paz, U. 1987. *The Birds of Israel*. Christopher Helm, London.

Peakall, D.B. 1962. The past and present status of the Red-backed Shrike in Great Britain. *Bird Study* 9: 198-216.

Peakall, D.B. 1995. The decline and fall of the Red-backed Shrike in Britain. *In* Shrikes (Laniidae) of the world: biology and conservation (R. Yosef and F.E. Lohrer, eds). *Proc. West. Found. Vert. Zool.* 6: 112-116.

Pearson, D.J. 1979. The races of the Red-tailed Shrike *Lanius isabellinus* occurring in East Africa. *Scopus* 3: 74-78.

Pearson, D.J. 1981. Field identification of Isabelline Shrike.

Dutch Birding 3: 119-122.

Pearson, D.J. 1989. Great Grey Shrike *Lanius excubitor* in the Ilemi Triangle. *Scopus* 13: 134.

Pearson, D.J. and Lack, P.C. 1992. Migration patterns and habitat use by passerine and near-passerine migrant birds in eastern Africa. *Ibis* 134 suppl. 1: 89-98.

Peet, N.B. and Atkinson, P.W. 1994. The biodiversity and conservation of the birds of São Tomé and Príncipe. *Biodiv. and Conserv.* 3: 851-867.

Penry, H. 1994. *Bird Atlas of Botswana.* University of Natal Press, Pietermaritzburg.

Peterjohn, B.G. and Rice, D.L. 1991. *The Ohio Breeding Bird Atlas.* Ohio Dept. Nat. Resources, Columbus.

Peterjohn, B.G. and Sauer, J.R. 1995. Population trends of the Loggerhead Shrike from the North American breeding bird survey. *In* Shrikes (Laniidae) of the world: biology and conservation (R. Yosef and F.E. Lohrer, eds). *Proc. West. Found. Vert. Zool.* 6: 117-121.

Phillips, A.R. 1986. *The Known Birds of North and Middle America.* Part 1. Published privately.

Poltz, W. 1975. Über den Rückgang des Neuntöters (*Lanius collurio*) *Vogelwelt* 96: 1-19.

Pons, P. 1993. Capture accidentelle d'une Pie-grièche à tête rousse (*Lanius senator*) par une graminée. *Nos Oiseaux* 42: 182-183.

Priest, C.D. 1936. *The Birds of Southern Rhodesia.* William Clowes, London.

Prodon, R. 1987. Incendies et protection des oiseaux en France méditerranéenne. *L'Oiseau et R.F.O.* 57: 1-12.

Prys-Jones, R.P. 1991. The occurrence of biannual primary moult in passerines. *Bull. Brit. Orn. Club.* 111: 150-152.

Rabor, D.S. 1936. Life histories of some common birds in the vicinity of Novaliches, Rizal Province, Luzon, I. The Large-nosed Shrike *Lanius schach nasutus* (Scopoli). *Philippine J.* 59: 337-353.

Rahmani, A.R., Shobrak, M.Y. and Newton, S.F. 1994. Birds of the Tihamah coastal plains of Saudi Arabia. *Bull. Orn. Soc. Middle East* 32: 17.

Raikow, R.J., Polumbo, P.J. and Borecky, S.R. 1980. Appendicular myology and relationships of the shrikes (Aves: passeriformes: Laniidae). *Annals Carnegie Mus.* 49: 131-152.

Ramadan-Jaradi, G. 1985. Les oiseaux non nicheurs observés en migration dans les Emirats Arabes Unis. *L'Oiseau et R.F.O.* 55, no. special.

Ramade, F. 1987. *Les Catastrophes Ecologiques.* McGraw-Hill, Paris.

Rand, A.L. 1957. *Lanius ludovicianus miamensis* Bishop, a valid race from southern Florida. *Auk* 74: 503-505.

Rand, A.L. 1960. Family Laniidae. In *Check-list of Birds of the World.* Vol. 9: 309-365. (E. Mayr and J.C. Greenway, Jr, eds). Mus. Comp. Zool., Cambridge.

Rand, A.L. and Fleming, R.L. 1957. Birds from Nepal. *Fieldiana: Zoology* 41: 189-192 (for Laniidae).

Rand, A.L., Friedmann, H. and Traylor, M.A. 1959. Birds from Gabon and Moyen Congo. *Fieldiana Zool.* 41: 221-411.

Rand, A.L. and Gilliard, E.T. 1967. *Handbook of New Guinea Birds.* Weidenfeld and Nicolson, London.

Ratcliffe, D. 1993. *The Peregrine Falcon.* 2nd ed. T. & A.D. Poyser, London.

Reeb, F. 1977. Contribution à l'étude de l'avifaune et des migrations en Afghanistan. *Alauda* 45: 293-333.

Rehsteiner, U. 1995. Raubwürger *Lanius excubitor* und Hermelin *Mustela erminea*: Neugierverhalten oder versuchter Kleptoparasitismus? *Orn. Beob.* 92: 81-85.

Richardson, C. 1990. *Birds of the United Arab Emirates.* Hobby, Dubai and Warrington.

Richardson, C. 1991. Breeding behaviour of Isabelline Shrike *Lanius isabellinus* in the UAE. *Emirates Bird Report* 15: 38.

Ricklefs, R.E. 1980. Geographical variation in clutch-size among passerine birds: Ashmole's hypothesis. *Auk* 97: 38-49.

Ripley, S.D. 1949. A new race of shrike from the Philippines. *Bull. Brit. Orn. Club* 69: 121-122.

Robbins, C.S., Bystrak, D. and Geissler P.H. 1986. *The Breeding Bird Survey. Its First Fifteen Years, 1965-1979.* U.S. Fish and Wildlife Serv. Res. Publ.

Robbins, S.D., Jr. 1990. *Wisconsin Birdlife.* University of Wisconsin Press, Madison.

Robert, M. and Laporte, P. 1991. History and current status of the Loggerhead Shrike in Quebec. *Progress Notes* no. 196, Canadian Wildlife Service.

Roberts, T.J. 1992. *The Birds of Pakistan,* vol. 2. Oxford University Press, Karachi.

Robertson, I. 1996. Recent reports. *Bull. Afr. Bird Club* 3: 139-140.

Robson, C. 1988. Recent Reports: Hong Kong. *Bull. Oriental Bird Club* 8: 33-34.

Rodwell, S.P., Sauvage, A., Rumsey, S.J.R. and Bräunlich, A. 1996. An annotated check-list of birds occurring at the Parc National des Oiseaux du Djoudj in Senegal 1984-1994. *Malimbus* 18: 74-111.

Rogacheva, H. 1992. *The Birds of Central Siberia.* Husum Verlag, Husum.

Root, T. 1988. *Atlas of Wintering North American Birds.* University of Chicago Press, Chicago.

da Rosa Pinto, A.A. 1965. Contribuição para o conhecimento da avifauna da região nordeste do distrito do Moxico, Angola. *Bot. Inst. Invest. cient. Ang.* 1: 153-249.

Roselaar, C.S. 1995. *Songbirds of Turkey. An Atlas of Biodiversity of Turkish Passerine Birds.* Pica Press, Robertsbridge.

Rothhaupt, G. 1991. Gefährdungsgradanalyse beim Raubwürger (*Lanius excubitor*) und Neuntöter (*Lanius collurio*). Diplomarbeit, Zool. Institut, Georg-August-Universität, Göttingen.

Rudin, M. 1990. Bruterfolg und Fütterungsverhalten des Neuntöters *Lanius collurio* in der Nordwestschweiz. *Orn. Beob.* 87: 243-252.

Safriel, U.N. 1995. The evolution of Palearctic migration – the case for southern ancestry. *Isr. J. Zool.* 41: 417-431.

Salomonsen, F. 1948. The distribution of birds and the recent climatic change in the north Atlantic area. *Dansk Orn. Foren. Tidsskrift* 42: 85-99.

Salomonsen, F. 1949. The European hybrid-population of the Great Grey Shrike (*Lanius excubitor* L.). *Vidensk. Medd. Dansk Naturh. Foren.* 111: 149-161.

Salomonsen, F. 1953. Miscellaneous notes on Philippine birds. *Vidensk. Medd. Dansk Naturh. Foren.* 115: 205-281.

Salvan, J. 1969. Contribution à l'étude des oiseaux du Tchad. *L'Oiseau et la R.F.O* 39: 38-69.

Sargeant, D.E. 1993. *A Birder's Guide to Gabon, West Africa.* Published privately.

Sargeant, D.E. 1994. Recent ornithological observations from São Tomé and Príncipe Islands. *Bull. Afr. Bird Club* 1: 96-102.

Schäfer, E. 1938. Ornithologische Ergebnisse zweier Forschungsreisen nach Tibet. *J. Ornithologie* 86. *Sonderheft.*

Schaub, M. 1995. Lebensraumansprüche des Rotkopfwürgers in der Nordwestschweiz. Diplom. Universtät Basel.

Schaub, M. 1996. Zum Ansiedlungsverhalten des Rotkopfwürgers *Lanius senator* in der Nordwestschweiz. *Orn. Beob.* 93: 163-168.

Schmidl, D. 1982. *The Birds of the Serengeti National Park, Tanzania.* BOU Check-list no. 5. London.

Schön, M. 1994a. Sex, age and individual characters in the plumage pattern of the Great Grey Shrike *Lanius e. excubitor* in comparison with other shrikes: on the effectiveness of optical signals. *Ökol. Vögel (Ecol. Birds)* 16: 11-80 (in German, detailed English summary).

Schön, M. 1994b. Breeding behaviour of the Great Grey Shrike *Lanius e. excubitor* in the region of the southwestern Schwäbische Alb (southwestern Germany): on pair-formation, pair dissolution, and pair-bond. *Ökol. Vögel (Ecol. Birds)* 16: 81-172 (in German, detailed English summary).

Schön, M. 1994c. Breeding biology of the Great Grey Schrike *Lanius e. excubitor*: clutch size, brood size, and breeding success in the region of the southwestern Schwäbische Alb in comparison with other populations. *Ökol. Vögel (Ecol. Birds)* 16: 173-218 (in German, detailed English summary).

Schön, M. 1994d. Density and trends, sex and age ratios, and group formation in a population of the Great Grey Shrike *Lanius e. excubitor* in the region of the southwestern Schwäbische Alb. *Ökol. Vögel (Ecol. Birds)* 16: 219-252 (in German, detailed English summary).

Schön, M. 1994e. Characteristics of the habitats of the Great Grey Shrike *Lanius e. excubitor* in the region of the southwestern Schwäbische Alb, southwestern Germany: seasonal utilization and territory-size, structural characteristics and their changes, micro structures and cultivation. *Ökol. Vögel (Ecol. Birds)* 16: 253-496 (in German, detailed English summary).

Schön, M. 1994f. On the structure of the nest sites of the Great Grey Shrike *Lanius e. excubitor*: types of nests, their environment and defence, change and reuse of nest sites. *Ökol. Vögel (Ecol. Birds)* 16: 497-566.

Schönwetter, M. and Meise, W. 1970. *Handbuch der Oologie.* Lief. 18. Akademie-Verlag, Berlin.

Schouteden, H. 1960. *Faune du Congo Belge et du Ruanda-Urundi.* 5 Oiseaux, Passereaux 2. Annales du Mus. Royal du Congo Belge, Tervuren.

Schüz, E. 1957. Vom Zug des Raubwürgers *Lanius excubitor* in Europa nach den Ringfunden. *Beitr. Vogelkunde* 5: 201-206.

Sclater, W.L. 1901. *The Fauna of South Africa.* Vol. 2. R.H. Porter, London.

Sclater, W.L. and Mackworth-Praed, C.W. 1918. A list of the birds of the Anglo-Egyptian Sudan based on the collections of Mr A.L. Butler, Mr A. Chapman, Capt. H. Lynes, R.N. and Major Cuthbert Christy. *Ibis* 10(6): 602-720.

Scott, T.A. and Morrison, M.L. 1990. Natural history and management of the San Clemente Loggerhead Shrike. *Proc. West. Found. Vert. Zool.* 4: 23-57.

Semenchuck, G.P. 1992. *The Atlas of Breeding Birds of Alberta.* Fed. Alberta Nat., Edmonton.

Severinghaus, L.L. 1991. The status and conservation of Grey-faced Buzzard-Eagles and Brown Shrikes migrating through Taiwan. In *Conserving Migratory Birds* (ed. T. Salathé) ICPB Technical Publication no. 12: 203-223.

Severinghaus, L.L. 1996. Territory strategy of the migratory Brown Shrike *Lanius cristatus. Ibis* 138: 460-465.

Severinghaus, L.L. and Liang, C.T. 1995. Food and foraging behaviour of the Brown Shrike *Lanius cristatus* in Taiwan. *In* Shrikes (Laniidae) of the world: biology and conservation (R. Yosef and F.E. Lohrer, eds). *Proc. West. Found Vert. Zool* 6: 194-199.

Shaw, T.H. 1936. *The Birds of Hopei Province.* Zoologia Sinica Vol. 20. Ser. B. The Vertebrates of China. Fan. Memorial

Inst. of Biology, Peking.

Shirihai, H. 1995. *The Birds of Israel.* Academic Press, London.

Shirihai, H. and Golan, Y. 1994. First records of Long-tailed Shrike *Lanius schach* in Israel and Turkey. *Sandgrouse* 16: 36-40.

Sibley, C.G. 1970. A comparative study of the egg-white proteins of passerine birds. *Bull. Peabody Mus. Nat. Hist.* 32.

Sibley, C.G. and Ahlquist, J.E. 1985. The relationship of some groups of African birds, based on comparison of the genetic material, DNA. In *Proc. Int. Symp. Afr. Vertebrates* 115-161, Bonn.

Sibley, C.G. and Ahlquist, J.E. 1990. *Phylogeny and Classification of Birds: a Study in Molecular Evolution.* Yale University Press, New Haven and London.

Sibley, C.G., Ahlquist, J.E. and Monroe, B.L., Jr. 1988. A classification of the living birds of the world, based on DNA-DNA hybridization studies. *Auk* 105: 409-423.

Sibley, C.G. and Monroe, B.L., Jr. 1990. *Distribution and Taxonomy of Birds of the World.* Yale University Press, New Haven and London.

Simonetta, I. and Sierro, A. 1996. Premier indice d'une deuxième ponte chez la Pie-grièche écorcheur *Lanius collurio* en Suisse. *Nos Oiseaux* 43: 307-308.

Slack, R.S. 1975. Effects of prey size on Loggerhead Shrike predation. *Auk* 92: 812-814.

Smith, K.D. 1955. Winter breeding in Eritrea. *Ibis* 97: 480-507.

Smith, K.D. 1957. Birds of Eritrea. *Ibis* 99: 307-337.

Smith, S.M. 1973a. An aggressive display and related behaviour in the Loggerhead Shrike, *Lanius ludovicianus* L. *Behaviour* 42: 232-247.

Smith, S.M. 1973b. Food manipulation by young passerines and the possible evolutionary history of impaling by shrikes. *Wilson Bull.* 85: 318-322.

Smythies, B.E. 1960. *The Birds of Borneo.* Sabah Soc. with the Malayan Nature Society, Kuala Lumpur.

Smythies, B.E. 1986. *The Birds of Burma.* 3rd ed. Nimrod Press, Liss, U.K.

Sokolow [=Sokolov], E.P. and Vietinghoff-Scheel, E.V. 1992. *Lanius sphenocercus* Cabanis. In *Atlas der Verbreitung Palaearktischer Vögel.* Lief. 18. (H. Dathe and W.M. Loskot, eds.) Akademie Verlag, Berlin.

Sokolov, E.P and Sokolov, A.V. 1987. On a rare case of hybridisation between two species of shrikes. *Ornitologiya* 22: 71-81 (in Russian).

Solari, C. and Schudel, H. 1988. Nahrungserwerb des Neuntöters *Lanius collurio* während der Fortpflanzungszeit. *Orn. Beob.* 85: 81-90.

van Someren, V.G.L. 1956. Days with birds. *Fieldiana Zool.* 38: 1-520.

Sonnenschein, E. and Reyer, H.U. 1984. Biology of the Slate-coloured Boubou and other bush shrikes. *Ostrich* 55: 86-96.

Stanclova, H. 1983. Interessantes über den Raubwürger. *Falke* 30: 242-243.

Stauber, W. and Ullrich, B. 1970. Der Einfluss des nasskalten Frühjahres 1969 auf eine Population des Rotrückenwürgers (*Lanius collurio*) und Rotkopfwürgers (*Lanius senator*) in Südwestdeutschland. *Vogelwelt* 91: 213-222.

Stegmann, B. 1930. Ueber die Formen der paläarktischen Rotrücken- und Rotschwanzwürger und deren taxonomischen Wert. *Orn. Monatsber.* 38: 106-118.

Steiof, K. and Ratzke, B. 1990. Hohe Siedlungsdichte des Neuntöters *Lanius collurio* auf der Mülldeponie in Berlin-Wannsee und Hinweise zur Erfassung der Art. *Orn. Ber. f. Berlin* 15: 39-48.

Stepanyan, L.S. 1978. *Sostav i Raspredelenie Ptitsi Fauny SSSR.*

Passeriformes. Moscow (in Russian).

Steyn, P. 1976. Protracted prelaying nest building by a Fiscal Shrike. *Ostrich* 47: 68.

Straka, U. 1991. Beitrag zur Winternährung des Raubwürgers *Lanius excubitor* L. in Ackerbaugebieten Ostösterreichs. *Ökol. Vögel (Ecol. Birds)* 13: 213-226.

Streich, E. and Sargatal, J. 1995. La Trenca al Parc Natural dels Aiguamolls de l'Empordà. *El Bruel* 13: 4-7.

Stresemann, E. 1923. *Lanius fuscatus* Lesson: eine Mutante von *Lanius schach schach* L.! *Orn. Monatsber.* 31: 79-82.

Stresemann, E. 1927. Die Wanderungen der Rotschwanz-Würger (Formenkreis *Lanius cristatus*) *J. Ornithologie* 75: 68-85.

Stresemann, E., Meise, W. and Schönwetter, M. 1937. Aves Beickianae. Nordwest-Kansu. *J. Ornithologie* 85: 375-576.

Stresemann, E. and Stresemann, V. 1971. Die postnuptiale und die praenuptiale Vollmauser der asiatischen Würger *Lanius tigrinus* und *L. cristatus*. *J. Ornithologie* 112: 373-395.

Stresemann, E. and Stresemann, V. 1972. Über die Mauser in der Gruppe *Lanius isabellinus*. *J. Ornithologie* 113: 60-75.

Svensson, L. 1992. *Identification Guide to European Passerines*. Published privately, Stockholm.

Swanson, G. 1927. The re-use of nesting material by the Migrant Shrike. *Wilson Bull.* 39: 235-236.

Takagi, M. and Ogawa, I. 1995. Comparative studies on nest sites and diet of *Lanius bucephalus* and *L. cristatus* in northern Japan. *In* Shrikes (Laniidae) of the world: biology and conservation (R. Yosef and F.E. Lohrer, eds) *Proc. West. Found. Vert. Zool.* 6: 200-203.

Tarboton, W.R., Kemp, M.I. and Kemp, A.C. 1987. *Birds of the Transvaal*. Transvaal Museum, Pretoria.

Telfer, E.S. 1992. Habitat change as a factor in the decline of the western Canadian Loggerhead Shrike *Lanius ludovicianus* population. *Can. Field Nat.* 106: 321-326.

Temple, S.A. 1995. When and where are shrike populations limited? *In* Shrikes (Laniidae) of the world: biology and conservation (R. Yosef and F.E. Lohrer, eds). *Proc. West. Found. Vert. Zool.* 6: 6-10.

Thiollay, J.M. 1985. The birds of Ivory Coast: status and distribution. *Malimbus* 7: 1-59.

Thomsen, P. and Jacobsen, P. 1979. *The Birds of Tunisia*. Odense.

Thonnérieux, Y., Walsh, J.F. and Bortoli, L. 1989. L'avifaune de la ville de Ouagadougou et de ses environs (Burkina Faso). *Malimbus* 11: 7-40.

Ticehurst, C.B. 1922. The Birds of Sind (part II) *Ibis* 11(4): 605-662.

Ticehurst, C.B. 1940. On *Lanius tephronotus*. *Ibis* (14)3: 714-715.

Took, J.M.E. 1966. The nest of Souza's Shrike *Lanius souzae*. *Ostrich* 37: 155-156.

Tucker, B.W. 1942. The Berkhamsted Grey Shrike. *British Birds* 36: 51-53.

Tucker, G.M. and Heath, M.F. 1994. *Birds in Europe. Their Conservation Status*. BirdLife International, Cambridge.

Tufts, R.W. 1986. *Birds of Nova Scotia*. Nimbus Publishing, Nova Scotia Museum, Halifax.

Tyler, J.D. 1992. Nesting ecology of the Loggerhead Shrike in southwestern Oklahoma. *Wilson Bull.* 104: 95-104.

Ullrich, B. 1971. Untersuchungen zur Ethologie und Ökologie des Rotkopfwürgers (*Lanius senator*) in Südwestdeutschland im Vergleich zu Raubwürger (*Lanius excubitor*), Schwarzstirnwürger (*Lanius minor*) und Neuntöter (*Lanius collurio*). *Vogelwarte* 26: 1-77.

Ullrich, B. 1974. Über die postnuptiale Mauser des Rotkopfwürgers (*Lanius collurio*) und Rotkopfwürgers (*Lanius*

senator). *J. Ornithologie* 115: 79-85.

Ullrich, B. 1987. Beringungsergebnisse aus einer Brutpopulation des Rotkopfwürgers (*Lanius senator*) im mittleren Albvorland, Kreis Göppingen und Esslingen. *Orn. Jh. Baden-Württ.* 3: 107-112.

Ullrich, B. 1993. Verhaltensweisen des Rotkopfwürgers *Lanius senator* zur Verringerung von Feindverlusten. *Vogelwelt* 114: 98-113.

Urban, E.K. and Brown, L.H. 1971. *A Checklist of the Birds of Ethiopia*. Faculty of Science, Haile Sellassie University of Addis Ababa.

Vande weghe, J.P. 1981. Additions à l'avifaune du Rwanda. *Gerfaut* 71: 175-184.

Vasic, V.F. 1974. Observations ornithologiques en Afghanistan. *Alauda* 42: 259-280.

Vatev, I.T., Simeonov, P.V., Michev, T.M. and Ivanov, B.E. 1980. The Masked Shrike (*Lanius nubicus* Lichtenstein) a breeding species in Bulgaria. *Acta Zoologica Bulgarica* 15: 115-118 (in Bulgarian, English summary).

Vaurie, C. 1955. Systematic notes on Palearctic birds, no. 17. Laniidae. *Amer. Mus. Novit.* 1752.

Vaurie, C. 1959. *The Birds of the Palearctic Fauna. Order Passeriformes*. H.F. and G. Witherby, London.

Vaurie, C. 1972. *Tibet and its Birds*. H.F. and G. Witherby, London.

Verheyen, R. 1951. La migration de la Pie-grièche écorcheur. *Gerfaut* 11: 111-139.

Verheyen, R. 1953. Exploration du Parc National de l'Upemba. Oiseaux. *Mission G.F. de Witte* 19: 1-687. Bruxelles.

Vincent, A.W. 1949. Breeding habits of African birds. *Ibis* 91: 111-139.

Vincent, J. 1935. The birds of northern Portuguese East Africa. *Ibis* 13(5): 707-762.

Voous, K.H. 1950. Klapeksters, *Lanius excubitor* L., met één en twee vleugelspiegels in Nederland. *Ardea* 37: 169-172.

Voous, K.H. 1960. *Atlas of European Birds*. Nelson, London.

Voous, K.H. 1977. List of recent Holarctic bird species. *Ibis* 119: 223-250, 376-406.

Voous, K.H. 1979. Capricious taxonomic history of Isabelline Shrike. *British Birds* 72: 573-578.

Voous, K.H. 1985. Shrike; Table of Classification. In *A Dictionary of Birds* (B. Campbell and E. Lack, eds). T. & A.D. Poyser, Calton.

Vorobiev [=Vorobieff], K.A. 1934. The desert element in the avifauna of the Astrachan steppes. *Ibis* (13)4: 160-164.

Vorobiev [=Vorobieff], K.A. 1954. *Birds of the Ussuri area*. Academy of Sciences of the USSR, Moscow.

Wagner, T. 1993. Saisonale Veränderungen in der Zusammensetzung der Nahrung beim Neuntöter (*Lanius collurio*) *J. Ornithologie* 134: 1-11.

Wagner, T. 1994. Brutzeitliches Beutespektrum des Raubwürgers *Lanius excubitor* auf Kahlschlag und Windwurfflächen im südwestfälischen Bergland. *Vogelwelt* 115: 179-184.

Wagner, T. and Hölker, M. 1995. Zum brutzeitlichen Nahrungsspektrum des Raubwürgers (*Lanius excubitor* L.) in der Medebacher Bucht (Südost-Westfalen) *Ökol. Vögel (Ecol. Birds)* 17: 233-242.

Wait, W.E. 1931. *Birds of Ceylon*. Ceylon Journal of Science, Ceylon and London.

Waite, H.W. 1948. The birds of the Punjab Salt Range. *J. Bombay Nat. Hist. Soc.* 48: 93-117.

Walsh, F. 1968. Emin's Bush Shrike in Borgu. *Bull. Nigerian Orn. Soc.* 5 (no pagination).

Walter, H. 1968. Zur Abhängigkeit des Eleonoren Falken (*Falco eleonorae*) vom Mediterranean Vogelzug. *J. Ornithologie* 109: 323-365.

Watson, G.E. 1967. Masked Shrike feeding on birds. *British Birds* 60: 303-304.

Welch, G. and Welch, H. 1984. Birds seen on an expedition to Djibouti. *Sandgrouse* 6: 1-23.

Western, R. 1992. Quail killed by shrike. *Emirates Bird Report* 16: 8-9.

White, C.M.N. 1946. The ornithology of the Kaonde-Lunda Province, Northern Rhodesia. Part. 4. *Ibis* 88: 206-224.

White, C.M.N. 1962. *A Revised Checklist of African Shrikes, Orioles, Drongos, Starlings, Crows, Waxwings, Cuckoo-shrikes, Bulbuls, Accentors, Thrushes and Babblers.* Government Printer, Lusaka.

White, R. 1992. Fiscal Shrike predation. *Honeyguide* 38: 129.

Wilbur, S.R. 1987. *Birds of Baja California.* University of California Press, Berkeley.

Wildash, P. 1968. *Birds of South Vietnam.* Charles E. Tuttle, Rutland, Vermont and Tokyo.

Williams, J. 1989. Icterine Warblers feeding White-crowned Shrike chicks. *Honeyguide* 35: 26.

Williams, M.D., Carey, G.J., Duff, D.G. and Xu Weishu. 1992. Autumn bird migration at Beidahe, China 1986-1990. *Forktail* 7: 3-55.

Williamson, K. 1973. The 'British' Red-backed Shrike. *Bird Study* 20: 142-143.

Williamson, K. 1975. Birds and climatic change. *Bird Study* 22: 143-164.

Winstanley, D., Spencer, R. and Williamson, K. 1974. Where have all the Whitethroats gone ? *Bird Study* 21: 1-14.

Winter, W. 1987. Die Ernährung des Keilschwanzwürgers *Lanius sphenocercus* Cabanis, im Mittleren Amurland. *Mitt. Zool. Mus. Berlin* 63. Suppl. Ann. Orn. 11: 13-34.

Woods, C.P. 1993. Variation in Loggerhead Shrike nest composition between two shrub species in southwest Idaho. *J. Field Ornithology* 64: 352-357.

Woods, C.P. 1995. Status of Loggerhead Shrikes in the sagebrush habitat of southwestern Idaho. *In* Shrikes (Laniidae) of the world: biology and conservation (R. Yosef and F.E. Lohrer, eds) *Proc. West. Found. Vert. Zool.* 6: 150-154.

Woods, C.P. 1996. Food delivery and food holding during copulation in the Loggerhead Shrike. *Wilson Bull.* 107: 762-764.

Woods, C.P. and Cade, T.J. 1996. Nesting habits of the Loggerhead Shrike in sagebrush. *Condor* 98: 75-81.

Yamagishi, S. 1982. Age. determination in the Bull-headed Shrike *Lanius bucephalus* based on buff tips of greater primary coverts. *J. Yamashina Inst. Orn.* 14: 96-102.

Yamagishi, S. and Nishiumi, I. 1994. Extrapair fertilization in monogamous Bull-headed Shrike. *J Ornithologie* 135: 289 (Abstract 21st Int. Orn. Congr., Vienna).

Yamagishi, S., Nishiumi, I., and Shimoda, C. 1992. Extrapair fertilization in monogamous Bull-headed Shrikes revealed by DNA fingerprinting. *Auk* 109: 711-721.

Yamagishi, S. and Saito, M. 1985. Function of courtship feeding in the Bull-headed Shrike, *Lanius bucephalus. J. Ethol.* 3: 113-121.

Yamashina, Y. 1961. *Birds in Japan. A Field Guide.* Shuburn International., Tokyo.

Yosef, R. 1992a. From nest-building to fledging of young in Great Grey Shrikes (*Lanius excubitor*) at Sede Boqer, Israel. *J. Ornithologie* 133: 279-288.

Yosef, R. 1992b. Behaviour of polygynous and monogamous Loggerhead Shrikes and a comparison with Northern Shrikes. *Wilson Bull.* 104: 747-749.

Yosef, R. 1993a. Prey transport by Loggerhead Shrike. *Condor* 95: 231-233.

Yosef, R. 1993b. Influence of observation posts on territory size in Northern Shrikes. *Wilson Bull.* 105: 180-183.

Yosef, R. 1993c. Effects of Little Owl predation on Northern Shrike post-fledging success. *Auk* 110: 396-398.

Yosef, R. 1994. Survival of Loggerhead Shrikes is negatively affected by fertilizer sprayed on their pastoral habitat. *J. Ornithologie* 135: 526 (Abstract 21st Int. Orn. Congr. Vienna).

Yosef, R. 1996. *Loggerhead Shrike.* In *The Birds of North America* no. 231 (A. Poole and F. Gill, eds). AOU, Academy of Natural Sciences of Philadelphia.

Yosef, R. and Grubb, T.C. 1992. Territory size influences nutritional condition in non-breeding Loggerhead Shrikes: a ptilochronology approach. *Conserv. Biol.* 6: 447-449.

Yosef, R. and Grubb, T.C. 1993. Effects of vegetation height on hunting behavior and diet of Loggerhead Shrikes. *Condor* 95: 127-131.

Yosef, R. and Grubb, T.C. 1994. Resource dependence and territory size in Loggerhead Shrikes. *Auk* 111: 465-469.

Yosef, R. and Lohrer, F.E. (eds.) 1995. *Shrikes (Laniidae) of the World: Biology and Conservation.* Proceedings of the 1st International Shrike Symposium, 11-15 January 1993, Archbold Biological Station, Lake Placid, Florida, USA. *Proc. West. Found. Vert. Zool.* 6.

Yosef, R. and Pinshow, B. 1988a. Nestling transfer in the Northern Shrike (*Lanius excubitor*). *Auk* 105: 580-581.

Yosef, R. and Pinshow, B. 1988b. Polygyny in the Northern Shrike in Israel. *Auk.* 105: 581-582.

Yosef, R. and Pinshow, B. 1989. Cache size in Northern Shrike influences female mate choice and reproductive success. *Auk* 106: 418-421.

Yosef, R. and Whitman, D.W. 1992. Predator exaptations and defensive adaptations in evolutionary balance: no defense is perfect. *Evol. Ecol.* 6: 527-536.

Zack, S. 1986a. Behavior and breeding biology of the cooperatively breeding Grey-backed Fiscal Shrike *Lanius excubitorius* in Kenya. *Ibis* 128: 214-233.

Zack, S. 1986b. Breeding biology and inter-territory movements in a Fiscal Shrike population. *Ostrich* 57: 65-74.

Zack, S. 1995. Cooperative breeding in *Lanius* shrikes. III: a reply in hindsight to Zack and Ligon I, II (1985). *In* Shrikes (Laniidae) of the world: biology and conservation (R. Yosef and F.E. Lohrer, eds) *Proc. West. Found. Vert. Zool.* 6: 34-38.

Zack, S. and Ligon, J.D. 1985a. Cooperative breeding in *Lanius* Shrikes. I. Habitat and demography of two sympatric species. *Auk* 102: 754-765.

Zack, S. and Ligon, J.D. 1985b. Cooperative breeding in *Lanius* shrikes. II Maintenance of group-living in non-saturated habitat. *Auk* 102: 766-773.

Zedlitz, O. 1915. Das Süd-Somaliland als zoogeographisches Gebiet. *J. Ornithologie* 63: 1-69.

Zheng Guang-mei and Wang Xiang-ting. 1985. On the intraspecific categories of Bull-headed Shrike (*Lanius bucephalus* Temminck and Schlegel). *J. Beijing Norm. Univ. (Nat. Sci. Ed.)* 3: 75-79 (in Chinese, English summary).

Zimmerman, D.A. 1955. Notes on field identification and comparative behavior of shrikes in winter. *Wilson Bull.* 67: 200-208.

Zimmerman, D.A., Turner, D.A. and Pearson, D.J. 1996. *Birds of Kenya and Northern Tanzania.* Christopher Helm, London.

Zink, G. 1975. *Der Zug Europaïscher Singvögel. Ein Atlas der Wiederfunde Beringter Vögel.* 2 Lief. Vogelzug-Verlag, Möggingen.

INDEX OF SCIENTIFIC AND ENGLISH NAMES

Species are listed by their English vernacular name (e.g. Great Grey Shrike), together with alternative names where relevant, and by their scientific names. Specific scientific names are followed by the generic name as used in the book (e.g. *excubitor, Lanius*) and subspecific names are followed by both the specific and generic names (e.g. *borealis, Lanius excubitor*). In addition, genera are listed separately.

Numbers in italic type refer to the first page of the main systematic entry and those in bold type refer to plate numbers.